Life, death and sacrifice
Women and family in the Holocaust

Edited by
ESTHER HERTZOG

gefen publishing house בית הוצאה לאור
JERUSALEM • NEW YORK

Life, death and sacrifice - Women and family in the Holocaust
Edited by Esther Hertzog

Technical editor: Deborah S. Jacobs (Ghetto Fighters' House)
Graphic design: Maya Bein-Nachal, *Cover design:* Roni Ben-Zioni
Cover background photo: courtesy of Yad Vashem, Jerusalem

ISBN 978-965-229-429-6

1   3   5   7   9   8   6   4   2

Gefen Publishing House, Ltd.
6 Hatzvi Street, Jerusalem 94386, Israel
972-2-538-0247
orders@gefenpublishing.com

Gefen Books
600 Broadway, Lynbrook, NY 11563, USA
516-593-1234
orders@gefenpublishing.com

www.israelbooks.com

Printed in Israel

Send for our free catalogue

The publication of this book in English was made possible by the generous contribution of the Friedrich-Ebert-Stiftung

Editorial board:
Batya Brutin (Beit Berl Academic College), Anita Tarsi & Yonat Klar (Beit Theresienstadt), Naomi Shimshi (Ghetto Fighters' House)

Several of the articles in this book have been published in Hebrew (*Women and Family in the Holocaust*. Otzar Hamishpat, 2006)

indexlaw@walla.com Tel. 972-3-6186141
www.ozar-hamishpat.co.il

To Eva – my mother

and in memory of
Bondi – my father
(1923–1971)

CONTENTS

Foreword

Introduction: Studying the Holocaust as a Feminist

Part 1: The Adaptations of Jewish Families to Horror

Gender and Family Studies of the Holocaust:
the Development of a Historical Discipline

Motherhood under Siege

"We're all well and hoping to hear the same from you soon...."
The Story of a Group of Families

1943: The Flight from Home

"Camp Families" in Ravensbrück and the Social Organization
of Jewish Women Prisoners in a Concentration Camp

Part 2: Gendered Persecution and Sexualized Violence

The Persecution and Murder of German and
German-Jewish Women between 1933 and 1945

Racialised Gender, Gendered Race and Gendered-Racialised Academia:
Female-Jewish Anthropologists in Vienna

Foreword

Though it is over sixty years since the end of the Second World War, more and more remarkable scholarly publications dealing with that historical period are making their appearance. This is despite the time that has elapsed since the liberation of human beings who were crushed and oppressed by the Germans, foremost of whom were the Jews of Europe as they experienced the utmost savagery of the Germans' systematic and unfathomable frenzy of annihilation. *Inter alia,* historical, sociological, and psychological studies address themselves with considerable energy and perseverance – particularly in Israel, in the USA and in Germany– to the similar but also perennially new questions posed about the grim history of the Shoah, since each generation attempts to investigate and evaluate history anew from its own perspective and against the backdrop of its experiences.

After an initial long period when research into the fate of women in the time of the Shoah was not granted any special attention, in the last two and a half decades academic works that focus particularly on women-centered themes have increased in number. This owes much, or perhaps is even entirely due to politically active feminist scholars' insistence that analyses of topics dealing with women's questions and phenomena should no longer be disregarded in academic research of the Holocaust.

For this reason, I am most appreciative that we, on behalf of the Friedrich-Ebert Foundation, were granted the privilege as foundation representatives in Israel to take an active part in the publication of the research on "Women and family in the Holocaust". Not only is the foundation involved with more than 90 international agencies in joint work with its partner organizations, promoting and extending the values of democracy, human rights and social justice. It also, under the auspices of its Center for Historical Research Bonn/Germany, endeavors to make an active academic contribution towards elucidating developments in German and European history. In this context, the investigation of the Shoah obviously holds a particularly prominent position.

The present volume contains an eminent range of seminal and significant contributions that explore the fate of women in the time of the Shoah. It should be emphasized here that the authors are especially concerned with investigating the variety of almost overwhelming challenges and pressures on women under conditions of persecution, incarceration, and when facing certain death by systematic annihilation. Also in this context both male and female readers are again confronted with the familiar and recurring phenomenon that women have to function in many diverse roles. First of all, as mothers they must take practical steps to protect their children in dangerous circumstances. As sisters they are aware of responsibility in a quasi-family context under concentration camp conditions; as daughters they are sometimes in direct proximity to offer help to their suffering parents; as wives they struggle for their husbands, and last but not least, they must maintain their own dignity as women in indescribable conditions of humiliation. The fact remains that women in the Holocaust were at times in a position to not merely contemplate active defiance of their tormentors; some also managed to implement their resistance, or at least tried to do so. These examples leave the readers in a state of astonishment and awestruck wonder.

Credit goes to all the contributors to this volume, who within the context of their scholarly research have erected a memorial for the women of the Holocaust. This is achieved through presentation and analysis of these women's suffering and resistance, which makes an impact at this present time; the topic does not just limit itself to a particularly appalling period in the history of the twentieth century.

The series of conferences on "Women and the Holocaust" is a contribution that must not be overlooked by those involved in studying and analyzing the Shoah, who desire to derive meaning from it that would influence our public political mores and private conduct today. For years now this event has been held, with great commitment, at the Beit Berl Academic College and two study centers devoted to the history of the Shoah, and with the participation of many prominent international researchers.

The fact that publication of this volume has now been achieved is primarily to the credit of Dr. Esther Hertzog of Beit Berl College, and I cite her as a prime example of numerous other outstanding women scholars. Her firm convictions of the imperative for a permanent debate about gender equality, and also about the role of women in historical and sociopolitical contexts, are not only noteworthy but represent one of the most important prerequisites within our understanding: how we can reshape our world today in a more just and humane way.

I hope that this book will have many readers, both men and women, so that questions about the fate and the role of "Women and the Holocaust" will continue to evolve and be grappled with in every era.

Hermann Bünz
Director of the Friedrich-Ebert Foundation Representation in Israel

Herzliya, January 2008

Introduction: Studying the Holocaust as a Feminist

Esther Hertzog

Both of my parents were Holocaust survivors and many of their relatives were exterminated in Auschwitz and in the Ukraine. However, only in summer 2000, when I found myself at an international conference on the Holocaust held in Oxford, did I first open up to the subject. This happened mainly due to my unanticipated exposure to studies on the subject that were presented by feminist researchers such as Dalia Ofer and Lenore Weitzman (1998), Esther Fuchs (1999) and Myrna Goldenberg (1996). I later learned of other prominent gender scholars who had studied the Holocaust from a feminist perspective, among whom were Joan Ringelheim (1985), Carol Rittner and John Roth (1993), Judith Tydor Baumel (1998) and Marion Kaplan (1998). It appears that being a woman sensitized by gender awareness made exposure to women's narratives and their feminist interpretation a compelling experience.

This book is, in a way, the outcome of the deep motivation and enthusiasm regarding feminist insights of the Holocaust that I gained from participating in the 2000 conference. Between 2001 and 2005, three international conferences on women and the Holocaust were organized in Israel by me and my colleagues at Beit Berl Academic College, Beit Terezin (Theresienstadt memorial center) and Beit Lohamei Haghetaot (the Ghetto Fighters' House museum). Many of the articles included in this book are based on papers that were presented in those conferences. They unfold the narratives of Jewish women who were degraded, tortured and murdered. The book therefore contributes to the commemoration of the personal and collective memory of those murdered; it affords them a kind of existence after physical and social death as individuals and as a group, as members of families and as active members of their communities. The book also highlights women's altruism and courage through narratives of self-sacrificing Jewish mothers who gave their lives to save their children or were exterminated with them, of Jewish and non-Jewish underground fighters and of non-Jewish women who saved Jews. It also brings the story of women who collaborated with the Nazi regime by denouncing Jewish families. The ongoing presence of Holocaust memories in the everyday lives of women survivors and in encounters with their new families is yet another perspective discussed here.

The Holocaust is depicted in the book as a period of ruptured frameworks, relationships, roles and values. Adjustments and changes in roles and status are described and analyzed. Hence, the emergence of alternative frameworks, adapted to the changing conditions and to the struggle for survival, is elaborated and associated with broader social phenomena. Obviously, in the case of the Holocaust, we are dealing with a total disruption of the social order and a bureaucratic machine that intentionally worked against the restoration of order, a context in which every individual is compelled to adjust continually. Despite widely accepted assumptions, I suggest that the Holocaust can be considered as another catastrophe in the history of humankind, like war or plague. At such times, social categories perceived as self-evident and supportive of the social order at large—especially the gendered division of power and roles—are breached. As old frameworks collapse, new social structures, adapted to the changing reality, emerge. Indeed, it must be repeatedly stressed that the reality of the Holocaust was far more extreme than any previously known social cataclysm; in response, changes were frequent, intense and unexpected.

The family is the most prominent social context with which the book deals. The upheavals that rocked the family did not occur at once but gradually, during and parallel to developments in Nazi racial, antisemitic policy. Several articles in this volume discuss the connection between these processes and changes in the family, although the transformations in gender roles and power described focus mainly on women. Several articles describe how women took on family responsibilities and leadership when the men were taken away or their positions undermined.

Feminist research suggests that in times of crisis and instability the social order, including gendered power relations, is shattered. In consequence, access to roles and status positions blocked to women in 'normal' times becomes viable. In other words, when prevailing frameworks are threatened, such as in situations of war and migration, gender relations and the social order at large change. New opportunities to realize their needs and skills, to take part in the political leadership, open up to women; even their customary role as caretakers and nurturers appears to gain recognition and prominence. As things settle down and social structures are re-established, gender stratification is restored and women are pushed back to the fringes of political-economic activity.

Implicitly—and sometimes explicitly—the articles in the book suggest that during war and other extreme social emergencies, women exhibit better survival social skills than do men. The resourcefulness, self-sacrifice, mutual support, and common sense that women demonstrated so often in the Holocaust are skills that are required for adaptation to the changing conditions associated with threats to individual and collective existence. This observation is compatible with claims made in studies on the adaptation of immigrant families. Some maintain that women adapt to the new situation with greater ease than do men and note women's prominent place in the integration of their families into new environments. These differences, if they actually exist, may be connected to the different social expectations and gender socialization that foster men's greater responsibility for family subsistence. As the expectations imposed on women are smaller in this respect, they may feel less threatened by failure and subsequently more at ease, when facing dramatic changes in their lives. Women may therefore be freer to make the most of every opportunity available to improve their families' socio-economic situation. Moreover, the political and occupational exclusion of women that prevails in 'normal' times is weakened at times of collective crises. The need to mobilize every possible resource for re-organization and survival compels the removal of social barriers and the elimination of mechanisms that in 'normal' times prevent women from attempting to accomplish their potential and realize their social skills. It seems absurd but the barriers, gendered power structure, discriminatory mechanisms and patriarchal norms return to their previous routine place when the crisis eases.

Studies such as those by Bloom (1991) on women in the Israeli army prior to and following the establishment of the State of Israel, by Talmon-Garber (1970, 1974) on Israeli kibbutz families, by Bernstein (1987, 1992) on Jewish women in pre-state Israel, by Swirski and Safir (1991) on the bluff regarding equality perpetrated in Israeli society, and by Giacaman and Johnson (1988) as well as Strum (1992) on the status of women in Palestinian society suggest that even before nation-building struggles are over and new social arrangements are stabilized, women are pushed back to the margins of the public arena, back to their traditional gender roles. Marx argues (1987) that economic crisis, which involves labor migration and the absence of men, increases women's economic independence and opens their way to leadership positions in the family and in society. The absence of men can occur as a result of employment opportunities or, sometimes, governmental actions such as going to war. South Africa's apartheid policy is an example of the impact of state policies on gender relations: The forced long-term separation between spouses inflicted far-reaching changes in gender relations in the black community.

An elaboration of the women's inclusion-exclusion processes practiced during the Holocaust shows that women were pushed outside the circles of social leadership soon after WWII began. This conclusion emerges from Baumel's study (1998) and from Chaim Hoffman-Yahil's testimony, cited by Baumel (ibid: 239), indicating that women's absence from the leadership of the *She'erit Hapleta* (Hebrew: Holocaust survivor community) and of the Displaced Persons (DP) camps continued after the Holocaust officially ended. Although some of the women who survived the Holocaust participated, as individuals, in various activities in the spheres of history, medicine, and welfare, women as a group did not participate in camp administrative bodies, apart from the central committee in Bergen-Belsen. Furthermore, no woman held a key position within the leadership of the DP camps in Germany after the war.

Baumel suggests that one explanation for the exclusion of women from leadership positions following the war is related to the fact that they were involved in caring for their children, born after the war as one outcome of their rehabilitation. Another explanation for their exclusion, still to be explored, emerges from the latent ways in which those in power prevented women from approaching the centers of power. One example supporting this argument in the context of the Holocaust is found in Reinhard Heydrich's orders ". . . regarding policy and taking steps against the Jews in the conquered lands", published in Berlin on September 21, 1939 ("Express letter to the heads of all *Einsatzgruppen* of the Security Police", in: *Documents on the Holocaust*: 139-140). In that document, Heydrich declares: "A Jewish Council of Elders should be established in every Jewish community, comprised, as far as possible, of authoritative figures and remaining rabbis. The Council of Elders shall number up to 24 male Jews". It appears, therefore, that women's exclusion can also be explained by state decisions and practices (or their absence).

Another perspective on social change in gender stratification relates to organized feminist struggles. The struggles for gender equality initiated by women's organizations can contribute significantly to promoting women's leadership. Both before and during the Holocaust, women's organizations played an important role in community affairs and in the struggle for survival (an aspect that Kaplan [1998] describes so well). The egalitarian ideology adopted by the women's revolutionary movement can, it appears, help breach the barriers of institutional leadership. This is illustrated in Baumel's study (1998) on women's leadership among Holocaust refugees. Women were part of the leadership in the pioneering Zionist movement (*Hechalutz*) that founded many kibbutz training programs in prewar Germany. Women similarly founded *Beit Yaakov*, the ultra-orthodox women's educational movement. These two evidently revolutionary groups were, each in its own way and context, challenging the status of women.

Feminist research on family and State relationships indicates that the family is one of the hubs of women's collective weakness in society. At the same time, women's weakness in economic-political spheres is reflected in and preserves their weakness within the family (Bernstein, 1992). A fundamental change in gendered power relations in the family depends on structural changes in the labor market, on the support afforded by state institutions and on the existence of a social movement "that offers an alternative to the prevailing relationships between woman, family and society" (ibid: 191). The connection between caring for children and gender stratification in the family and in society appears to be particularly significant. In this area as well, the role of the State is decisive, although usually invisible, because it can encourage the sharing of responsibility for children between mothers and fathers by providing opportunities and suitable childcare facilities. The part played by government authorities in constructing female responsibility for childcare emerges, for example, from my study (1998) on the impact of the bureaucratic systems on gendered power relations among Ethiopian immigrants in Israel.

The book supports this line of analysis. The struggles to survive the horrendous experiences and traumatic changes that Jewish families and communities were put through by the Nazi regime indirectly strengthened women's position in the family and their participation in leadership in the camps and in the underground. While living conditions of families enormously deteriorated, women's social skills and resourcefulness were exposed. However, some of the articles appearing in the book seem to imply that the changes in gender roles did not, in fact, entail long-range transformations in the social order and gendered power relations. This implication is compatible with the feminist discourse, which emphasizes the stability of the patriarchal domination embedded in most human societies, which prevails over temporary changes and circumstantial diversity. Moreover, the role of the family in regaining social stability and reinforcing traditional stratification and gendered power structures within the framework of the state appears to be a crucial contributor to this process. One of the clearest statements of this mechanism is found in Kate Millett's (1969) ground breaking *Sexual Politics*. Millett suggests that the family is "patriarchy's chief institution" and argues that:

> It is both a mirror of and a connection with the larger society; a patriarchal unit within a patriarchal whole. Mediating between the individual and the social structure, the family effects control and conformity where political and other authorities are insufficient. As the fundamental instrument and the foundation unit of patriarchal society, the family and its roles are prototypical. Serving as an agent of the larger society, the family not only encourages its own members to adjust and conform, but acts as a unit in the government of the patriarchal state which rules its citizens through its family heads. ...As co-operation between the family and the larger society is essential, or else both would fall apart, the fate of three patriarchal institutions, the family, society, and the state are interrelated.
>
> ...Radical social change cannot take place without having an effect upon patriarchy. And not simply because it is the political form which subordinates such a large percentage of the population (women and youth) but because it serves as a citadel of property and traditional interests. Marriages are financial alliances, and each household operates as an economic entity much like a corporation. As one student of the family states it, "the family is the keystone of the stratification system, the social mechanism by which it is maintained". (Chapter 2).

How Jewish families adapted to horror

While the association of terms such as 'Women's Studies' and 'Family Studies' with the Holocaust are relatively new, the phenomena they describe are not. Judith Baumel's article on the development of women's, gender and family studies of the Holocaust as a discipline within history provides evidence for the phenomenon. Other examples can be found in the work of the Jewish historian Emanuel Ringelblum (1993), who began to study the lives and behavior patterns of women and children in the Warsaw ghetto in 1941-1942. His study on women as mothers and wives was nipped in its prime with the liquidation of the ghetto and the murder of the women.

Women's writing on their Holocaust memories and experiences appeared soon after the war and in considerably greater volume than male compositions. Baumel links this phenomenon to the social training of women, which encourages them to write memoirs as a 'feminine' occupation. (In her 1998 book, Baumel notes that women played a "guiding force in Holocaust commemoration". Yet, they were "the least commemorated body within the *She'erit Hapletah*". p. 245.)

Nevertheless, documentation of the women as mothers, caring for and saving their children, is extremely limited and connected primarily to the testimony of surviving children and family members. The sources have therefore been written and researched mainly by men. This becomes apparent from Dalia Ofer's article, which argues that the voices of mothers are most rare and, accordingly, it is difficult to present a reliable historical account of their experiences and of the diverse perspectives relating to motherhood held by women during the Holocaust.

Since the mid-1970s, research into the narratives of women, children and families during the Holocaust has increased consistently. The main explanation for this development, beyond the emergence of a Holocaust awareness, is the academic interest in 'women's culture' and in family studies, disciplines that began to gain recognition during that period. Current feminist study assigns the family to a distinctive research category, contrary to the past, when women were studied as a sub-category of the family in Holocaust research. Baumel considers this to be "coming full circle".

As mutual dependence and the institutionalized partnership of men and women are embedded in the social framework of the family, it could be argued that a common analytical basis should be applied when discussing the family. However, the articles in the book focus mainly on women, dealing only tangentially with changes and processes pertinent to children and even less so to men. I nevertheless suggest that in the future, feminist research of the Holocaust should also focus on the transformation of men's roles in the family and explore the processes by which they regained their place as the heads of families and society after the war. The (meanwhile slow) entry of male scholars into gender research of the Holocaust may well bring new insights and perceptions, based on male perspectives, to the study of victims, Jewish and others, as well as perpetrators, whether Nazis or their collaborators.

Women's adaptability during the struggle for survival during the Holocaust emerges as a prominent phenomenon in the articles that focus on family issues, Women mitigated the edicts that dismantled families, they maintained routine as family life disintegrated, found alternative strategies for survival and constructed new family-type frameworks that replaced the old family support structure. The shifting social roles of women are described as closely associated with the changing circumstances, and as flexibly responding to the changing reality, to available opportunities, as well as to the inevitable constraints. The articles imply that the family's existence was dependent on the presence of a woman and on her presumed advantage in making decisions under crisis situations.

Marion Kaplan (1998) argues that women were similarly better equipped to handle threats. She maintains that during the Holocaust, women revealed their skills in maintaining 'normality' in chaotic conditions by making relevant decisions, preparing escapes and finding alternative means for saving their families. Kaplan's analysis thus supports the claim that women's social-adaptive skills served their families during the Holocaust, when the men were taken from their places of work, expelled to the camps, and emotionally collapsed when their status as providers eroded.

The articles by Dalia Ofer, Irith Dublon-Knebel and Lidia Sciama confirm, in different ways, the conclusions derived from Kaplan's study. Ofer focuses on women's identity as 'mothers' in Jewish communities in the years prior to the Holocaust and on the changes experienced with the Nazi destruction of Jewish family life. She describes the different impacts of tradition and culture when compared with conditions of place, economic opportunities, status, etc., on issues of gender identity. She claims that motherhood and family do not have the same meaning in all Jewish communities, or even among the various groups within them. On the other hand, Nazi policy presented all mothers with similar dilemmas, fatal to their most basic social training as caretakers of their children and to the inherent urge to hold on to their identity as mothers. They were forced to decide between leaving their children and protecting them under onerous conditions that endangered themselves and other family members. Ofer perceives the emotional strength of the Jewish mother in the Holocaust, her heroism and readiness to sacrifice for her children as a key feature of the Holocaust experience.

The changes observed in gender role division in Jewish families during the Nazi era were, apparently, incorporated into the existing social order, which did not necessarily match the image of 'traditional' reality. In such circumstances, the position of women in the family and society, and the opportunities that were opened up to them before and during the Nazi era, differed by location—Western or Eastern Europe—and wealth and social status, as suggested by Ofer (following Kaplan's study, 1991). Concrete circumstances apparently affect the opportunities and roles of women (like others) in their social surroundings, sometimes in contrast to seemingly explicit norms. Women (and children as well) therefore took upon themselves the responsibilities that men, now absent or emasculated by Nazi policies, had formerly filled.

Irith Dublon-Knebel emphasizes the crucial role of the mother in the family's struggle for survival. She tells of families transported to the concentration camps, with fathers and husbands separated from their families and sent to Buchenwald while women and children were removed to Ravensbrück. As the father's position crumbled, the 'normative mother' became the 'head of the family'. Against this background, Dublon-Knebel elaborates on the tragic conflict between women's struggle for their personal survival and their intrinsic obligation for their children's survival. On the one hand, the fact that the children's survival was dependent on their mothers' continued endurance afforded significant motivation in the women's struggle to stay alive. On the other hand, this dual struggle for survival often endangered them. That is to say, motherhood in the Holocaust context meant extended vulnerability and personal jeopardy.

Lidia Sciama's personal story about life in a shelter-refuge with an Italian couple illustrates the change in gender relations and roles in wartime conditions, far from home and familiar routine. Men who did not actively participate in the war but lived under foreign conquest lost their authority but still demanded deference; they often needed support and sometimes even had to be restrained. Looking back on those days, Sciama states that the behavior of the women—the mother and the landlady—was more adaptive and aroused respect. Her mother's conduct was skillful and resourceful in preserving balance and routine; this she compares to, her father, who lost his power and consequently acted in a confused manner. She depicts her father as an almost childish figure, who should be protected from his careless behavior. The two women, in contrast to the men, developed the ability to communicate comfortably. Under the peculiar circumstances that linked Sciama's family and the Italian couple, common sense, intuitive understanding and the sensitivity of women prevailed. The end of the story illustrates that the return to routine after the war marked the return to the familiar family framework as well as the return of children, women and men to their pre-war positions and roles. It should be noted, however, that although the 'traditional' family framework, with its gender and age divisions, was apparently restored after the Holocaust, the return to the familiar, conventional social order was affected by the specific circumstances in which people found themselves after the war.

The horrific living conditions in the concentration and death camps, on the one hand, and the loss of family relationships and support on the other, imposed the need to develop alternative support groups. The phenomenon of 'camp families' has emerged on this background. Women (and men as well, quite probably) adopted surrogate families and relationships, to replace those that were destroyed. Judith Buber Agassi's article on Ravensbrück's Jewish prisoners' 'camp families' demonstrates this phenomenon. Consequently, Agassi ascribes a different meaning to the concept family, which is not only a social unit based on biological links and kinship ties, recognized by state institutions. In the case of 'camp families', the family is a small group of women that provides mutual help, organizing itself *ad hoc* as a means of adaptation and support for individuals, and so often contributing to their survival.

Buber Agassi argues that this kind of social organization thrived among the Jewish female prisoners in Ravensbrück as it emerged from their gendered socialization as girls. They were trained to take responsibility and show concern for others, namely, the weaker and more dependent members of their families. Nevertheless, since Buber Agassi examines 'camp families' as a social phenomenon that took place among women from diverse origins, her analysis may also apply to indicate women's social skills in facing hazardous situations in general. By introducing the concept of an *alternative family*, Buber Agassi offers support to perceiving the 'family' in more dynamic terms, as a social formulation, which adjusts itself to its social surrounding, and accommodates itself in changing conditions and situations. This observation implies that at times of social crisis, the self-evident components of the 'family' are exposed as irrelevant and its cultural-ideological dimension is broken up.

Gendered persecution and sexualized violence

Research on women in the Holocaust has enjoyed growing recognition in the academic and public realms over the last decade. The increasing number of historical and social studies on 'Women's Holocaust' discuss, among other things, the degrading experiences that distorted their human existence and femininity, the way in which they reacted to the loss of family members, how they coped with daily problems, and the way in which their past roles changed and adapted to the rapidly changing situations. These studies also had a political objective: To afford a voice and place to women who vanished and were silenced, to confer prominence on the unique experiences of women as a collective and to develop the subject of women's Holocaust as a legitimate and significant field within Holocaust research. This stream of research also implied a protest against the male discourse, which often ignored women's perspectives, silenced and overlooked their personal and collective existence.

Feminist scholarship on the Holocaust claims that women, those who perished and those who survived, were frequently perceived in academic publications and in the arts as an anonymous group among the victims. Against this background, it is not surprising that many feminist publications discussed women in the Holocaust in isolation from men and often as responding better to the horrendous situations. They suggested, implicitly or explicitly, that women coped better with starvation (e.g. Myrna Goldenberg, 1998) and with problems of hygiene (e.g. Rochelle Saidel, 2004). Others insisted that women tended to be more altruistic (Sara Shalev, 2003). Some scholars pointed to women's different type of memory, which is "always complex, always multiple, dynamic and fragmented", as Lentin (2006) proposes. (Her essay is published in the Hebrew version of this volume). She further argues that "in contrast to men's linear chronologies, women's tales are often multiple, ambivalent and recursive. If men's stories tend to follow the main traits of idealized auto/biographies, women's stories are often deviant, subverting the collective's story" (ibid: 274).

As the importance of feminist perspective has been acknowledged and as voices and experiences of women survivors became an inseparable part of the Holocaust commemoration, it appeared that feminist research could have adopted a more integrated approach. And yet, research on 'women and the Holocaust' seems to have not exhausted itself as yet. On the contrary: the articles in this book indicate that studying narratives and memories of women from the Holocaust offers divergent outlooks and insights that necessitate a distinct feminist focus. The special and independent emphasis on women's experiences and representations affords an opportunity to expand the knowledge of what happened to women, as women, in the Holocaust. It enables, for example, the revival of the life stories of women who did not survive, as does Herta Nöbauer in her article on two Jewish anthropologists, Marianne Schmidl and Eugenie Goldstern, and Rochelle Saidel in her essay on political prisoners in the Ravensbrück concentration camp.

Another significant feature of Holocaust research from a feminist perspective is the analytical framework it offers for associating various aspects of women's experiences during that period with universal gender issues. Nöbauer's work, for instance, on the two women anthropologists dismissed from Austrian universities, stresses gender discrimination in the academia in general. With this in mind, her tragic heroines become trailblazers in a struggle that has since become an obvious issue on the feminist agenda.

Focusing on women's perspectives likewise calls for a broader (and universalistic) feminist outlook. It enables us to break down politically constructed divisions between women, as if they belonged to essentially distinct, hostile collectives. Thus, whereas conservative Holocaust research relates to the Jewish genocide and places all Jews (men and women alike) in total opposition to all Germans (men and women) under the Nazi regime, a feminist/gendered approach highlights a common fate—the oppression of women on both sides—inflicted by a patriarchal chauvinist regime, which Nazism was. Deconstructing the Jewish/non-Jewish dichotomy introduces, I suggest, a more complex understanding of the Holocaust and the Nazi era's other human contexts.

Such an argument is supported by Riane Eisler (1987), who suggests that the last 5000 years of human culture is eminently androcratic (differing from *gylany*, the social system characterized by equality and peace that preceded it). Building on Marija Gimbuta's (1977) archaeological findings from "Old Europe", Eisler argues that the term *androcracy (andros* in Greek means man) describes the social system in which men's domination is based on power or on the threat of exercising force, a system in which half of humanity is dominated by the other half. Moreover, she argues (1992), the rise to power of the Nazis in Europe illustrates:

> . . . [a] return to the dominator configuration, the core configuration of top-down authoritarian rule, be it in the family or the state, the ranking of the male half of humanity over the other half, and a great deal of socially condoned and officially perpetrated violence... You see it was not by accident that getting women back into their traditional place was one of the *leitmotifs* of the Nazi rise to power.

Eisler also suggests that Hitler's *Mein Kampf* (1962) is the most prominent neo-androcratic document of the twentieth century. Millett's analysis supports this argument in suggesting that "patriarchal societies typically link feelings of cruelty with sexuality, the latter often equated both with evil and with power..." (ibid). Andrea Dworkin's provocative book, *Scapegoat: The Jews, Israel, and Women's Liberation* (2000) offers further support to this analysis. She suggests that throughout history, women and Jews have been stigmatized as society's scapegoats. According to Dworkin, the previous millennium witnessed a terrifying period of misogyny and antisemitism. She compares the Nazis' terror, whose aggression was both race- and gender-motivated, to the inquisition, which targeted women as witches and Jews as heretics.

Helga Amesberger and Brigitte Halbmayr offer a striking example of this line of argumentation. In their paper, they suggest that in no other ideology has sexuality played such an important role as in National Socialism. The enforcement of its racist goals made it necessary to control the sexual behaviour of the population of the German Reich, especially that of women. Women's sexuality and their reproductive ability were subjected to the racist paradigm of generating and preserving the 'Aryan race' and the 'German national community'. Amesberger and Halbmayr show how the patriarchal base of the Nazi regime destroyed the social boundaries between women who belonged to the 'right', 'proper', 'Aryan' race and those who were outcasts, the 'non-Aryans', with all sexually controlled on the basis of their gender. Women from both 'sides' were disgraced as whores and punished in relation to their fertility, as mothers and pregnant women, although Amesberger and Halbmayr emphasize the differences in the extent of punishment inflicted on the various groups.

Kirsty Chatwood also contributes to blurring the distinctions between perpetrators and victims, as Jewish men were found to be able of carrying out acts of sexual assault on their Jewish female partners. Sexual assaults were committed mainly against women, but also against children and men, such a phenomenon is common in human society. Nonetheless, the main message of Chatwood's work lies in the fact that the patriarchal social order and the gendered division of power in Nazi Germany—and in contemporary society at large—makes women a highly vulnerable group in terms of sexual assault and persecution. Their sexuality and femininity plays a major role in constructing categorical distinctions and social boundaries for the sake of establishing community, nationhood and the 'purity of the superior race'.

Thus, the essays by Amesberger and Halbmayr as well as Chatwood foster the understanding that evil does not reside exclusively in one specific camp and goodness does not automatically belong to victims of any kind of persecution, whether sexual or otherwise.

Vandana Joshi's article on women denouncers provides another illuminating example for casting doubts on the gendered essentialist approach. While Eva Fogelman's article argues that women risk their lives to save others no less than men, Joshi shows how women can be vicious in contrast to the compassionate-protective and altruistic stereotype attributed to them. Joshi describes women as serving the Nazi regime within the private domain of the family living room. Women contributed their share by informing on Jewish families in their neighborhoods; they were thus capable, no less than men, of destroying Jews. They acted like watchdogs in their racist community. Within the German patriarchal structure, women could enjoy society's esteem if they adopted an immoral conduct consistent with the sexist and racist system controlled by men.

Barbara Distel's account of the persecution of German and German-Jewish women in Nazi Germany demonstrates other advantages of a research approach that undermines constructed dichotomies. Distel notes the ongoing disinterest of Holocaust research in the persecution of women in Germany as members of families opposed to the regime and as half of the country's Jewish population. Bearing in mind the few protests against the regime, she describes the courage of German women who dared to demonstrate against the arrest of their Jewish partners.

Gendered altruism and women's leadership

Gender research of the Holocaust also contributes to scholarship of women's leadership, both Jewish and non-Jewish, under the Nazi regime, which is poorly documented.

Saidel's essay on Jewish political prisoners is one example. She tells the stories of seven women with differing political views who arrived at the Ravensbrück concentration camp at various times during the six years of its existence. While most of the non-Jewish female political prisoners brought to the camp in its early years survived, the Jewish political prisoners were exterminated in the gas chambers. Jewish women were persecuted by the Nazis both as political activists and as Jews. The stories of Olga Benário Prestes, the German Communist, and Dr. Käthe Pick Leichter, the Austrian Social Democrat, clearly reveal the heroism of those women and describe their leadership prior to their arrival in the camp and throughout their lives there. Like Schmidl and Goldstern in (Nöbauer's essay), Käthe Pick Leichter was also rejected by the University of Vienna because women were not accepted there. Her work for women's rights—organizing discussion groups as the head of the Department of Employment in the Austrian government—and her study of working women indicate extensive feminist activity as early as the 1920s. Jewish women participated and apparently even led many of these activities.

Sophie Scholl's story, told by Annette Dumbach, offers a fascinating portrait of a young woman's courage while taking part in activities that led to her capture and execution. Sophie was a member of a student group called the White Rose, a famous group active in the resistance during the Nazi era. Dumbach suggests that "her story is uniquely her own; there are no generalizations to be made". However, German women ("hundreds, perhaps thousands", as she notes) took part in "some act of resistance, of kindness, of decency amid existential perils. Many were tortured and killed. A large number of these women were Social Democrats, Communists, some Catholic nuns, and many who remain unnamed and unknown". Dumbach's paper supports other arguments such as that made by Eva Fogelman. Fogelman's concern rests with the gender perspectives of courage, namely that both men and women were involved in daring acts of self-sacrifice while endangering themselves to save others. Her work also supports the implied argument made in the Amesberger and Halbmayr article that righteousness and evil are not distributed between the 'persecutors' and the 'victims'; rather, both are found across all social divisions and borders.

Similar to Saidel and Dumbach, Fogelman elaborates on women's heroism. However, she rejects any argument of essentialist gender differences with respect to the types and motives of rescue and heroism. She argues that in saving Jews, women took risks that are generally attributed to men. Moreover, she maintains that there are no real gender differences in compassion and ethical motives for rescue, as attributed mainly to women in some studies. Fogelman also emphasizes aspects of personality and of personal motivation alongside the social roles and circumstances underlying altruistic behavior in the Holocaust. She concludes that Carol Gilligan-style dichotomous gender differentiation lacks any evidentiary basis. Women, like men, endangered their lives in the Holocaust for the sake of others. Both genders had altruistic motives, a common voice expressing decency and simple humanity.

Nevertheless, the dispute over the significance and implications of gendered perspectives for studying the Holocaust stems from the gendered debate itself. It appears, therefore, that distinguishing Holocaust narratives by gender contributes significantly to Holocaust scholarship. The approach comparing men's and women's experiences in the Holocaust context in terms of moral behavior by attributing a kind of superior moral conduct to women, as victims, saviors, family members and so forth, or as having essentially different and better skills, has become the focus of heated discussions. Eva Fogelman's essay on altruism provides one example for objecting to arguments about essential gender differences.

Gender and womanhood in Holocaust representations

Remembering is instrumental in feminist research into the Holocaust, as in Holocaust research in general. It is perceived as a way of affording life after death to those whose physical existence was annihilated, and as a way of memorializing the experiences of the survivors. Documenting women's experiences, raised from memory and processed within a context distant from the historical events, reaffirms, vitalizes and actualizes them. This is what I do in my article based on my mother's memories as they were recounted to me. The importance of this analysis is in actualizing things that took place in the past, even if it is not clear what 'really' happened. It appears that efforts to unveil any "truth" or "real facts" behind the stories has been found, time after time, to be impossible. "Memory is not History" suggest Martin Davies and Claus-Christian Szejnmann (2007). They, further argue that:

> The history of reactions to the Holocaust reveals a basic reality: that history, though it keeps the past present, manages a world that is constantly changing. It is a basic truth: the human world is by definition temporal, hence transient. The 'truly stated' facts history preserves are—to use classical, Aristotelian terminology—accidents in time as a process of degeneration. (ibid: xxxii).

My article implies that remembering, like any other human performance is affected, among other things, by gender dictates. It appears that social, intellectual, emotional and other aspects involved in remembering, reflect gender-based differences. This argument is clearly supported by Ronit Lentin's analysis (as presented in her paper in the Hebrew version of this volume, Hertzog 2006). Following Mary Gergen and Ken Gergen's work (1993: 195-196), she suggests that women's recollection is different from men's. According to the Gergens, males' auto/biographies tend to follow the classical lines of fundamental Western 'monomyths'—the sagas of a hero who triumphs over many obstacles—whereas most women's lives are characterized by multiple and parallel trajectories, affected by their mothering and nurturing roles. Lentin consequently claims that:

> ... in contrast to men's linear chronologies, women's tales are often multiple, ambivalent and recursive. If men's stories follow the traits of idealised auto/ biographies, women's stories are often deviant, subverting the collective's story. The narratives of Israeli women Shoah survivors often deviate from the arguably male linear Shoah narrative, the trajectory of which begins prior to the Shoah, and continues via Shoah (and often *gevurah*: acts of heroic resistance), to *tekumah* (redemption) in the State of Israel. (ibid: 274).

My mother's narrative offers evidence to this claim, although its analysis broaches key social issues that are, apparently, relevant and meaningful beyond gender. Applying past memories to her daily life serves my mother, so it seems, in handling disturbing situations in the present. The instrumentalization of Holocaust memories enables her to deal with the past, whether to cope with her memories of incredible suffering or to fulfill the commitment to remember those who perished. Her ability to 'humanize' the Holocaust, her insistence on remembering events through positive lenses and her tendency to soften her memory of the events indicate, in all probability, modes of recall that are compatible with ways of thinking perceived as 'feminine'.

Esther Fuchs discusses the cinematic creation of woman as either sex object or sexual subject. She argues that Nazi racism is condemned in cinematic representations through the glamorized Jewess who nevertheless embodies danger and fatal risk for those who are attracted to her. She suggests that the Jewish protagonist of Holocaust romances is constructed in sexual terms, whether virgin or courtesan, heterosexual or lesbian. The Jewess is both redeemed and doomed by her romantic attachment to gentile men and women, who are portrayed as valiant resisters of the Nazi regime, or as naive collaborators. By establishing the virgin/ whore dichotomy, the Holocaust romance succeeds in normalizing the Holocaust as a story about sexual innocence and experience. Moreover, shifting the blame for her death to the 'reckless' victim herself, the Holocaust romance implies that the tragic heroine is the victim of her own actions; blame is thus shifted from the (male) perpetrator to the (female) victim.

The articles in the book have been divided into four sections: "The adaptations of Jewish families to horror", "Gendered persecution and sexualized violence",

"Gendered altruism and women's leadership", and "Gender and womanhood in Holocaust representations". The concept underlying this division is one of expanding circles, at whose heart is the woman: in the narrow but dynamic and open circle of the family, she is portrayed as responsible for other members and improvising opportunities and connections; in the expanded circle, the woman is facing authoritative and powerful agents, who control her freedom, social status and sexuality; in the wider circle of the encounter with more distant social environments, she appears as saving and leading others; the widest circle relates to the memory of the past that is linked to the present and the future, where the annihilated woman-mother is perceived as a symbol of humanity, the persecuted Jewish woman is represented through sexist stereotypes and the memories of the woman survivor are incorporated in her daily interactions.

This is, of course, not a strict division, and readers are invited to approach the articles in the different sections from various perspectives and according to their needs and preferences.

References

Arad, Y., Gutman, Y., Margaliot, A. 1978. *Documents on the Holocaust: Selected Sources on the Destruction of the Jews of Germany and Austria, Poland and the Soviet Union*. Jerusalem: Yad Vashem. (Hebrew).

Baumel, T. J. 1998. *Double Jeopardy, Gender and the Holocaust*. London & Portland, OR: Valentine Mitchell.

Bernstein, D. 1987. *A Woman in Eretz Israel: Striving for Equality during the Period of the Yishuv*. Tel Aviv: Hakibbutz Hameuchad. (Hebrew).

____. 1992. (ed.). *Pioneers and Homemakers: Jewish Women in Pre-state Israel*. Albany, NY: SUNY Press.

____. 1992. "Human Being or Housewife? The Status of Women in the Jewish Working Class Family in Palestine of the 1920s and 1930s". In D. Bernstein (ed.). *Pioneers and Homemakers: Jewish Women in Pre-state Israel*. Albany, NY: SUNY Press.

Bloom, R.A. 1991. "Women in the Defense Forces". In B. Swirski and M. P. Safir (eds.). *Calling the Equality Bluff. Women in Israel*. New York: Pergamon Press.

Davies, M.L., Szenjnmann, C.C.W. 2007. "Introduction". In *How the Holocaust Looks Now, International Perspectives*. New York: Palgrave Macmillan.

Dworkin, A. 2000. *Scapegoat, The Jews, Israel and Women's Liberation*. New York: Free Press

Eisler, R. 1987. *The Chalice and the Blade: Our History, Our Future*. Harper Collins Publishers.

____. 2001. "Toward an Economics of Caring". Lecture delivered at the Boston Research Center (BRC), March. *http://www.partnershipway.org/html/subpages/*

articles/brckeynote.htm#top

Fuchs, E. (ed.). 1999. *Women and the Holocaust: Narrative and Representation.* Lanham & Oxford: University of America Press.

Gergen, M.M., Gergen, K.J. 1993. "Narratives of the Gendered Body in Popular Autobiography". In R. Josselson and A. Lieblich (eds.). *The Narrative Study of Lives.* Newbury Park: Sage.

Giacaman, R., Johnson, P. 1988. *Building Barricades and Breaking Barriers: Palestinian Women in Politics in the Occupied Territories.* Birzeit, West Bank: Birzeit University.

Gimbutas, M. 1977. "The First Wave of Eurasian Steppe Pastoralists into Copper Age Europe". *The Journal of Indo-European Studies.*

Goldenberg, M. 1996. *Lessons Learned from Gentle Heroism: Women's Holocaust Narratives.* Thousand Oaks, California: Sage.

___. 1998. "Memoirs of Auschwitz Survivors – The Burden of Memory". In D. Ofer and L.J. Weitzman (eds.). *Women in the Holocaust.* New Haven: Yale University Press.

Hertzog, E. 1998. *Immigrants and Bureaucrats: Ethiopians in an Israeli Absorption Center.* Oxford and New-York: Berghahn.

___. (ed.). 2006. *Women and Family in the Holocaust.* Beit Yitzhak: Otzar Hamishpat. (Hebrew).

Hitler, A. 1962. *Mein Kampf.* Boston: Houghton Mifflin.

Kaplan, A.M. 1998. *Between Dignity and Despair: Jewish Life in Nazi Germany.* New York & Oxford: Oxford University Press.

___. 1991. *The Making of the Jewish Middle Class: Women, Family and Identity in Imperial Germany.* New York: Oxford University Press.

Lentin, R. 2006. "Women Survivors Narrate Transnistria". In E. Hertzog (ed.). *Women and Family in the Holocaust.* Beit Yitzhak: Otzar Hamishpat. (Hebrew).

Marx, E. 1987. "Labour Migrants with a Secure Base: Bedouin of South Sinai". In J. Eades (ed.). *Migrants, Workers and the Social Order.* London: Tavistock.

Millett, K. 1969. "Theory of Sexual Politics". In K. Millet, *Sexual Politics.* UK: Granada.

Ofer, D., Weitzman, L.J. (eds.). 1998. *Women in the Holocaust.* New Haven: Yale University Press.

Ringelblum, E. 1993. *Diary and Notes from the Wartime Period – the Warsaw Ghetto: September 1939 - December 1942.* Jerusalem: Yad Vashem and Beit Lohamei Haghetaot. (Hebrew).

Ringelheim, J. 1985. "Women and the Holocaust: A Reconsideration of Research". *Signs.* 10 (4): 741-761.

Rittner, C., Roth, J. 1993. *Different Voices: Women and the Holocaust.* New York: Paragon.

Saidel, G.R. 2004. *The Jewish Women of Ravensbruck Concentration Camp.*

Madison, WI: University of Wisconsin Press.

Shalev, S. 2003. *The Altruistic Dialogue: Ethics, Women and Politics*. Haifa: Pardes. (Hebrew).

Strum, P. 1992. "The Women are Marching". *Brandeis Review*. 12(2),

Swirski, B., Safir, M.P. (eds.) 1991. *Calling the Equality Bluff: Women in Israel*. New York: Pergamon.

Talmon-Garber, Y. 1970. *The Individual and Society in the Kibbutz*. Jerusalem: Magnes. (Hebrew).

___. 1987. "The Family in the Kibbutz". In: D. Roth-Heller and N. Naveh (eds.). *The Individual and the Social Order*. Tel Aviv: Am Oved. (Hebrew).

Part 1

The Adaptations of Jewish Families to Horror

Gender and Family Studies of the Holocaust: the Development of a Historical Discipline

Judith Tydor Baumel

Introduction

In the beginning there was Anne Frank. Ever since her diary was first published in 1947, millions of readers have been introduced to the inner world of the Holocaust's most famous victim.[1] Initially, some did not connect her with that cataclysm, never before having heard the term; others intentionally universalized her story, portraying it as a symbol of humanity in a world filled with oppression and terror. However, the *Diary of a Young Girl*, as the 1950 English language edition was entitled, was first and foremost the story of a Jewish child and later, young woman, living in hiding with her family during the Holocaust. Many of its better-known entries focused upon the interrelationships of mothers, children and families in wartime. It was therefore natural to assume that the interest surrounding the diary's publication might generate a number of gender and family studies examining Jewish life under Nazi domination.[2]

What happened in reality? When did historians began to pursue gender and family (or child-oriented) studies of the Holocaust? How did they integrate the examination of family and women's culture into ongoing Holocaust research? Why did they initially concentrate upon certain aspects of these topics while completely ignoring others?

This article will discuss four waves of publications dealing with gender and family issues during the Holocaust that appeared during the second half of the twentieth century up to the present (2004). My argument is that the appearance of each wave of publications was connected to a number of factors which affected its timing and the nature of its contents. Such factors may have included public events, political changes, research developments and survivor status. Furthermore, the publications appearing within each wave often had topical common denominators affected, once again, by the factors listed above.

Any serious historical analysis of gender and family Holocaust research necessitates a few basic definitions. The term "Holocaust" entered the English language in the late 1950s to describe the fate of Jews under Nazism. Thus, by definition, gender or family studies of the Holocaust, as opposed to those of the Second World War, must concentrate primarily upon *Jewish* women, children or families in Nazi lands. Following the recent growth of interest in the refugee and postwar survivor phenomena, "Holocaust studies" has expanded to include those topics as well. Consequently, I will also refer to those studies concentrating upon women and child refugees and survivors.[3]

The idea to group gender and family studies of the Holocaust together had its genesis in the early conception of gender studies being an outgrowth of the more familiar category known as "family studies". Indeed, a number of the early women's Holocaust studies were actually part of a complete study of the family, such as the research on these subjects that was carried out in the Warsaw ghetto. As time progressed however, gender studies earned its own niche, making it into a separate category from family studies, with its own disciplinary tools. The two groups of studies are therefore not synonymous, each having its own characteristics and trajectory. Contemporary studies of women during the Holocaust are no longer just studies of "women and children" but are instead studies of women's society, female behavior, gendered socialization and other facets of women's lives. Nevertheless, the two topics are dealt with together in this article as both were long considered almost subaltern topics, having little to do with the "major" Holocaust issues. Furthermore, for many years the two topics developed along similar lines, being considered part of the study of "daily life". Consequently we have almost come full circle, with family studies often seen now as a part of gender studies, just as five decades ago almost all studies of women were considered to be part and parcel of family studies.

The first wave of gender and family Holocaust historiography

The first books on women, children and family life under Nazism began to appear in Germany shortly after the end of the Second World War.[4] However, almost without exception, their subjects were *German* women and children living in the Third Reich and not *Jewish* women and children under Nazi domination.[5] Non-Jewish women and children from Nazi-occupied lands were likewise excluded from most historical research conducted until the late 1980s. One exception was Kiryl Sosnowski's pioneering study, documenting the fate of Polish children in Nazi-occupied Eastern Europe.[6] Another was the numerous volumes written on women and youth in the European resistance movements.[7] However, most of this resistance literature can not be considered family- or gender- oriented as its primary focus was *resistance* and not *women* or *family*. Furthermore while all of these studies concerned themselves with Nazi Germany or the Second World War, few of them could truly be labeled "Holocaust research"—family, gender or other.

When did the study of Jewish women and children during the Holocaust begin? While the terms "gender and family studies of the Holocaust" are new, the phenomena they describe are not. Using a technique which had become popular in inter-war Polish social research, more than half a century ago the late Dr. Emanuel Ringelblum began studying the lives of Jewish women and children in the Warsaw ghetto. During 1941 and 1942, the staff of his clandestine *"Oneg Shabbat"* archives distributed questionnaires to women living in the Warsaw ghetto, inquiring into their lives as women, mothers and wives under ghetto conditions. Their answers, together with the interviewer's own historical observations, were supposed to serve as the basis for a comprehensive examination of ghetto family life. However, before Ringelblum could bring this project to fruition the ghetto was liquidated and the subjects of his study were sent to Treblinka. Today, only a handful of questionnaires and some preliminary conclusions remain as mute testimony of this early attempt at a gender and family study of the Holocaust.[8]

The first wave of publications about Jewish women, children and family during the Holocaust began within a year of the war's end. During the early postwar period (1945-48), little synthetic Holocaust research—gender, family or other— was pursued. Those historical essays which appeared usually documented life in ghettos and concentration camps. Only a few of these focused upon women's experiences—for example, Denise Dufurnier's 1948 study of the women's camp at Ravensbrück.[9] What *did* characterize the period were memoirs: first-person stories by survivors who had experienced life in hiding, ghettos, camps and the resistance. Broadly speaking, it appears that during this early period more memoirs were being written by young girls and women than were being penned by men. Was it because women had a heightened historical consciousness, a greater need to record their experiences, or just because more of them survived the Holocaust? There is no way to be certain. One argument states that the sexual disproportion of memoirs may stem from the fact that women were often granted a longer rehabilitation period than were men before having to rejoin productive society. However this is not a convincing explanation, as, for example, many women became mothers shortly after being liberated from the camps, which clearly could not allow them any gradual rehabilitation. A more coherent explanation may be the gendered socialization that encouraged female activities such as writing memoirs. Thus, after an initial stage of physical rehabilitation, it appears that women devoted more time to emotional recovery, recording their wartime experiences as part of a postwar catharsis.

Some of the better-known memoirs published during this period are those by Rozka Korczak and Zivia Lubetkin—both members of Eastern European Zionist underground movements; books by Olga Lengyel and Gisella Perl, Jewish physicians who had survived Auschwitz; recollections of Auschwitz survivor Kitty Hart; the diaries of Mary Berg and Justina Davidson[10] and, of course, the posthumously published diary of Anne Frank.

It is interesting to note that many of the memoirs written during this early period, as opposed to the more randomly preserved diaries, were those of pivotal figures in the Eastern European Jewish resistance movements or women who acted as camp functionaries. Not only did members of these groups have a better chance of survival; their stories were also considered of greater public interest than those of "ordinary" survivors. This was particularly true in the case of memoirs written first in Palestine and later in Israel by women who had been active in the Zionist underground movements. For more than two decades after the Second World War, the Israeli public remained "resistance oriented", expressing reservation about what it considered to be the passive "Diaspora" behavior of most Holocaust victims. These were the years when the accusation of "going as sheep to the slaughter"[11]—a description coined by Abba Kovner in the Vilna ghetto—was hurled in the face of more than one Holocaust survivor in Israel.[12] This was also the period when the Holocaust Memorial Day in Israel was still entitled *Yom Hashoah ve-Hamered*—Holocaust and Resistance Memorial Day—as opposed to the more moderate name adopted later, *Yom Hashoa ve-Hagevurah*—Holocaust and Heroism Memorial Day—thus placing the armed uprisings on an equal if not higher plane than other Holocaust experiences.[13] These were also the years when Israeli political movements actively encouraged members who had belonged to the Zionist resistance groups in Europe to record their memoirs for posterity.[14] Again it appears that initially, more women than men took up this challenge.

What characterized the early memoirs penned by women who had survived the Holocaust? Firstly, their authenticity. Memoirs written right after the war were often a more accurate description of their authors' experiences than later recollections, as memory had not yet been blurred by the passage of time. Secondly, the absence of moralizing. Although often referring to the author's ideological background, early memoirs were usually a factual, if often emotional reconstruction of the author's wartime experiences, devoid of the moral preaching or long-range ideological conclusions that characterized many of the later Holocaust memoirs. Thirdly, many of the early women's memoirs concentrated upon experiences belonging solely to women's culture. This was highly unusual at a time when it was uncommon to conceptualize gender. Fourthly, a majority of the early women's memoirs began in September 1939, providing only a short description of the author's prewar life. In this they differed from the early men's memoirs which usually devoted at least a few paragraphs to the inter-war period. Finally, virtually all of these women's memoirs written during this early period emphasized the role of female self-help and mutual assistance in their author's survival. The key to survival would later help scholars in analyzing women as historical subjects in wartime. Examples of this are the recent studies on women's mutual assistance during the war, particularly in women's camps, as an explanation of their ability to survive under conditions which were often worse than those which men were forced to endure.[15]

The first wave of publications focusing upon Jewish youth during the Holocaust followed a different pattern than those concentrating upon women. Only a handful of children's diaries had survived the war and most were not published until the 1960s or even later.[16] The same held true for memoirs, During the early postwar years more child survivors had not yet reached the stage of writing memoirs, although at least one appeared in Poland as early as 1946.[17] However, although no Holocaust-related gender studies were being conducted during this period, two research projects involving children were then underway. The first was headed by Ernst Papanek, a German-Jewish educator who had found refuge in France and later in the United States. In 1945 Papanek was commissioned by the Columbia School of Social Work to examine the history and acclimatization of child Holocaust refugees in America. His preliminary findings were published by Columbia University in 1946. Papanek then appropriated the source material for his personal collection. Eventually, the entire collection was donated to the New York Public Library where it became a gold mine for scholars seeking authentic documentary material on the history of child refugees in the USA.[18]

The second research project focusing on children was conducted by Dr. Mark Dworzecky, a Lithuanian physician who abandoned the medical profession after the war in order to devote the rest of his life to Holocaust research. Dworzecky's projects were of a completely different nature than Papanek's and focused on children in ghettos. In early 1942 Dworzecky began documenting the health and welfare of Jewish children in the Vilna ghetto where he was incarcerated. In 1946 he published his first articles on the fate of Jewish children and families under Hitler.[19] Although not of standard historical quality and often medically oriented, these articles were an example of early academic studies about children and families during the Holocaust.

Both Papanek and Dworzecky's studies were based on circumscribed sources— material provided by the child refugees themselves in one case; Jewish wartime and postwar observations concerning children and families in ghettos in the other. This source material was supplemented by the readily available German documentation captured by the Allies, upon which most early postwar studies were based. Neither project could make use of Jewish sources such as children's diaries, registers of Jewish welfare organizations or communal records, as these had either been destroyed or were as yet unavailable.

Publications of the 1950s and 1960s

The second group of publications about women, children and family during the Holocaust began to appear in the early 1950s and continued for almost two decades. These years are often considered a semi-dormant period between two waves of "Holocaust consciousness", the first encompassing the immediate postwar period and the second beginning in the mid-1970s. With the exception of those monumental works based primarily upon German documentation,[20] little systematic Holocaust research, and virtually no gender or family studies, was conducted until the late 1960s. Exceptions were the socio-historical studies of refugee children during the Holocaust, many of which were commissioned by child welfare organizations to mark a milestone in the institution's history. An example of a book about children appearing during this period is Freier's history of the Youth Aliyah movement.[21] These studies were largely based on non-German documentation, such as those of Jewish child welfare organizations in France, England, Israel and the United States. Thus they differed from the earlier studies on children which were forced to rely primarily on Jewish observations supplemented by Nazi documentation. Furthermore, the fact that many of the studies were commissioned by the same organizations whose achievements they were supposed to document, often influenced the author's conclusions. Finally, the authors were usually unable to interview more than a few former refugee children, and thus their studies lacked a dimension which was necessary for a balanced analysis.

As for Holocaust memoirs by women and children, these appeared sporadically throughout the years in question, growing in number from the late 1960s onward. A high proportion of the women's memoirs then being published were still those of resistance member or wartime functionaries. Several collections of children's testimonies also appeared during this period. One such book was Karen Gershon's collective autobiography of German-Jewish refugee children in Britain.[22] These volumes provided the very dimension which was missing in the studies of refugee organizations—that which could only be provided by the survivors themselves. One interesting book published during this period combined women's and children's Holocaust-related experiences: Lena Kuchler-Zilberman's account of her postwar attempts to rehabilitate Jewish children in Eastern Europe.[23] This book, originally published in Hebrew and later translated into English, made a great impact upon early Holocaust consciousness in Israel of the 1960s.

Why was there such a dearth of Holocaust scholarship and memoirs during these years? Firstly, many survivors had overcome their immediate psychological need to bear witness and were now busy rebuilding their lives.[24] Furthermore, some survivors who had originally intended to record their story began to realize that they had a dwindling or almost non-existent audience. One must also bear in mind the sociological and cultural framework in which many of the survivors, particularly the young ones, functioned. Until the growth of multiculturalism during the early 1970s, a great number of survivors attempted to play down their past and assimilate into the culture of their adopted country. Thus, while there were probably those who recorded their memoirs for "home consumption", few were willing to actually publish the results and emphasize their foreign origins. Finally there was the economic aspect of publication. Prior to the mid-1970s when a resurgence of "Holocaust awareness" put the topic back on the literary map, few publishing houses considered Holocaust literature to be a lucrative venture. Therefore, they did not actively solicit manuscripts from survivors, as would be the case a decade or so later.

The lack of synthetic Holocaust research during the 1950s and 1960s, particularly on topics concerning gender and family, was intrinsically connected to the historical and cultural climates of the period. The state of source material, dearth of memoirs, lack of historical awareness regarding the importance of gender and family history, and even political considerations, were all factors which discouraged the systematic study of women's and children's Holocaust history during these years.

The absence of Holocaust studies focusing on gender and family contrasts sharply with the extensive research then being conducted about German women, children, and families under Nazism. One explanation cites the Nazi preoccupation with motherhood and feminism as having provided the impetus for the immediate postwar gender and family studies. A second conjecture places these studies within the context of the postwar research being conducted on life under Fascism. Examinations of women and children under Nazism were therefore considered to be just another facet of such research and not forerunners of gender and family studies as we know them today. Yet a third explanation concentrates on source availability. The profusion of Nazi documentation regarding German women and youth made these topics extremely "researcher-friendly". Finally, one must not overlook the cultural aspect. German interest in topics concerning women and family dates back to the early years of the Weimar Republic. Thus it was natural for postwar scholars to continue where their predecessors had left off.

Publications of the 1970s

A third group of publications began to appear in the mid-1970s. These were directly related to two worldwide phenomena: the growing interest in issues pertaining to the Holocaust and the academic development of women's and family studies. Three major categories of Holocaust literature dealing with gender and family appeared during this period: individual memoirs, collected testimonies and academic studies.

Ever since the end of the Second World War, the overwhelming bulk of Holocaust literature had consisted of survivor's memoirs. With the development of "Holocaust awareness" in the mid- to late 1970, dozens of these memoirs began to appear. Many survivors who had toyed with the idea of recording their experiences now took up the challenge in a world receptive to their stories. Others who had never considered such a venture were encouraged to do so by friends, family, Holocaust centers and astute literary agents.

Women's Holocaust memoirs appearing from the mid-1970s onward strongly emphasized gender-related experiences. Similar to the earlier groups of memoirs, women survivors writing in the 1970s and 1980s continued to emphasize the unique female experience during the Holocaust. Once again, almost all authors cited women's mutual assistance as a primary factor in their survival. Secondly, while earlier women's memoirs usually began with the outbreak of war, later memoirs often included a certain number of the author's prewar experiences. This expanded chronological framework usually stemmed from the authors' heightened sense of historical awareness. Consequently, the reader was not only provided with necessary background material but was also introduced to Jewish women's culture during the inter-war period. Third, this group of memoirs was characterized by a comparative degree of modesty in sexual matters. Although they tended to be emotionally revealing, many of the later women's memoirs were reticent about physical intimacy among women and matters concerning female sexuality during the Holocaust. This contrasts sharply with literature written by female survivors in the 1940s and 1950s which was often surprisingly revealing about such matters. What caused this turnabout? One conjecture notes that the sexually explicit *"Stalag"* literature was at its zenith during the earlier period, creating a tone and cultural framework for all Holocaust literature then appearing. Another connects it with the authenticity of early memoirs whose authors did not attempt to "beautify" their experiences for their potential audience. A final characteristic of both men's and women's memoirs was the absence of an ideological ballast. While memoirs of this later period were frequently tinged with religious or moralistic overtones, most were devoid of the ideological beliefs which accompanied many of the earlier publications. This stemmed from the fact that memoirs were now being written by "plain, ordinary survivors" as opposed to political ideologues or former resistance members.

What characterized the *women* writing Holocaust memoirs after the mid-1970s? They were survivors of concentration camps, ghettos, transit camps, family camps; had lived in hiding, assumed false identities and fought among the partisans. Some had written before, some had not; some had written for their families only. In short, any and every type of female—or for that part, male—survivor was writing Holocaust memoirs. The same held true for children's Holocaust memoirs. People who had never considered putting their stories into print were suddenly publishing intimate recollections of their prewar and wartime experiences. Many of these children were now entering their sixth decade and able to finally devote time to dealing with their past. Part of their catharsis assumed a written form, creating children's Holocaust memoirs written 30 years or more after the fact. Thus, all of those writing memoirs became links in a worldwide chair reaction caused by "the need to bear witness".

A second category of Holocaust literature during this period which dealt with gender and family was the collected volumes of women's and children's memoirs.[25] An example is Lore Shelley's story of the Jewish women who worked at the political bureau at Auschwitz.[26] Some of the collected memoirs are annotated, others are solely narrative. All provide unique source material for gender and family historians examining Holocaust-related experiences.

These collected volumes of testimony differed from earlier memoirs in several ways. Firstly, almost all were prepared by historians and Holocaust scholars and not just by the survivors themselves. Thus they heralded a surge of academic interest in gender and family studies of the Holocaust. Secondly, most of these collected testimonies required the cooperation of a group of survivors willing to bare their private experiences for the public eye. This could only occur during a period of heightened Holocaust awareness when participants understood the importance of making their stories known to the public. Finally, the collected testimonies were usually thematic, thus paving the way for later academic research on gender and family during the Holocaust.

In addition to the individual and collective memoirs, analytical research on women and children during the Holocaust began to appear from the mid-1970s. An example of books dealing with children is my study of the rescue of Jewish refugee children and their resettlement in the United States.[27] These studies attempt to view children as subjects and not solely as objects of history, thus opening a new dimension of child-oriented Holocaust research. All are written by scholars familiar with both Jewish and non-Jewish sources, most rely on both written and oral documentation, and most important: many adopt an interdisciplinary approach in examining their topic.

An example of a historical study of women appearing during this period is Marion Kaplan's social history of Jewish women and family in prewar Germany. It is interesting to note that for the first time, a number of these gender-oriented studies were being written by historians who were not themselves survivors of the Holocaust. Furthermore, with few exceptions, the aforementioned studies dealt with women, children and families during the Holocaust from a predominantly historical perspective. Most drew upon the numerous memoirs and diaries which had become available over the previous two decades. Some adopted an interdisciplinary approach, integrating the scientific tools and methods of the social sciences into a humanities framework. Finally, all were typical of the new wave of historical gender and family studies appearing during the late 1970s and throughout the 1980s—studies which made women and children subjects, and not just marginal objects of history.[28]

Publications of the mid-1990s and onward

Since the mid-1990s an additional wave of gender and family Holocaust studies has appeared, expressing itself in numerous literary and academic forms: diaries, memoirs, collective autobiographies, poetry, media studies, historical works, sociological analyses and the like. Similar to the previous wave, it is characterized by a plethora of publications, primarily in English, Hebrew and German, linguistically corresponding to the major populations where "Holocaust awareness" had become ingrained.[29]

By the last decade of the twentieth century, Holocaust research, writing and commemoration were already commonplace phenomena. Tens of thousands of books had already been published on the subject and many more were underway. Holocaust research centers and memorials had become integral fixtures in Israel, Europe, and throughout the English-speaking world, and even in a number of cities outside of the West, such as in Fukuyama-City, Japan.[30]

Simultaneously, the political uses and misuses of the Holocaust continued to develop along lines that had emerged during the early- to mid-1980s, affecting the cultural and literary spheres as well. In Germany, the "historians' debate" *(Historikerstreit)* over Germany's culpability regarding the Second World War, stemming from an attempt to create a new historical reading of the Holocaust, initiated a reappraisal of German complicity and guilt for the results of the Second World War.[31] A steady growth of Holocaust revisionist publications in Europe, Canada and the United States catalyzed the enactment of legislation forbidding its dissemination.[32] The death dance and ultimate fall of Communism in Poland was an impetus for discussions of the Polish role during the Holocaust. One of their expressions was a debate that raged on the pages of the Catholic newspaper *Tygodnik Powszechny* during the late 1980s, centering around Polish poet and novelist Czeslaw Milosz's (1911-2004) poem, "A Poor Pole Looks at the Ghetto".[33] Even in Israel, there were those who presented the growing tendency to evoke the Holocaust outside the historical realm as a legitimate justification for military and political actions, while others considered it to be a demonic manipulation of Jewish history.[34] All of these factors played a role in keeping the Holocaust alive as a dynamic topic of literary and scholarly worth, expressing itself in contemporary events.

Academia and literature were also intrinsically connected. Throughout the 1990s, academic study of the Holocaust continued the process that had begun a decade earlier in which topical focus shifted from the heroic to that of daily life. The growing symbiosis between academic publishing and trade press led to a search for new Holocaust memoirs by those who were once considered "unheroic" figures. By publishing such memoirs, publishers strengthened the already existing scholarly trend towards examining the lives of groups which had once been seen as marginal in Holocaust study: refugee children, those who survived the war living under false identity, *mischlinge* girls and young women, and Aryan women in mixed marriages.

Four factors characterized the gender and family studies of the Holocaust appearing during this period. In the literature from the 1970s and 1980s there was almost no common denominator among the authors of autobiographical women's literature other than the fact of their having survived the Holocaust. Now one could note a chronological tie among the authors in terms of age. As time progressed, the majority of women's autobiographies and memoirs were no longer being written by adult survivors but by those who had been children and teenagers during the Holocaust.

Two and three decades earlier, when the major wave of Holocaust first person memoirs was being published, these young survivors had been in their late 30s and 40s, busy with the fabric of daily life, professional development and economic advancement. By the mid-1990s these child survivors were often facing retirement, giving them time and perspective to re-evaluate their wartime experiences and consider the importance of leaving a testimony for future generations. As the years progressed and the number of survivors who had experienced the war as middle-aged adults dwindled, these teenage and young adult survivors had become the majority of those still alive. Consequently, publishers began to focus their sights on these groups as potential autobiographical authors. One example of such books is Jana Renee Friesova's memoirs of her life as a teenager in Terezin.[35]

A second factor characterizing the gender and family studies of the Holocaust appearing from the 1990s onwards were the authors' wartime experiences. A large number of authors writing in the earlier decades had been survivors of ghettos and Nazi camps. As opposed to this group, authors of this new wave of memoirs and autobiographies had often spent most of their war years in hiding, under an assumed identity, or even outside occupied Europe. For years they had considered their story to be secondary in importance to those of concentration camp survivors, forced laborers, underground couriers and the like. The historical re-evaluation of Holocaust experiences, which were broadened to include Jews who had not been incarcerated in ghettos and camps and even those who had escaped Europe during the Nazi era, enabled these young survivors to redefine themselves and their connection to the Holocaust. Consequently, growing numbers of them now felt ripe to express their wartime experiences in autobiographical form. Memoirs and studies in this category include Philip K. Jason and Iris Posner's collected autobiographies of refugee children from Europe who had found refuge in the United States during the Holocaust.[36]

A third factor characterizing this new wave of Holocaust literature was the result of a growing trend to broaden and even universalize the Holocaust experience. While non-Aryan Christians or Christian women married to Jews had rarely received literary acknowledgement in the earlier waves of Holocaust literature, these groups now were the focus of memoirs, autobiographies and historical studies. A spinoff of this group were memoirs that were being written by non-Jews and particularly non-Jewish women who in their youth had been incarcerated in Nazi camps for political and religious reasons. Although by definition "Holocaust" was originally a term relating only to Jews, they, too, became part of the new trend of Holocaust and Nazi-related literature. An example of such literature is Nanda Herbermann's account of her experiences as a German Catholic woman imprisoned in Ravensbrück for resistance work.[37]

These first three factors that I have mentioned delineate the age, historical background, and religious-racial definition of the authors but do not explain why a large proportion of them were women. This may be explained by a fourth factor, the authors' growing sociological and psychological awareness of gender and self. The age of these young survivors had made them into part of the generation that had been influenced to a certain degree by the nascent phenomena of gender equality and self-expression of the 1960s and onward. The feminist movement, affecting not only those women who had come of age during that decade, but also those who had undergone that process half a generation earlier. Thus, not only were members of this group often more in touch with their personal need to write down their experiences as an expression of closure in terms of their Holocaust traumas, but awareness of the importance of writing Holocaust testimony among female survivors in this age group was also becoming an expression of their female self.

The result was a growing number of children's and young adult Holocaust autobiographies and memoirs, in which women appeared even more prominently than men. This may be explained by factors slightly different than those evidencing themselves in previous groups such as an earlier retirement age for women and greater gender- and self-awareness due to the later waves of the feminist movement.

In addition, a new wave of historical studies appeared during this period, focusing on the experiences of special groups of women during the Holocaust and the Second World War and particularly those who actively participated in the military campaign. An example of such a study is Nigel Fountain's account of women at war, a large portion of which focuses on the Second World War.[38] This book was also combined with a recent exhibition at the Imperial War Museum in London, about Women and War.

Another phenomenon evidencing itself in this wave of Holocaust literature were studies being written about women or children during the Holocaust and its aftermath. Some, such as my study of gender and the Holocaust or Dalia Ofer and Lenore Weitzman's collected volume of studies about women during the Holocaust, were written by scholars either born outside Europe or after the war.[39] A number of them, however, were being written by historians and social scientists who had themselves been teenaged or young-adult women survivors who successfully merged the personal with the professional. An example is Felicja Karay's autobiographical study of young women in the HASAG-Leipzig labor camp.[40] Similar to studies appearing from the 1970s onward, these studies also often integrated tools of the humanities and social sciences, presenting the readership with a truly interdisplinary book.

The symbiosis between academia and publishing, both scholarly and trade, had its affect on the academic development of gender and family as well. The plethora of literature which by now had appeared on these subjects granted them academic legitimacy and made it possible to compose comprehensive bibliographies on their various aspects. Although each discipline developed separately, sometime during the early 1990s initial attempts were made in the United States and Israel to prepare courses that incorporated themes from Women's Studies or Gender Studies into the study of the Holocaust.[41] The result was a number of courses dealing with women and Holocaust that focused upon the fields of history, sociology, or literature. Taught initially in only a few institutions, the topic was slowly picked up by scholars throughout the world. For example, my course on "Women during the Holocaust", which I began teaching in Israel during the mid-1990s, was the first of its kind to be offered in that country. Yet within a few years, the topic was being taught by scholars at various Israeli universities and colleges who had been drawn to the topic of gender studies and began dealing with topics pertaining to women during the Holocaust.[42]

* * *

In the preceding discussion we have examined four cycles of interest in family and gender Holocaust studies. We have shown how the first publications dealing with women and children during the Holocaust were usually memoirs or studies being conducted by survivors. While memoirs and diaries continued to be published and even grew in number, they were augmented by analytical studies, appearing as part of the second cycle of publications. Finally, another group of historians, most of whom were born after the Second World War, are now involved in synthetic gender and Holocaust family research, thus providing us with a conceptualization of these topics.

Nevertheless, our survey leaves several questions yet unanswered. What generated each of these cycles? Were they connected to world events, new historical interpretations or other academic developments? What common denominators do we find among the topics chosen for family and gender scholarly research? What limitations hindered their examination and analysis?

The various surges of interest in gender and family studies of the Holocaust do not seem to have been influenced directly by world events connected to the Holocaust, the Second World War, Jewish identity or Jewish survival. Neither the Kastner nor Eichmann trials gave birth to specific Holocaust research concerning women, children and families. The same holds true for the ratification of relations between Israel and Germany, the Israeli debate over accepting German restitution or the Six-Day, Yom Kippur or Lebanon wars. The only factors which appear to have generated a growth of interest in these topics were the development of "Holocaust awareness" during the mid-1970s and the simultaneous growth of academic interest in women's culture and family studies.

Historical enthusiasm is contagious. As interest in family and gender studies of the Holocaust grew, it assumed distinctive forms depending upon source availability, researchers' personal inclinations and subject popularity. As a rule, it appears that these studies began more as appendices to the general Holocaust research rather than being conducted as independent historical examinations. For example, the studies conducted during the late 1970s on refugees in the Free World gave birth to research in the 1980s on refugee children and women in exile. Similarly, research conducted during the mid-1980s on religious life during the Holocaust has now given birth to studies on the lives of Orthodox women's groups in ghettos and camps. It also appears that the general trend in the mid- to late 1980s to examine daily life and death in various Nazi camps led to specific studies of women in camps or studies of women's camps in the late 1990s. Gender and family studies of the Holocaust have thus been primarily reactive, responding to existing research patterns and academic fields of interest. Nevertheless, most research on the topic of gender and family has remained within the realm of social history, barely touching upon what many Holocaust historians consider the nexus of Holocaust research: women in the Final Solution, gender and Jewish leadership during the Holocaust, and so on. Only recently did historians truly begin broadening their interpretation of what were now considered major Holocaust topics. Consequently, until the latest wave of Holocaust publications, the topics of gender and family had remained marginalized as compared to what was once the "hard-core" Holocaust scholarship. Only now have steps been taken in order to integrate the topics into the mainstream of Holocaust research.[43]

Why did synthetic gender and family studies of the Holocaust begin to appear only at such a late date? Two factors which played a major role in their timing were topic awareness and source availability, something which held true for all Holocaust studies being limited by similar factors. However, while general Holocaust research began to flourish during the early 1970s after Jewish source material became available, the problem was much more acute with regard to gender and family studies. These were heavily based upon oral documentation and memoirs, source material which began to appear in quantity at an even later date. Thus, gender and family studies of the Holocaust have only recently taken their place on the academic map, due to the growing awareness of feminist and family history and the abundance of newly available sources. As a result, historians are only just beginning to integrate the examination of family and women's culture into general Holocaust research. Numerous challenges face historians specializing in gender and family research of the Holocaust. One is to look actively for sources and topics instead of merely responding to existing ones. Another is to give their research an interdisciplinary focus, as most of their primary sources, such as memoirs and testimonies, are best studied on the interdisciplinary level. There is also a caveat. Several of the early gender studies on the Holocaust exhibited a tendency towards excessive exploration of speculative tangents. These included, for example, an early tendency to claim that women suffered *more* than men and not *differently* than them. Serious historians would do well to avoid such pitfalls, concentrating instead upon analytically probing their designated topic.

The question of research themes brings our historiographical survey to a close. Until recently one could state that most research concerning women during the Holocaust was in its infancy while that pertaining to children is better developed. This is primarily a factor of source availability, as researchers have been privy to a plethora of sources concerning Jewish children and family life during the Holocaust. A second reason stems from the earlier historical awareness of the centrality of family experiences to understand the human basis of the Holocaust, and only a later acceptance of the importance of women's experiences in order to round off the fuller historical and sociological picture.

Many themes still remain to be covered. Little has been written about the rescue of children by resistance organizations. Early research has now begun on the question of women as leaders during the Holocaust. Other research projects in their infancy concern women's religious lives during the Holocaust, motherhood in camps and ghettos, women's and children's culture during the Holocaust, and the Jewish woman in Nazi ideology.[44]

What direction will the new research on gender and family during the Holocaust take? Will it be incorporated into existing fields of research such as studies of the resistance movement, rescue activities and the Displaced Persons problem, or will it become an independent academic discipline? Will the choice of themes be dependent upon the historian's personal inclination or will we witness an attempt to coordinate research and share information about sources and studies in order to avoid duplication and to streamline projects?

One thing appears certain. In spite of the rise of new Holocaust scholarship, particularly since the 1990s, junior researchers at the beginning of their academic career often still face what I did twenty-five years ago when I spoke of my desire to specialize in women's Holocaust experiences. At the time, one of the more prominent Holocaust historians in Israel gently suggested to me to choose a "more suitable and serious" topic, in his words, so as not to become a laughingstock in the eyes of my more senior colleagues and ruin my academic career. Today, criticism of the topic is not as broad, but there are still critical voices being raised against it.

After a decade of research and teaching the subject in highly acclaimed academic centers throughout the world, when researchers of the subject were convinced that there was no longer a need to justify their choice of topic, they suddenly found themselves facing opposition from unexpected corners. The most noteworthy of these was *Commentary* editor Gabriel Schoenfeld, who in 1998 published an extensive essay examining the topic and questioning the legitimacy of study that combined the issues of Holocaust and gender.[45] The revival of calls to halt the academic study of women during the Holocaust was a wake-up call for some of the scholars involved in that undertaking who realized that there was still a need to "fine-tune" some of the gender research that was being carried out.

While a portion of the criticism is justified, particularly that having to do with faulty methodology, other parts, focusing on publications, now have less of a basis in reality. It is an academic fact of life that courses require syllabi and bibliographies. As I have shown, for many years there had been a large body of research literature about women and the Second World War, and particularly women and Nazi Germany. However, only from the early 1990s onward, after a minimal number of academic studies dealing with women during the Holocaust could be found on university library shelves, did it become possible to develop academic courses dealing with the Holocaust and gender.[46] Yet, there was also a catch: these studies were not congregated in one academic discipline. Some were historical, others were literary, a third group was sociological or psychological and a fourth category of studies was interdisciplinary. Furthermore, the number of studies in each discipline was still minimal.

Until collected historical studies about women during the Holocaust were published towards the mid- to end of the 1990s, historians preparing a reading list for a course on the history of women during the Holocaust sometimes found it necessary to include selections from other disciplines—a move that was frowned upon by those diehard purist historians examining course syllabi, shaking their heads in dismay when encountering selections from sociology or literature.[47] In addition, there was still a fair amount of academic criticism being directed against some of the newer studies—usually those from sociology, whose historical background or methodology was questionable. One of the arguments that critics such as Schoenfeld leveled against Holocaust scholars interviewing women about their gendered Holocaust experiences, was that by prodding and directing their interviewees, they had created issues where none had actually existed. Other arguments focused on what was seen as faulty methodology, which in certain cases was actually the use of social science methodology by humanities scholars.[48]

Both of these difficulties—the bibliographical and the methodological—were used to dampen the enthusiasm of younger historians wishing to specialize in gendered Holocaust studies. More often than not, historians of all ages (and usually women) proposing to teach the topic, were subjected to criticism by their less adventurous peers and by senior historians who claimed that they were surrendering to popular fashion rather than developing a sturdy academic discipline. This phenomenon was far more common in Israeli and European universities than in American ones, as they often lagged behind their American counterparts in matters of gender and other historical topics. Even senior historians who were favorably disposed toward the topic sometimes found it necessary to warn their colleagues teaching or researching the subject, of the need to rebut their critics. Even at the time this article is being written, voices are still being raised against studies dealing with the Holocaust and gender.

As Rochell Saidel writes in her recent review essay of academic literature about women and the Holocaust, the fact that scholars dealing with the topic still have to preface their studies with a justification of their choice of topic accentuates the realization that a gendered perspective on the Holocaust is far from having become the norm.[49] Where does this leave gender and family studies of the Holocaust as we enter the twenty-first century? Firstly, as I have shown here, with a growing body of sources and studies that is being added to constantly, in the form of additional survivor memoirs and research being conducted by scholars throughout the world. Secondly, despite the aforementioned scholarly criticism, with growing numbers of university based and independent scholars who are focusing their research on these topics. The result is seen in the form of books and articles dealing with the topic, Internet sites devoted to it and research institutes that gather and encourage the production of additional studies dealing with women and family during the Holocaust.[50] It therefore seems that at the beginning of the twenty-first century, with the numbers of survivors dwindling and Holocaust revisionism reaching new peaks, gender and family studies of the Holocaust are nevertheless becoming legitimate historical disciplines. Having ultimately taken their place alongside other topics of Holocaust studies, they continue to expand our knowledge of a period about which we will continue to learn but will probably never truly understand.

Notes

1   Millions of copies of Anne Frank's diary were eventually published in a total of 36 countries. For the history of her diary and its various editions see the complete annotated edition, first published in 1986: *De Dagboeken van Anne Frank*.

2   On similar integration of these and related topics see K.K. Sklar, "A Call for Comparisons", in *The American Historical Review*. 95:4, (October 1990), p. 1114.

3   For the history of the term "Holocaust" see G. Korman, "The Holocaust in American Historical Writing", *Societas* 2 (Summer 1972), pp. 251-270. For a development of this theory see: Y. Bauer, *The Holocaust in Historical Perspective*, Seattle: University of Washington Press, 1978.

4   Long before women's history took root in the mid- to late 1970s, German scholars were exploring gender- and family-related issues within the political, social, economic and military contexts of the Third Reich. These investigations were augmented by similar research projects being conducted outside Germany, some of which had their

roots in wartime and even prewar studies.

5 If an essay *did* refer to Jewish women and children, it usually mentioned them in passing and confined itself to those living in Germany. Later research projects about the German family and feminism during the Weimar and Nazi periods—particularly those conducted during the 1980s—began to include more serious references to the lives and fates of Jewish women and children. Again, however, they confined themselves geographically to Germany, thus excluding close to 95 percent of European Jewry from the scope of their scholarly examination. See, for example, R. Bridenthal, A. Grossmann, and M. Kaplan (eds.), *When Biology Became Destiny: Women in Weimar and Nazi Germany*, New York: Monthly Review Press, 1984.

6 K. Sosnowski, *The Tragedy of Children Under Nazi Rule*, Poznan-Warsaw: Zachodnia Agency Prasowa, 1962.

7 Many of these studies had their roots in a desire to refute accusations of wartime collaboration.

8 Regarding the history of the *"Oneg Shabbat"* archive, see J. Sloan (ed. and trans.), *Notes from the Warsaw Ghetto: The Journal of Emmanuel Ringelblum*, New York: Schocken, 1974, pp. ix-xxvii. The portions of the archive which were found after the war are in the Yad Vashem archive, Microfilm collection MJ.

9 D. Dufurnier, *Ravensbrueck, the Women's Camp of Death*, London: Allen and Unwin, 1948.

10 R. Korczak, *Lehavot BaEfer (Flames in the Ashes)*, Tel Aviv: Sifriyat Hapoalim, 1946; Z. Lubetkin, *HaAharonim Al Hahoma (The Last Ones on the Wall)*, Ein Harod: Hakibbutz Hameuchad, 1947; Olga Lengyel, *Five Chimneys*, Chicago, 1947, London: Mayflower, 1972; G. Perl, *I was a Doctor in Auschwitz*, New York, 1948, Place Tamarac: Berger, 1987; K. Hart, *I Am Alive*, London: Abelard-Schumann, 1946; M. Berg, *The Diary of Mary Berg*, New York, 1945; G. Draenger, *Pamietnik Justyny*, Cracow: Centralna Zydowsky Komisja Historyczna przy C.K. Zydow Polskich, 1946.

11 The phrase appearing in Abba Kovner's famous proclamation in the Vilna ghetto calling for revolt on 1 January 1942. The proclamation's text appears in Y. Arad, et. al, *Documents on the Holocaust*, Jerusalem: Yad Vashem, 1981.

12 On the attitude towards survivors in the newly established State of Israel, see H. Yablonka, *Survivors of the Holocaust*, New York: NYU Press, 1999.

13 On the history of this day and its national and religious significance see J. Baumel, *A Voice of Lament: The Holocaust and Prayer (Kol Behiyot: Hashoa Vehatefila*, Ramat Gan: Bar Ilan University Press, 1992.

14 See for example, D. Porat, "Beslicha Uvehesed: Hamifgash Bein Rozhka Korchak leven Hayishuv Umanhigav" ("In Forgiveness and Kindness": The Meeting between Ruszka Korczak and the Yishuv and its leaders"), *Yalkut Moreshet* 52 (1992), pp. 9-33.

15 See, for example. J. Baumel, "Social Interaction Among Jewish Women in Crisis: A Case Study", in *Gender and History* 7:1 (1995), pp. 64-84.

16 Two which did appear during this period were actually diaries of young women: Mary Berg and Anne Frank.

17 Hanka H. [sic.], *W ghetcie I obozie, Pamietnik dwunastoletniej dziewczyny*, Cracow 1946.

18 Much of this source material was used later by Iris Posner in starting the OTC (One Thousand Children) Organization in 1999, focusing on the thousand Jewish refugee children from Europe who found refuge in the United States during the Holocaust. See also the Ernst Papanek Collection, New York Public Library; Manuscripts Division.

19 For example in *Medical Notes*, special edition, September 1946; *The Jewish Frontier*, November 1946, *Mahbarot (Notebooks)*, October 1946.

20 R. Hilberg, *The Destruction of the European Jews*, New York: Harper and Row, 1961.

21 R. Freier, *Let the Children Come: the early history of Youth Aliyah*, London : Wiedenfeld and Nicolson, 1961. Other books of this period are K. Close, *Transplanted Children*, New York: Victor Gollancz, 1953; N. Bentwitch, *They Found Refuge*, London: Cresset, 1956; D. Lowrie, *the Hunted Children*, New York. W. W. Norton, 1963; J. Bernard, *The Children You Gave Us*, New York, 1973; and P. Leshem, *Strasse Zur Rettung 1933-1939: aus Deutschland vertrieben – Bereitet sick Juedische Jugend auf Palaestina vor*, Tel Aviv: Verband der Freund der Histadrut, 1973.

22 K. Gershon, *We Came as Children: A Collective Autobiography*, London : Gollancz, 1956. See also: B. Bellak (ed.), *Donne e bambini nei lageri nazisti*, milan 1960.

23 L. Kuchler-Zilberman, *My Hundred Children*, New York: Pan, 1957.

24 On the emotional rehabilitation of survivors in the United States see W. B. Helmreich, *Against all Odds: Holocaust Survivors and the Successful Lives they Made in America*, New York: Simon and Schuster, 1992.

25 One early example is *Lohmat Nashim (Women's Resistance.)*, Tel Aviv 1979. The collected memoirs of Jewish women prisoners in the A.E.G. camp in Germany.

26 L. Shelley (ed.) and trans), *Secretaries of Death: Accounts by Former Prisoner who worked in the Gestapo of Auschwitz*, New York: Shengold, 1986. See also: J. Baumel, *Voices from the Canada Commando*, Jerusalem: Emunah, 1989; A. Eisenberg, *The Lost Generation: Children in the Holocaust*, New York: Pilgrim, 1982.

27 J. Baumel, *Unfulfilled Promise: The Rescue and Resettlement of Jewish Refugee Children from Germany in the United States 1934-1945*, Juneau: Denali, 1990. Other studies include: J. Walk, *Hinuho Shel Hayeled Hayehudi BeGermaniya (The Education of the Jewish Child in Germany)*, Jerusalem; Yad Vashem, 1975; C. Shatzker, "Reality and Imagination – Perceptions of the "Organized Jewish Youth During the Holocaust", in Asher Cohen, Joav Gelber, Charlotte Wardi (Eds.), *Comprehending the Holocaust*, Frankfurt, Bern, New York, Paris: Peter Lang, 1988, pp. 215-223; D. Dwork, *Children with a Star: Jewish Youth in Nazi Europe*, New Haven and London: Yale UP, 1991.

28 M. Kaplan, "Jewish Women in Nazi Germany: Daily Life, Daily Struggles, 1933-1939", *Feminist Studies* 16 (1990), pp. 579-606; G. Kreis, *Frauen in Exil. Dichtung und Wirklichkeit*, Duesseldorf: Claassen, 1984; A., Lixl-Purcell (Ed.), *Women of Exile: German-Jewish Autobiographies since 1933*, New York, Westport, London: Greenwood, 1988; J. Ringelheim, "The Unethical and the Unspeakable: Women and the Holocaust", *Simon Wiesenthal Center Annual* 1, Chappaqua, NY, 1984, pp. 69-87.

29 D. Michman, "One Theme, Multiple voices. The Role of Linguistic Cultures in Holocaust Research", in Shmuel Almog, David Bankier, Daniel Blatman, Dalia Ofer (eds.), *The*

Holocaust: The Unique and the Universal. Essays Presented in Honor of Yehuda Bauer, Jerusalem, Yad Vashem and the Institute of Contemporary Jewry, 2001, pp. 8-37.

30 The Holocaust Education Center, Japan (In Memory of 1.5 million Jewish children), founded in June 1995 by Mr. Makoto Otsuku who had met with Otto Frank, Anne Frank's father, in 1971 and already then expressed the desire to found such a center.

31 Articles by M. Broszat, E. Notle, Y. Habermas, H.. Meier, E. Yekel, Y. Gutman in Yad Vashem Studies 19 (1989).

32 R. Knoller, "HaTofa'a shel Hakhashat HaShoa" (The Phenomenon of Holocaust Revisionism") *Mahanayim* 9 (December 1994), pp. 238-247.

33 J. Blonski, "Poor Poles Look at the Ghetto", (Heb.) Yad Vashem Studies 19 (1989), pp. 271-281.

34 Y. Elkana", Bizhut Hashihiha" ("On the Right of Forgetting"), *Haaretz* 2 March 1988, p. 13.; B. Evron, "Hashoa – Sakana La'am" ("The Holocaust – a Danger to the Nation"), *Iton 77* (21), June 1980, pp. 12-17; D. Michman, "Dimuyei Hashoa Bavikuah Hatziburi Hayisraeli: Mishkaim Umanipulatzia" ("The Image of the Holocaust in the Israeli Public Debate: Sediment and Manipulation"), in *Gesher*, 135 (Summer 1997), pp. 52-60.

35 J.R. Friesova, *Fortress of my Youth: Memoir of a Terezin Survivor*, Madison: University of Wisconsin Press, 2002. Other such books include: S. M. Whiteley, *Appel is forever: A Child's Memoir*, Detroit: Wayne State UP, 1999; A. Brostoff, *Flares of Memory: Stories of Childhood During the Holocaust*, Oxford: Oxford UP, 2001.

36 P. K. Jason and I. Posner, *Don't Wave Goodbye: The Children's Flight from Nazi Persecution to American Freedom*, Westport: Ct and London: Praeger, 2004. Other books include: V. Samuel, *Rescuing the Children: a Holocaust Memoir*, Madison: University of Wisconsin Press, 2002; L. J. Rozenberg, *Girl with Two Landscapes: The Wartime Diary of Lena Jedwab 1941-1945*, New York and London: Holmes and Meier, 2002; A.K. Schieber, *Soundless Roar: Stories, Poems and Drawings*, Evanston: Northwestern UP, 2002; F. Walker and L. Rosen, *Hidden: A Sister and Brother in Nazi Poland*, Madison: University of Wisconsin Press, 2002.

37 N. Herbermann, *The Blessed Abyss: Inmate #6582 in Ravensbrueck Concentration Camp for Women*, Detroit: Wayne State University Press, 2000; C. Crane, *Divided Lives: the Untold Stories of Jewish-Christian Women in Nazi Germany*, New York: St. Martins, 2000.

38 N. Fountain (consulting ed.), *Women at War*, London: Michael O'Mara Books Ltd., 2002. See also: R. Pennington, *Wings, Women, and War: Soviet Airwomen in World War II Combat*, Lawrence, University Press of Kansas, 2001.

39 J. T. Baumel, *Double Jeopardy: Gender and the Holocaust*, London: Frank Cass, 1998; D. Ofer and L. J. Weitzman, *Women and the Holocaust*, New Haven and London; Yale UP, 1998; See also: Marion Kaplan, *Between Dignity and Despair: Jewish Life in Nazi Germany*, New York and Oxford: Oxford UP, 1998, pp. 62-73; R. G. Saidel, *The Jewish Women of Ravensbrueck Concentration Camp*, Madison, University of Wisconsin Press, 2004.

40 F. Karay, *Hasag-Leipzig Slave Labour Camp for Women: The Struggle for Survival Told by the Woman and their Poetry*, London: Frank Cass, 2002. See also: J. Hemmendinger

and R. Kress, *The Children of Buchenwald: Child Survivors of the Holocaust and their post-war Lives*, Jerusalem and New York: Geffen, 2002; N. Tec, *Resilience and courage: Women, Men and the Holocaust*, New Haven and London: Yale UP, 2003.

41 Although I have been unable to find the date of the first of such courses in the United States, I have been told that it was taught sometime in the period between 1990-1992.

42 I first taught the course at the University of Haifa and at Touro College, Jerusalem in 1994, and later at Bar-Ilan University from 1999 and onward. A similar history course has been taught by Prof. Dalia Ofer at the Hebrew University in Jerusalem since the late 1990s.

43 See for example, B. Throne with M. Yalom, *Rethinking the Family: Some Feminist Questions*, New York: Longmans, 1982; Hunter College Women's Studies Collective, *Women's Realities, Women's Choices: An Introduction to Women's Studies*, New York, OUP, 1983; E. C. DuBois et al, *Femnist Scholarship: Kindling in the Groves of Academe*, Urbana: University of Illinois, 1984.

44 D. Dwork, *Children with a Star: Jewish Youth in Nazi Europe*, New Haven and London: Yale UP, 1991.

45 G. Schoenfeld, "Auschwitz and the Professors", *Commentary* 105 (1998), pp. 42-46; G. Schoenfeld, "Controversy - Holocaust studies: Gabriel Schoenfeld and critics", *Commentary* 107 (1998), pp. 14-25.

46 J. T. Baumel, *Double Jeopardy: Gender and the Holocaust*, London: Frank Cass, 1998.

47 D. Ofer and L. Weizmann (eds.), *Women and the Holocaust*, New Haven and London: Yale University Press, 1998.

48 This issue was expressed in the workshop on teaching about women and the Holocaust, held in Jerusalem in 1995.

49 R. Saidel, "Women's Holocaust Experiences – New Books in Print", *Yad Vashem Studies* 28 (2000).

50 See, for example, Judy Cohen's internet site about studies dealing with women and the Holocaust and Rochelle Saidel's recently founded "Remember the Women" Institute.

Motherhood under Siege

Dalia Ofer

Introduction

The perspective of mothers and motherhood issues in the Holocaust presents an important aspect of the tragedy of the individual and the community. It is connected to the history of the family during the Holocaust, to issues of gender and the cultural role of women, wives, and mothers in Jewish societies. Therefore, it requires for a multidisciplinary approach.

In this, as in any proper study of motherhood, the institutional and individual perspectives are treated in tandem and as intertwined. In the historical description, the approach of the community and its institutional and social frameworks including Judenrat policies, self-help organizations, support for mothers without a spouse, etc., are all factors to be integrated with the personal narratives of mothers. The title expression 'Under Siege' is appropriate to Jewish life during the Holocaust in general. With the description of mothers and motherhood, I focus on a single issue in order to illuminate the perspective of the individual as part of the Jewish collective.

As historical works stress, the particularity of the events presents a difficulty in the analysis of motherhood as a general concept during the Holocaust. Therefore, the description of motherhood in the various Jewish communities of different countries must take into account their differing historical circumstances, and examine the developments and conditions that emerged under Nazi rule and those that affected the Jewish family unit. Theoretical concepts are useful to better understand and formulate a comprehensive explanation of motherhood and family in times of crisis.

Researchers have vast amounts of documentation, though fragmentary, on Jewish life under German rule. There are contemporaneous formal documents, such as the minutes of Judenrat meetings and reports of various committees and self-help organizations, which provide information on numerous topics of daily life. There are also personal letters sent to family members living in other parts of occupied Europe, or between Jews in different ghettos and forced-labor camps. All provide a great deal information about the writers' cultural milieu, the community and social environment. In addition, there are many survivors' testimonies that were recorded at the end of war, which capture their still-fresh memories. A final source of valuable material is Holocaust survivors' postwar testimonies, collected either several or many years after the event. These latter testimonies may reveal new perspectives reflecting the survivors' postwar life experiences as well as the integration of their broader knowledge of the events of the Holocaust into their personal histories. With all these sources at hand, the historian can combine the approaches of an ethnographer, a sociologist, and a psychologist, in order to produce a rich and complex depiction of an individual's history and that of an entire community. Yet the historian must remain aware that the narrative s/he is writing is also a product of his/her own personal and cultural milieu.

The testimonies and other sources of information may lead to seemingly contradictory impressions. Different conditions in each ghetto, different phases of ghetto life, the variety of ghettos, concentration and forced-labor camps, the stages of the war, and shifting policies towards Jewish labor, all leave one with a great sense of apprehension about making generalizations.

By contrast, within the vast amount of documentation there exists only a small amount of contemporaneous material written by individuals—men, women, fathers and mothers. This issue must be addressed empirically. As seen in this paper, the documentation left by mothers is very much smaller, as women left fewer accounts than men and were often depicted through the eyes of men. In her study, *Family Frames,* Marianne Hirsch notes that in Art Spiegelman's book, *Maus:*

> "Anja" [the mother] is simply recollected by others; she remains merely a visual presence and not an oral one. She speaks in sentences that are only imagined by her son or recollected by her husband. In their memory, she is mystified and objectified—shaped to the needs and desires of the one who remembers.[1]

Written memoirs and recorded testimonies of young people describing their families are often filled with statements expressing guilt for having been rescued and surviving. This can also be seen in the testimonies of child survivors who were placed with families in order to be saved, with the unfulfilled promise that one or both parents would come back to retrieve them. These recollections carry a sense of anger and disappointment. Whether expressed by a young person or a child, the longing for the parent is painful. As a result, the representation of the family—and of the mother in particular—is often idealized in testimonies.

We have very little knowledge about the individual families, of whom just a few letters or a single diary were left. Thus, we must be wary of attributing all family behavior as a response to wartime circumstances. It may be that the ties that connected a couple were already thin and fragile before the war and that the wartime crisis simply enhanced its breakup. Usually our conception of a normal family during this period includes a married couple with children; therefore, mothering and motherhood are studied within the context of the family unit. Prior to World War I and its aftermath, family units without a paternal figure had begun to emerge among Eastern European Jewish households. This was in part due to the tragedies of deportation during the First World War and to the large-scale population migrations during the first decades of the twentieth century. Husbands left home for lengthy periods to work, study, or to celebrate a holiday at a Rabbi's court. Some husbands simply abandoned their wives and children. Therefore, in a great number of families during the 1920s and 1930s a different structure came into being, composed of either a mother with her children or a grandmother who became the head of the multigenerational household.[2] However, the concept of the normative family had both mother and father, which comprised the majority of Jewish families.

I would like to include a few more notes about methodology that relates to the theoretical foundation of motherhood as presented by the sociologist William Goode. Every culture has an ideal of motherhood embedded within its tradition. People relate to this ideal from the perspective of their place within their own society. There are differing models of motherhood between different societies and among diverse groups within the same society. Motherhood should be studied within its cultural, social, and historical context. It should also be analyzed from the perspective of economic class and gender differentiation.[3]

I find the theoretical conception of William Goode to be helpful here. I will employ it in relating to the similarities and differences in the practice and concept of motherhood among Jews in different parts of Europe. Two additional theoretical concepts will be used in my analysis.[4]

In a study of the family structure, Wally Seccombe relates to the interdependence between the way families organize their lives and the economic system of their society. In his view, the development and relationship between the nuclear family and the extended family and the different roles of its member were a reflection of economy and culture of the society. Seccombe's perception may assist in understanding the changes within Jewish families when Jews were cut off the surrounding economy.

The third theory that I will use relates to the historical experience of Jews and its impact on the family and particularly upon mothers.[5] In his study on the "Jewish Family in Retrospect: What's Past is Prologue", Benjamin Schlesinger states that the often violent assaults against Jews throughout their history prompted the development of a particular defense mechanism and a strong instinct of mothers to protect their children. This became, in his view, a cultural code within the Jewish family. In relation to the Holocaust and to the experience of Jewish families in Eastern Europe in the twentieth century, one may conclude that the tragic experience of deportation during World War I and the Nazi assault were precursors that reinforced the need for such a protective mechanism. These theories will guide the empirical findings that relate to mothers behavior under Nazi assault.

Motherhood in Jewish tradition and the move to modernity

In Jewish tradition, the ideal figure of a wife and a mother is depicted in the biblical Book of Proverbs (Chapter 31): *"Eshet chayil"* ("woman of valor") a standard part of the Sabbath liturgy in the traditional Jewish home. She is described as devoted to her husband and children, sees to all the needs of the home, and is active economically in providing for the family's livelihood. She is praised by her children and husband, and is known in public for her achievements and her love of the Almighty.

William J. Goode writes about the role relations within a family and in society in his book, *The Family*. He states:

In all societies, a range of tasks is assigned to females and another set is given to males, while still others may be performed by either sex. Both sexes are socialized from the earliest years to know what these roles are, to become competent in doing them, and to feel that the division of tasks is proper.[6]

In modern times, Jewish mothers were greatly influenced by the conventions of the societies in which they lived. Therefore, they were expected to promote the socialization of their children in both the Jewish and the non-Jewish societal spheres. We may observe this in Marion Kaplan's work on the Jewish middle class in Germany during the Second Reich, wherein she described the tension prevailing in the mothers' social messages:

> Faced with the contradictions and constant flux, mothers had to raise proper German children while affirming and redefining Jewishness, to present a family in the appropriate light to a society intolerant of differences, and to create a refuge for a minority to come home to.[7]

Middle-class Jewish mothers had to function as keepers of the religious tradition by modeling Judaism as a way of life: keeping the Sabbath, celebrating holidays, observing dietary rules. They were responsible for their children's good conduct both in school and in the broader non-Jewish society.

Among both Eastern and Western Europe Jews, the home was of major importance in one's integrating into the Jewish tradition. In Eastern Europe, the study of religious texts and rituals was conducted in a more formal educational setting, such as a Jewish afternoon school for boys and occasionally for girls, or in a traditional Jewish school known as the *Heder.* While Jewish identity varied among Jews in the different European countries, the sense of living apart from the general society was more prominent in Eastern Europe. In the traditional Jewish family, the role of a mother was concentrated within the private sphere of the family. (This actually contradicts the image of the proverbial "woman of valor" mentioned above.) However, the private and public spheres were not completely separated. Many wives helped to provide for the family, many being involved in the family business. They often had contacts with customers and their activities in the marketplaces were often considerable. During the 1930s, about one-third of the Jewish women in Poland were employed outside the homes, comprising about 20 percent of the Jewish labor force.[8]

There was a public sphere of great importance, particularly among middle-class families, which involved extending aid to those less fortunate and the poor. This was a more modern form of the *tzedaka* (charity) tradition, which here involved working through institutions, collecting goods and money for contributing to the poor, or doing direct social work among the lower classes. Many women were involved in these activities.

Under Nazi rule and during the war, the Jewish family went through a period of grave crisis. The lives of its members were constantly threatened. Every part of the family unit was greatly devastated by starvation, displacement, and death. One must ask how women, as wives and mothers, coped with the crisis. In the following, I shall pursue major themes of women's self-understanding by describing the major changes in the economic and social situation of the family and how these affected the fulfillment of traditional roles and women's behavior towards their children. I shall also demonstrate how each concept of motherhood was besieged by the Nazi onslaught. In conclusion, I will investigate the legacy of motherhood in the wake of this experience.

Identity: Woman, housewife, mother

Leaving Home

In Eastern and Western Europe, the home was the source of pride and a representation of one's identity in both traditional and non-traditional Jewish families. Housewives would accumulated household items such as furniture, linens and dishes through hard work and painstaking savings. These material acquisitions were a source of self-esteem. Among the middle- and lower-middle classes, the collecting for dowries was a major symbol of devoted mothers and prosperous housewives. Therefore, leaving one's home either by flight or by being forcefully relocated into a ghetto, leaving behind treasured belongings, had a devastating, severely traumatizing affect on women. They felt as if they had lost their anchor in life; they were bereft at having to leave the home that was their safe haven, their natural environment. Thus, for many women the first major humiliating crisis—excepting the loss of a family member—was the expulsion from or need to flee one's home. This happened to tens of thousands of women in the first months of the war when expulsions took place from the regions in Western Poland that had been annexed to the German Reich. (Such actions affected tens of thousands of non-Jewish Polish families as well.) Many women and other family members became refugees, uprooted from their homes within their own country.

Another phenomenon of uprootedness was caused by the massive destruction of cities that were heavily bombed and shelled by the invading German army. In Warsaw, for example, one-third of its houses were hit in German air raids and shelling, with a large number being completely destroyed. As a result, many residents lost all they had and became refugees in their own city. This was the case also in smaller cities and towns, becoming more visible when the Jews were ordered to concentrate in specially designated areas even before a ghetto was established.

Still another group of refugees were comprised of Jews who had been deported from other countries. They were, in fact, exiles: strangers to the new environment, lacking knowledge of the local language, considered as 'others' even by the local Jews. In Poland prior to the mass killing, thousands of Austrian and German Jews were sent to the General Government (the non-annexed, Nazi-administered part of Poland), many to the Lublin area, and housed among the local Jews. I will elaborate on these refugees further on. The extreme case in which the majority of the Jewish population was comprised of such exiles was in Transnistria, the southern part of the

Ukraine that Germany handed over to the Romanians.[9]

Although most became destitute, class differentiation and the extended family situation still mattered. Among those families who remained in their own homes, economic distinctions of the past continued to be meaningful. Families that managed to take household items or other valuables with them, even if they had been deported from their homes, were able after some time to find a room to rent. Families with relatives nearby or in the same city were better off than those who moved to places where they were utter strangers.

Family ties were one of the most important sources of aid. Letters that were sent from one ghetto to another indicate how families in different places endeavored to assist each other. These letters often contained requests for financial assistance from family members or expressed gratitude for money received. A telling example is a letter dated January 1, 1942, from Mirl in Grabow to her brother in Warsaw. She asks him if he had received the money that she had sent him, and informed him of the destruction of the community in coded words, such as *"What Haman planned to do, happen in our place"*. She told about the death of their mother and her own children, and asked him to report on what was happening with them.[10] Loyal non-Jewish friends were often able to assist. Handing over one's household belongings and other valuables for safekeeping was a way to save some material goods and sources of funds, and thus helped reorganizing life, though an uprooted one.

After the establishment of the ghettos, which occurred in each city and town at a different time and place, the economic situation of most families notably worsened, and the number of uprooted families increased considerably. However, there were families whose homes were in the section that was subsequently designated as the ghetto, thus did not have to relocate. These relatively fortunate families were thus were able to sublet rooms and obtain some income thereby.

Under these circumstances, the matter of keeping the family together became dominant. From the mother's point of view it involved the effort to maintain a normative life, to go on with the regular routines even if providing only the basic necessities for the family: food, cleanliness, childcare, assisting one's husband, keeping a sense of a home and some intimacy. All these were the building blocks of a ghetto mother's identity and sense of purpose. This applied to the periods before the beginning the mass killings and deportations to the death camps. In the areas where mass killings commenced with the occupation, it applied to periods of relative quiet in the ghetto or when the deportations to the camps would be suspended for an interval.

Refugees and the lower class

The worst conditions were suffered by those who had to live for long months in the public housing shelters [in Yiddish: *Punkten*] set up for refugees. Situated in public buildings that had no residential accommodations, the physical and sanitary condition in the makeshift living quarters were extremely difficult. They were overcrowded and lacked privacy, making the situation unbearable. Many tried to move out to apartments, but those too were overcrowded.

Women were constrained by being unable to perform their daily duties and the chores associated with being a wife and a mother. With few regular homemaking duties remaining to be performed, women felt stripped of their central role as both mothers and wives and left some of them feeling completely worthless.[11]

The central responsibility of keeping the living quarters clean was beyond attaining in these refugee centers. Lack of hot water and soap made washing and laundry extremely difficult. People became infested with disease-bearing lice, and soon the typhus spread wildly throughout the refugee centers and in the overcrowded apartments. As a result, health issues and epidemics became a major concern for the refugees. The high mortality rate among young children left mothers desolate over their bereavement, and there was not even a proper burial due to the family's lack of money and the large number of deaths. (The percentage of child mortality in the Warsaw ghetto in 1941 was 9.4% and during the first three months of 1942 this rose to 14.8%).[12]

From the Warsaw ghetto we have chilling descriptions of dead bodies in the streets, often left naked and covered by newspapers.

Mothers felt that they were deprived of the ability to fulfill their basic responsibilities and saw how their children were deteriorating in front of their eyes. Poverty, high food prices and the lack of facilities all worked against them. Contemporary records of the period document that the rise in price for bread, potatoes, and other food, resulted in starvation on a large part of the population.[13]

Historian Dr. Emanuel Ringelblum, who initiated the massive documentation project and archive that would enable future historians to write the wartime history of Polish Jewry, noted in his diary on May 20, 1941, that bread prices had increased to 15 zloty for a one kg. loaf. This increase, he added, would bring the majority of the ghetto's inhabitants to the point of starvation.[14]

Isaiah Trunk provided the following prices for a number of basic products on the Warsaw ghetto black market during the first six months of 1941:[15]

Product	Price per kilogram January 1941	Price per kilogram June 1941
Brown bread	3.45 zl	18.15 zl
Rye bread	5.00	27.60
Barley	8.00	25.00
Beans	6.50	29.95
Sugar	9.20	35.80
Potatoes	1.20	6.75
Horsemeat	5.00	20.30
Pork fat (lard)	15.50	72.30

Source: Trunk, Epidemics, Table 3, p. 70

The analysis of the June 1941 prices demonstrates that in order to have the basic nourishment and avoid starvation, a family of four required about 1,200 zloty per month. However, even workers in demand such as carpenters or brushmakers did not earn more then 750 zloty per month, so that even those who worked hovered on the verge of starvation.[16]

For mothers to prepare a meal from the meager products available was a major challenge. Many had come from established, middle-class homes and had no prewar experience of living in poverty.

The problem of starvation was most critical in the large ghettos of Lodz and Warsaw. In places with smaller populations, or in those regions where ghettoization did not occur until the end of 1941, the situation was somewhat easier. However, most records from all parts of occupied Eastern Europe describe the hunger and food shortages as the major issue, even before ghettoization and prior to 1941. The case of Transnistria is even more telling. The first wave of exiles arrived there in the fall of 1941, just before the most difficult winter months. Most of them lacked financial means and had few if any items to barter. The places where they were concentrated were not supplied with food and the majority of these refugees were unable to purchase food from the local population, either due to lack of means or because of the harsh regulations of isolation. Fifty percent of the exiles died in the first winter of 1941/42 because of the starvation and typhus. The records about desperate mothers are shocking. Many sent their children to beg for food in the surrounding villages, despite the danger of being shot by the Romanian or Ukraine gendarmes for leaving the enclosed confines of the ghetto. The extensive death toll left between 5,000-7,000 orphans in the various ghettos of Northern Transnistria.[17]

More women had to work outside the home, either because their husbands were unable to provide or were absent. Work shifts were very long, often from dawn to dark. A few descriptions of the homes of working mothers demonstrate the neglect that often plagued these families. However, working mothers were obliged to maneuver between work and the care of their children during work hours. Avraham Lewin described how working mothers would have to leave their little children at home alone all day. These children often went hungry and cold, having little to wear nor adequate bedding in the freezing, unheated apartments. Often mothers returned home to find a child dead. This situation caused mothers terrible distress and would leave them feeling completely helpless.[18]

A description of medical treatment administered by a nurse to a poor family depicts a family unit consisting of a mother and four children, living under appalling conditions in the basement of an apartment house. The basement had no windows and no light, and no furniture except for a few dirty blankets and several mattresses. The mother had to support her children, so she found work as a laundress for a family that was better off and could pay for the service. Meanwhile her own children were left alone in the neglected and filthy basement.[19] The nurse showed no sympathy for this mother, and her report includes criticism and a sense of estrangement. Twice she emphasizes that the mother was not around to take care of her sick child because she would go out to her workplace. But what were the alternatives for this mother, who had four little ones to take care of? It should be left to the historian's imagination to construct a story of such a family in the Warsaw ghetto or in other similar situations where single mothers struggled to keep themselves and their children alive.[20]

In Warsaw was very difficult for women to find employment. Fragments from the Ringelblum archive depict recently widowed mothers who became hysterical when they were left alone with little children, since they did not know how they would be able to endure. Many asked themselves more than once about the possibility of joining their deceased husbands, but the responsibilities of caring for their children usually took precedence over such thoughts.

A report dated June 21,1942 from the Refugee Committee in Warsaw to Yitzhak Giterman, head of the Central Aid Committee (ZSS), just one month before the mass deportation from the ghetto, reported that 3,500 women and 1,800 men were unemployed in one refugee shelter, with an additional 3,200 children under fifteen years of age.[21] How many of these 3,500 women were mothers with children is not known.

In her research on women, Cecilia Slepak presents the narratives of 16 women and their lives in the ghetto.[22] Several mothers were among the interviewees. One of the mothers previously a middle-class housewife, worked as a cleaning woman in the household of a well-to-do family. One day her husband was taken by the Germans, and she did not know what had happened to him. Despite the great pain this caused her, the only way she was able to provide for herself and her ten-year-old daughter was through her work. She took the child with her to the workplace. She was worried about her daughter's education, but no other solution was available. As a middle-class housewife in the past, who could afford help in her own household, it was difficult and in some respect humiliating for her to work as a maid, but she accepted this. She would comfort herself with the thought that it was a temporary situation, that other people were suffering even more, and that her husband would return. This mother had not lost the sense of being part of a family and a community.

Another narrative included by Slepak was that of a mother of two who became a surrogate mother to the two children of her sister who had died of typhus. She too was without a husband, but her family had already dispersed before she moved to the ghetto. Prior to the war she had been a vendor of vegetable produce, and she continued to sell in the marketplace until she was forced into the ghetto. There she tried to resume her business in order provide for the children. From Slepak's description, we learn that the whole family took part in the enterprise—the mother, her sister and the four children—until the typhus epidemic infected all of them. All recovered except for her sister, who died, leaving this woman with four children to provide for.

Slepak described her with great respect, in particular her struggle to work: as a laundress, a vendor, a cleaning woman—anything to avoid becoming a beggar. She endeavored to take care of the children and was proud that they were not swollen from hunger, though they were very weak.[23]

Sara Selver-Urbach describes her mother before the war as being weak and utterly dependent on her husband. He was the leader of the family, made all the decisions, and was the provider. Things did not change until her father was deported to a forced-labor camp and never returned.

At first her mother was in shock and barely functioned. Her older brother started to work in order to provide for the family's livelihood. However, after the baby brother fell sick, their mother pulled herself together and started to search intensively for ways to provide for her family. Part of their room had a big window facing the street, and this she turned into a shop, hoping to sell used items. After this venture was unsuccessful, she mended clothing and also taught her daughter. Despite the fact that she continued to be bitter and complained constantly about her misery, she went on to keep the children and the family intact. Despite being a religiously observant woman, she was ready to feed horsemeat to her older son, who fell ill, to give him strength. This demonstrated her adaptability to the hardships she experienced.[24]

In addition to the heroic efforts of mothers to take care of their children, there were also cases of a different nature. Some mothers left their starving children in a children's shelter or beside an orphanage door, hoping that their child would be better fed there and would survive. However, that was often an illusion. The increase in the numbers of children at the 39 Dzielna Street children's shelter in Warsaw, according to a report in the Ringelblum archive, demonstrates how many mothers abandoned their children since they felt unable to take care of them. In January 1941, the shelter housed 480 children; six months later in June it sheltered 625 children. (During those months 135 children died in the shelter).[25]

Peretz Opoczynski describes the situation of these mothers as follows:

> There is no doubt that these mothers do this only after anguished self-searching. No doubt their hearts are torn within them as under cover of darkness they sneak away, leaving their babies on the stairs of a CENTOS corridor or the community council building, or just out on the street. The Judenrat together with CENTOS established a home for abandoned children but their numbers increase every day.[26]

Among poor families, children often became the providers. This, however, was true also in families whose situation was slightly better than those described in the preceding paragraphs. The following should therefore be seen as relating also to the middle class, or at least the lower middle class in the ghetto.

The most famous cases are the smuggler children, immortalized by ghetto poet Henryka Lazowert.[27] Smuggling food for their families, these youngsters risked their lives each time they crossed the ghetto's boundaries. This phenomenon of children who became supporters of their families is characteristic of many ghettos throughout Eastern Europe. Testimonies from Transnistria tell that often the local population was more generous to the children than to the adults. And even when they would not let them enter their homes because of the lice with which they were infested, the householders would hand them a bowl of soup and some bread. These situations caused mothers to have intense inner conflicts: on the one hand, they were thankful for the food brought in, but on the other, they felt guilty for the risks that their children were taking.

Bajli Kaselberg was a 15-year-old girl in Warsaw who engaged in smuggling. She described how her mother would stand on the corner of a certain intersection in the ghetto and Bajli would give her a sign from the streetcar when crossing to the Aryan side.[28]

Mothers were often unable to maintain any type of control over their children, especially the ones who had become street children. Lacking a real home, they would wander around all day trying to find something to eat, even to the extent of grabbing food from passersby.[29] The mothers' helplessness brought them so low when they became depressed and starved, that they were no longer able to give a thought to their wandering children.[30]

The lower middle class and middle class

In having some funds at their disposal, the lower-middle- and middle-class families were somewhat better off than those in the lower classes. Even though their income might have been very meager, they were able to exchange household items for food in order to support themselves. As long as a family remained together within its own city, even if moved from their original residence, and had managed to save some of their household items or keep some ties with non-Jewish friends and acquaintances, they had a better chance of surviving—at least until deportations began. These generalizations must, however, be limited by taking into account other factors not discussed here, such as age and health, the size of the family and its social connections.

Barter became a major factor in the economy of the family, and usually these transactions were carried out by women. The common items to be offered were garments and household goods. The latter, as mentioned above, had often been acquired by painstaking efforts during the prewar years, so parting from them took an emotional toll on the mothers. In smaller ghettos such as Kovno and Vilna in Lithuania, Blechatow near Lodz, and Deblin near Lublin, the situation was usually better. This was notably the case in places where the ghetto was not sealed off by a fence or wall, and where some of the workplaces were situated outside the ghetto.[31] In those circumstances, Jewish workers were able to contact non-Jews in order to exchange various items for food to take back with them into the ghetto. It is important, therefore, to bear in mind that situation was different in each ghetto and that the progression of the "Final Solution" in each region and locality had a crucial impact on the control over the ghetto.

Living conditions in all ghettos were dire, and most families lived in one room. Sometimes a family had to share its room with two or more other families. The average occupancy in Warsaw was 9.2 people per room, in Vilna 5.8 – 7, and in Lodz, 7.[32] It is hard to imagine how families could manage in such crowded living conditions. As mentioned previously, there were problems in the refugee centers with the lack of the intimacy, but the circumstances were not much better the crowded apartment. It took a heavy toll on relationships within the family. If one considers Goode's theory mentioned above: in the culture of the Jewish middle class, the wellbeing of the family was the overall responsibility of the wife and mother. It is therefore appropriate to see this problem as worrisome to women more than to men. Women had to share cooking time in the apartment's kitchen, which often served up to ten families. Dividing cooking time or cooking together was a cause for both contention and friendship and solidarity. Under the severe shortages and constant hunger, even if not outright starvation searching in one other's cooking pot could result in agitation. Sometimes mothers who could spare some food were sensitive to the needs of their neighbors and shared their food or helped to feed another family's child.[33] Families invited refugees or children who had lost a parent to eat with them, which resembled the middle-class mothers' prewar involvement in social welfare aid, now in the ghetto setting.[34]

Under these harsh conditions, caring for the children was still a primary concern. Mothers, even when left alone, did their utmost to protect their children from cold and hunger, to provide hygienic conditions for their health, and endeavored to pay attention to the children's emotional and intellectual needs.[35] They utilized all services that were available for children in some ghettos such as Lodz, Vilna, and Kovno: special food rations for young and schoolaged children, or for those recuperating from a serious illness.

All this notwithstanding, the fact is that often very young children of the middle- and lower-middle-classes had to work to support the family. Many survivors testify that mothers felt guilty for sending them to do hard manual work, at the tender age of ten or less, out of necessity. Documents of the ghetto period describe the children's willingness to take responsibility for their family and do all kinds of work for a livelihood. Young children pushed carts, toiled in workshops, went out to peddle saccharin or homemade cigarettes, and the most famous 'occupation' of all: smuggling. On occasion, the fact that the children were at work and not at home prevented or reprieved them from being deported when a roundup of Jews occurred).[36]

The strength of mothers can be seen illustrated in two contemporaneous diaries. The first quote is from the diary of Fela Szeps. She was a 22-year-old from Dabrowa Gornica and wrote about her home until she and her sisters were deported to the Grünberg forced-labor camp in Upper Silesia. This passage is quite telling for many middle-class Jewish families. She wrote:

> In slow stages the normal life returned within the war conditions. These were lives in constant fear, in which one had to hide while walking in the streets. These were days of fear and nights of anxiety [...] our small family was

still holding. Despite the storm outside my mother knew how to create an atmosphere of care and warmth. It was quiet and pleasant in our apartment. "Would you remember my sister?" Not once while reading we completely forgot the outside reality. There always was the threat of being kidnapped to the camps in front of us, but our code (slogan) was "always, everywhere and in all situations—together". Our mother particularly fought to keep us next to her, under her protecting wings, with all her might. And the day came that our nest was destroyed.[37]

It is important to pay attention to the expression "normal life returned" in the opening of the quotation. The description of the quiet time in the diary is far from what one would ordinarily consider a normal daily routine. Only in view of the reality of the labor camp and distance from home, life under Nazi terror could be imagined or reconstructed as normal.[38]

The second quotation presented as a general statement of evaluation is from the diary-memoir of the artist Esther Lurie, who was interned in the Kovno ghetto. Lurie, who lived in Palestine, was caught by the war while visiting family in Kovno. Unmarried and childless, she lived with her married sister in the ghetto after their parents were deported:

I could not stop wondering how delicate women, who were often ill in the good days, became strong under these conditions. In particular, women who had children had to mind their energies. And one can say that children prosper in the ghetto. [...] The only joy that was left for parents were the children. And if we remember that so many mothers were left without the spouse, all that was left for them were the children. They were ready to risk their life for the children, without thinking twice. The fact is that women in the ghetto demonstrated more energy and larger adaptation to the harsh conditions than men. [...] In most cases women were the providers for the family.[39]

These quotations sum up the courage that mothers often displayed when faced with being responsible for their children and the family. This should be read in the larger context of problematizing gender in the narrative of the Holocaust.

Families who were deported to Poland from other countries

Another group of refugees were the Jews deported from European countries to occupied Poland. Often they were deported directly to the death camps, but some were first deported to ghettos or forced-labor camps. As mention above, Austrian Jews were deported to the Lublin region in the fall of 1939 and again in early 1941; German Jews were deported to the ghettoes of Lodz, Kovno, Riga, Minsk and to forced-labor camps.

Abraham Lewin writes about the German Jews in Warsaw:

Between us and them there still stands a wall of many hundred years of prejudice and linguistic division. In the final analysis, it is difficult for a Jew from Hanover to have a conversation with a Jew from Piaseczno or Gryca and vice versa.[40]

What follows is the story of once such deported family. The story of the Berger family from Prešov, Slovakia, as told by Esther Neuman Berger, the daughter who survived, is an example of the plight of a deported mother. The Berger family was a middle-class Jewish family who kept a religious home. They had five children, two boys and three girls, ages 8 to 18. Esther was 10 years old when the war begun. Her 16-year-old sister was deported to Auschwitz in March 1942 with the first group of Slovakian Jewish girls. (It was discovered after the war that having been unable to adapt to camp life, she perished shortly after her arrival.) Two months later, the Bergers were rounded up in Prešov's main synagogue with thousand of other Jews scheduled for deportation to Poland.[41]

When the news of the upcoming deportation came out, the father was unable to exempt his family, despite his good relations with the authorities. The mother prepared a rucksack for each member of the family. In each rucksack she put some bread, which she hoped would last them for a while. She also stitched some money into each of the children's bags and in their clothes. She made sure they remembered by heart the address of her sister who lived in the United States. The father showed the children where he hid the family's valuables and told them about items he had entrusted to his non-Jewish friends. Having lived through the experience of the First World War, the father assumed that he would not return but that the children would, and that they should be able to recover the family's home and assets.

Upon reaching Poland they were brought to the small town of Deblin, near Lublin, from which a few weeks earlier the local Jews had been deported to the Sobibor and Belzec extermination camps. The Berger family received one room in the deserted home of a family that had been deported. Additional rooms in the house and elsewhere were given to other families from Prešov. Jewish homes in Deblin had already been stripped of all the possessions of previous residents. (According to various testimonies, Poles entered the recently vacated houses and stole everything they could take).

The residence was very crowded and dirty. The mother started to clean and tried to obtain some of the necessities to give the small dwelling a semblance of a home. Mrs. Berger found the courage to adapt herself and her family to the new situation. She encouraged her husband and children to go work in the camp near town. She agreed that 12-year-old Esther would replace a Polish Jewish woman who had a work permit, which was considered to be a lifesaver. The woman paid Esther an extra fee for taking her place. Esther worked on a farm near the Deblin airfield and she managed well with her work. The youngest brother started to pack small saccharin sweets and sell them in the streets of the ghetto or to sneak them over to the 'Aryan' side for sale, as the Deblin ghetto was not walled off. The Bergers had no household items to barter for food, but they did have some money and valuables that they smuggled into the ghetto upon entering it. An uncle in Prešov, who had not been deported yet, sent them some aid via a special emissary. Thanks to all of these factors, they managed to get by.

The mother was responsible for cooking, laundry, and cleaning, together with her mother-in-law. Despite the radical change from her previous life, she was able to use her skills as a housewife and a mother, and to offer help to her husband.[42] She often encouraged their children who were engaged in hard physical labor, while remaining concerned for their health. After a few months in Deblin, the older sister, Lea, age 18, contracted typhus. She had worked in a construction center carrying 150 buckets of water daily for the making of special concrete blocks. Twelve-year-old Esther replaced her for a few days, since this work paid higher wages than her job on the farm. After several days, the mother—who had been watching Esther—realized that the work was far too difficult for such a young girl, so prohibited her from continuing. Esther thus returned to her previous work on the farm, which paid less but was more suitable and safe for a young girl to perform. The mother kept her older daughter at home and fed her as best she could. This, however, meant putting the other members of the family on a more meager diet. Even after Lea regained her strength, her mother kept her from returning to the harsh workplace. This act had unfortunate consequences, as she was not working when the third deportation surprised the Jews in Deblin and she was taken to her death.

The mother did not have many months to test her adaptability, since all family members—except for Esther and her father, who were at work—were deported to the Treblinka camp in October 1942, only five months after their arrival in Deblin.

Eastern and Western Europe: Separation for rescue

This next section presents what I consider one of the most difficult aspects of besieged motherhood during these years. Separation for the purpose of rescue was perhaps the most heartbreaking in its contradictory significance. The following is a passage from the memoir of Shalom Elati, a 10-year-old boy from the Kovno ghetto. He described the event of his leaving the ghetto in the spring of 1944:

> I didn't really want to leave that morning, to emerge from the dim warmth of Mother and our only room, to prepare for departure. But I had to. All the arrangements had been made, and now everything depended on getting past the sentries successfully. [...] But this time my exit was fast and smooth. The German officer was not there, and only our people supervised the roll call, with no interference from the guards. A few more steps and we had already reached the riverbank. [...]
> Her [i.e. Mother's] instructions were clear: once we reach the other bank I was to march without stopping through the Lithuanians standing there, cross the

road, and go up the path that led into the hills. I was to walk all alone, without raising suspicion and without looking back. Further up the path, a woman would meet me and tell me what to do.

All this occurred so quickly and so easily that I scarcely grasped what had happened to me in such a short while. [...]

Like Moses in the bulrushes I was cast by Mother onto the shore of life. I therefore dedicate this story to my mother, who gave me life twice, but was unable to save herself even once.[43]

This is a description of separation—a departure to the unknown—which included both sadness and joy. In this case, it resulted in a successful outcome: the child was rescued. Mothers knew the hardships and uncertainties that followed their children. It made the dilemma of separation even more distressing. To separate from her child when s/he was in great danger was against motherhood's most basic instinct. In times of fear and danger, it is most natural for a mother to embrace her child and hold it close. She wants to offer comfort, to ease the pain, to provide protection. However, when great disaster threatened the Jews during the years of destruction, the mothers had to act contrary to their basic instincts. This was a calculated and most painful act, filled with anxiety and frustration. The mothers who decided to separate from their children had weighed this against the alternatives, which seemed far more dangerous for their children.

In the early years of Nazism before mass killings of Jews, many thought that their separation would only be temporary and would alleviate the children's miserable conditions. However, as the annihilation process progressed, separation created some hope for possible rescue.

Not all mothers were ready to take such a drastic step. Not all were sure that this was the right way to help their children. Esther Lurie, for example, talked about her sister, who had a little girl whom she refused to send to live with a Christian family, as she was unable to accept the idea that her child would grow up among non-Jews and thus learn to hate Jews. Her slogan was: we must stick together.[44] In any event, only a small number of Jewish mothers were able to relinquish their children to foster families. Usually these Jewish mothers were from middle- or upper-middle-class families who either had money or had professional connections with non-Jews. This complex situation was indicative of the dilemma that confronted Jewish mothers and fathers from the early years when the Nazis rose to power.

Prewar separation

Thousands of parents separated from their children and sent them off to strange places, sometimes in a different country with a different culture and language. Ten thousand children were sent to England on the well-known *Kindertransport*. Another six thousand were sent to the Land of Israel by the Youth Aliyah, an organization established to take German Jewish youth away from persecution so that they would grow up in freedom. Their parents knew that they would live in institutions or on a kibbutz (collective farm), far from the middle-class environment in which they had been reared. They would have to learn a new language and struggle with difficult conditions in an untamed environment with a totally different climate.[45]

"My darling Klarinka," wrote Sara Kofler to her 16-year-old daughter who had been sent in January 1939 with the Youth Aliyah to Palestine, when the conditions in Vienna became desperate:

> I must confess that I miss you very very much [emphasis in the original], however, I hope, that if I could be sure that you felt really happy, I would be happy with you. I am sure that you are also longing for us, this is fine, and you can admit it.[46]

These lines in her letter, and in other mothers' letters, reveal the inner conflict they went through. Sara Kofler was comforting herself with the "real happiness" of her child, while knowing very well that her child was yearning to be with her and would have to endure very traumatic days.[47]

From letters of other mothers we learn how they endeavored to remain involved in the details of their children's experiences. They asked about friends and social activities. They advised their children what vocation they should learn, and how to manage their daily affairs. Physical distance did not seem to be an obstacle to mothers' following and understanding their children's development.[48]

In addition, parents, who sent their children on illegal immigration voyages to Palestine were uncertain whether the children would actually arrive at their final destination. This was the feeling of the parents of a group of children known as the Villa Emma group. These children left Germany and Austria before the outset of the war, and were stranded first in Yugoslavia and then were moved to Slovenia. When it became too dangerous there, they were transferred to Italy where they lodged at Villa Emma in the small village of Nonantola (this is how the group received its name.) Following the occupation of Northern Italy, they were successfully moved to Switzerland. It was only after the war's end that they did finally set out for Palestine. Their parents, who said good-by to them in the hopes of being reunited one day, had meanwhile been deported to the East, never to return.[49]

Ten thousand children were sent to England on the *Kindertransport*. Some of them were sent to institutions while others were placed with non-Jewish families. The parents did not know in advance where their children would end up or even for how long. The mothers and fathers knew that they would not be around to offer them support during the difficult times of transition. We know that both parents and children missed each other very much, but as it was primarily the responsibility of the mothers to care and support their children physically and emotionally, their guilt feelings were strong. However, in an almost dialectical way, they were convinced that they took the correct step to save their children.

One may conclude that the life stories of these children had a happy ending. In the context of the total annihilation of their communities, they at least were saved, as their parents had wished. We must also remember that during the 1930s, for most lower- or middle-class Jewish families, the physical wellbeing of children was what mattered. Parents of that time did not pay as much attention to psychological considerations. During the 1930s and 1940s, there was no established theory of family education or a clear consideration of what was important for a child's emotional development. It was simply accepted that it was important to provide a child with physical security.[50]

Many children suffered greatly from the abrupt separation from their parents, and they waited in vain for years in the hopes that their parents would fulfill their promise and be reunited with them. Only long years later, after these children grew up to be parents themselves, could they comprehend the pain of their mothers and fathers who send them away. Only after realizing the full magnitude of the Holocaust and its scale of human destruction were they able to find some form of compassion for their lost parents. Only then, in many cases, did the pain of loss and the endless longing somewhat subside.[51]

Separation during the war years

After the outset of the war and when the deportations began, separation became a complete rupture. Very few of the parents were able to keep in touch with the children and with those to whom they had been entrusted, such as a non-Jewish family, convent nuns or the monks of monasteries where they were hidden. In Belgium, for example, where a large number of Jewish children were hidden through the resistance organization, parents were not even informed where their children had been placed.[52] The fear that they would be caught by the Germans and interrogated and forced to give the children's address was too great a risk to take, for both the child and the protective family. In Eastern Europe, often the protective families themselves did not know that the child they were keeping was Jewish. In most cases, a child's identity had to be kept secret. Sometimes, desperate mothers would leave their babies on the doorstep of a non-Jewish home or institution in the hope that somebody would be kind and humane enough to take them into their care. It is even known that mothers threw their children out of the train en route to the death camps. This was their ultimate endeavor to rescue the child while taking the supreme risk that the child might not survive the act. These cases were desperate behavior completely contradictory to what a mother would have acquired through culture, socialization, and values.

A mother left this most shocking note with her little son, who had probably been thrown off a deportation train taking them to be murdered. Published in a collection of "Last Letters," it reads:

Merciful People:
Save the child, May God repay you, don't hand over the child to the

murderers!

Everything will be paid for, he has two pieces of property in Lukow, everything will be paid for.

Have mercy on the miserable child!

This is the request of a mother unable to do otherwise.

The distressed mother, H/P/[53]

We have very little documentation from the time, of mothers or fathers on child/parent separation. It is therefore heartrending to read the letters from parents to their children published by Frederick Raymes and Menachem Mayer, *Are the Trees in Bloom over There?* The Raymes family of Hofheim in southern Germany were part of a group of over 6,500 German Jews deported from little towns and villages in that region. In October 1940, the Raymes arrived at the Gurs concentration camp in France. After four months in the camp, their two sons were taken by the French-Jewish children's aid organization, *Oeuvre de Secours aux Enfants* (OSE), to an orphanage in the South of France.

The parents wrote to the children from March 1941 until August 1942, when they were deported to Auschwitz. Hilde Raymes, a mother who experienced the uprootedness and duress of a refugee in a German concentration camp in France, wrote most of the letters. Like Sara Kofler, she too expressed her great concern over the daily details and asked herself constantly about her children's health and food situation. She was planning to send them fruit and other things that they loved. In most of her letters, she pleaded with them to be kind to each other. The father appealed to the younger son, age 8, to listen to his older brother who was 12 years old. The parents begged the brothers to stay together, as if that would compensate for their own distance from the children.

In a letter dated August 10, 1942, just before her deportation to Auschwitz, the hopeless mother wrote, contemplating their separation while confronting the journey to the unknown:

> Just a few lines before the voyage. I do not know to where we are going to be transported. We are not at all sorry that we are leaving you behind. You are better protected; perhaps later you will know everything. Take care of your health.
>
> All the best, my children, and kisses from your mother.
>
> P.S. My dear Manfred and Heinz, be good to each other, these are my concerns.[54]

Reading the letter we ask, what was the meaning of the sentence, "Perhaps later you will know?" Was the mother alluding to her fears that the children did not understand why they had been separated from their parents? Is she hinting at the fact that she already knew her and their father's doomed fate and that the children had a better chance to survive?

In some small places, where ghettos were transformed into forced-labor camps, Jews managed to bribe the Germans to let them keep their children with them.[55] The children were not registered and thus did not receive food rations, but neither were they deported. We already noted this fact in the labor camp near Deblin: eighty children were living there until the camp's liquidation in July 1944.

Hannah Szientprout Topolski testified that her mother forced her out of the march to the *Umschlagplatz* (German: assembly area) and told her to run away and find a safe haven in the labor camp.[56] She was only twelve years old and already worked in the camp, but she was afraid to run away on her own and felt unsure about the surrounding. Her mother, though, did not give up. This was the third deportation from Deblin. Most of her extended family had already been deported to Sobibor, and the mother had previously found out about the death camp. She was determined that her daughter should run away and mingle with the Polish crowd that was standing on the sidewalks, watching the Jews being marched to their death. The child had fair hair and was small, so her mother thought that she had a good chance not to be noticed in the midst of the crowd; she told her to go back to the labor camp and find her father.

In desperation, the mother tried to escape first with her nine-year-old daughter, but was chased back by a German guard. After her mother's failure, Hannah was convinced to try, trusting her mother to follow with her little sister. Successfully, she left the line and stood for a few hours amid the crowd watching the Jews march off. Then she sought a way to get to the labor camp, but was unsuccessful. She wandered in the fields. When evening approached, she knocked desperately on a farmer's door but was chased away. Frightened and hungry, she walked unsure of her next steps, feeling the chill of October evening, when in the distance she saw the image of her mother. Was it true or an illusion?

Hannah started to run to that direction and called her mother desperately, when suddenly she heard her mother's voice faintly coming from a certain ditch. Yes, Hannah was lucky. Her mother did fulfill her promise and managed to escape from the death march. Her mother's embrace calmed her, and they remained in hiding for many hours until the trains loaded with the Jews departed from the Deblin railroad station.

Hannah was with her family in the labor camp in Deblin until the summer of 1944, when they were sent on a transport to Czestochowa. These were difficult years of hard work, illness and lack of food, but they did not starve to death. It was always the mother, with her ingenuity and resourceful manipulations, that kept up the spirit of hope. She did not let the struggle to survive fade away. The father was deported from Czestochowa to Buchenwald just days before liberation. He did not survive. When the Soviet army came to Czestochowa they liberated the mother with her daughters and one son.

Conclusion

> On one matter there was full consensus: To take a child out of the ghetto was
> considered a solemn, holy task. The Jewish policeman, or another official at
> the gate, would sometimes offer what help he could, even at the risk of his
> own life. Those who were able might send a child to an acquaintance or to
> a stranger whom they would pay, but for many this option was simply not
> possible. However, there were many parents who did not want to send their
> children away and declined to do so. Parents debated this matter extensively,
> some arguing that on principle they would not send their child to a gentile.
> Mothers said that they would rather die with their children than send them
> away. They were unable to imagine the ensuing separation if their children
> were taken from them. Others said that if the Nazis would lay their hands on
> them, they would ask to be killed with their children. The most popular way
> to rescue children from the ghetto was to arrange for underground hideouts
> – *malines,* as they were called in the ghetto.[57]

This is a testimony from the Kovno ghetto, which is supported by many other
documents. In Kovno and in Shavli, before the liquidation of the ghetto, the Germans
raided the ghetto during working hours. While most of the mothers were away at
work, the Germans deported their children to death camps. The devastated mothers
returned from work only to find out that their children were gone.

Dr. Aharon Pick from Shavli reported that women in the ghetto were unable to
conceive that their children were murdered.[58] They endeavored throughout all these
long and horrible years of the ghetto to save them, and then, when the Soviet Army
was almost at the gates of Lithuania, they were murdered. Rumors spread through
the ghetto every day that the children had been seen, or that they were deported to
Germany, or that they were living safely in some remote camp and at the liberation
they would be reunited with their parents. Ringelblum, mentioning the experiences
of mothers who lost their children in the Warsaw ghetto and would listen to rumors
of their whereabouts, noted sadly that all these reminded him of the old Jewish
legend of the Ten Lost Tribes of Israel.[59]

Were these mothers who experienced the Nazi annihilation policy blind to the reality
that their children were lost forever? Was this a psychological defense mechanism that
helped them endure the present and long for the future? These mothers endeavored for
long and trying months to shelter their children, and it became the anchor of their life.
Were they unable to accept the abrupt and cruel disappearance of their children? Were
they trusting the tradition of the Jews as a "people of remnant" (Hebrew: *She'erit*) and
thought that they and their children would become such remnants? Could Schlesinger's
theory reinforce such assumption? I leave it as a question.

And yet mothers also deserted their children to rescue themselves, and some
were ready to put their babies to sleep in order to get a place in a hideout. Mothers in

the ghetto workplaces ("shops") in Warsaw, during the days of the mass deportation of summer 1942, sometimes faced a choice to either go to death with their children or to hand them over for deportation. Their decisions varied. I shall end with a quote from Ruth Bondy on mothers in Auschwitz-Birkenau in June 1944, who had come there from the Theresienstadt ghetto:

> Although many of the women of Theresienstadt were privileged to live in the family camp in Auschwitz-Birkenau with their children, by June 1944 they knew they were going to be sent to the gas chambers. Because the Nazis needed working hands, they held a selection: the mothers of young children had the choice of presenting themselves to be selected as workers – or staying with their children and thus be sent to the gas chambers. After six months in Birkenau they had no illusions about saving their children – they knew that their children were going to be sent to the gas chambers. Only two of about 600 mothers of young children appeared for the selection; all the others decided to stay with their children to the end.[60]

What is the legacy that these mothers bequeathed us? Is it a story of dignity and despair, a story of courage and struggle against all odds? It certainly leaves us with great wonder about those women and their children who survived the war and created new families. From the testimonies of survivors, fathers and mothers who lost children during the war, we know that the pain of loss never disappeared. The lost child continued to live in the parent's heart, beside those children who were born into new families that were formed after the war. Often these children learned about their parents' losses when they grew up and became adults or after the death of one of the parents.[61] The deep memory that Lawrence Langer describes in his work was one mechanism that enabled mothers and fathers to live with the pain of loss alongside the joy of new life.[62]

Notes

1   Marianne Hirsch, *Family Frames: Photography, Narrative and Postmemory.* Cambridge: Harvard University Press, 1997, p. 33.
2   An interesting illustration of the family situation emerges from the collection of autobiographies of Jewish youth in Poland initiated by YIVO, in 1932, 1934, and 1939. An anthology of the autobiographies that survived were published in *Awakening Lives: Autobiographies of Jewish Youth in Poland before the Holocaust.* Jeffrey Shandler (ed.), New Haven: Yale University Press, 2002.
3   William J. Goode, *The Family.* Englewood Cliffs: Prentice Hall Foundation of Modern Sociology Series, 1982, second edition, pp. 1-14.
4   Seccombe Wally, *A Millennium of Family Change: Feudalism to Capitalism in Northwestern Europe.* London, New York: Verso, 1992, Introduction, pp. 1-7.

5 Schlesinger Benjamin, "The Jewish Family in Retrospect: What's Past is Prologue," in: *Jewish Family Issues: A Resource Guide*. Benjamin Schlesinger (ed.) New York: 1987, 13-17.

6 Goode, p. 71.

7 Marion A. Kaplan, *The Making of the Jewish Middle Class: Women, Family and Identity in Imperial Germany*. New York: Oxford University Press, 1991, p. 31.

8 See Bina Garnazarska-Kedari, "Temurot bamazav hahomri shel shekhavot ha'ovdim hayehudi'im be-Polin (1930-1939," [The changes in the material condition of the Jewish working class in Poland] *Galed 9* (1986), 169, table 8; Louis Briner, "Some Speculations on the Emotional Resources of the Jewish Family," in: *The Jewish Family in a Changing World*. Gilbert S. Rosenthal (ed.), New York: T. Yosselof, 1970, pp. 307-320. Paula E. Hyman, "Gender and the Jewish Family in Modern Europe," in: Dalia Ofer and Lenore J. Weitzman (eds.), *Women in the Holocaust*. New Haven: Yale Univ. Press, 1998, pp. 31-36.

9 Transnistria was the southern part of the Ukraine occupied by the German and Romania army in the summer of 1941. In September 1941, an agreement was signed between the German and the Romanian in Tiginia and the region was given to the rule of the Romanians and named Transnistria. The Romanians nominated a governor to the region and it became the depot area for some 150,000 Jews from Bessarabia and Bukovina that the Romanian government wanted to deport from the State. A few thousand Jews from the Regat were also sent to Transnistria and some 20,000 Roma.

10 Rutha Sakowska (ed.), *Archiwum Ringelbluma, Listy o Zaladizie*. Warsaw: ZIH, 1994, Letter from Mirl from Grabow to her brother in Warsaw, dated January 1, 1942; see also February 13 1942, a letter of Lenczycki from a labor camp near Posen to her sister and brother-in-law, Gelernter, in: *Warsaw*. Lenczycki was in a labor camp with nothing of her belongings and she is asking to send her parcel. She also informs her sister that she is allowed to receive up to 5 marks and that it is permissible to send this in a regular letter.

11 M-10 ARI/77 bulletin for the Joint Distribution Committee (JDC) describing the situation in Poland during the first 13 months of the war September 1939; November 1940; M-10 ARI/ 211 bulletin of the Joint Distribution Committee (JDC) describing the situation in Poland during the year 1941. (Yiddish) See also M-10 ARI/309 *"Vi azoy "lebe" di heymloze oyf di punkten"* (Yiddish: How the homeless live in the shelters).

12 Isaiah Trunk, "The struggle of the Jews against contagious diseases" (Yiddish: Mikhome keygen Yidn durk farspreiten krankayten) *YIVO Blater,* 37, 1953, p. 93.

13 Yad Vashem AR-309, " How the homeless live in the *Punkten*".

14 Yad Vashem AR-309, "How the homeless live in the *Punkten*"; Emanuel Ringelblum, *Diary and Notes Vol I.* (Hebrew) Jerusalem: Yad Vashem, 1993), p. 282. "May 9th, the prices are skyrocketing again, bread 12 zloty potatoes 3.4-4 zloty per one kilogram," p. 284; "the price of bread 14.50 zloty (May 18th)", p. 285; "May 20th, the price of bread is 15 zloty."

15 Isaiah Trunk, "The struggle of the Jews against contagious diseases" (Yiddish). *YIVO*

Blater 37, 1953, pp. 53-100; An English version appeared in English in *YIVO Annual of Jewish Social Science*, 8, 1953, pp. 92-204 .

16 Ibid, p. 71.

17 Avigdor Shachan, *Burning Ice: The Ghettos of Transnistria.* New York: East European Monographs, 1996, pp.190-271; Ruth Glasberg Gold, *Ruth's Journey: A Survivor Memoir*. Gainesville: University Press of Florida, 1996, pp.62-117; Jan Ancel , *Transnistria 1941-1942*. Tel Aviv: Goldstein-Goren Diaspora Research Center, Tel Aviv University, 2003, pp. 339-428.

18 Avraham Lewin. See the description of the apartment and four little children alone and in misery, *"Vi azoy "lebe" di heymloze oyf di punkten"* (Yiddish: How the homeless live in the shelters) YVA, M-10 AR-309, p. 9.

19 YVA M-10 ARI/196, Maluba Regina, "A report of one medical treatment".

20 A cruel description of a poor family and the neglect and poverty in the home, described by Rozycki. YVA M10/ 429.

21 Yad Vashem Archives (YVA) M-10 ARII/85.

22 Slepak report, YVA JM/215/3, band 3. Cecilia Slepak belonged to the *"Oneg Shabbat"* underground research group organized by Emanuel Ringelblum in the Warsaw ghetto. Slepak's job was to carry out in-depth interviews with a cross-section of women in the ghetto. She interviewed sixteen women, who were asked to describe their lives prior to the war and after the outbreak of the war, and how they and their families coped with life in the ghetto. Many of Slepak's questions dealt with the economic situation of the women's families, their children, their work, and details about their everyday lives. For a more extensive account of the actual report and on the lives of women in the Warsaw ghetto as ascertained from the report, see Dalia Ofer, "Gender Issues in Diaries and Testimonies; also, Dalia Ofer "Her View through My Lens: Cecilia Slepak Studies Women in Warsaw", in: *Gender, Place and Memory in Modern Jewish Experience.* Judy Tydor Baumel, Tova Cohen (eds.), London, Portland, OR: Vallentine Mitchell, 2003, pp. 29-50.

23 Ibid.

24 Sara Selver-Urbach, *Miba'ad lahalon beiti: zikhronot megeto Lodz* (Hebrew: Through the window of my home; memoirs of Lodz Ghetto). Jerusalem: 1964).

25 YVA M-10 ARI/223 1941. I would like to thank Ms. Lea Priess for providing me with this document.

26 Peretz Opoczyski, *Sketches from the Warsaw Ghetto* (Hebrew). Tel Aviv: Hakibbutz Hameuchad, 1970, p. 105.

27 Henryka Lazowert, "The Little Smuggler" in: *And They Will Call Me : Poems from the Holocaust in Yiddish and English Translation.* Waltham Mass: Brandeis University, 1982, pp.10 -11.

28 YVA M-10 ARI/470; See also the following comment by Ringelblum: "This is the way stuff is smuggled through Sienna Street: The street cleaner stands on the Other Side of the Wall diligently sweeping. He pushes various objects through the rain-water culvert with his broom; he receives money through the same channel. Emaciated three- or four year-old children crawl through the culverts to fetch merchandise from the Other Side.

Imagine what a mother must go through when her child is in mometary danger of death." Emanuel Ringelblum, *Notes from the Ghetto: The Journal of Emanuel Ringelblum*. New York: McGraw Hill, 1958, p.172.

29 On street children, see Rachel Auerbach, *In the streets of Warsaw: 1939-1943*. (Hebrew) Tel Aviv: Am Oved, 1954), p.24; Ringelblum 1 p. 299; Dalia Ofer "Children and Youth During the Holocaust: Issues for Research," in: *The Holocaust: History and Memory: Essay Presented in Honor of Israel Gutman*. Jerusalem: Yad Vashem, 2001, pp. 72-74.

30 YVA, M10 426, Rozycki p.24

31 David Silberklang, *Hashoah bemahoz Lublin* (Hebrew: The Holocaust in the Lublin District). Ph.D. dissertation, Hebrew University of Jerusalem, 2003, pp. 93-117; YVA M1/E 874, Testimony of Sumer on his life in Deblin and the ghetto; YVA M1/E 1627, Testimony of Moses Klawer on his life in Deblin and the ghetto; YVA MIQ 101, Testimony of Adam Kostecki and many more; see also Avraham Lewin, "On the deportations from Deblin," p. 71, 78-79.

32 For further information about living condition in the ghettos of Vilna, see Aharon Einat, *The Internal Life in the Vilna Ghetto* (Hebrew: Hachaiim hapnimiim begeto Vilna). Ph.D. dissertation, Hebrew University of Jerusalem, 2006. For Lodz, see Michal Unger, *Lodz, aharon ha-getaot bePolin* (Hebrew: Lodz: the last ghetto in Poland). Jerusalem: Yad Vashem, 2005. For Warsaw, see Abraham Lewin, *A Cup Of Tears: A Diary from the Warsaw Ghetto*. Antony Polonsky (ed.) Oxford: Blackwell, 1988, pp. 4-7.

33 Helena Szerszevska, *Haperek haaharon* (Hebrew: The last chapter). Tel Aviv: Lohamei Haghetatot, 1980, pp.104-127.

34 Mary Berg, *The Diary of Mary Berg: Growing Up in the Warsaw Ghetto*. S.L. Shneiderman (ed.) Oxford: OUP, 2006, p. 38-9 Feb. 5 1941, p. 41 Feb. 20, p. 99-101 October 1941, p. 110 Dec. 1941.

35 Tamar Lazarszon-Rostovski, *Yomanah shel Tamara* (Hebrew: The diary of Tamara). Tel Aviv: Lohamei Haghetatot, 1975, pp. 71, 82, 87; Shalom Elati, *Lahazot et hanhar,* (Hebrew: Crossing the river). Jerusalem: Yad Vashem, Carmel, 1999, pp. 89-91 Esther Lurie, Memoirs of the Kovno Ghetto (Hebrew) YVA 03/637, and many more places.

36 See Esther Neuman Berger's testimony, Yad Vashem Archive (YVA) 033c/4154; Hannah Topolski, (Yad Vashem) (YV) 03/9295; see testimonies in note 29.

37 Fela Szeps, *Ba-lev ba'arah ha-shalhevet: yomanah shel Felah Sheps, mahaneh ha-avodah Grünberg* (Hebrew: A Blaze from Within: The Diary of Fela Szeps, the Grünberg Forced-Labor Camp) Bella Guterman (ed.), Jerusalem: Yad Vashem, 2002, pp. 41-42, Hanukkah, no date.

38 For some elaboration on this matter see, Dalia Ofer "Cohesion and Rupture: The Jewish Family in East European Ghettos during the Holocaust", in: *Studies in Contemporary Jewry*, Vol. XIV, 1998: 143-165.

39 YVA 03/637.

40 See for example what Lewin is writing about the German Jews in the Warsaw ghetto, Abraham Lewin, *A Cup of Tears: A Diary of the Warsaw Ghetto*. Antony Polonsky (ed.), Oxford: Blackwell, 1989, pp. 85-86, entry (May 21, 1942).

41 Esther Neuman Berger, Yad Vashem Archive (YVA) 033c/4154, the story of the Berger family is based on her testimony, which I shall not mention again in the notes.

42 A number of testimonies of survivors from Prešov who were deported to Deblin are in the Yad Vashem collection. Some were taken in the DP camps in Germany right after liberation and some were taken years later. They have different narratives but are similar in the larger contour of the description on the arrival to the Deblin ghetto and the state of the houses that they were put in. Many describe the mothers' efforts to clean the place, the care to give the place some resemblance of home, and in general their naiveté in regard to their future. See for example YVA 03/6303 Shosha Klapus, born in Prešov in 1925, and was deported to Deblin in May 1942; Israel Shapira M49E/139; Avraham Weingarten, 03/6751, was born in 1928 and deported to Deblin in May 1942.

43 Shalom Elati, *Lahazot et hanahar,* pp. 11-12; translation provided by the author.

44 Esther Lurie, YVA 03/620, pp. 140-141.

45 Sara Kadosh, *Ideology vs. Reality: Youth Aliyah and the Rescue of Jewish Children During the Holocaust 1933-45.* Ph.D. dissertation, Columbia University, 1990.

46 *Za'akah beterem shoah* (Hebrew: A scream at the outset of the Holocaust) translated from the German and edited by Klara (Hedwa) Koppler Yuval, Jerusalem: private publication, (2000) p. 22. This collection of letters is a striking example of feelings of parents (the Kopplers) who sent their daughter to Palestine. She left Vienna on January 1, 1939 with the Youth Aliyah. The parents tried to conceal from their daughter the hardships that they were experiencing in Vienna during 1939. The mother's letters expressed concern over the difficulties that her daughter experienced in the new country. She endeavored to be involved in all details of daily life, without expressing distrust in her daughter's ability to manage. On November 1939, after the war broke, the parent too boarded an illegal immigrant ship that was stranded in Yugoslavia and never reached Palestine. The parents, together with their younger daughter, were murdered by the Nazis in Yugoslavia.

47 I have dealt with the issue of personal letters and with letters of mothers in another study. "Personal Letters in Research and Education on the Holocaust," *Holocaust and Genocide Studies* 4, no. 3 (1989), pp. 341-55; *The Dead-End Journey: The Tragic Story of the Kladovo-Sabac Group.* Lanham: University Press of America, 1996 (with Hannah Weiner).

48 Dalia Ofer, Hannah Weiner, *The Dead-End Journey.* Lanham, MD: University Press of America, 1996, pp. 58-60, 69-72. Of significant interest are the letters from Ghaje Weinstock to her children from October 1939 to April 1941 (private collection); see also the letters of Jacob and Sara Rotman to their children, (private collection).

49 Yael Nidam-Orvieto, *Parashat Yaldei Vila Ema berei hazalat yeladim bitkufat hashoah"* (Hebrew: the story of the children of Villa Emma as a reflection of the rescue of children during the Holocaust). *The Twelvth World Jewish Congress,* section 5) Jerusalem 2001. pp. 145-154; *Parashat Yaldei Vila Ema: hahatzala shel kevutzat yeladim bitkufat hashoah* (Hebrew: The Story of Villa Emma: a rescue of one group of children during the Holocaust). Jerusalem: Yad Vashem, 2005; on illegal immigration see Dalia Ofer, *Escaping the Holocaust: Illegal Immigration to the Land of Israel.* New York: OUP, 1990.

50 Dan Baron, Julia Chaitin, *Parenthood and the Holocaust.* Jerusalem: Yad Vashem, 2001, p. 17.
51 Koppler, *A Scream at the Outset,* p. 13; Frederick Raymes, Menachem Mayer, *Haim Ha`ezim Porhim ezlachem?* (Hebrew: Are the trees blooming over there?). Jerusalem: Yad Vashem: 2001 pp. 13-14, 16-17; Sharon Cohen Kangisser, *Finding their Voices: Child Survivors of the Holocaust in Israel: Social Dynamics and Postwar Experiences.* Portland, OR: Sussex Academic Press, 2005.
52 Testimony of Mrs Fanny Eisenberg, USHMM, signature, May 31, 2007 "One Person."
53 *Last Letters from the Shoah.* Zvi Bachrach (ed.), Jerusalem: Yad Vashem and Devora Publishing, 2004, p. 269. See also USHMM RG 10.249 letters, Diary of Frida and Reinarch 1939-42, entry of the mother, May 1 1942, entries of the father May 24 1942, October 20 1942.
54 Meir, Menahem, Frederick Raymes (Manfred Mayer) and Menachem (Heinz) Mayer note l; pp.102-103.
55 YVA, testimony of Abraham Weingarten 03/67; Salzman Mayer, M49/1168.
56 YVA 03/9295.
57 Esther Lurie, pp. 140-141.
58 Aharon Pick. *Reshimoth migai haharega* (Hebrew: Writing from the death land: memoirs from the Shavli Ghetto 1942-1944). Tel Aviv: 1988, p.202.
59 Ibid. p. 202; Lurie, p. 181.
60 Ruth Bondy, "Women in Theresienstadt and the Family Camp in Birkenau" in Ofer and Weitzman, 1998, p. 324.
61 See for example the book of Baruch Milkh, *Ve-ulai hashamayim rekim* (Hebrew: And the Heavens may be Void). Jerusalem: Yad Vashem, 1999. Of particular interest is the introduction by his daughter Shosh Milch-Avgial, pp. 9-22.
62 Lawrence L. Langer, *Holocaust Testimonies: The Ruins of Memory.* New Haven: Yale University Press, 1991, pp. 1-38.

"We're all well and hoping to hear the same from you soon…" [1]
The Story of a Group of Families

Irith Dublon-Knebel

Prior to the physical extermination of the Jews, the social frameworks of their lives – from the broad, formal ones to the most intimate – were gradually dismantled and broken down. One of the stages on the way to extermination was the separation of the sexes and the breakdown of the family. The first arrests of Jews inside Germany, which occurred between 1933 and 1939, marked the beginning of the separation. The deportations to the ghettos and transit camps in 1939 and 1942, during which the family was uprooted from its home, constituted an additional stage in the attack. The onslaught reached its peak with the deportation to the concentration camps and the separation of the men and the youths from the women and children that took place either at the gates of the camp or when they were sent to different camps. Separation as a stage in the "Final Solution" is rooted in the decisions that were made at the Wannsee Conference in January 1942, stating that "the Jews will be taken to work in the East in large groups and with separation of the sexes".[2]

This paper deals with the breakdown of the Jewish family, with Jewish children, and with motherhood during the Holocaust. Its focal point is the exceptional story of a group of families with Romanian or Hungarian citizenship who resided in Holland. During the German occupation, their citizenship provided them with a certain measure of protection against the extermination policy because the Third Reich occasionally displayed some flexibility. In spite of the extensive racial laws, the regime introduced considerations of internal and external policy into the extermination policy. Jews who were citizens of neutral countries or countries that were friendly to Germany were classified not only according to their race, but also according to their national affiliation. Those Jews who happened to live in the occupied countries were not subjected to the same regulations to which the indigenous Jews were subjected. The "neutral Jews"[3] were granted an extension, during the course of which they could return to their countries of origin. However, even when they could not meet the deadline and remained in the occupied country, they were treated less severely than the local Jews. A directive that was issued in March 1943 stated that all Jews who were citizens of the friendly or neutral countries and were living in German-controlled regions, but had not yet returned to their countries of origin, would be included in the deportation regulations. Since they could not be deported to the East, men over age 14 would be transferred temporarily to the Buchenwald concentration camp, and women and children would be taken to the Ravensbrück concentration camp.[4] The members of the families focused on in this article were transferred to the above-mentioned camps at the beginning of 1944 from the Westerbork transit camp in Holland.

During the first stages of the persecution, up to the time they left the transit camp, the history of the families in this article is similar to that of other Jewish families. However, when they left the Westerbork camp, their fate differed from that of most of the Jews of Holland. While the latter were transferred to the extermination camps in the East, the members of the families with foreign citizenship were sent to concentration camps in Germany, where the children, including infants, remained with their mothers until they were liberated. They lived as family units – albeit broken and damaged – within the camps.[5] The story of the women and children from these families is exceptional because of the anomalous phenomenon of Jewish mothers, children and infants living together for over a year in the reality of a Nazi concentration camp. Their survival affords a discussion of concepts such as "motherhood" and "childhood" and the relationship between them in the extreme conditions in which they existed.

While the racial policy certainly affected both sexes, there was no impartiality with regard to sex and gender.[6] "When Nazism elevated race to a crucial political concept, gender was not erased but relegated to a kind of underground", wrote Gisela Bock, adding that "This is where historians need to discover the dynamics of gender – in terms of gender history as well as Holocaust history..."[7] The reasons for the differences in the Nazis' attitude toward Jewish men and women were biological and sexual as well as gender-related. Among the main reasons for those differences was motherhood, which was imbued with a new meaning under Nazi rule. While Aryan motherhood was glorified, Jewish motherhood was its diametric opposite, thereby becoming fraught with peril.

From the biological point of view, men and women alike were capable of propagating the Jewish race, and for that reason the Nazis performed their sterilization experiments on both sexes. However, Jewish women who were already pregnant with the next generation were in particularly grave danger as compared to men of the same age group. In such cases, the difference in the way pregnant women were treated was biological. The source of the additional danger that threatened a Jewish mother was mainly gender-related. When the sexes were separated, children under age 14 remained with their mothers in accordance with the traditional social and cultural outlook that defined the role of the mother as the principal caregiver in the parental role distribution.[8]

As the next generation of Jews and as non-productive elements, the children were targeted for extermination almost automatically. They were a nuisance, since they disrupted the Nazi routine and order, were difficult to supervise, did not obey orders, and cried a lot.[9] Rudolf Höss, commandant of the Auschwitz concentration and extermination camp, wrote that it was extremely important for the prevailing atmosphere to be as calm as possible when the transports arrived and were dealt with.[10] It was easier to cope with the group of mothers and children without separating them. When the mass transports reached Auschwitz, loudspeakers instructed the mothers and children to turn left.[11] Even though doctors were present, the selection was performed according to categories, and the category of mothers and children was targeted for extermination.[12] Mothers were thus more vulnerable than the men; only children who were alone were more vulnerable than they were.[13]

The article is based on documents and on the testimonies of people who were children during the war. Most of the parents were no longer alive when the material that constitutes the story of the group was collected, and therefore this is, to a great extent, the story of the events from the special point of view of children. Most Holocaust research focuses on the world of the adults, according to Debórah Dwork. This is not surprising since the concept of "society" usually refers to the world of adults – productive and decision-making individuals. However, in view of the fact that a million and a half children were killed in the Holocaust, and their murder represents the quintessential of Nazi evil, historical research fails if it does not properly recognize the place of the children in the Holocaust.[14]

The Initial Damage

The initial damage to the families was characterized by the disruption of the internal order of the family prior to the final separation, particularly the damage inflicted on the father figure – whether by separating him temporarily from his family or by undermining his position and his role.

Before the war, the traditional roles in the K. family were clear and defined. The eldest son's testimony reveals the story of how these roles were undermined when the Germans invaded in 1940.[15] According to Kerstenberg and Brenner, the greater the child's admiration of the parent, the more profound the trauma that accompanies the damage to and the humiliation of that parent.[16] Indeed, the collapse and traumatic disintegration of this admiration are expressed in the words of the son, who was eight years old at the time, when he described the first days after Holland had been occupied: "My father, who always knew what to do and how to do it, who I could always turn to with any question I could possibly think of – didn't have answers! And at that moment, my world caved in... and at that moment I stopped being a child".[17]

Before the war, the role of the father as the head of the family, as the intermediary between the family and the world, as the one who understood and explained how the world functioned, and as the protector of the family against it, was clear to the child. Similarly, the mother's lack of expertise in the face of what was occurring outside of her home was another basic assumption within the existing family setup. It was clear to the son that his mother "... didn't understand anything about the war".[18] With his father's brief enlistment in the Civil Defense, he understood that the disposition of power and the authority of the family had changed. The parents' helplessness as well as the father's inability to answer his son's questions and his temporary absence, constituted the first stage in the gradual decline of the son's childhood. It was clear to him that from then on, he would have to protect his mother and his three- and five-year-old siblings. At this point, he was still laboring under the naïve illusion typical of the way children perceive things, that he could conquer the world and overcome enemies and hostility as easily as he was accustomed to conquering his familiar environment.[19]

After the first days of the war, family life resumed some kind of routine. The second disruption occurred in 1942, when four Dutch policemen appeared at the family's home. The three children reacted in accordance with their ages. Young children who are not aware of danger or impending disaster display fewer signs of anxiety when they are close to their parents, while slightly older children and teenagers are more aware of the dangers and display more signs of distress.[20] The eldest son, seeing the policemen approaching the house, was aware of the danger and tried to prevent his mother from opening the door. Nevertheless, the policemen were let into the parlor, where they announced to the family that they were about to be arrested.[21] The two younger children remembered the policemen as congenial, apologizing for the task that they had been forced to do. There was no brutality. The youngest, a girl, even remembers that she sat on one of the policemen's knees. The traumatic aspect that was etched in the memories of the two sons focused on the father's weakness and impotence.[22] In the case of the younger son, the father's inability to fulfill his traditional role and protect his family was linked to the betrayal on the part of another authority that was supposed to protect him – the Dutch state.[23]

The father, who was crushed by the absolute power facing him, was evidently in a state of shock. His annihilation as a person with civil and legal rights and the shattering of the illusion that his family was protected by his Hungarian citizenship left him powerless. Out of a childish belief that he could protect his family, the eldest son tried to fill the void that had been created and function as the representative of his family in the face of the representatives of power, by explaining to the policemen that he and his family were Hungarian citizens and that the notice of their arrest was a fundamental error.[24]

The mother wept, but accepted the decree as a fait accompli. She did not lose control, and displayed resourcefulness and creativity with regard to the practical and immediate organization of the family's departure from the house. She gathered belongings, obtained a suitcase from the neighbor, and, in order to take additional clothes for the children above and beyond the permitted quota, dressed them in several layers of clothing. The family, including the grandparents, was transferred to the Westerbork transit camp.[25] Leaving the home was a crucial stage in the course of the persecution. At the moment of departure, life as they knew it ended.[26] The physical framework that bordered, defined, and protected them as a family, collapsed.

In August 1942, a daughter was born to the M. family, a sister to their ten-year-old son and six-year-old daughter. When the police arrived to arrest them in September 1942, only the father was arrested. He was transferred to the Westerbork transit camp. Because of the infant's tender age and the fact that the mother had just given birth, the mother and her children were granted an extension before being arrested.

Even after the extension had lapsed, the mother tried to prevent their arrest. To this end, she resorted to two courses of action – one that was immediate and short-term, and the other a long-term solution. She obtained a certificate stating that the children were ill with an infectious disease and hung it on the door of the house in order to prevent the Germans from entering. In addition, she searched for a hiding place for herself and the children. The father, who would occasionally come to visit his family from the detention camp, evidently objected to the mother's plan to go into hiding, since he feared for his family's lives if they were caught. Despite his objections, the mother accepted the offer of one of the neighbors to hide in her house. The hiding-place turned out to be a trap. To this day, the sound of the police banging on the door of their hiding place still echoes in the eldest son's ears, and he remembers his mother spitting in the neighbor's face before they were arrested and taken to Westerbork.[27]

The eldest child in the D. family was 12 years old at the time of the family's dramatic and violent arrest. The destruction of the family's life began when the window of their house was shattered in September 1942 while they were sitting down to dinner. The Dutch policeman who broke the window opened the door, entered, and ordered the father to let the German soldier who was standing outside into the house. Even though the eldest son's testimony does not relate on an ethical or emotional level to the role of the father during this event, it clearly evokes aspects of the negation of the father's role as the family protector, of his inability to fulfill his traditional role, and of his helplessness. While the representative of the authorities did address him as the head of the family, his order to let the German soldier into the house, not only voided the father's role of any meaning but actually turned the father into his intermediary.[28]

The Dutch policeman and the German soldier ordered the family to prepare for departure in 15 minutes. The family's belongings were already packed. They had in fact been waiting for the arrest since they had witnessed arrests around them, a fact that nonetheless did not diminish the shock.[29]

The Camps
Westerbork

The Westerbork transit camp in northeast Holland, where the families were brought, was established in 1939 by the Dutch government for German Jews who had entered Holland illegally. At the end of 1941, the Germans converted the camp into a transit camp. The Dutch police, reinforced by an SS unit, controlled the camp. The camp commandant was German, initially a civilian, and later, from September 1942, a member of the SS. Everyday life was run by the German Jews, who had been there since the establishment of the camp.[30]

The barracks were divided into two halls. One section housed the women and the young children, and the other the men and the older boys. The toilets were situated at the end of the barracks. The beds were arranged in two-story rows along the length of the hall. The barracks were constantly full of sand, and in the winter, they were freezing. A "barracks elder" was responsible for life and discipline inside the barracks. Morning and evening roll calls were announced by means of a siren.

At this stage, after being uprooted from their homes and becoming a part of a group that was subjected to the totalitarianism of all strata of the camp regime and its various lackeys, ranging from the camp commandant to the barracks elder, the families ceased existing as independent units. In addition, there was the physical separation of the sexes. While this was not yet absolute, it harmed the family unit.

"National Socialism tried, with some success, to do away with the traditional separation between the private and the public sphere, between the personal and the political" thus wrote Gisela Bock about German society during the Third Reich.[31] In its attack on Jewish society, Nazi Germany succeeded in breaking down this separation totally. From the moment the families were rousted from their houses, the individual aspect of their existence was eliminated.

The violation of the family, its destruction as an intimate unit bounded by the borders of its home and by it members, caused the eldest son in the K. family to feel completely exposed and defenseless when he arrived in Westerbork: "I felt like an apple that had been peeled and thrown into the street. Other than the clothes I was wearing, I didn't have anything of my very own... wherever I was, there were fifty other people with me. Even my very own family was no longer mine".[32]

However, even in this exposed place, the mother managed to separate her family from the rest of the prisoners by physically delineating the area around her family's beds with blankets. She arranged the clothes in boxes, thereby creating an illusion of a barrier on the one hand and intimacy on the other – the things that form the basis of the existence of every family. "Mother made a home for us", her son recalls. "One of the wonders of the world. How can a woman make a home for her family in two hours with almost nothing? Later on, Grandpa and Grandma also joined us, and the family was complete".[33]

The arrival of the mother and children from the M. family, who had been caught in their hiding-place, at the camp was particularly traumatic. The father's earlier arrest had already split up the family, and because they had been captured while in hiding, the mother and her children were incarcerated in the punishment barracks.[34] The shock of the transition to the closed world of the detention camp was severe and was further exacerbated by their incarceration in the punishment barracks. It took several weeks for the father to manage to have them transferred to a regular barracks. The connections the father had established with influential people in the camp during the months he had spent there prior to the arrival of his family gave him a relative advantage that enabled him to fulfill his role as the protector of his family once more.[35]

Parents were required to provide their children with some kind of explanation with regard to the structure of their new lives. Some of them clung to the reality they had left behind them in order to minimize the horror of the incarceration of their children and the threat that loomed over them. They did so by explaining that the policemen were guarding them and making sure that they didn't get lost. While the older children did not believe the explanation, some of the young children, as they were transported from one camp to the next, paradoxically felt that the guards and the policemen were not only filling the void that had been created, but also constituted the very authority, power, and protection of which the parents had effectively been deprived.[36]

The process of undermining the family structure that had commenced at the beginning of the war continued in the transit camps. In view of the loss of the prisoners' power on the one hand and the absolute power of the camp command on the other, the parents' authority collapsed and the children's perception of their parents changed radically. A central part of parenthood – the ability to protect one's children – was lost. However, even though parents lost their authority, they did not always lose the ability to give emotional support. This was particularly true with regard to the little children, but all the children derived comfort from the fact that they were in the vicinity of their parents, even though the hierarchical structure had changed.[37] Nevertheless, the severe overcrowding in the barracks created tension and friction, and children were frequently the objects of the adults' wrath. A large part of their day was spent outside of the barracks. Many of them spent several hours studying in a setting that included all age groups.[38] Other children found work in the camp and quickly became cognizant of the rules and regulations there, sometimes more so than the adults, who were physically and emotionally exhausted by the conditions that prevailed.[39] The feeling of satisfaction that accompanied those achievements was mixed with pain for the harm done to the adults, who had been stripped of their power:

> They took everything my parents had away from them. My father was not allowed to earn, my mother was not allowed to make a home for us, and Grandpa and Grandma were not allowed to take care of us. On the contrary: I went with Grandpa to show him where everything was in the camp... I would even speak on his behalf... All this threw me into a state of great confusion.[40]

The middle child in the K. family, who was seven at the time, also recalled the blow that deprived the adults of respectability as the factor that shaped his memory of the Westerbork transit camp: "It was ... not at all nice. I remember that. Not at all respectable". These feelings were linked to the loss of confidence in the adult world and in the parental protection that was concentrated in the figure of the father, as the sons of the K. family perceived it. The undermining of their confidence in him was so fundamental that in an interview that was conducted over 50 years later with the son who was seven at the time, the latter was still amazed that his father, who was occasionally allowed to leave the camp, would actually return to his family in the camp. After all, his father could have escaped and disappeared.[41]

For the children, life in the camp was ambivalent. On the one hand, it was the beginning of a process of adaptation to a world that was unprecedented, in which they were obliged to detach themselves from the template of the rational, protected, and predictable world they had known in the past. On the other hand, signs of the regular world existed there;[42] there was a school, a hospital, and even a cabaret and an orchestra. The type of evil that would come later did not yet exist. Looking back, Rudi K., who was seven at the time, concluded that that camp was a kind of intermediate stage between health and illness.[43] Although there was a situation in which the foundations of family life had been undermined by uprooting, detention, destruction of the adults' self-respect, and the fact that they were stripped of power and protection, there were no executions, and people did not die of starvation.

The most traumatic event in Westerbork occurred once a week when the transports departed for the concentration and extermination camps. The lists of deportees were read out on the eve of departure, auguring further separation and suffering for the families. Even though the destinations of the transports were inscribed on the trains, the prisoners did not grasp the full significance of the names of the concentration camps. Anyone who had ties with the Jewish leadership of the camp did anything in his power not to be included on the lists. One of the lists included the grandparents of the K. family. The preparations for the forthcoming journey took all night. Here, too, it was the mother who played the central role in the preparations, displaying the same resourcefulness she had shown at the two previous stages in the family's breaking-down process. Once again, her actions engendered wonder and admiration in the memory of her son, who did not understand where she had obtained the supplies with which she equipped her parents.

The night before their departure, the grandparents sorted out their belongings and debated as to what to take with them and what to leave behind. Objects that were laden with memories and significance passed back and forth between two piles – the pile that would be left behind for safekeeping and the pile that they would take with them. That night, they also entrusted the history of the family to the family members who were to remain behind, and some of it was etched into the memory of the eldest son. The feeling that prevailed that night was one of a final farewell. In the morning, the grandparents were put on to a train inscribed with the word "Auschwitz".[44]

The breakdown of the nuclear family occurred when the fathers were transferred to Buchenwald. The fathers from the K. and D. families were sent on the same transport. The son from the K. family remembers his father and his mother in a state in which he had never seen them before. They embraced for a long time, and he felt the intervention of "a great and terrible power, greater than the power of my father". Although he wrote his memoirs almost 60 years later, when his father's powerlessness was clearly understood, there is still some residual accusation with regard to what was perceived as capitulation in the child's and later in the adult's eyes:

> The power broke him but had no effect on me, even though I saw him broken.
> . . I saw him denuded of the slightly distant mystical image of Father. . . He

tried to say something but did not succeed. How can a grown-up person tell a child that he has capitulated and is transferring his role to him?...I told him, "I'm not ten years old any more", and with those words I parted from him and he parted from me.[45]

The disintegration of the father figure reached its peak during their final farewell, and it contained all the elements that had been present during the entire process of the undermining of the father figure that had begun three years previously, at the beginning of the war. There we find the vestiges of the child's admiration for his father, the humiliation with the attendant pain and feeling of affront, and the child's naive belief in his own power. The child and his friend tried to approach the train that was departing for Buchenwald in order bid their fathers farewell, but were unable to do so because of the huge commotion that was in progress there. The father's "capitulatory" stance and the physical separation from him constituted the moment pinpointed by the son as the one in which his life changed completely.

There is a considerable difference between the way in which circumstances such as those were etched in the memories of the children whose families survived and were reunited and the children who had lost their parents. The annihilation of the family by Nazi Germany and the breakdown of parental protection and authority constituted the central factors that shaped the rest of the lives of the people for whom the situation became final and absolute. The manner in which the parental figures during the Holocaust were perceived in retrospect was also dictated by this fact to a large extent. People whose families survived and were reunited and rehabilitated glorified the image of their parents during the war, whereas people who lost their parents remained eternally entrenched in a feeling that linked parental impotence to the subsequent state of orphanhood. This feeling revolved mainly around the father figure. The residual anger of a child whose father perished is still recognizable in the adult's testimony, which opens with the words: "The clearest memory is of my father … promising me a bike. To this day I haven't received it".[46]

Ravensbrück

A fortnight after the men were taken away, the first transport of women and children with Hungarian nationality departed for Ravensbrück, arriving there on February 7, 1944. There were 65 in the transport: 46 women and 19 children. Four women died during the journey.[47] They traveled in an old but comfortable passenger train that was divided up into compartments. Each person had a suitcase. During the passage from Westerbork to Ravensbrück, they passed through the "ordinary" world, but only visual contact existed between the two worlds; beyond that, the detachment was absolute.[48]

Another transport with 35 women and children in possession of Romanian papers reached Ravensbrück almost two months later, on April 6, 1944.[49]

The biggest child on the first transport, the eldest son of the D. family, was then

13 years old, and remembers the armed Germans who warned the group of women and children that they would be shot if they tried to escape.[50] In spite of that, the mother of the K. family considered fleeing with her children while the train was stationary during the night. Although the idea was abandoned, the fact that the son mentioned it in his memoirs highlights his feeling about his father's helplessness.[51]

The scenes that met the eyes of the women and children upon their arrival at Ravensbrück were unlike anything they had ever seen before. They were placed in isolation for a short time. On the other side of the fence stood hundreds of women who were yelling to them. Initially, the cacophony of shouting made it difficult for them to make out what these women were saying, but gradually they managed to grasp the crux of the matter. The inmates on the other side of the fence were instructing them to eat all the food in their possession and to hide jewelry and gold inside their bodies. The K. family's son summed up the spirit of the message the veteran inmates were trying to convey to the mothers as follows: "Forget the past, the outside world, forget everything you know. You will be reborn, you will come into the world as you came into it the first time, completely naked, physically and mentally".[52]

The mothers reacted by plunging into feverish activity. They gave their children the remaining food – bread with a lot of sugar on it. All their belongings were confiscated. One of the children had a silver teaspoon engraved with his initials forcibly taken away from him. He had received it from his grandparents, and it was the last thing that remained from his previous life.[53] Tiny earrings were removed from the ears of an eight-year-old girl.[54] A female SS overseer entered and ordered everyone to strip. One of the mothers tried unsuccessfully to hide a small passport photo of her husband inside her body.[55]

All the children recall the situation as being threatening and frightening, but the exposure of the mothers in their nakedness was particularly traumatic for the boys in the group who were old enough to remember it. The situation contained an additional stratum, that of the desecration of the parent's honor – the mother's, this time – in which another line was crossed and the relationship between the mother and her children was fundamentally breached. According to the K. family's son, his mother's enforced nakedness contained an element of sacrilege.[56] During the first moments, neither mothers nor sons knew how to cope with the humiliation and embarrassment that had been forced on them. For the sake of the values of the past, one of the mothers ordered her son not to look, but the present was stronger, and although he tried not to peep, every now and again he was compelled to look up, if for no other reason than to avoid tripping. Aware of her son's distress, the mother did the only thing that could save him from his terrible embarrassment. She managed to overcome her own embarrassment and ordered him to look at her. The ensuing relief was enormous, and the shame evaporated.[57] Another child who stared in amazement at the scene before him remembers that he was harshly scolded by his mother. A fear of death prevailed in the hall, and from then on he associated it with the nakedness he saw for the first time in his life.[58]

After the nakedness came the shaving of some of the women in the group. By stages, the identities of the women were stripped and destroyed in their own and in their children's eyes. It seemed to the older children that the stage following the shaving was when the women internalized their situation. The hair on the floor was collected meticulously and the seven-year-old child told himself that they had come to a very tidy place.[59]

The women were issued prison uniforms. Since the camp warehouses did not contain clothing in children's sizes, the children were permitted to keep their clothes and the blankets they had brought from Holland. The mothers subsequently made use of these clothes and blankets as well, since they were bitterly cold in the uniforms they had been issued.

One of the factors upon which the lives of the women and children depended was the attitude both of the women who were in charge of the block and of the other prisoners. Upon their arrival, the women in charge explained the camp rules to them. They also quickly learned the inmates' hierarchy, which was determined according to the categories of imprisonment. The generalizations pertaining to the bad treatment meted out by the Polish and Ukrainian inmates and the good treatment they received at the hands of the Russian inmates, who were Red Army soldiers, recur throughout the testimonies. However, when the individual descriptions are analyzed, these generalizations are shattered, and they reveal a range of attitudes that do not always match the overall division according to nationality. There were inmates who would beat the children and treat them cruelly,[60] but on the other hand there are testimonies, both from the group of mothers and children and from other inmates, to acts of assistance and rescue. A Polish inmate who worked in the kitchen would keep food for one of the mothers and her children every day. Another saved the life of a little girl who had fallen ill.[61] In yet another case, German inmates recounted how inmates who worked in the camp's offices changed the age of an 11-year-old girl in order to enable her to join a group of inmates who worked in the Siemens plant. By so doing, they saved her life.[62]

The Red Army POWs were a source of attraction for the children. They maintained their military routine, executed military drills amid the barracks, and sang in a choir. They would throw birthday parties for the children, the focal point of which was bread and a little jam that they siphoned off from their rations.

The inmates would often burst into tears when they encountered the children, both because of the horror of the very fact of their incarceration in the camp and because of the memories the children evoked. Many of the children's memories of the other inmates were good. It seems that the children were placed above the hierarchy that existed among the inmates, which was based on racial affiliation and nationality. One of the children related that the yellow triangle that attested to their Jewishness was of no interest to German inmates. The latter rejoiced in them because they had not seen children for a long time.[63] The children, well aware of the reactions they sparked in the inmates, would go from barracks to barracks, begging for food.

The mothers tried to minimize the disturbance caused by the children to the other inmates as much as possible, and when one of the babies began teething, her mother would stand holding her at night near the latrine so that her crying would not awaken the other inmates.[64]

The attitude of the children toward the SS personnel was complex. On the one hand, the latter constituted the focal point of the terror, but on the other – surprisingly – they were also a source of admiration. In the reality in which the children lived, the manner in which they perceived themselves, their relatives, and the Nazi criminals was occasionally distorted. This distortion was reflected in the games they played, among other things. When playing the roles of the Nazis, they were on the "correct" side of the concentration camp world for a moment.[65] The contrast between the polished uniforms and cleanliness of the Nazis and the wretchedness of the inmates was extreme. The power they wielded and their ability to impose order were also facets of the children's admiration. They possessed something from the world of fairy tales – the type of fairy tale that contains an element of cruelty, as one of the children recalled.[66]

The distortion can also be seen in the attitude of some of the SS personnel toward the children, and can be perceived as a part of the distorted yet complex behavior of the Nazi criminals. The continuous flow of their regular lives, with their love and affection for their families, their pets, music, and in the case below, infants, existed alongside the atrocities they committed. One of the SS overseers, a good-looking young woman of about 20, would amuse herself with one of the babies every morning by bathing and pampering her. She completely disregarded the atrocities she had committed a short time previously and seemed to detach herself from them.[67]

In another case, an SS man gave an toddler of about two years old a cube of sugar. Her mother taught her to smile at that particular German, and he came back and gave her more sugar cubes on subsequent days as well. The mother also taught the child to hold the cube at the front of her mouth and give it to her without sucking it, so that she could divide it up between the rest of her children.[68]

Descriptions of beatings suffered by the children at the hands of the SS are rare. The mothers were the ones who were beaten, in most cases because of incidents involving their children. The day began at three a.m. in the summer and at four a.m. in the winter for the inmates and children. The women, huddling together for the morning roll call in the bitter cold, resembled sheep, as one child saw it. The roll calls represent a particularly bad memory, both because it was extremely difficult to remain standing for so long in the bitter cold, and because of the additional danger that was inherent in the very situation. Mothers of infants would hold them in their arms during the interminable hours of standing. One of the children recounted that during the period of waiting, he was haunted by the terrible fear that his mother would collapse and fall and would then be beaten by the overseers. Emmi K. remembers her mother fainting during the roll call and lying on the floor without any possibility of anyone coming to her aid.[69] Another child, who was six at the time, relates that during one of the roll calls, she whispered something to her mother. An SS man who was passing by hit the mother with his whip. "They hit her because of me", she recalled, "and I remember thinking at that moment, How dare you hit Jews, you're nothing but a *goy* [Yiddish: gentile], even if you're well-dressed".[70]

These descriptions exemplify and unite two approaches. The first approach deems the child's staying with the mother a significant factor in diminishing his trauma,[71] while the second approach claims that it was precisely the incarceration with the parents that was liable to intensify the trauma since the child was afraid for his parents and experienced his parents' fear.[72] As emerges from the testimonies, both approaches are correct and existed concurrently. While the mother's centrality and significance in the children's lives is undoubted, the worry and fear for her safety, as well as the insult and the humiliation, constituted a central component in the world of the children in the concentration camp. The child's total identification with his mother was sometimes expressed in similar physical reactions.[73]

After the roll call, the women would march in line back to the barracks. The children were permitted to run, so they could reach the barracks first and get hold of one of the few chairs for their mothers. For breakfast, they received a slice of bread, and anyone who did not work did not get any more food until the evening. The older children debated whether to eat all the bread in the morning or to save some of it for the afternoon and risk having it stolen during the day. In the evening, they were fed beet soup.

One of the advantages of detention in a concentration camp in Germany was the possibility of keeping in some kind of contact with the outside world and with the fathers, who were incarcerated in Buchenwald. Once a month, every female inmate could receive or send a postcard or a letter that was limited to the number of lines in it. Naturally, it was subjected to censorship and therefore had to be written in a clear handwriting. According to the information that was stamped on the postcard by the camp command, any postcard that was not written legibly would be destroyed. At least two families still have a few postcards and letters that were sent to and from Buchenwald and Ravensbrück in their possession. One of them was written in the clear, rounded handwriting of the eldest son. The message in the majority of the missives was similar: "We're all well and hope to hear the same from you soon", and their main objective was to serve as a sign of life for faraway family members. Sometimes a few lines were dedicated to a description of the children's development: the two-year-old daughter who had just begun to talk called every man she saw "Daddy".[74]

A relative of the D. family who was in Switzerland during the war attempted to transfer parcels to the family in Ravensbrück. The attempt was evidently successful, according to letters from a Dutch Jewish organization whose headquarters were in Geneva.[75]

Death was an inseparable part of the children's daily lives, and one of the witnesses recounted that when she fell ill and was placed in the sickroom *(Revier)*, she lay next to a woman who constantly admonished her not to move because she was preventing her from sleeping. "Until one night, when she didn't say anything," she said. "I was happy that she was quiet, that she didn't say anything to me, and in the morning it turned out that she was dead". "Children were accustomed", she added, "at that time they were accustomed to people dying around them". Her fear of death was not as great as her fear of the inmates who had lost their sanity and were tied to the sinks during the day. She recalls the terror that gripped her when she had to pass by them on her way to the lavatory.[76]

Emmi K. remembers the feeling of death that accompanied her as she lay in the *Revier* not as a bad feeling, but rather as a good and comforting one.[77] The commonplace nature of death made it less threatening and frightening to the children than to the adults.[78] "Death games" were a part of the repertory of children's games during the Holocaust and served as a means of coping with the fear of death as well as with the wish to die.[79]

Several mothers had jobs, some of them in the Siemens plant close to the camp. Others stayed with the children. The feeling that persisted in the memory of some of the children was that the mothers helped one another and the family atmosphere that was created imbued them with a sense of belonging. Because of the need to obtain food, the mothers sought additional jobs. One of them would bring the food from the kitchen to the barracks and distribute it. Another volunteered to work in the crematorium commando.

The fact that the mothers relinquished some of their food for the sake of the children is frequently mentioned in the various testimonies. One of the girls compared her mother's behavior to that of an animal taking care of her young. In order to safeguard her children while she was sleeping, she would tie her little daughters to her body during the night.[80]

Besides attempting to meet the most basic prerequisites for their children's survival, the mothers had to cope with their physical and emotional hardships as well. When one of the little girls complained that she was hungry, her mother instructed her to suck her fingers. She sucked them so hard that she hurt herself.[81]

Subjected to the concentration camp reality, some of the mothers tried to give the children tools that would enable them to overcome it. The mother in the D. family, who was of English origin and a teacher by profession, taught children in a kind of class she held in the barracks. Beyond the act of teaching, which exemplified an attempt to introduce a modicum of normality into the children's lives, she tried to somewhat minimize the terror of the camp, the sight of the dying women, and the piles of corpses. Her son still remembers a song that she taught him. It began with the words: "Stone walls do not a prison make. If your spirit is such that you can overcome it, then the stone walls won't mean anything".[82]

In another testimony, a person who was seven years old at the time of his sojourn in Ravensbrück describes how his mother helped him overcome his fears by getting him to internalize the idea that what was going on around him was not really happening; it was a kind of play that was being staged there. He says:

I didn't have fears. People call it her indoctrination, that I was observing my entire surroundings, all those things, even in the camps, as clowns... I have a feeling that that's what Mother succeeded in... not to take things seriously... that it was not a serious world.[83]

Reciting the family history and the names of the family members was an additional method of rising above everyday life in the camp. The mother of the M. family recited the names of the family members to her children over and over again. While this had the practical objective of drilling the children's identity and origin into them in case of further separation, it was also a way of detaching them from the reality in which they were trapped and characterizing it as temporary and unimportant. What was worth remembering was the family history, the past from which they came.[84]

Two traumatic incidents for which there is no corroboration are reported in the children's testimonies. Debórah Dwork relates to the problematic nature of this kind of discrepancy in interviews with child survivors, maintaining that it is mandatory to examine it in the framework of constructing the reality of the narrating individual. Dwork raises the question of what reality actually is. She differentiates between the "objective" historical past (what "really' happened), the "subjective" psychological experience (that which the child believed, or the one the now-adult survivor believes to have occurred), and the narrative part. These three components – historical truth, psychological truth, and the truth of the narrative – are not always discrete and isolated entities, and the historian must analyze how the story was chosen and constructed in order to explain it and give it meaning.[85]

The first incident that recurs in the stories of some of the survivors is the story of the Christmas celebration in December 1944. According to the testimonies of the children and of the non-Jewish inmates, the inmates organized a party for the children of the camp. Scraps of food were collected and hoarded, gifts for the children were prepared, and there was even a puppet show. That is the undisputed objective reality. The non-Jewish inmates recounting the event stress the act of solidarity as well as the joy of doing and the excitement it engendered.[86]

Some of the children's testimonies state that during or after the celebration – in any event after they themselves had left the scene – the Germans threw a hand grenade into the barracks where the party was being held, killing all the children who were still there.[87] Naomi M. related that she was singing in the choir with all the other children while her mother and another mother were waiting outside. When they had finished singing, the mothers removed their children from the party, with the excuse that it was not their holiday. Naomi's brother, on the other hand, related that their mother had not allowed them to go to the party at all, and that the next day, she told the children that at the height of the party, hand grenades had been thrown into the barracks. Judith H. recalled that she sang at the party. While she did not remember anything about the hut being blown up, she mentioned that the memory of the Christmas celebration evoked a negative feeling.

The celebration was held during a period in which the mass transports from Auschwitz were arriving. Among the female arrivals was a relative of the M. family. They located her and took her to their barracks, where she reported what had happened to her in Auschwitz:

> First she said: I don't believe that there are still children in the world! How come there are children here? Because all the children who had been with them had gone up the chimney. There were no children... She told us about the gas chambers, she told us about the crematorium. And then, when we saw what the Germans had begun to do at the end of 1944, we were gripped by fear... Suddenly we saw that the Auschwitz end was coming to us as well because of the construction and preparation of the gas chambers and the crematorium that she told us about in Auschwitz.[88]

It is possible that it was the fear that gripped the children upon hearing the reports from Auschwitz that accounted for the story of the liquidation of the children at the 1944 Christmas celebration. In the reality in which they lived, such an incident was possible. The story of the liquidation of the children reflected the deterioration in the living conditions in the camp as a result of the arrival of the transports from the East, the Germans' alarm with regard to the situation on the front, and the information that Jewish children were targeted for elimination – information that the children had internalized thoroughly. It is further possible that the conflict involving the participation of Jewish children from a religious family in a Christian celebration, and the objection of the mother to their remaining in that situation, was also a component of that story.

Another story that lacks "objective" corroboration or supporting testimonies is the story of the accidental killing of a female SS guard by Menachem K. Five children, among them Menachem, were playing a game of throwing the lids of tin cans. These lids were large and had sharp edges. When he threw the lid, a scream was heard. The children did not see what the lid had hit, but it was clear to them what had happened. Shortly afterwards, they were all summoned to a special roll call. Their mothers were at work and they stood alone with other women and felt worse than ever. The commander of the roll call shouted that a female German soldier had been killed and if the perpetrators of the murder did not give themselves up, everyone would be punished. There were small, sharp stones scattered over all the paths in the camp, and the camp command issued an order that until the murderer had been found, the inmates would all go barefoot. The children held a vote in which they decided not to reveal Menachem's involvement. A few weeks later, the inmates were allowed to resume wearing shoes.

In this incident, too, it is obvious that the component of fear constitutes the basis of the story. It is possible that the various elements of the story are true – the game, the roll call, and the punishment that was meted out to the inmates – but their combination and the way the child interpreted them cast doubt on the "objective" truth. On the other hand, there is no doubt whatsoever regarding the subjective psychological truth or the repercussions of the palpable terror that doubtlessly haunted the child, who believed that he had killed an SS guard.

No less than the historical facts, both incidents attest to the reality in which the children lived in the camp. Perpetually in danger, taking part in activities and games that were forbidden or disapproved of, the children constructed a reality other than the "objective" one. This other reality was no less tangible, disturbing or threatening, and its effect on them was obvious.

According to camp regulations, when the boys grew up and reached the age of 12 or 13, they were transferred to the small men's camp that was situated next to the women's camp. The world of the women and children was therefore subjected to a further upheaval. The youngest of the transferees was an 11-year-old boy, who links the transfer to his rape by one of the Red Army POWs. The woman, who lived in the barracks, enticed him to her bunk with bread and honey. While the children did indeed observe sex scenes in the camp, said the boy, he had not made any connection between those scenes and his own body until then.[89] As he interpreted it, the Germans saw what was going on and decided that he and his older friend would be transferred to the men's camp. Notice of the transfer was delivered unexpectedly and without any advance warning. His mother, who was in a state of shock, made the eldest son from the D. family, who was also being transferred, swear that he would look after her son. This additional crisis was another stage in the breakdown of the family, and from the point of view of the children who were transferred it was the final stage in the loss of parental protection. Despite the extreme conditions in which they had lived until the transfer, the fact that they had remained with their mothers and siblings made the place "relatively warm": "However difficult it was, we had a place where we were looked after. There were people to talk to, there were people who were concerned, there were people who told us what we could and couldn't do, and there was Mother, who always spread her wings over us".[90]

Similar to the other crossroads in the decline of Menachem K's childhood, the feeling of orphanhood that accompanied the transfer was counterbalanced – and, to a certain extent, contradicted – by his pride in his maturity: "I imagine that for our mothers it was a terrible blow, but we felt very important and grown up".[91]

The transfer altered the structure in the families that remained in the women's camp, and in the K. family, the younger brother became responsible for his little sister when his older brother left. The weight of the responsibility was such that for a long time, he did not even remember that his older brother had been with them in the women's camp.

Bergen-Belsen

In March 1945, the group was transferred to Bergen-Belsen in freight trucks. The conditions that prevailed in the camp at the time are described in a letter written by Camp Commandant Kramer to the headquarters in Oranienburg in response to the announcement that 2,500 women were being transferred to Bergen-Belsen from Ravensbrück. Kramer informed headquarters that the barracks already exceeded their maximum capacity by 30 percent. The women could not lie down to sleep, but rather had to sleep sitting up on the floor. A typhus epidemic was raging in the camp, and the number of dead, which had been 60 or 70 a day at the beginning of February, was now approaching 300. There were no disinfectants in the camp to eliminate the disease, and food supplies had run out on February 20.[92]

The camp was in a shambles, recalls one of the witnesses. In contrast to Ravensbrück, where discipline and terror ruled, Bergen-Belsen was on the verge of disintegrating. The new inmates did not even undergo the camp reception procedures, there were no beds, and roll calls were no longer held. Starvation and disease reigned supreme.[93] There were piles of corpses all over. The mother from the M. family volunteered again to evacuate the corpses here as well:

> …You went to sleep at night and you didn't know whether you would get up in the morning. Every morning, a few more people didn't get up. They were taken out of the barracks. I remember my mother and a few other people each grabbing an arm, a leg, and taking them outside and throwing them on the pile, like garbage. Such a thing is indescribable. That's why I say that what I saw in a month and a half in Bergen-Belsen, I didn't see in a year in Ravensbrück.[94]

The camp command no longer saw to anything. It seemed to the child that the inmates no longer interested the Germans, who were only concerned with saving their own skins. They gazed with admiration at the SS personnel who, in spite of everything, still tried to impose order.[95] The members of the group, both the mothers and the children, fell ill.

On April 15, 1945, the British liberated the camp. A few days elapsed before they recovered from the shock of entering the camp and began to organize aid for the survivors. The mother of the K. family was dying. She handed her son a note to give to the British, requesting that they provide her with medical assistance. The child remembers that he tried to deliver the note, but in the terrible commotion, he failed to accomplish his mission. His failure to deliver the message haunted him for many years. The medical assistance came too late, and his mother died five days after the liberation. Suddenly, she was no longer there, he related. Initially, he felt angry, because she had always been there for him, and suddenly she disappeared. Later, he told himself that now she was free; it was the only thing she had done for herself – and she had only done it after ascertaining that her children had been rescued.[96] The two children, the boy and his little sister, were at her side when she died. Other women testified that they would never forget the wails of the two children. The boy bent over his mother's corpse, said his little sister, and removed her eyeglasses – the only thing she had left.[97]

Her body lay there for a few more days until it was buried. The boy, intoxicated with freedom, would go out on expeditions all over the camp and run around freely, but he would return to the barracks in which his mother lay: "It was the only home I had", he said, "the place where I lived, and that's where she was lying, and it wasn't her".[98]

Conclusion

The history of the families who form the central core of this article exemplifies the classification of groups of Jews as exceptions to the Third Reich's extermination policy. Nevertheless, many characteristics in the undermining and breakdown of the families, from the moment Nazi Germany burst into their lives until their incarceration in the concentration camps, are similar to those of other Jewish families who were not classified as "exceptions". The survival of mothers and children, some of whom were infants during the war, from among the group under discussion has provided us with unusual testimonies regarding the lives of women, mothers and children in the world of the concentration camps.

The breakdown of the family occurred gradually and began with the undermining of the family hierarchy and internal order. Already at that stage, the impairment of the father's function and the ensuing perception of the father figure account for the principal damage. During the first stages, the mothers were required to continue playing their traditional role, and in all the cases described above, succeeded in doing so. As the public domain increasingly crushed the private domain, additional roles that deviated from conventions and from their regular frameworks of activity were added to their traditional roles.

As the domains in the gender-based distribution within the family broke down, so the boundaries between the adults' world and the children's world became blurred. The way the children perceived events and experiences depended on their ages. When the family, which constitutes the first circle of the child's security,[99] was undermined, the children's world was also undermined. The concept of parenthood underwent an upheaval when it was deprived of two central components: the parental ability to protect, and respectability. With the re-division of the world into victims and perpetrators, children sometimes assumed responsibility for relatives, adults and children, and in all cases, the parents became the objects of the older children's concern.[100] For these children, the collapse of parenthood, in the traditional sense, occupied a central place in their memories. In parallel, they went through a process of the decline of their childhood and even of aging.[101] The memories of people who were small children and infants at the time are characterized by flashes of sensation. Since they had no memory of a fixed template of normal relations with their parents, they also did not remember the collapse of these relations.[102] In both age groups, "screen memory" conceals many of the traumatic experiences,[103] but may also expose the forms and the strata of the fear that was these children's lot. Strata of subjective reality were constructed in order to save themselves from the objective reality and as a process of interpreting the components of that reality. At the base of those two poles lay profound fear.

Within the objective reality to which the children were subjected in the concentration camps, the basic concepts of behavioral and social morality and norms were distorted, as was the concept of death, and the clean, orderly, and powerful world of the SS personnel sometimes became an object of admiration.[104]

The mother is the central figure in all the children's testimonies. There is no doubt that this statement can be explained by the fact that she was with the children in the concentration camps.[105] However, when the gender-based distribution of roles in the family was in the process of being undermined, mothers played a crucial role right from the onset of the persecution. Their functioning in the world of the concentration camp included the fight for their children's and their own survival, mediation with their surroundings, and their work in the camp. It is almost certain that the fact that the children's survival depended on the mothers' continued survival served as significant motivation in their fight for their own survival. The double fight for survival that they fought often endangered them. In retrospect, however, the other female inmates and even, in isolated cases, the SS personnel, occasionally displayed a spark of positive feeling toward the children. In a few cases, the somewhat tolerant attitude toward the children was useful for the mothers as well. This is exemplified in the case of the children being permitted to keep their clothing and blankets.

In a reality in which the borders between the private and the public domains were totally annihilated, the mothers succeeded in creating a private, emotional, and spiritual bubble of privacy for brief periods. They attempted to detach the children temporarily and mentally from the horrors of the camp and to instill the family heritage in them. In addition, the religious mothers tried to inculcate something of the religious heritage into their children.

The way in which the Nazis classified gender as a sub-section in the racial category was among the factors that determined the place and fate of the women during the Holocaust. By leaving children with their mothers, their fate was sealed – in most cases, in the concentration and extermination camps in the East. In the cases presented in this article, motherhood assumed the central role in the existence of the women in their history of the Holocaust. The fight for survival – their own as well – was first and foremost a fight for the children's survival, and the concept of motherhood took on its most extreme significance.

Notes

1   From a postcard that was sent by Frieda M. and her children from the Ravensbrück concentration camp to the father of the family, Ben-Zion M. in the Buchenwald concentration camp in the spring of 1944. It was printed in a booklet written by Uriel M., *My Father, My Teacher, The Righteous Late Rabbi Ben Zion M.* (unpublished) This article was written in the framework of a research project on the Jewish women in

the Ravensbrück concentration camp that was conducted at Tel Aviv University and the Freie Universität Berlin, and funded by the Israel Germany Fund for Research and Development (GIF). It was thanks to the cooperation of the survivors that the research about them could be conducted, and I am grateful to them for that. In order to safeguard their privacy, I have not revealed their full names. Due to constraints of space, it was not possible to present all the testimonies and their analyses here. A broader version of this article is about to be published in the forthcoming (2008) publication *A Holocaust Crossroads: Jewish Women in Ravensbrück* edited by Irith Dublon-Knebel.

2   The English translation of the protocol can be found in: Yitzhak Arad, Israel Gutman, Abraham Margaliot (eds.), *Documents on the Holocaust* (Jerusalem, 1981).

3   This is what the head of the Department of Jewish Affairs in the Foreign Office called those Jews in a letter dated Dec. 15, 1942. Yad Vashem Archive JM 3122.

4   The regulation was issued by the German Security Police and the Security Service in coordination with the Foreign Office. Office of the United States Chief of Counsel for Prosecution of Axis Criminality, *Nazi Conspiracy and Aggression* (Washington, 1946), document PS-3319.

5   The Ravensbrück concentration camp was officially inaugurated in May 1939. During the six years of its existence, it housed approximately 140,000 inmates, 15 percent of whom were Jewish women. Adjacent to the women's camp was a small men's camp. The estimated number of children who were incarcerated in the camp from the day of its establishment until the liberation is over 800, among them Gypsies, Russians, Ukrainians, Czechs, Poles, a small number of Germans, and Jews. The latter almost certainly constituted the largest group. While in most cases the children came to the camp with their mothers, there were also children who came with other female relatives or who arrived alone and were "adopted" by other female inmates. About the Ravensbrück camp, see the articles of Judith Buber Agassi and Rochelle Saidel in this collection.

6   Gisela Bock, *Frauen in der Europaeischen Geschichte* (Muenchen, 2000), p. 282.

7   Gisela Bock, "Ordinary Women in Nazi Germany", in Ofer Dalia and Lenore Weitzman (eds.), *Women in the Holocaust* (Yale, 1998), p. 96.

8   See the instruction regarding the transfer of the women and children to Ravensbrück and of the men and boys over 14 to Buchenwald, p. 2 of this article.

9   Debórah Dwork, *Children with a Star: Jewish Youth in Nazi Europe* (New Haven and London, 1991), p. xvii.

10   *Commandant of Auschwitz: The Autobiography of Rudolf Hoess* with an introduction by Lord Russel of Liverpool (Cleveland and New York, 1959), p. 164. The SS doctors were required to advise whether it was necessary to separate the mothers from the children in order to perform the selection as smoothly as possible. Robert Jay Lifton, *The Nazi Doctors: Medical Killing and the Psychology of Genocide* (New York, 1986), pp. 147, 149.

11   Robert Jay Lifton, *The Nazi Doctors*, p. 176.

12   Debórah Dwork, *Children with a Star*, p. 253.

13   Joan Ringelheim, "Women and the Holocaust: A Reconsideration of Research", in Rittner, Carol, Roth, John K. (eds.), *Different Voices, Women and the Holocaust* (New

York, 1993), p. 378. Lydia Vago wrote that when the transports reached Auschwitz, the directive issued was that all children would remain with their mothers. Veteran prisoners, who received the transports, instructed the young women to give their children to their grandmothers since they knew that both the elderly women and the children were targeted for extermination, while young childless women had a chance of surviving. Many women refused, and as a result went to the gas chambers with their children. From the manuscript of Lydia Vago's memoirs that were handed to the research group, "Female Jewish Prisoners in the Ravensbrück Concentration Camp" at Tel Aviv University.

14 Debórah Dwork, *Children with a Star*, p. 253-254.

15 Born in 1932.

16 Judith S. Kerstenberg and Ira Brenner, *The Last Witness: The Child Survivor of the Holocaust* (Washington and England, 1996), p. 139.

17 Menachem K., *Diary of Memories* (unpublished), p. 10.

18 Ibid., p. 9.

19 Barbara Bauer, "Die Immoralität der Nazi-Welt aus der Sicht von Kindern and Jugendlichen", in Barbara Bauer und Waltraud Strickhausen (Eds.), *"Für ein Kind war das anders": Traumatische Erfahrungen jüdischer Kinder und Jugendliche im nationalsozialistischen Deutschland* (Berlin, 1999), p. 241.

20 Everett M. Ressler, Neil Bothby and Daniel J. Steinbock, *Unaccompanied Children: Care and Protection in Wars, Natural Disasters, and Refugee Movements* (New York, Oxford, 1988), p. 148.

21 Menachem K., *Diary of Memories*, pp. 15, 16.

22 Interview conducted by the author and A. Kemp with Menachem and Emmi K. Yad Vashem 03/230939; and an interview with Rudi K. that was conducted by Sabine Kittel on 26.2.1999 in Saarbrücken, Germany.

23 Interview with Rudi K.

24 Menachem K., *Diary of Memories*, p. 16.

25 Ibid.

26 Debórah Dwork, *Children with a Star*, p. 26.

27 The testimony of Uriel M. Yad Vashem 03/10515; and the testimony of Naomi M. in an interview conducted by the author and A. Kemp. Yad Vashem 033C/5583.

28 An interview with Don K. conducted by Kathrine Roller in South Africa, 5-6.8.1997. Yad Vashem 03/10835.

29 Ibid.

30 The civilian was Erich Deppner and the SS officer was Josef Hugo Dischner. Joseph Michman, "Westerbork", in Israel Gutman (ed.), *Encyclopedia of the Holocaust* (New York, London, 1990). About Westerbork, see also Jacob Presser, *The Destruction of the Dutch Jews* (New York, 1969);, Jacob Boas, *Boulevard des Misères, The Story of Transit Camp Westerbork* (Hamden, Conn., 1985).

31 Gisela Bock, "Ordinary Women in Nazi Germany: Perpetrators, Victims, Followers and Bystanders", in Ofer, Dalia and Weitzman, Lenore (eds.), *Women in the Holocaust*, p. 91.

32 Menachem K., *Diary of Memories*, p. 17.

33 Ibid., p. 18.

34 The fact that anyone caught hiding was sent to the punishment barracks in Westerbork recurs throughout the testimonies. See Frieda Menco-Brommet's testimony in Debórah Dwork, *Children with a Star*, p. 115.

35 Yad Vashem 03/10515.

36 Menachem K., *Diary of Memories*, p. 18; interview with Rudi K.

37 Debórah Dwork, *Children with a Star*, p. 122.

38 According to camp directive no. 40 from July 1943, an education system was supposed to be established in the normal format, which included kindergarten and school. However, such a framework did not in fact exist because of the lack of teaching materials and the constantly changing population. Jacob Presser, *The Destruction of the Dutch Jews*, p. 446; Debórah Dwork, *Children with a Star*, p. 122.

39 See Judith S. Kerstenberg and Ira Brenner, *The Last Witness*, p. 22.

40 Menachem K., *Diary of Memories*, pp. 20-21.

41 Interview with Rudi K.

42 Debórah Dwork, *Children with a Star*, p. 116.

43 Interview with Rudi K.

44 When the camp became too overcrowded, people who enjoyed preferential status, among them the families with Hungarian or Romanian nationality, were transferred to another camp (Amersfoort or Vught) for a few weeks. The conditions there were better; the camp was smaller, and the prisoners all had families.

45 Menachem K., *Diary of Memories*, p. 26.

46 Yad Vashem 03/9814.

47 *Ungarn-Sonder-transport vom Lager Westerbork*, Archive of the Memorial Site of Ravensbrück.

48 Interview with Judith H. conducted by Adriana Kempff. Yad Vashem 03-10838 [03/ 10838?]; Menachem K., *Diary of Memories*, p. 28.

49 *Sondertransport 6.4.1944*. Archive of the Memorial Site of Ravensbrück.

50 Interview with Don K.

51 Menachem K., *Diary of Memories* (2000), p. 17.

52 Ibid., p. 29.

53 Ibid.

54 Yad Vashem 033C/5583.

55 Menachem K., *Diary of Memories*, p. 29.

56 Ibid.

57 Ibid.

58 Interview with Rudi K.

59 Ibid.

60 Irene P.'s testimony. She was interviewed by Katherine Roller [See FN 28], South Africa 5.8.97.

61 Yad Vashem 033C/5583; Yad Vashem 03/230939.

62 "Solidarität Deutscher rettete ein niederländisches Jüdisches Kind". Archive of the Memorial Site of Ravensbrück, StBG Bu/Bd.34/609.

63 Yad Vashem 03/10515.

64 Yad Vashem 033C/5583.

65 Barbara Bauer, "Die Immoralität der Nazi-Welt aus der Sicht von Kindern und Jugendlichen", in Barbara Bauer und Waltraud Strickhausen (Hrsg.), *"Für ein Kind war das anders": Traumatische Erfahrungen jüdischer Knider/Kinder und Jugendliche im nationalsozialistischen Deutschland*, p. 230.

66 Interview with Rudi K.

67 According to the baby's brother, one of the Jewish women collapsed during the roll call one day. The same female SS overseer beat her, let the dogs loose on her, and killed her. Immediately after the roll call, she took his little sister and played with her and pampered her as she did every day – as if nothing had happened. Yad Vashem 03/10515.

68 The author's interview with the L. family, Jerusalem, Jan. 30, 2001.

69 Yad Vashem 03/230939.

70 Interview with the L. family. Another witness recounted that her mother had been brutally beaten by a female overseer twice – once because a prayer book had been found in her possession, and the second time because she brought a chair for her sick son so that he could sit down during the roll call. Interview with Naomi M.

71 Hans Keilson, *Sequentielle Traumatisierung bei Kindern: Deskriptiv-Klinische und quantifiezierend-statistische follow-up Untersuchung zum Schicksal der Jüdischen Kriegswaisen in den Niederlanden* (Stuttgart, 1979), pp. 45-46.

72 Eva Lezzi, "KZ-Haft in früher Kindheit und ihre literarische Evozierung", in Barbara Bauer und Waltraud Strickhausen (Hrsg.), *"Für ein Kind war das anders": Traumatische Erfahrungen jüdischer Kinder und Jugendliche im nationalsozialistischen Deutschland*, p. 257. Lezzi quotes Hans Keilson, who wrote that the main trauma was the separation from the mother, and that staying with her diminished the trauma. She also quotes Reinhart Lempp, who felt that the very fact of being imprisoned with the parents was traumatic.

73 Eva Lezzi, "Verfolgte Kinder: Erlebnisweisen und Erzählstruktur", in *Menora* (1988), pp. 181-223, p. 198.

74 The correspondence between Frieda M. and her family and Ben Zion M. Uriel M., *My Father, My Teacher, The Righteous Late Rabbi Ben Zion M.* (private memorial booklet).

75 Joodse Coordinatie Commissie, Geneve. Yad Vashem, Arolsen documents, Ravensbrück, individual documents.

76 Yad Vashem 033C-5583.

77 Interview conducted by the author and Adriana Kempff with Menachem and Emmi K. Yad Vashem 03/230939.

78 Yad Vashem 03/10835.

79 Judith S. Kerstenberg and Ira Brenner, *The Last Witness*, p. 189.

80 Interview conducted by the author with the L. family, Jerusalem 30.1.2001.

81   Ibid.

82   Yad Vashem 03/10835.

83   Yad Vashem 03/9814.

84   Interview conducted by the author with the M. family 2.7.1997.

85   Debórah Dwork, *Children with a Star*, pp. xxxv ff.

86   Ravensbrück-komitee (eds.), *"Nur deshalb sind dem Tode wir entronnen, damit wir an dem Frieden bau'n"* (Ravensbrück, 1949), p. 6; Frauen-Konzentrationslager Ravensbrück: Geschildert von Ravensbrücker Häftlinge (Vienna, 1946), pp. 23-24; Britta Pawelke, "Als Haeftling geboren-Kinder in Ravensbrück", in Claus Füllberg Stolberg, Martina Jung, Renate Riebe, *Frauen in Konzentrationslagern. Bergen-Belsen Ravensbrück* (1994).

87   Interview with Naomi M.; the words of Uriel M. at a group meeting, Givatayim May 9, 2001.

88   Yad Vashem 03/10515.

89   Menachem K., *Diary of Memories*, pp. 36, 40. The son from the D. family also ascribes the transfer to the "sexual attention" the boys received from the Russian inmates; interview with Don K. It is worthwhile analyzing and relating to the description of the rape more broadly and profoundly. This cannot be done in the framework of the present article – in particular, anything to do with the gender difference between the descriptions of women and girls who experienced similar incidents and the description that appears here.

90   Menachem K., *Diary of Memories*, p. 40.

91   Ibid.

92   The Vienna Library archive, Tel Aviv University 7/D.

93   Interview with Rudi K.

94   Yad Vashem 03/10515.

95   Interview with Rudi K.

96   Ibid.

97   Interview with Emmi and Menachem K.

98   Interview with Rudi K.

99   Everett M. Ressler, Neil Bothby and Daniel J. Steinbock, *Unaccompanied Children*, p. 147.

100 This concern was already expressed in the testimony of someone who was six years old at the time of the event. Interview with the L. family.

101 Judith S. Kerstenberg and Ira Brenner, *The Last Witness*, p. 132.

102 Interview with Emmi and Menachem K.

103 Judith S. Kerstenberg and Ira Brenner, *The Last Witness*, p. 60.

104 Judith S. Kerstenberg and Ira Brenner, *The Last Witness*, p. 160.

105 See also: Iris Berlazky, "Characteristic Features of Child-Survivors' Testimonies as They Appear in Their Narration", in: *International Journal on Audio-Visual Testimony* (Brussels, 1999), p. 141.

1943: The Flight from Home

Lidia D. Sciama

This narrative is one of many fragments I have written but then abandoned, to give my attention to research and academic writing. I am an anthropologist – not a Holocaust scholar – and what I am offering here is just a report from personal experience. It was written a long time after the events. It is about remembering, but it may also reflect a fear of forgetting and an attempt at recording the feel of those years between childhood and adolescence, and the speech habits, modes of address and mannerisms I associate with my Jewish childhood and with wartime Abruzzo. It is, in Derrida's words, an 'autobiographical anamnesis, an *autobiogriffure*' (2001: 183. See also Okely, J. and H. Callaway, 1992).

Initially I had given the story a subtitle, 'My First Fieldwork', because it was in Abruzzo I first met people of different types and social classes, and first witnessed popular religion. Previously, in our Jewish school in the Venice Ghetto, most of us children had had little or no occasion to meet people outside the community.

On re-reading the story through the lens of gender, and thanks to the development and refinement of gender perspectives, I can now see that gender implications are of great interest, and their exploration can undoubtedly sharpen our understanding. However, given that in narrative, as distinct from sociological work, the facts should simply 'speak for themselves', I shall add my brief reflections on changes in gender and family relations in times of oppression and war at the end, as a postscript.

* * *

When in the early evening of 8 September 1943 it was announced on the radio that General Badoglio's government had signed a 'short armistice' with the Allies, I was staying with my sister and parents at a small country house near the river Brenta. It had long been our habit to protract the summer holidays into early autumn, so we children could join, or at least watch, the grape harvesters and be free to cycle round the warm, flat country lanes, before returning to the confined existence of Venice in winter. But that year our parents' decision to keep us away from the city had been mainly due to the uncertainties of war.

Mussolini's government had fallen on July 25th and in many Italian cities people celebrated as if they had been sure that the war too would end very soon. But, in fact, the Fascist regime had been turned into a hopeless military dictatorship, and, while a treaty with the Allies was being prepared with disastrous inefficiency, General Badoglio, in his absurd attempt not to alienate the Germans, had declared on the radio that the war was to continue. Meanwhile, during the forty-five days between the fall of Fascism and the September armistice, Badoglio had communicated to anxious Jewish leaders that racial laws 'could not be immediately repealed, but they would temporarily remain inoperative.' With ironical irrelevance, an official amendment of August 31, 1943 stated that 'the prohibition for Jews to sojourn in certain health resorts or holiday places' was repealed, and they would now be free to legally own radios and to apply for passports.

Nothing really had changed, but vague and sinister rumours about the imprisonment of Jews in Germany and Poland were reaching Italian communities with increasing frequency. Euphoria at the first news of the September armistice had rapidly given way to suspense and uncertainty for most Italians, but for many Jewish families fear and a sense of impending disaster had soon prevailed over all hope that the war might truly have come to an end.

Yet for those few days of early September – and with that half-knowledge of things that must have been quite typical of our eleven and ten years of age – at first my sister and I had shared in the excitement of an unexpected and speedy demobilization. The mood throughout the Venetian countryside was one of mirth: the boys were coming home. The war was going to be over within a matter of days: just in time for the harvest. But it was not very long before the population were again overtaken with anxiety and with a fear of worse things to come. The day after the armistice had been announced, the man who usually delivered our milk had come rather unexpectedly in the late afternoon to ask mother if she could spare any men's suits, shirts or shoes. Civilian clothes were urgently needed to help soldiers, then disbanded and spread through the countryside, quickly divest themselves of their uniforms so they could go home and escape the danger of being taken off to labour camps in Germany. Mother had been glad to provide all she could, but, as we heard that German divisions were pouring into Northern Italy through the mountain passes, it was not very long before our parents decided that it was time for us too to leave.[1]

One of the family's long-standing employees encouraged us to escape to his native Abbruzzi, where, as we all hoped, we would soon be joined by the Allies. We left at dawn, and, after an interminable train journey, repeatedly interrupted by air raids, and, in the coastal area south of Ancona, by machine gun fire from perilously low-flying Allied planes, in the evening we arrived at Pescara. Our plan was to reach Castel di Sangro, but we would first stop at Lanciano, a small town a few miles inland, to try and gather some information about the war, because in the general confusion of the last few days the news was often contradictory and unreliable. From Pescara we reached Lanciano that same evening quite undisturbed, in a pleasantly speedy horse-drawn carriage, and booked in for the night at a hotel near the station. But when on the following day we should have been ready to continue our southward journey we were told that the Germans had destroyed all bridges, and the charming railway over the Sangro Valleys had been systematically blown up and dismantled.

The small city now stood isolated and apparently calm. Its station, rendered quite useless, looked more than ever toy-like, and the fact that it should be guarded by heavily armed German soldiers appeared quite unnecessary and entirely baffling to my naive eyes, still unused to the strangeness of war. Crossing the lines at this point, we were told, was all but impossible. That we should remain in Lanciano, then, seemed almost fate. We were disconcerted, but we still hoped that the Allies, who on October 8th had successfully landed at Termoli, only twenty five kilometres away from us, would soon make another landing at Pescara, or San Benedetto del Tronto, north of Lanciano: the Germans, as we then hoped, would naturally leave in order not to find themselves encircled and the small town would be bypassed by the war.

We had no choice other than to wait. With the help of relatives of the man who had in the first place directed us to Abruzzo, we found rooms in the house of a woman whose husband, an army officer, was in a British prison camp in Africa. To give ourselves an occupation we would often go to the market, where we marveled at the variety and abundance of fruit. After the long journey, the bustle, confusion and crying at Pescara station, Lanciano in its warm autumn days seemed to offer a fullness of life that made the noise and anguish of war seem all the more absurd and unreal. Not that one could forget or ignore the war, since the rumbling of cannons in the nearby valleys, the sudden dry sound of machine guns, the stirring roar of airplanes and the continual shouting of soldiers, kept it forever present in people's hearts. But there were moments when (perhaps just to my childish perception) the sight of upright, darkly clad women, balancing their laden baskets firmly on their heads and walking over miles of uncertain ground to carry their produce to market, conveyed a feeling of unconcern and of generosity, one which, however, was soon to change to stubborn endurance and resignation as oppression became harsher and more protracted.

On the evening of October 5, after German soldiers started sacking the shops in the city's main street, several young men set fire to German vehicles heading south for the front. By the following morning, from some of the town's high points, there had developed a violent street battle. A hope that the Eighth Army might land on the coast, or even that British paratroops might come to the aid of insurgents, was soon to prove quite unfounded, and it was not very long before German artillery had regained total control over the main streets. The uprising was then violently repressed and was immediately followed by house-to-house searches, reprisals and executions.

In the first days of occupation, German requests, injunctions and threats were communicated through edicts appended to walls and shop-fronts in the center and side streets of the town, while, in order to contravene or ignore their orders, a large part of the population deliberately exaggerated the extent of their illiteracy. The military commanders then decided to resume an older tradition and have their requests broadcast by the municipal town crier, a robust tenor who often embellished even the most peremptory of martial communications with salacious witticisms at the expense of his new masters. But there certainly was no humour when, ordered to raise his carefully modulated voice through the semi-deserted streets, so it could reach behind closed shutters and doors, he announced that Lanciano was to be cleared of all civilian population by October 25th.

While that evening I stood almost motionless, my forehead glued to a windowpane, gravely watching some of the city's buildings, as well as a mill on a distant hillside, go up in flames, I once more heard my mother and father trying to work out what we should do. Still hoping that the whole region might soon be taken over by the Eighth Army, they then decided that we should make our way to a nearby hillside village. (So near the front lines that, father said, we need not fear the bombs, for they would fly right above our heads like firebirds and land much further north). Meanwhile, under a violent rain, the flames gradually turned to smoke; we went to bed while mother stayed up to pack and to organize some food for the journey.

Our hope that the advance of the Allies would be as sharp and speedy as it had been from Bari to Termoli was soon disappointed. Then, as it was the Germans' policy to push the population northwards when they foresaw some strenuous battle and when their own slow retreat from front line villages was impending, we too were forced to join a convoy of peasants and were ordered to march towards Chieti. At any other time, the haphazard and disorderly line of refugees could have been mistaken for a religious procession. But, on that occasion, the shouting from military vehicles at the sides of the long line of people, and the clipped guttural voices ordering us to take cover on the grassy banks and lie flat in the roadside ditches, when Allied planes flew over and from time to time sprayed German vehicles with sudden outbursts of machine gun fire, would not have left viewers in any doubt.

As evening was beginning to come down, and it was clear that we could not possibly have reached Chieti that day, it was decided that we should spend the night at one of the hillside villages on our route. Indeed, that last part of our journey had been speeded up, when after a long day's walking we were picked up by the driver of a German lorry, who insisted we should all take a few sips from one of numerous bottles of Marsala wine he had just collected from an abandoned farm. We spent the night in a cold, high-vaulted church, each family group huddled together, some weeping and praying, others in desperate silence, while the sound of artillery seemed to get closer and more intense as the night grew deeper. Finally we had some rest near dawn. Although nobody dared to say so, there was a hope in the air that we might wake to find that the Allies had arrived... Instead we were roused by the now familiar shouting: "Out! Out! You must all make for Chieti!" followed by the customary threat, "Anyone contravening... will be executed on sight..."

I now cannot remember at all if our sojourn in Chieti was one of months or weeks. We had been able to rent a room from a couple whom I then regarded as rather old, Don Edoardo and Felicetta. The woman always wore thick black cotton dresses with long skirts, woolen stockings and rather square black leather shoes, like those usually worn by nuns. She usually covered her skirt with a thick apron of a slightly different black, which faded to dark greens and browns at its folds and edges. Her face was a heavy highly expressive oval with shining brown eyes, her figure was wide, and her hands had the hardness of peasant's.

Felicetta had taken a liking to me and she often begged for my mother's permission to take me out with her on errands. Much as she feared and dreaded such outings, my mother thought that also total refusal might have been dangerous and have alienated the goodwill of our hosts, so that several times I joined the woman when she went to seek food for all of us in the nearby countryside and at the city's outskirts. It was not as if one could actually go out very much: as well as the constant rumbling of artillery, and the fear that it might at any moment become closer, the occasional air raid, and the unnerving visits of Allied reconnaissance planes, we had much to fear from the threats of shouting and drunken Germans, who, sometimes just back from the front, perpetuated the noise and violence of war in the streets of the small city.

Sometimes I quietly wondered what Felicetta's relation with Don Edoardo might be. Naturally we all thought of them as husband and wife, but other possibilities were not entirely unimaginable, or so I thought. Clearly that was not a time when I could ask my parents 'stupid' questions. It was, as mother had explained, a time for reserve and silence. Don Edoardo – the woman never omitted his title, Don – was a man of very few words. He always wore knickerbockers over brown woolen kneesocks, and his shoes were scrupulously polished, as is the mark of a gentleman. Every morning, as he appeared in the parlour, he seemed to be just about to start on some long journey, but, when he did leave the house, it was usually to reappear a few minutes later. I could not make my mind up if I should be frightened of him. In any case it was clear that it was best not to get in his way, so that, often confined in the same rather small living space, I made it a firm rule never to cross his path.

In order to leave our true identities completely undisclosed, we had explained to our hosts that our home was in Naples, then in the hands of the Allies, and that, finding ourselves in Abruzzo when the Germans invaded, we had been forced to join the refugee contingent, and thus had arrived to Chieti. Now, having to share their house, we had settled to a routine by which irritation and interference might be minimized. Every day, Don Edoardo would have his lunch and supper before us, while my sister and I entertained ourselves with our parents in our large bedroom.

The man ate alone ('happen what may', or, to use his own, and, given the increasing rhythm of air raids, more appropriate, Italian expression, *'caschi quel che ha da cascare'*[2]) while Felicetta busied herself in the kitchen, or ran up the stairs to wait on him in the parlour. She would first serve him a warm soup, then an egg or tinned meat with whatever vegetable she had been able to find. When Don Dua' reached his second course, it was time for Mother to go down to the long narrow kitchen and prepare our meal. Felicetta then sat in a corner at its far end to eat something, while Mother finished putting together whatever we had been able to buy, mostly from our hostess or from occasional brave street traders. We often had to make do with cauliflower, tomatoes, dried pimentos; but once or twice Felicetta offered to make us fresh pasta. When she was not too exhausted, she would even make her special version of pizza, which she tossed up into the air, out of a shiny black pan, and then enriched with tiny bits of fat, herbs, and dried pimentos – an incongruously delicious and festive meal, which filled us with a vague sense of absurdity. Felicetta had firmly established that mother should address her by her first name, while she would never think of calling mother anything but 'Madam', *Signuri*`. I was in no doubt that both women quietly enjoyed a few moments of rest and silence together in the old darkened kitchen.

Don Edoardo's coffee, like everybody else's at that time, was brewed from toasted barley or chicory, but brought up to the parlour by Felicetta on an elegant silver-plated tray, then poured into a tiny china cup at the approving nod of his head, it seemed to represent an important moment of their daily ritual. Sometimes Felicetta joined him (the tray was usually laid with two cups, but she did not always partake), he would first drink a sip, pass some derogatory comment on the flavour, or condemn it outright with the then current definition, '*caffe - caffœ*', then pick up a newspaper and bury himself in his reading.

When Papa` came into the room, he and Don Dua' would acknowledge each other loudly, as was the local custom:

'Don Giulio'
'Don Edoardo'
'Don Giu', may Christ blind you!'
'Don Dua', may you go down with a fever!'

I attended to the two men's exorcisms with slight feelings of trepidation: Don Edoardo had a heavy glass eye, which always made his mention of blinding particularly poignant and even rather daunting.

When finally our turn arrived to settle round the table, and we four had our meal together, the man would sit quietly in his armchair and, with an old pipe and his coffee beside him, he would watch us eating with an air of contentment, as if he felt that he himself had provided for us and had once more fulfilled a necessary yet very pleasant duty. After lunch the room was rapidly cleared, the table was covered with a yellowy thick cotton damask cloth, representing a lively hunting scene, gaily populated with deer and knights. We all remained in the room together for a while, often in silence. I usually tried to avoid looking straight at Don Edoardo, because I found his intense one-eyed glance most disconcerting; he and Papa` would exchange grunts and pages of newspaper, while my sister and I, following Mother's whispered instructions, knitted gloves and socks for the 'soldiers' (I did not know which soldiers) out of some intensely greasy gray wool that had been brought round to the house by an elegant woman on behalf of the Red Cross. I was very proud of my new skill in knitting with four pins and I had rapidly learnt to make 'heels' and 'toes'. I worked away in silence, and always tried to beat my sister in speed and precision.

I also owned a copybook in which I occasionally wrote my observations or laboured over some composition on themes set by my mother. Indeed, throughout our various moves and departures, I had even managed to salvage a small sketchbook and a few crayons, which I was rather dismayed to see growing shorter and shorter. Often, on long afternoons, I would get totally absorbed in sketching imaginary castles, with peaked towers and drawbridges. One day, just as I was trying to shape a farm animal on a brilliant green lawn, Don Edoardo had directly addressed me. Taking the pipe from his mouth, and pointing it firmly towards a picture on the wall opposite his armchair – an old print image of a cone-shaped mountain with smoke rising from its peak, over a bay crowded with all manner of boats, he said, *"Napœle..."*

"Oh, yes", Papa had replied breaking very quietly into song, *'Quando spunta la luna...'*[3] while Mother's grave gaze rested on him with just a hint of apprehension. Was the man's unexpected communication with me a subtle signal of incredulity about our alleged Neapolitan origin? But Don Edoardo had quietly brought the conversation to its natural close: *'... quanto se' bella, Napœle'*.

I had turned to a new page in my sketchbook and tried to copy the print, but, as the result was utterly monotonous, I decided to get back to my walled castles, surrounded with lawns and fields. Waiting, I thought, one could be nothing other, or more, than a dull silent child.

Felicetta had not had any children. She often mentioned a relative whose wife she used to visit, usually in the afternoons when all housework was done. Because she almost never stayed away for longer than an hour, I had reached the conclusion that her relations must have lived in the vicinity. I wondered why, then, she had never taken me with her.

One evening she had come back with a man, who, she explained, would spend the night with us. He was a pleasant man, and, although he was slightly graying near the temples, I thought he looked younger than Papa'. That evening he had supper with us. Felicetta had carefully laid him a place on a large white napkin, but he had eaten mostly his own food, some tinned meat and dried fruit. From time to time he would look at his rucksack, which he had kept by the side of his chair, then, when the meal was over, and after he had joined Don Edoardo and my father too in the ceremonial coffee drinking, he started removing and tidily repacking his folding camping fork, knife and can opener – unexpected reminders of family summertime expeditions. He then produced a map of the area; he opened it wide on the table (did he not know that the mere possession of a map was dangerous and could make him look very suspect?) and he minutely studied it in a totally self-absorbed and intent way.

From the opposite side of the table I could see the tortuous and meandering lines of the river Sangro. It was light blue, but I imagined its waters dark red with blood. The man had extracted from his coat pocket a small brown leather book, and he made some notes in it. Then, after meticulously folding up the map, he replaced all things respectively in his sack or his jacket, and he seemed almost ready to start on his way at any moment. We looked at him in silence. I could almost hear my heart beat. Then Papa` said in his casual friendly way, "Lovely places". "Oh, yes", said the man, "So lovely. Soon the Sangro valley will be covered with flowers". Then, looking sad, he said gallantly "Lovely, like these girls". I knew that the man was going to venture across the front lines. "Big blue eyes", he said, "Oh, but how serious!"

Mother got up. It was time to go to bed. Anyway, we would soon be woken up again by the noise of war. Saying good night, I had smiled at the guest. That evening I undressed very quickly, climbed up into my tall cold iron bed, turned towards the wall, and thought I should have liked to cry. If the man had children, I thought, they must be younger than me. I imagined him in a beautiful home, playing with a little girl and a boy, I could almost feel the sensation of being in a warm sweet-smelling room, and for some reason that commonplace fantasy was enough to make me want to weep. After about two hours, when we were woken up by an explosion louder than usual, we gathered again in the small living room, but I did not see the man again, and then I thought he must have started on his way in the late evening, after a very brief rest.

Life continued from day to day in relative calmness, all of us clinging to our new cautiously shared domesticity, while more and more refugees kept arriving in Chieti. Felicetta continued to take me out with her on her adventurous shopping expeditions as often as she could. However concerned, my parents had had to agree that to always refuse their permission would have been an unpleasant sign of hostility. She was, after all, getting food also for us, and they had to trust that she would not expose me to too much danger. What is more, the fresh air would do me good. On clear days one could see the snowy peaks of the mountains, and even the sea at Ortona. Both views filled me with a keen longing to wander much further afield than we could ever go... I had been told by my parents that I was never, ever to mention Milan, nor Venice, nor even Padua or Verona; no northern city was ever to enter my conversation... only "Napœle... Napœle, Napœle..." Little did my parents realize that the names of Italian cities were of no relevance whatsoever to the woman's world.

My sister could not go out much at all. She would sometimes take a short walk with the rest of us in the morning, but she certainly couldn't venture out casually with Felicetta, because although she was just a year my senior, she was a tall, attractive, already 'well-developed' thirteen-year-old, and – as the woman had been the first to point out – it would not have been wise to risk exposing her to the attention of the soldiers. Indeed, when a group of Fascists and Germans had come to search the house, she had had to hide inside a large wicker trunk, which was then hastily covered with old rugs and blankets. Thanks to my immaturity – I was almost twelve, but, as I suspected, I was considered physically rather backward – I enjoyed a measure of freedom, and, as a token of trust and friendship, I was allowed to circulate with Felicetta.

After lengthy negotiations between the German commander and representatives of the town, it had been decided that on the day of Corpus Christi, the population would be allowed to hold their traditional procession. Hanging in suspense and uncertainty, it was as if all their nervous expectancy had been focused on a deep-seated and overwhelming need to take the Holy Host, as well as the effigy of the city's patron saint out through the streets, to pray and to perform their customary ritual to the full. The city's main street, usually semi-deserted, was suddenly full of people. Two men, one a priest, the other a graying, modestly dressed, ageless man, carried the dark rigid figure of the saint over its painted wooden stand. From time to time they would stop and slowly turn the effigy towards different directions to face the people, who responded with an intense unison of discordant implorations and songs.

The saint's image, a large silver bust, was almost lifelike, but the face was the colour of dark gold. Old men, women and children followed the procession. "Let us pray", said the priest. The saint's face looked rather young. Some moments it looked impassive, gleaming eerily in the cold winter light, other moments it almost seemed to absorb the crying, the singing, and the confused implorations of the people. Felicetta held my hand very tight, fearing the crowd might separate us. From time to time she broke the "Hail Marys" and "Holy Fathers" intoned by the priest, to utter her own prayer to the saint: *"San Giusti', O, San Giusti'... San Giustino mio,* oh, let them arrive this evening!"

We had walked for about half an hour when it started raining. Large drops were pouring down so hard that we took shelter under a doorway, when German soldiers on four heavy motorbikes rushed dangerously into the Street to disperse the crowd. "My child", Felicetta looked at me. "Come away, let us go home", and we returned in silence.

* * *

Slumped on one of the high parlour chairs, Felice' had her back towards the window. Her head was lowered on her breast. Against the light, her body and arms looked darker and heavier than ever. Through some strange association (or perhaps to evade the full intensity of Felicetta's sorrow) I thought of the geometrical figures in one of my schoolbooks and the beautiful crystal solids in my old class room, set against the light. With Don Edoardo standing silently by her side, the woman emitted a suffocated cry, while we four stood motionless before her, like a muted choir, without knowing what to say or do. Mother tried to loosen her clothes, and then she ran down to make a warm drink. "Felicetta, for the Lord's sake, what is it?" Her guttural cry had changed to uncontrollable sobbing. "For mercy's sake, Felice', what happened?" Don Edoardo continued to stand firmly, ashen-faced, beside her. Only after emitting a long pitched cry was the woman able to utter a phrase: 'The four boys. They have killed the four boys'.

I had never realized that the relatives of whom Felicetta had frequently spoken had four sons. The previous evening, two of them had been caught by Black Brigade soldiers in possession of a radio transmitter, while they were sending messages out to the Allies. Their brothers were found hiding at a nearby deserted farmhouse and all four had been taken to prison. Their mother had hoped that they would have been released after a few days, perhaps sent to dig trenches, or even away to a labour camp in Germany. But, instead, the following morning she heard voices calling her from the street and she rushed to the window. The boys were tied to the back of a lorry and shot one by one. "The youngest", Felicetta was breaking down into sobs again – a dark figure of sorrow. "The youngest?..." "They threw him off the lorry, covered in blood, and shouted, "You come and get him, old woman!"

Felicetta had exhausted her capacity to speak and she seemed only to find her breath through a long, deep cry, like an ancient lament, in which mixed with her pain was the full violence of hatred and of desperate impotent rage. "Felicetta. . ."

Don Edoardo persuaded gently, "We can't..."
"I know, we cannot even mourn, we cannot cry... May Christ... "

That evening she had come down as usual to make some soup. Nobody spoke a word. We continued to live like that for some time. Food was growing very scarce. Felicetta continued to climb up and down the stairs, gasping, murmuring prayers and invocations or curses, pale, and disfigured with tears. She still called me "my child", but her eyes had lost their vivacity. She continually ran to visit her relatives, and, when she came home, she seemed almost incapable of communication, she often went down to the kitchen to sit with my mother, but, unless she dropped into a doze, she was never still for very long. Her unshakable respect for Don Edoardo's needs and timetables kept her going.

Now the man almost never left the house. Food was so scarce that a group of ladies from the Red Cross had set up a soup kitchen in the *piazza*. There, chatting and joking with a few Black Shirt supervisors, the women, absurdly clad in their starched white uniforms, distributed a liquid maize soup, enriched with bits of meat and pork fat. I had fallen ill, and then, once more, my parents decided that we had to leave. The Allies were not coming. We had to move back to the North, where it was hoped I might get some treatment. We had to leave Felicetta and Don Edoardo.

Chieti was crowded with confused, starving peasants, and the Germans were continuing their policy of pushing the population northwards. In their absurd attempt to keep order, they instructed all refugees to fill out a form, on the basis of which they would issue them with travel documents. In a small crowded shop, which, as its sign showed, had been one of the town's betting offices, an Italian clerk with two German soldiers standing stiffly behind him was handing out forms and helping those who were not able to write, to fill in the required information. Taking advantage of the noise and disorder, Papa` managed to persuade the clerk that he could not satisfy the request to show his identity card, because it was lost: he did not have one. Then, on the spur of the moment, he firmly filled in the forms with the first local surname which he could conjure up in his mind. That is how, from that moment on, I was no more L. D.: I had suddenly acquired a new family name – one unmistakably marked with the sound of that region, and which, despite our having lived in that area for several months, still sounded strangely, almost shockingly, harsh and foreign.

Postscript

Like Dan Segre (1985), I could call myself a 'fortunate Jew': I never suffered imprisonment and, thanks to my parents' foresight, I escaped almost certain death in a concentration camp. Less fortunate, however, in realizing immediately after the war ended, that so many of my cousins and schoolmates had died and a great catastrophe had befallen the Jewish people. But, for most of the period of German occupation of Italy, between 8 September 1943 and 30 May 1945, while I certainly shared in my parents' distress and suffered some illness, I was incredibly lucky in not being separated from my immediate family, and protected from fear by my father's good-tempered sense of humour and patience.

It was an evil war and Italians were hopelessly divided, but, although no one could be trusted, most of the people we came close to, were actually humane and kindly. Their resistance and their hatred of the occupying Germans certainly was no guarantee that they would have sympathized with our plight. However, in the course of time and despite our inevitable silence about our identity, awareness of our common suffering certainly gave rise to a sense of sharing and of solidarity.

Away from home and from the usual routines of family life, gender relations naturally changed. As a child, I had never seen much of my father, whose time was taken up with business, and who then appeared a rather elusive, somewhat authoritarian figure. Forced to live in hiding, father spent large part of the day with us, trying as best he could to entertain us with some game or light-hearted conversation. On the other hand, after September 1943, our mother seemed to have been forced to take on a strongly controlling role: she knew that father was impulsive and she was often watching him to prevent some incautious and tactless action that might compromise our safety.

Because the Germans were rounding up Italian men of all ages to dig trenches, or be transported to Germany's labour camps, it was Mother who had to be responsible for the cash that was essential to our survival. Always carrying around with her a purse with all the money we had been able to take with us (and we had no idea how long our exile was to last!) must have felt like a very heavy burden. It was she who negotiated terms with our hosts, and who managed to observe the strictest economy, while endeavouring to keep us adequately nourished.

It is of interest to note how her relationship with our landlady, Felicetta, was different from that of father with Don Edoardo. The men always behaved with civility, but also with great circumspection, they usually exchanged stereotyped greetings and grunts, or at most shared a barley or chicory coffee substitute, partly to uphold the symbolic value of male hospitality by drinking something together. By contrast, the women soon developed an ability to interact with ease. At any other time, sharing the kitchen might have created all manner of difficulties, but under the circumstances, common sense, as well as a feeling of sharing the same dangers, under the same oppressor, seemed to have greatly sharpened the women's intuitive intelligence and sensitivity.

Felicetta would venture out into the nearby countryside to buy food, part of which she sold to Mother. Sometimes, as I mentioned, she would take me along. She said my company gave her courage, but after we came very close to being machine-gunned from an Allied plane, our trips had to stop. And while especially at the beginning of our stay in Chieti, no comments were made about the political or military situation, Felicetta, who had heard about several cases of rape, was more explicit than mother in her advice to us girls, especially my older sister, who was just over thirteen. She, for example, stated very firmly that we should never speak or even make eye contact with 'those men in uniform'.

Father considered it his task to lessen our sense of fear, entertaining us with stories and jokes, and pretending things were not too different from normal and we should soon return to our habits and our homes.

After the war ended, like other adolescents who had lived through similar experiences, both my sister and I found it difficult to settle down to 'normal' bourgeois school and family life. It took a great deal of good will and forbearance for our parents to partly reassert their control and authority.

Notes

1 "My mother was a delicate, yet strong-willed woman, she was somewhat secularized, but attached to the Jewish community and Jewish traditions. My father was a very gentle, sociable, man. He was a respected businessman – a wholesaler, who kept Venice's shops well-provided with detergents, perfumes and spices (I shall never forget the fragance of saffron!). He was captured by the Germans in 1944 and deported to a labour camp – I think in Hungary, but I am not sure because after the war we did not talk about it very much (I think the name of the camp and date of my father's deportation are recorded in a book by L. Picciotto Fargion, 1991)".

2 *Cascare*, to fall.

3 'When the moon rises... How beautiful you are, Naples!'

References

Derrida, Jacques. 2001. 'Sarah Kofman (1934-1994)', in *The Work of Mourning*. Chicago.

Okely, J. and Callaway, H. 1992. *Anthropology and Autobiography*. London

Segre, Dan Vittorio. 1985. *Memoirs of a Fortunate Jew: an Italian Story*. Halban: London

"Camp Families" in Ravensbrück and the Social Organization of Jewish Women Prisoners in a Concentration Camp

Judith Buber Agassi

Before describing the small groups that are the focus of this article, it is essential to discuss the problem of why there was so little group-wide social organization among the Jewish prisoners of Ravensbrück. What kind of social organization could concentration camp prisoners establish? It has to be remembered that the SS intended to prevent not only any initiative at grass-root prisoner organization, but even simple ties of friendship among them. The prisoners were intended to be nameless numbers, ruled by a hostile hierarchy of members of the SS, of persons hired and trained by them or under their authority. The rulers of the camp could at will change the barracks and the place of work of any prisoner, decide on their transfer to other camps, send them to the *Strafblock* ("bunker"), punish them by flogging, and "select" them to be killed.

In order to maintain their kind of order and discipline, they used a system of so-called *Häftlingsselbstverwaltung* (prisoner self-administration), appointing prisoners to the positions of *Stubenälteste* (room leader), *Blockälteste* (block leader), and *Lagerläuferin* (camp runner). Usually the holders of these positions, the *Funktionshäftlinge*, did not belong to the group that they had to supervise.

In Ravensbrück, we know of a time between 1940 and 1941 when all or most of the Jewish prisoners, about 1000, lived in one block and had a remarkable Jewish *Blockälteste*, Olga Benário. Group-wide cultural and educational activities took place only during that time. The intention of the SS was to bribe the *Funktionshäftlinge* by small improvements in their conditions of housing and clothing and by granting them some freedom of movement in the camp, to make them serve as loyal enforcers of the SS policies and disregard the interests of their charges. Any contravention of the orders of the SS by the *Funktionshäftlinge* that the camp authorities discovered resulted in cruel punishment. An additional system of the prevention of attempts of prisoners to organize was a network of informers.[1]

Nevertheless, we know of several categories of non-Jewish prisoners with well-developed and very effective group-wide organizations that were tight-knit and even exclusive. Thus, the German political prisoners were well organized, and their mainly Communist leadership enforced its decisions by measures of strict discipline, including even the ostracism of members of their group who disregarded orders of their leadership, or of disliked prisoners outside their group. With the help of its strict organization, the German "political" group certainly was effective in ensuring a somewhat better standard of housing and nutrition for its own members. Its leadership decided on the form and extent of measures of help and support to members of other groups according to their judgment of their relative "value". Obviously, they considered Communist and other left-wing prisoners of other nationalities, as well as all the prisoners from the Soviet Union, as their natural friends and allies. Many members of the German "political" group had been imprisoned for many years and thus had acquired positions of power. Naturally, they had no language problems of communication with the camp authorities.

Whereas the German Communist prisoners were used to strict centralized discipline from the party practice of "democratic centralism", the Jehovah's Witnesses *(Bibelforscherinnen)* based their group organization in the camp on continuing the extremely disciplined way of life of their religious sect. This way of life ruled out any fight over scarce food, stealing, untidiness or neglect of work duties. They saw themselves as "the chosen few" and considered it their sacred duty to choose martyrdom over (even formal) betrayal of the sect. This restricted their contacts with members of other groups to missionary efforts and caused them to sacrifice the lives of seriously sick members that could have been saved by signing a formal declaration of leaving the sect. Different interpretations of their sacred texts caused division among those demanding more or less extreme refusal to perform any work duties that could be construed as helping the war effort. This resulted in a group of their "radicals" first to be sent to Auschwitz and then to return to Ravensbrück to be executed.

The Red Army group of prisoners impressed their fellow prisoners by their strict military-style discipline, and by their collective refusal to perform any work for the camp authorities except for work in the camp hospital *(Revier)*.

Perhaps the most effective organization of any national group of prisoners was that of the Poles; it has been documented in two books.[2] From the beginning of the arrival of Polish political prisoners in 1942, the initiative for their internal organization came from the Roman Catholic political resistance. Their central and most active cores were the seven groups of the Catholic Scout Movement (Murów) and the organization of the "Friends of the Scouts".[3] Their main strength lay in their religious and patriotic ideology and practice. They organized regular educational activities (preparing young girls for school-leaving exams), as well as prayer and religious services, all of which the camp authorities strictly forbade. In the later stages of the camp, after larger numbers from the Polish left-wing socialist/ Communist underground had arrived in the camp, they even succeeded to establish a common platform with them. By gaining access to the most important places of work, they succeeded to obtain enough food and clothing in order to save many of the weakest members of their group. These were the youngest, the oldest, and especially the *"Kaninchen"* ("guinea pigs"), those Polish political prisoners on whose legs horrible "experimental" bone-transplant operations had been performed. They established a widespread illegal correspondence with their families in Poland. They also established contact with the International Red Cross in Switzerland through Polish POWs, stationed near the work places of some of the Polish women, and even succeeded to inform the BBC about the "selection" of a large group of old and sick prisoners and their deportation to the death camps of Majdanek and Auschwitz.[4] They were effective in hiding *"Kaninchen"* from being executed, but could not prevent the execution of more than 160 of their members, who had been condemned to death while in Polish prisons.[5]

One of the most amazing group activity of the Polish organization, initiated by Ursula Winska, was the theft of copies of hundreds of arrival lists from the *Massar Nähstube* (the sewing workshop[6]) with the declared intention "to let the world know what happened".[7] The lists were packed in 70 small parcels, to be carried by 70 Polish prisoners under their clothes. Most of these were evacuated on the last train of the Bernadotte humanitarian rescue mission,

This highly organized Polish group was composed nearly exclusively of women and young girls who had been arrested for political resistance activities, and thus were ideologically motivated. There were in the camp, however, thousands of Polish prisoners who had reached Ravensbrück as deported "civilians", and many who had been working in Germany as foreign laborers, either forced or voluntary, and had been charged with some offence and imprisoned. This group was not organized at all.

The Austrian, the Czech and the French groups, as well as the Norwegian group, were composed mainly of women arrested for resistance activities. They also had well-developed group organizations that were not (or only partially) dominated by the Communists.

Was it at all possible for the Jewish prisoners of Ravensbrück to develop an organization including all or most of the Jewish prisoners in the camp at a certain time, or at least an organization or organizations of the major "national" Jewish groups? As conditions changed radically and as there was little continuity between the Jewish populations at different times, I find it convenient to divide the six years of the existence of the camp into five periods. First, from 1939 to the end of January 1942, when nearly the entire Ravensbrück Jewish population was killed in the euthanasia gas chamber of Bernburg; second, from February 1942 to the end of February 1943, when the last of the Jewish women were sent to Auschwitz and the camp became *"judenfrei"*; third, from March 1943 to the end of July 1944, when special groups of Jewish women and children arrived; fourth, from August 1944 to the end of the year, when thousands of mainly Hungarian and Polish Jewish women arrived for the express purpose to be sent as slave laborers to the war industry in external labor camps; finally, fifth, from the beginning of 1945 to the beginning of May – the end of the camp and of the war – when Ravensbrück was an extermination camp.

Was it possible for the Jewish prisoners of Ravensbrück to organize? Obviously the Jewish prisoners of Ravensbrück lacked the elements that served as the basis of the successful group organization of the non-Jewish groups mentioned above. They lacked a common homeland, a shared patriotism: they came from 15 different countries. Even in those countries, where many Jewish inhabitants had considered themselves not only loyal but even patriotic citizens, as for instance Italy and Hungary, the local political leadership had eventually collaborated with the German allies or occupation forces in the rounding-up, imprisonment, deportation and destruction of their Jewish population. Not only did all the Jewish prisoners, but also the members of each of the "national" Jewish groups, lack a common political ideology, but even a common religious belief, practice and organization. Zionist ideology and Zionist youth organizations had affected only a minority. Only from the large group of survivors from Lodz, several young women remembered early affiliation with Zionist organizations.

As for religion, a considerable number came from traditional Jewish families, especially those originating from Poland, from the Hungarian rural areas, from those parts of Romania and Slovakia occupied by Hungary, and also from Belgium and the Netherlands. For many of them home life had been that of closely knit large families. Their families had still observed Jewish holidays and the dietary laws, and were opposed to marriage to non-Jews. They accepted the fact of their being Jewish. Yet this common traditional religious background of part of the Jewish women and girls from different countries apparently did not serve as a sufficient basis for a common social organization. We have to remember two additional factors. First, communication, even between those with a traditional Jewish background but coming from different countries, was often difficult. Second, Jewish women traditionally play a much less active role than men in religious ceremonies, services, prayer and especially studies.

Many of the better-educated and urban Jewesses came from a more or less assimilated background.[8] What all or most of the Jewish prisoners knew of Jewish culture including religion, history, literature and music, was evidently not enough to serve as a substantial bond among them. Yet for some of them their cruel experiences caused them to develop a kind of Jewish national pride or consciousness. One Israeli survivor, who was as a child in Ravensbrück, housed with her mother in a "Block" together with Yugoslav non-Jewish women, reports that when these women, who had all been arrested for resistance activities, constantly performed small acts of sabotage at work, and the whole "Block" was punished, she asked her mother, "Why do they do this?" Her mother answered: "Because they have a Fatherland". She then decided that she too wanted to have a fatherland, and would go there. The US survivor, Halina Nelken, describes in her remarkable diary from the Krakow ghetto and from the Plaszów concentration camp, how, as a 17-year-old girl, who had grown up in an upper-middle-class cultured and assimilated family, she developed a Jewish national consciousness. After a massacre in the ghetto, she writes: "What words could describe how we are being driven to slaughter? Worse than cattle. Why? What fault is it of ours? ... Of course I know – we are Jewish. Suddenly, with the broom in my hand, I straightened up, as though the suffering of my nation had given me strength and pride. At this moment I realized what a powerful bond common suffering is. My nation! My *Jewish* nation, no longer just my *Polish* nation, as I had felt until now".[9]

Most important, the Jewish prisoners lacked the conviction, common to all those non-Jewish prisoners imprisoned for political and/or religious opposition to the Nazis, that their suffering was the result of their previous effective actions against the regime of their persecutors and jailers. Only in the first and the second periods (from 1939 to the end of 1942) the SS still maintained the fake division of the Jewish prisoners into groups with different reasons for arrest. The persecution and imprisonment of nearly all of them in fact rested on their belonging to a group defined by the Nazis as "racially inferior". With the outbreak of the War, all members of this group were declared enemies of the German people and condemned to death by the Nazi leadership.

During all five periods, most of the Jewish prisoners were housed together and worked in separate Jewish work groups. Contacts between them and non-Jewish prisoners were rare, discouraged, and even banned by the SS. Circumstances permitting or hampering internal Jewish group organization varied very much from period to period.

During the first period, the Jewish prisoners, though from various social backgrounds and political convictions, nearly all spoke German and had lived in Germany or Austria and the Czech Protectorate of Bohemia and Moravia. Nearly all of them were housed in the *Judenblock* (*Baracken* 9 or 11) and in 1940 and 1941 had a Jewish *Blockälteste* (barrack leader).[10] Thus in this period, before the general conditions of housing, hygiene and food, deteriorated considerably, in spite of the segregation, the especially onerous work-tasks and the special humiliations meted out to the Jewish prisoners, the internal life of the *Judenblock* was relatively orderly. For some time it was still possible to conduct some regular cultural and educational activities, secretly organized by several courageous and well-educated women. Thus, in spite of the constant threat of punishment and persecution by the camp authorities, a certain Jewish prisoner society existed during this period.

After the mass murder of nearly all the Jewish prisoners of the first period between February and April 1942 in the gas chamber of Bernburg, it could hardly be expected that the few survivors from that first period, together with the several hundreds of new arrivals, could develop a new Jewish camp society before the mass deportation to Auschwitz on October 5, 1942.

During the third period of 1943 to the end of July 1944, the period of the "special groups", we know about a surprising measure of social organization within the family groups that had arrived from the Dutch internment camp Westerbork, sufficient to establish a school-class for their children in Ravensbrück.[11] These families obviously had known each other for some time in Westerbork. We also know about children's birthday parties, friendship groups, some outdoor play, and the availability of paper and pencils for the children.[12]

There is, however, no evidence for a similar social organization of the Belgian group, most of whom claimed Turkish citizenship and were of Sephardic or part-Sephardic origin and had arrived from Brussels and from the Malines (Mechelen) internment camp.

As to the group of *Mischlinge*, who had arrived together from Auschwitz and most of whom had originated from the "German Reich", there is no evidence of any special group solidarity within the entire group, despite their unusual common fate. The remarkable larger group of friends (about 20) that later formed at the Siemens factory was not based on any special ties between the several members of the *Mischlingstransport* working there and later also living there. It included many other fellow workers, Jewish and also some non-Jewish.[13] There was little chance that the thousands of Jewish arrivals of the fourth period (the five months of August to the end of 1944) would develop a common social organization for all or most Jewish prisoners. The basic reason for this was their instability. Over 30% of them stayed in Ravensbrück for only a short time, often less than a month, before being sent on to – at least – eight different external labor camps.

But also for many of those staying in Ravensbrück until the end of the fourth period and into the fifth, there existed serious problems of communication. Most of those classified as Hungarian or as Polish, the two major "national" groups of Jewish arrivals, had no common language. Obviously most Hungarian Jews did not speak Polish and Polish Jews certainly did not speak Hungarian, but, most important, most Hungarian Jews neither spoke nor understood Yiddish. Most Romanian Jews and many French and Belgian Jews could communicate in Yiddish, and German Jews could at least understand it. For Polish Jews with a secondary education and for those living in Polish cities with a large German-speaking population, German was another important language of communication in the camps, not only with their German jailers, but also with many Jewish and non-Jewish prisoners. A minority of the Hungarian and Romanian women and girls had learned German at school. Many Czech, Slovak and Dutch Jews spoke German, and of course all German and Austrian Jews too. Yet the hard-core of the Hungarian, as well of the Italian and the Greek-Jewish prisoners, suffered from serious communication problems. The hard-core of the two largest groups of Jewish Ravensbrück prisoners of the fourth and of the fifth periods from Hungary and from Poland could not understand each other. This proved a serious obstacle to the development of a general group-wide Jewish social organization, among the Jewish prisoners in the main camp of Ravensbrück as well as in its two major external camps – Malchow and Neustadt-Glewe.

Who were the Hungarian-Jewish women who remained in Ravensbrück at least for several months? Only a very few had arrived in August and September 1944. The rest had arrived with the direct transports from Budapest in November 1944 and also with the nearly 1,700 arrivals from the cruel labor camp of Frankfurt/Walldorf. All of them suffered from the horrendous housing and sanitary conditions, and the starvation diet accorded to new arrivals towards the end of 1944. The physical condition of the arrivals from Frankfurt/Walldorf was especially bad.

Who were the Polish groups who remained in Ravensbrück for at least several months? Out of the 500 arrivals directly from the Lodz ghetto on October 22, 1944, 200 women had been sent to Wittenberg, and the children were eventually sent to

Königs Wusterhausen. The members of the Ghetto Piotrkow direct transport of December 2, 1944 remained in the camp until March 1945, when many of them were sent to Bergen-Belsen.

Many of the Polish arrivals of the last two transports from Auschwitz in November and December 1944, and of the transport from Czestochowa at Christmas 1944, were soon sent to Malchow. The fact that many women from these three transports were eventually evacuated to Sweden from Malchow, raises the possibility that this Polish-Jewish group that spent four months together in Malchow may have developed group-wide ties.[14]

Apparently there was no wider social organization among the Hungarian Jews staying in Ravensbrück. In the infamous tent and later in the rundown blocks where they were housed, they lived not as a separate group, but together with other groups. Among them were especially Polish-Jewish women with whom they did not succeed to communicate and to overcome mutual animosity and suspicion. They were unable to protect themselves from the extremely bad *Blockälteste* and *Stubenälteste* who systematically stole their food and prevented them from using the scanty washing and sanitary facilities of the block. Although among the Hungarians small groups appear to have played an important role, we hear little about any wider group activities. Seren Tuvel reports having told to larger groups stories about her childhood and her rural, traditional Jewish family, stories that involuntarily tended to end in descriptions of the wonderful food eaten at holidays and festivals.[15]

Surprisingly, even within the large group (originating from different countries) of those that arrived as survivors of the "Auschwitz *Todesmarsch*" (death march) of January 1945, many had a common history of living and working at the "Union" factory in Auschwitz. This included even the participation of several of them in underground activities. Nevertheless, the ties broke down during and after the "Auschwitz *Todesmarsch*"[16] due to sheer exhaustion. Although at least 81 of the "Union" workers were sent to Neustadt-Glewe, under the extreme conditions of starvation and epidemics, even the common history of this group was not sufficient to permit the creation of a larger group there. After the war, the "Union" survivors established a worldwide organization.

There was no large-scale social organization, and hardly any medium-scale social organization, among the Jewish prisoners of the fourth and fifth periods. The affinity between those from the same country of origin, and especially those from the same hometown, such as those who had come from Lodz, Piotrkow, Krakow, or Budapest, facilitated cultural activities. These were telling the contents of books, reciting poetry, singing songs, and listening to one of the astonishingly many artists in the camp. Among a larger group of women and girls from Poland and the Ukraine, starving in Malchow, the common greeting in the morning was, "What are you cooking today?" While some described pierogi or knishes, everybody knew that two of them "kept kosher", and listened to their chicken soup and noodles recipes.[17]

To sum up, we have seen three major obstacles to the formation of wider group ties and activities among the Jewish prisoners of Ravensbrück in the fourth and fifth periods: the instability resulting from the constant transports to labor camps, the appalling conditions that caused apathy and extremely high mortality, and the tensions resulting mainly from communication difficulties.

Nevertheless, there were rare instances of overcoming the animosities and tensions between different Jewish groups, as well as instances of leadership and initiative. Examples are: the heroic leadership by speech and by singing of Franka on the Burgau transport,[18] the story of Irmgard Judith Berger, now Becker, who reports that in Malchow her mother, Pepi Berger, prevented the throwing out of the dying typhoid patients, who were soiling their surroundings, from the block, by convincing her block-mates that as Jews it was their duty not to abandon the dying.

One exception of a successful larger group organization that existed during the fourth and fifth period was that of the nearly 500 women and girls who had been sent from Auschwitz to the small all-Jewish labor camp at Krupp/Neukölln, which arrived in Ravensbrück as late as April 1945. Their group organization carried over to Ravensbrück during the short time they stayed there, facilitated their evacuation to Sweden as a group and persisted there.

As to the problematic role of those designated *Funktionshäftlinge* (prisoners appointed as functionaries), most non-Jewish functionaries prevented the forming of any solidarity among the Jewish prisoners. Later, in the labor camps, there were also some Jewish *Blockälteste* and even a *Lagerälteste* (camp leader). Several survivors mention Jewish women whom they call "the Auschwitz élite" who behaved badly when appointed, but they also mention several very decent and resourceful Jewish *Blockälteste*, *Stubenälteste* and *Lagerläuferinnen* in labor camps, who encouraged the formation of positive ties among the prisoners.[19]

Only one medium-sized group for special purposes had been mentioned by the survivors of the fourth and fifth periods. This group was the "burial-*kommando*" (special work crew) that was organized by Rena Kornreich in Neustadt-Glewe. It included ten girls who, each at her own initiative and request, volunteered to move each day the dead bodies that lay outside the *Revier* on a cart with a box to a burial place, first in the Neustadt-Glewe cemetery, and later in the woods.[20]

Now to my main point, that is the crucial role of small-group ties or "camp-family" ties. My claim is that in the life of the Jewish women prisoners of Ravensbrück, a special form of social organization played a crucial role. I called it here the small group or the camp family. This was other than the ties that existed between mothers and their young children under age thirteen. The arrival of family transports, including mothers with their young children, or even mother-substitutes, especially aunts with nephews and nieces, were the exception in Ravensbrück. Late in 1943 and early in 1944 such family transports arrived, especially from the Netherlands and Belgium. Among the flood of thousands of arrivals, starting in August 1944, such family transports, one from France, several from Slovakia and from Italy,[21] as well as three direct transports from Polish ghettos (i.e. not via Auschwitz),[22] were the exception. Although maternal caregiving was extremely difficult under concentration camp conditions, it was considered by all to be the natural behavior of women. This caregiving was truly heroic and certainly contributed to saving the lives of many of the children.

My intention here is not to describe these maternal-child relations, but to elaborate on a special form of small group, sometimes called "camp-family".

From August 1944 the thousands that were transported to Ravensbrück from Auschwitz, as well as the arrival with the direct transports who had walked from Budapest to the Austrian border, all were of working age. They rarely included girls under 16 or women over 50. Among the 2305 names of arrivals, survivors of the "Auschwitz *Todesmarsch*" of January-February 1945 known to us, we know of only 23 children up to 13. Yet a great number of mothers with daughters either teenage or in their early twenties, and even many more sisters and cousins from the same city, small town or ghetto, arrived from August 1944 to the end of the camp in the first days of May 1945. There were also groups that included sisters-in-law. Many young women had been working in the same workplace or had gone to school together. Middle-aged women played the role of mother-substitutes to the daughters of their neighbors. This was the basis of small real-family and substitute-family groups, usually not larger than four people. Sometimes a larger group of sisters, for example, the 6 Schreiber sisters (from the Frankfurt/Walldorf transport) and the 6 Stern sisters (from the Krupp/Neukölln transport), formed such a family group.

The most common small group was that of two sisters, two best friends,[23] or of a mother with one or two daughters.[24] If a woman had only one sister or friend, a separation may have proved fatal. Kato Gyulai, who was deported from Budapest with her younger sister Evi, was separated from her when Kato was "selected" for work in Spandau. The fact that she could not prevent this separation and that she never saw her sister again, was for her the most tragic event in her Holocaust experience.[25]

Lidia Vago (Rosenfeld) describes her frenzied attempt not to be separated from her sister Aniko (who was away to have the bandage on her freshly operated hand changed) at the roll-call for the transport from Ravensbrück to Neustadt-Glewe. She had tried to reserve a place in a row of five for her sister. She writes: "this was not an easy task, considering that lonely women were a rarity in the camps, because being alone meant near certain death. Everyone without a close relative, or a good friend, had to have a *Lagerschwester* (camp sister), or the younger girls whose mothers had been gassed, were adopted by mature women".[26] Seren Tuvel described the danger of separation at the time of the selection for the Burgau transport as follows: "A great cry went out, a moan that welled up from the bottom of despair. Each pair would be cut in two, leaving every woman far less than half of what she had been in a pair. Having a sister, a cousin, or a friend in the camp with you was sometimes the only thing that gave you the courage to go on; each lived solely for the other".[27]

Even Silvia Grohs, the actress and singer, who had a gift for making friends, needed the friendship of an older woman, a "camp-mama". She was Gemma Glück the

Hungarian-Jewish twin sister of Fiorello La Guardia, the then mayor of New York.[28]

Several memoirs describe the adoption of single girls by a mother-daughter "small group". Erika Kounio Amariglio describes how her mother "adopted" three Greek girls at the beginning of the "Auschwitz *Todesmarsch*", and thus a "camp family" of five was formed. It lasted through the death march, their stay at Ravensbrück, the months in Malchow, the evacuation march from Malchow, until their arrival to the American Occupation Zone.[29]

Lidia Vago also described how after existing for some time as just a small group of two sisters, in Neustadt-Glewe they found two women known to them from the "Union" factory of Auschwitz and formed a group of four. Somewhat later they found another congenial group of four and regularly told each other stories and relieved the hunger pangs by exchanging extravagant recipes.

Substitute-family groups could also form on the basis of a common unusual background, such as the Eva Dános group of four baptized Jewish women from Budapest, who together read a French prayer book that they had found in the Ravensbrück garbage.[30]

Groups of this size played a crucial role in "organizing" minimal food and clothing, trading them against other necessities such as medicine, protecting its members against aggressive others and the theft of essentials, supporting them in case of illness, dragging them along during the cruel foot-marches and preventing suicide.

Why did well-organized small groups usually not try to include additional members? Seren Tuvel's answer was: it was dangerous to make friends with more people, even if they appeared congenial, because you were always in danger of losing them, as mortality was so high.[31]

The small groups tended to be a combination of stronger and weaker members. There usually was one stronger woman whose authority was accepted and who forbade any behavior that she considered as life-threatening. As Seren Tuvel described it: "I felt completely responsible for these three young girls; to me we were all sisters. I had to do everything in my power to enable us to remain alive. Survival became a matter of establishing rules and adhering to them religiously. I was the oldest; I made the rules. We were of the old European school of thought: you listened to the oldest even if she was a fool".[32] A basic rule was that the members of the group should stay together against all odds, when being assigned to a workplace or being "selected" to an external labor camp.[33] It was the combination of receiving help and feeling responsible for the wellbeing of others that played an important role in the will to live, as well as of avoiding many dangers.

Yet even the best organized small group could not guarantee survival. Three of the four members of Eva Dános' group succumbed to typhoid fever in the locked wagon of the Burgau death-train; one of the four members of Seren Tuvel's group died in the same wagon.

Yet, a small group of sisters, cousins and friends, sometimes even succeeded to save one of their members from certain death. Klara Landau, later Bondy, succeeded together with her cousin and her friend to convince the S.D.G. (*SS-Sanitätsdienstgrad*; medical orderly) to remove her sister's name from the list of those already "selected" to be returned from the *Revier* in Neustadt-Glewe to Ravensbrück to be gassed there[34]. Yet, Lea Schwalb-Kisch, also a member of a small group of sisters, who did not know of the danger of "selection" from the Neustadt-Glewe *Revier*, continues to blame herself for not having saved her sister Blimi from the *Revier*, a mere two weeks before liberation.[35]

It is interesting that many of the memoirs and interviews with survivors mention that at the time of liberation or soon after, in spite of their physical weakness, they found enough energy to form larger medium-sized groups of friends or acquaintances. These groups, with between 8 and 20 members, undertook the tasks of finding temporary housing, food, clothing, and most important – of organizing the journey to wherever they wanted to travel or to return.[36]

Finally, as I cannot compare this large group of Jewish women concentration camp prisoners to a group of Jewish men prisoners under equal conditions, I can only speculate that the proliferation and vitality of "small-group" or "camp-family" social organization among the Jewish Ravensbrück women prisoners was a phenomenon facilitated by the widespread socialization of girls towards a high degree of responsibility, support and care of others, especially of weaker, younger or older family members, including even a sense of obligation towards those not especially loved by them.[37]

Notes

1   Buber-Neumann, Margarete, *Als Gefangene bei Stalin und Hitler*, Munich 2002, p. 295.
2   Wanda Kiedrzyńska, *Ravensbrück, kobiecy obóz koncentracyjny,* Warszawa, Książka i Wiedza, 1961; a full length German translation, Die Werte siegten, in the Ravensbrück archive, and Ursula Wińska, *Zwiciężyły wartosci: Wspomneinea z Ravensbrück: Wyd 1.* Gdansk: Wydawn. Morskie, 1985.
3   Wanda Kiedrzyńska, op. cit., pp. 233-234.
4   Wanda Kiedrzyńska, op. cit., p. 234.
5   Wanda Kiedrzyńska, op. cit., p. 150.
6   Wanda Kiedrzyńska, op. cit., pp. 7-8.
7   In this sewing workshop the cloth triangles designating group affiliation and prisoner number were prepared. To that end copies of all arrival lists were deposited there.
8   Sara Tuvel Bernstein writes (in: Sara (Seren) Tuvel Bernstein, *The Seamstress*, Berkley, New York, 1997, p. 228): "Lily and many of the other women in the camp were children of mixed marriages where Jewish customs had ceased to be observed generations ago."
9   Halina Nelken, *And Yet I Am Here!*, Amherst, 1999, pp. 173-4. Italics in the original text. After Plaszów she was imprisoned in Auschwitz, Ravensbrück, Malchow and HASAG-Leipzig.
10 This was the only case of a Jewish block leader in Ravensbrück itself. In the external

camps there were several of these

11 According to Israeli survivor Judith Harris, war name Judith Hirsch, interviewed 26.08.1997 by A.K. "Mrs. Kraus taught the children in Dutch".

12 Story that the late Professor Arthur Abraham (Buma) Stahl told in an interview with J.B.A. on 16.03.1998.

13 Interview with Israeli survivor Judith Taube, war name Jolanta Arato (Aufrichtig), by J. B. A., 10.09.1997.

14 It is significant that hardly any of the Polish-Jewish women who had arrived before the end of 1944, were sent from Malchow to HASAG-Leipzig.

15 Sara (Seren) Tuvel Bernstein, op. cit, pp. 229-230.

16 Vago, Lidia Rosenfeld, *One Year in the Black Hole of our Planet Earth*, Petah-Tikva, Israel, 1995 (119 pp., unpublished), pp. 43, 52.

17 Halina Nelken, op. cit., pp. 249-250.

18 Dr. Eva Danos Langley, *Prison on Wheels: From Ravensbrück to Burgau*. Daimon Verlag, Einsiedeln, Switzerland; 2000, pp. 76-79.

19 Examples are: Edita Kornfeld, the Czech lawyer who was appointed head of the office or *Blockälteste* at Krupp/Neukölln, see chapter VIII/6, and Paula Katz-Eisen in Neustadt-Glewe - Anna Szyller-Palarczyk states that she and another Polish prisoner, Wanda Marosanyi, survived the camp due to her (in: Karl Heinz Schütt, *Ein vergessenes Lager? (I) – Über das Aussenlager Neustadt-Glewe des Frauen- KZ Ravensbrück,* 1997, p. 28).

20 Kornreich-Gelissen, Rena, in: Karl Heinz Schütt (I), op. cit., pp. 60-61.

21 With the family transport from Toulouse came 15 children and 4 young teenagers; in the various Slovak transports there were 32 children and 13 young teenagers; and in the Italian transports – 6 children and 2 young teenagers. All of these transports also included older women.

22 Ghetto Czestochowa (on 03.09.1944) – 5 children, Ghetto Lodz (on 22.10.1944) 36 children and 10 young teenagers, most of whom were transferred to Königs Wusterhausen, and the Piotrkow ghetto (on 02.12.1944) – 55 children and 15 young teenagers.

23 Goldberg-Blumen, Regina: "Each of us had a small group of friends she felt belonging to", in: Schütt, op. cit., p. 37.

24 An example was Irmgard Judith Berger, later Becker, and her mother Pepi and sister Marlit.

25 Gyulai, Kato, *Eine einfache Deportiertengeschichte*, Budapest 1947 (Xeroxed version), pp. 37-38.

26 Vago Rosenfeld, Lidia, op. cit., p. 55.

27 Tuvel Bernstein, Sara, op. cit., p. 243.

28 Grohs-Martin, Silvia, Silvie, New York, 2000, p. 316.

29 Kounio Amariglio, Erika, *From Thessaloniki to Auschwitz and Back,* London, 2000, pp. 120-137.

30 Dr. Eva Danos Langley, *Prison on Wheels: From Ravensbrück to Burgau,* Daimon Verlag, Einsiedeln, Switzerland, 2000, pp. 31, 47, 48.

31 Tuvel Bernstein, Sara, op. cit., pp. 215-216.

32 Tuvel Bernstein, Sara, op. cit., p. 210.

33 When not all the four members of Seren Tuvel's group were "selected" to be sent to Burgau, they exchanged coats with Ravensbrück numbers with others who wanted to stay in Ravensbrück and had been "selected". Eventually all were sent to Brugau (in: Tuvel Bernstein, Sara, op. cit., pp. 244, 245).

34 Israeli survivor #425/270011 Landau Bondy Klara, in: Karl Heinz Schütt (I), op. cit., pp. 62-63.

35 Testimony of Lea Schwalb-Kisch, in Karl Heinz Schütt (I), op. cit., pp. 114-115.

36 Testimonies of: Margita Schwalbova, in: Karl Heinz Schütt, *Ein vergessenes Lager? (II),* June 1998, p. 24; Lea Gelbgras-Ferstenberg, in Karl Heinz Schütt (I), op. cit., p. 48, Jutta Pelz-Bergt, in Schütt, op. cit., pp. 75-78, Lidia Vago, in Karl Heinz Schütt (I), op. cit., p. 103, and Irene Kluger-Hajos, Karl Heinz Schütt (II), op. cit., p. 57. A group of 20 set out from Neustadt-Glewe in the direction of Czechoslovakia - in: Karl Heinz Schütt (II), op. cit., p. 8.

37 Thus Halina Nelken's camp-family of six included from beginning to the end also her sister-in-law Genia, towards whom she felt an obligation although she was not at all congenial (Nelken, Halina, op. cit., p. 251).

Part 2

Gendered Persecution and Sexualized Violence

The Persecution and Murder of German and German-Jewish Women between 1933 and 1945

Barbara Distel

During the summer of 2003 a new film by a well-known director, Margarethe von Trotta, whose oeuvre includes a filming of the life of Rosa Luxemburg, became the subject of controversial and intense discussion in Germany. *Die Rosenstrasse* tells the story of the protest staged by a group of 200 to 300 non-Jewish women against the imprisonment of their Jewish husbands in Berlin.

In February 1943, all Jews still living in the German Reich, were arrested without any warning at their workplace during the so-called *Fabrik-Aktion* ('the factory operation'). The goal of this operation was to deport them to the East. Jewish men who lived in so-called 'mixed marriages' were interned in a building in the Rosenstrasse. Their wives gathered together and protested in the Rosenstrasse for a week, defying intimidation and attempts to drive them away. Eventually their husbands were released. Besides another public protest by a group of some 300 women at Witten in November 1943, the Rosenstrasse protest was presumably the only public demonstration against the unjust regime. The film tells the story as a melodrama and shows too little consideration for the historical facts. Nevertheless, today, more than 60 years after the actual event, this film has set off a public discussion about why there was so little resistance against the Nazi dictatorship in Germany and how great the role played by women was in this.

My short look back on the persecution of women in Nazi Germany begins a decade before the protest staged by the women in Berlin's Rosenstrasse. The suffering of those women in Germany who were deemed to have no place in the so-called '*Volk* community' began immediately after the appointment of Adolf Hitler to German Reich Chancellor on January 30, 1933.

Who were these women? Firstly there were the politically engaged women who opposed the new regime, mainly from the left, but also in isolated instances from liberal and conservative parties; wives, mothers, girlfriends and daughters of Nazi political opponents also belonged to this group. If the men had fled Germany or gone underground, in many cases the wives were persecuted, taken hostage and deprived of their freedom.

There were also of course the Jewish girls and women, who numbered some 260,000 and thus made up more than the half of the some 500,000 Jews living in Germany in 1933 (or 0.77% of the population).[1] They directly felt the full brunt of the anti-Semitism that had an effect on every area of life. The first warning was the boycott ordered by the regime on April 1, 1933; this boycott was directed against Jewish businesses, doctors and lawyers and ended in looting and attacks. Another initial sign was the law for the 'Restoration of the Professional Public Service' that came into force on April 7, 1933; this law removed Jewish persons from their positions in the public service. The next point in the history of persecution and exclusion before the Holocaust was the enactment of the Nuremberg Laws in September 1935, which made marriage and extramarital sexual relations between Jews and non-Jews a punishable offence as 'racial defilement'. Sinti and Roma women, who had already suffered under persecution and discrimination in Germany before 1933, were also oppressed and excluded from the very beginning. Also subjected to the dictates of the Nuremberg Laws, these women were imprisoned in camps especially set up for them as early as 1936. Only a few years later they shared the fate of the Jews in Auschwitz-Birkenau and elsewhere.

Ill and disabled women also belonged to the victims. After the law 'for preventing genetically ill offspring' came into force in July 1933, their forced sterilization was ordered. And immediately after the start of the war, the state-organized murder of the ill and disabled began, a murder operation described as 'mercy killing' and which took the lives of at least 200,000 persons. As in the case of males, female members of the Jehovah's Witnesses, banned as an organization in April 1933, were exposed to extreme persecution. From the 25,000 members of the Jehovah's Witness who lived in Germany in 1933 some 1,200 were murdered. At least 2,000 were sent to the concentration camps, many of them women.[2]

And finally, mention needs to be made of those women who did not match the racist ideal of the Nazis, for example prostitutes, women who had committed a criminal offence or those without a permanent place of residence. These women were harassed, forcibly excluded from society and sent to concentration camps as 'asocials'. There are hardly any traces or information left regarding their fate.

Insofar as there was no overlapping between the Nazi categories, for instance Jewish and political or disabled and Jewish, all these women lived in situations isolated from one another. Hence, only in retrospect did the common features of their fate as persecuted persons become visible. However, there were soon institutions in Nazi Germany where these persecuted women, who came from different social and political backgrounds, did encounter one another. These were the prisons of the regime, which became one of the most important state instruments of persecution and suppression before, in the course of the war years, camps were set up for the exclusive purpose of carrying out the factory-like killing of humans.

Until the spring of 1938, as Austria became part of the German Reich, only Germans were imprisoned in the camps – the exception being non-German nationals living in Germany. At the end of the war however, only 5 to 10% of the prisoners in the concentration camps were German nationals, while 90 to 95% came from the areas occupied and annexed by the Germans. On January 15, 1945, there were 714,211 registered prisoners in all concentration camps, 202,764 of whom were female.[3] How high the proportion of female German nationals was at this point in time is not known; it was in all likelihood very low.

But the gigantic concentration camp system, which culminated in 25 main camps and some 1,200 subsidiary camps stretching across almost all of Europe, was begun in 1933; the passing of the law 'for the protection of people and state' in this year created the basis for taking political opponents and undesirables into so-called 'protective custody' for an indefinite period. No sentencing by a court was required. In the first year of the dictatorship, early forms of concentration camps or so-called protective custody sections within prisons were set up at over 100 sites; the great majority of these existed only for a few weeks or months, and some 80,000 persons were incarcerated in them in the course of 1933. Established on March 22, 1933, the Dachau concentration camp was, by the way, the only one of these early camps that existed for the full 12 years of the Nazi dictatorship. It was a camp for men; only in the last years of the war were female prisoners also sent to the Dachau subsidiary camps.

Women were first imprisoned in the so-called protective custody sections of prisons, such as in the Stuttgart prison Gotteszell,[4] where 60 to 80 women were sent between March 1933 and January 1934. At this stage physical violence against women was still the exception. However, the women were placed under enormous emotional and psychological pressure – arrested without warning by the Gestapo, they had to leave behind their children without knowing how long they would remain under arrest. Beginning in November 1933, a large number of women were transferred from Gotteszell and other protective custody sections, in other German states, to the first central concentration camp for women at Moringen, in Lower Saxony.[5] Until its closure in March 1938, approximately 1,400 women were imprisoned at this camp. With almost 50% of the imprisoned women, the female members of the Jehovah's Witnesses formed the largest group; there were also many political prisoners from the German communist and social democratic parties and a far smaller number of Jewish women, as well as the so-called 'asocials', 'professional criminals' and 're-immigrants'. At this camp too, under the command of a civilian director and not the SS, physical violence was yet to be inflicted on the imprisoned women. The work they were forced to do was monotonous and supplies were inadequate, leading to undernourishment. But here as well, the greatest burden was the uncertainty about their fate and the worry about the children they had been forced to leave behind, and about their husbands, friends and fathers, who often were also imprisoned.

In December 1937, the Renaissance castle at Lichtenburg,[6] where previously male prisoners were incarcerated, was turned into a concentration camp for women, and the women imprisoned at Moringen were transferred there. Like the other concentration camps, Lichtenburg was under the control of the Inspectorate for Concentration Camps; female SS guards were deployed here for the first time. The daily routine was regulated with military precision down to the last minute, as in the male camps. Roll calls, controls, harassment, and abuse characterized the lives of the imprisoned women. At Lichtenburg the different treatment of the various prisoner groups also began. Jewish women were treated the worst: they had to do the hardest and dirtiest work and they were subjected to the cruelest torments.

There were, however, no SS-owned commercial companies, and only 22% of the women were forced to work. During the existence of the Lichtenburg women's concentration camp, which lasted for almost 18 months, a total of 1,400 women were imprisoned here. However, the dilapidated Lichtenburg castle was to play no further role in the plans to extend the concentration camp system that were drawn up as part of the preparations for war. In the spring of 1938, plans instead were begun to set up the central concentration camp for women at Ravensbrück near Fürstenberg,[7] located in what today is Brandenburg. In May 1938, 867 women from Lichtenburg were transferred there, amongst them a group of Austrians. By the start of the war around 3,000 women had been sent to the concentration camp. The Ravensbrück camp was no longer any different from the other main camps in the territories under German rule. Up until the spring of 1945, 107,753 women were registered as prisoners, 18% of whom were German and Austrian women (or at least those registered as German nationals); 20,086 male prisoners were registered. The female German political prisoners assumed a strong position in the prisoner hierarchy. Like the men, but often using different means, they offered one another support and were always looking for ways of surviving the hell that was the concentration camp. How many German women died in total in the concentration camps is not known.

In the years between 1933 and 1939, the deprivation of rights, the exclusion and the discrimination of all women who did not belong to the Nazi ideal of the '*Volk* community', increased continually. The elimination and ousting of Jews from German economic life was as good as complete by the end of fall 1938. After the pogrom of November 9, 1938, called the *'Kristallnacht'* ('night of broken glass'), 30,000 Jewish men were sent to the concentration camps. The goal of state policy at this time was to force Jews into immigration and to appropriate Jewish property and assets. Thus it was mostly left to the women, isolated in a situation of existential anxiety, to fight with the authorities for the release of their imprisoned husbands, to procure the papers necessary for the hoped-for emigration, to sell their property and assets at giveaway prices, to comfort their traumatized children, and to prepare for life in a foreign country. Supported by Jewish welfare organizations, in 1938/39 around 10,000 Jewish children were sent to England, rescuing them from murder.[8] Most of these children never saw their parents again. By 1938, 266,000 Jews had left Germany, whereby the proportion of men who were able to flee into exile was greater than that of women. Above all, elderly and single women remained behind. After the so-called *'Kristallnacht'*, by 1941 another 23,000 Jews were able to flee the deathtrap that was Germany. By then the systematic murder of Jews had long begun, an operation that threatened the Jews of all countries falling under German control. In Germany itself they were forced into slave labor, driven out of their apartments and homes, and pressed into collective accommodations. From September 1941, they were forced to wear the yellow Star of David; in October 1941 the systematic deportations to the East began. Faced with near-certain death, more and more people committed suicide upon receiving notification of their imminent deportation – in

Württemberg the figure was 10%. One exception was the deportation of around 6,000 Jews from Baden and the Saarland to the Gurs[9] internment camp in southern France in October 1940. From there, a considerable number were able to flee before the internees were sent on to Auschwitz in 1943. Only about a half of the some 42,000 German Jews sent to Theresienstadt managed to survive. In the summer of 1943, 30% of the German-Jewish population was still living in Germany, the majority of them the elderly and women. At the end of 1943, Germany was declared to be *'judenfrei'*, 'free of Jews'. In total, around 165,000 German Jews were murdered in the genocide; the number of women was some 20% greater than men[10] what According to estimates, some 15,000 persons were able to survive within the German Reich[11]. German Jewry had been exterminated.

After the liberation of the death camps, the extent of the National Socialist murder policy became clear. The German women who were among the first victims had either been murdered or now lived, apart from a few exceptions who had survived in the underground or returned to Germany, dispersed across the globe. In Germany there was hardly any interest in the fate of the survivors for decades, whereby the fate of women was granted even less attention. But in other countries as well, for understandable reasons, everything that was German – or once had been German – was only viewed in connection with the perpetrators. Only in the last two decades has a worldwide interest developed in the history of the Holocaust and the individual fates of the victims. "The task is to recapture lost stories"[12] – this is the demand made by the American historian Sybil Milton with regard to all women who were victims of Nazi crimes. I consider it to be the special task of German society to preserve and uphold the remembrance of the first victims of barbarism and herein the remembrance of women in particular.

Notes

1   Ino Arndt und Hans Boberach, Deutsches Reich, in: Wolfgang Benz (Hg.). *Die Dimension des Voelkermords*, München, 1991, S.23.
2   Detlef Garbe, Der Lila Winkel. Die "Bibelforscher" (Zeugen Jehovas) in den Konzentrationslagern, in: Wolfgang Benz, Barbara Distel (Hg.), *Dachauer Hefte* 10 (1994), S. 3-31.
3   Bundesarchiv Koblenz (BAK) NS3/439, Aufstellung über die Zahl der Waschmannschaften und Haftlinge in den Konzentrationslagern vom Januar 1945.
4   Markus Kienle, Gotteszell – das fruehe Konzentrationslager für Frauen in Württemberg, in: Wolfgang Benz, Barbara Distel (Hg.), *Terror ohne System. Die ersten Konzentrationslager im Nationalsozialismus*, Berlin 2001, S.65-69.
5   Hans Hesse, Von der 'Erziehung' zur 'Ausmerze'. Das Konzentrationslager Moringen 1933-1945, in: Wolfgang Benz, Barbara Distel (Hg.), *Instrumentarium der Macht. Fruehe Konzentrationslager 1933-1938,* Berlin 2003, S. 111-147.
6   Stefanie Endlich, Die Lichtenburg – Haftort politischer Prominenz und Frauenkonzentra

tionslager 1933-1939, in: Wolfgang Benz, Barbara Distel (Hg.), *Herrschaft und Gewalt. Fruehe Konzentrationslager 1933-1939*, Berlin 2002, S.11-65.

7   Bernhard Strebel, *Das Konzentrationslager Ravensbrück 1939-1945*, Paderborn, 2003.

8   Rebekka Goepfert, *Ich kam nicht allein. Die Rettung von zehntausend jüdischen Kindern*, München 1994.

9   Gabriele Mittag, 'Das Ende sind wir'. Leben und Tod in Gurs, der, Vorhalle von Auschwitz, in: Barbara Distel (Hg.), *Frauen im Holocaust*, Gerlingen 2002, S. 49-70.

10 Monika Richarz (Hg.), *Jüdisches Leben in Deutschland. Selbstzeugnisse zur Sozialgeschichte 1918-1945*, Stuttgart 1982, S.60f.

11 Ino Arndt, Hans Boberach, Deutsches Reich, in: Wolfgang Benz (Hr.), *Die Dimension des Völkermord*, München 1991.

12 Esther Katz, Joan Miriam Ringelblum: Proceedings of the Conference "Women Surviving the Holocaust", New York, 1983, S.36.

Racialised Gender, Gendered Race and Gendered-Racialised Academia: Female-Jewish Anthropologists in Vienna

Herta Nöbauer

Abstract

This chapter examines the significance of gender and 'race' for female-Jewish anthropologists in the context of Nazism in Vienna. By focusing on two anthropologists, *Eugenie Goldstern* and *Marianne Schmidl*, I propose that they died a 'triple death': their social-professional death as a result of anti-Semitism and racism was followed by physical death by assassination in a Nazi camp in Poland. Subsequently, however, they died an 'institutional death' by being 'forgotten,' neglected and ignored in their professional field, anthropology, for an extended period of time. It is argued that their 'institutional death' largely corresponds with the organisation of academia and anthropology, areas that require more critical reflection. Consequently, the significance of gender in its intersections with 'race', class, religion/confession and nationality, and the impacts of this on Goldstern and Schmidl is demonstrated in more detail. In doing so, the chapter contributes to writing against a representation of anthropology's *his*tory that is mainly based on a male bias.

Introduction: Constructing national identities

While I was writing this chapter in the early weeks of 2005, Austria announced its intentions to dedicate this year to a broad commemoration and remembrance of its postwar nation-building. Although the fiftieth anniversary of the signing of Austria's State Treaty after the end of occupation during and after the Second World War indeed provides considerable grounds for celebration, like elsewhere, in this regard commemoration and remembrance are contested. Whose voices are to be heard and acknowledged? It is not really surprising that until now it has mainly been men's and ethnically dominant voices that are represented in Austria's media. There are two popular phrases that particularly represent national identity, and which are of great juridical, symbolic and emotional significance: 'Austria is free'[1] is one, and 'Never again (fascism)!', the other. These two statements present two perspectives that have not always been seen in conjunction with one another in Austria. As a result, heated discussions are also underway about the denial of particular 'dark spots' in the past of Nazism, the lack of formal recognition of resistance efforts,[2] and contemporary forms of racism and xenophobia. At the same time, two renowned historians (Neugebauer and Schwarz 2005) have published a new book that is attracting great attention. They have offered the first analysis of the 'dark and neglected aspects' of an Austrian political party: The Society of Social Democratic Academics (BSA), which is an organisation for academic party intellectuals, promoted and (re-)integrated a whole range of members of the National Socialist Party and Nazi persecutors after the Second World War.

The liberation of Auschwitz sixty years ago is also currently commemorated along with the last five decades of sovereignty and neutrality. The opposition parties and some public sectors have criticised that only the federal president and not also the current chancellor of the coalition government attended this memorial ceremony. And last, but not least, there is a controversial review that analyses the five-year coalition between Austria's People's Party (ÖVP) and the far-right Freedom Party (FPÖ). Opponents of the current coalition government recall, among other things, that this was the first postwar government to face such deep-rooted opposition that it was forced by massive civil protests to travel through an underground pathway to the site where it was sworn into office.[3]

Dying a 'triple death'

Anthropologists in the German-language area, by and large, have only in the past two decades begun to study the history of anthropology in relation to Nazism. A critical reflection on the complex relationship between anthropology and politics, and the ethics of anthropology, results from a systematic analysis that distinguishes the vastly different roles of anthropologists during Nazism and their impact on anthropology. (Details on the disciplinary division and distinction in Austria will follow). This chapter argues that with a few exceptions, anthropology's reconstruction in the context of Vienna still tends to neglect and ignore female anthropologists and the significance of gender before and during the Nazi era.[4] In particular, the first generation of female anthropologists in Vienna and the innovative and pioneering research of Jewish female anthropologists among them tends to remain hidden. Thus, a mainstream/malestream anthropology also simultaneously covers the various processes of marginalisation and exclusion of women with different socio-cultural backgrounds and their work; and last but not least, it does not take into account a differentiated *her*story of female-Jewish victims murdered by Nazis, on the one hand, and those forced into emigration/exile, on the other.[5]

While especially from the 1990s on, a number of critically thinking men and women anthropologists representing the second and third postwar generation of anthropologists have begun to shed important light on anthropology's involvement with Nazism, a majority still tends to neglect gender as a critical category therein and as a meaningful structure contributing also to cultural hegemony alongside political and institutional structures in science. In order to write against this 'forgotten' aspect of cultural hegemony, I focus on two female-Jewish anthropologists who were among the murdered victims: *Eugenie Goldstern* and *Marianne Schmidl*. By expanding the concept of 'social and physical death' of Jewish women as formulated by Kaplan (2001),[6] I claim that these two anthropologists died a 'triple death': Their social-professional death as a result of anti-Semitism and racism was followed by physical death by assassination in a Polish concentration camp; they subsequently died an 'institutional death' by being 'forgotten', neglected and ignored in their professional field, anthropology, for an extended period of time. Their 'institutional death', I further argue, is significantly grounded in a male-biased approach to anthropology's history, which is related also to an implicit and explicit concept of 'key persons' (Fischer 1990).[7]

By proposing a concept of 'triple death', this chapter therefore contributes to an analytical review of distinct but interrelated stages of the experiences of female researchers that have mainly been shaped by anti-Semitism, racism and gender. This discrimination, however, which resulted in assassination, must not be understood as 'additional'. Rather, gender, anti-Semitism and 'race' intersect with each other in the same way as they are mutually informed by other experiences and categories like class, religion/confession, nationality, academic/institutional ties and positions.[8]

Considering Goldstern's and Schmidl's passion and identities as researchers, this chapter will give special attention to significant aspects of their institutional and social-professional death as they are specifically linked with each other within and because of the academic context we focus on here. Accordingly, subsequent sections will outline and discuss some aspects of Goldstern's and Schmidl's 'triple death' as it is to a considerable extent informed by anti-Semitism, 'race' and gender. Before that, however, the following sections will introduce these two pioneers, Eugenie Goldstern and Marianne Schmidl, and compare them to each other in more detail. A particular emphasis is laid on their family backgrounds, their various roles as women and their own understanding of their gender and Jewish identities. In doing so, I will not only outline some significant similarities and differences between these two anthropologists, but will also make explicit a set of requirements for academics, on the one hand, and the obstacles and discrimination these women faced in the academic realm, on the other.[9] Anthropology's institutional establishment will also be highlighted in order to provide the context for the discussion that follows.

Introducing the pioneers: Eugenie Goldstern and Marianne Schmidl

Eugenie Goldstern

Eugenie Goldstern was born into an upper-middle-class merchant family in Odessa (Ukraine) in 1884. She was the youngest of fourteen children. Both her parents were Jewish. Her mother was Marie Goldstern, née Kitower, and her father Abraham Goldstern. Although her family was rooted in a traditional religious elite in Poland, the Goldsterns lived a liberal lifestyle. Through her wet nurse and travels with her father, Eugenie became acquainted with the peasant sphere. This may have had an impact on her later research interest and focus on folk studies. Along with her family, she was a member of the Jewish third of Odessa's population in the late nineteenth century. After a Jewish primary school, she attended a Russian secondary school, from which she graduated with a certificate. However, Eugenie Goldstern's educational background was oriented more towards German-language-based cultural realms due to her German-speaking father, in particular. Accordingly, she was fascinated by German literature and philosophy. German was also the language of Odessa's intellectual elite at the time. In addition to Yiddish, Russian, Hebrew and German, Eugenie Goldstern spoke several other languages including Polish, French and Italian. Finally, because of her later fieldwork she was also able to speak Patois, the dialect of the people she studied in the French Alps. Along with several of her ancestors, brothers and sisters as well as friends she had a strong interest in emancipatory and revolutionary issues. She increasingly identified with Western European-informed education, which became a symbol for emancipation for many Jewish women in Eastern Europe. Her intellectual self-understanding thus might have been a reason why she never married or had children. Without marriage and children she was the only family member who lived contrary to and kept a distance from what was expected of her according to traditional Jewish gender roles. It seems that the men in her family in particular did not respect her because of this (cf. Ottenbacher 1999). Socio-economic and political crises and especially anti-Semitism and pogroms in Russia at the turn of the century would lead to the first major rupture in Goldstern's biography. In 1905, shortly before the outbreak of the revolution, Eugenie Goldstern and several of her family members were forced to emigrate. While some of her brothers and sisters had already left Russia to disperse throughout various European countries, she first (im)migrated to Vienna at the age of twenty-one. Her second oldest brother, Sima, who was a dentist living in Vienna, became her guardian. However, Eugenie lived in a large house in which her eldest brother, Samuel, and his family also lived, and which he ran as a prominent sanatorium. Eugenie Goldstern had a small, irregular income from translating and private teaching but no income from anthropological work. However, her financially secure brothers supported her economically. At the age of twenty-six, in 1910, she began to study anthropology at the University of Vienna.

Marianne Schmidl

Like her colleague Eugenie Goldstern and many other students at that time Marianne Schmidl came from a wealthy and intellectual family, which moved between Austria and Germany. She was born in Berchtesgaden, Germany, in 1890. Her mother was Maria Schmidl, née Friedmann and the daughter of a Protestant mother and a Jewish father. Marianne's father, Dr Josef Schmidl, was a lawyer who had converted from Judaism to Protestantism shortly before marriage to his Protestant wife. His parents were Jewish. Like her younger and only sister Franziska, Marianne Schmidl was baptised a Protestant. The two girls were raised in Vienna. As converted Protestants still considered Jewish by their friends, they represented a minority vis-à-vis Vienna and Austria's large Catholic majority. Anti-Semitism was a social and political reality in Vienna at that time. Unlike the majority of Austrian girls of her era, but similar to Eugenie Goldstern, Marianne Schmidl received a humanistic education in an exceptional school for girls, based on educational reform. There she developed close relationships with artists, socialists and members of youth movements alike. She graduated school with a certificate in Graz (Austria) in 1910. This certificate enabled her to enroll as a student at an Austrian university. In the same year, at the age of twenty, Marianne Schmidl began to study mathematics and theoretical physics at the University of Vienna. However, three years later she switched to anthropology.

We can assume that Schmidl's social background also considerably shaped her understanding of herself as an intellectual and emancipated woman. Like Eugenie Goldstern, she never married nor did she have children. Indeed, she lived a life fully dedicated to her profession – as was also the case with Goldstern. Like the latter, she was socially integrated into her extended family. She shared a house with her sister's family in Vienna's Twelfth District. After her sister's death upon the birth of her third child in 1925, Marianne Schmidl took over ownership of the house together with her brother-in-law, who was a professor at the Vienna University of Technology. In contrast to Eugenie Goldstern, Marianne Schmidl was able to earn her own income after many years working as a volunteer and searching for a job. Getting a job – let alone a tenured university position – was even more difficult for female anthropologists back then than it is today.[10] With the strong support and intervention of a few powerful anthropology professors, she finally got a tenured position at the Austrian National Library in 1924 – which granted her a regular income until 1938. It is also important to mention that in addition to her full-time job at the National Library, Marianne worked as an ethnographer and as an ethnologist. She also received some funding for her anthropological research, which she carried out in several European museums. However, it was one of her research grants that would later become the cause of a hate campaign against her, led by a professor a few years later (details below).

Challenging male (-Catholic) academia: Female (-Jewish) students entering university

When both Eugenie Goldstern and Marianne Schmidl began to study at the University of Vienna in 1910, they belonged to the first generation of female students in Austria.[11] They were among those 20 percent of students in these early days who were women. While about 69 percent of female students at the Faculty of Philosophy were Catholic, 20 percent were Jewish.[12] Due to increasing anti-Semitism, however, this percentage dramatically decreased in the mid-1930s (Heindl and Tichy 1990; Kossek and Habinger 1993)[13] and led in 1938 to the complete banishment from the universities also of all Jewish men and women. Unlike their female predecessors, Goldstern and Schmidl had already been allowed to attend a higher school (*Gymnasium*) and graduated with a certificate (*Abitur/Matura*) as mentioned above. However, it is important to emphasise a considerable difference between them, which indeed had serious consequences for Eugenie Goldstern. Unlike Marianne Schmidl, she was not allowed to enroll as a student but instead had visiting-student status. The reason was that she had received her certificate from a Russian and not an Austrian school as required for study at an Austrian university. The educational system, which was based on national certificate identity, also later prohibited her from submitting her Ph.D. in Austria. As a result, she graduated in Switzerland.

Thirteen years after the University of Vienna had finally opened its gates to female students, beginning with the Faculty of Philosophy in 1897, both our anthropologists entered a traditionally 'men-only' field. The fact that women's participation in higher education became possible was largely an achievement of the Women's Movement, which had long fought for this right. Although only privileged men and women could afford to study at the time, entrance into the scientific community was still no easy matter for these pioneering women. The mere physical presence of women within academia remained a strongly contested matter. Women had to fight and resist a broad range of deep-seated prejudices from male professors and male colleagues alike.[14] They were excluded from particular lectures and also lacked powerful networks, which were (and are) of undeniable significance for the support and careers of male academics, to name but a few disadvantages and forms of discrimination. In other words, the first generation of female students and academics had to prove their intellectual abilities in a field characterised by male-only and male-dominated societies; a male-biased knowledge of dominance and male interpretations of intellectual women as *Mannweiber* (literally 'menwomen') (Bandhauer-Schöffmann 1990; Heindl and Tichy 1990).[15]

Referred to as *Mannweiber,* these students were blurring the boundaries between male and female as constructed by the Western European middle-class ideology of the nineteenth century. But specifically, *Mannweiber* were constructed as socially and physically dangerous by those scientific discourses sharing Gobineau's racist and anti-Semitic ideology[16] since female connoted 'sensuality' (sexuality) – in opposition to male, which connoted 'culture' – these women would demand 'free love', the result of which would be the initiation of a process of 'racial mixture'. Such a process of 'hybridization' (Fuchs 2003; 2005) was politically identified with liberalism and socialism. Indeed from the late nineteenth century onwards the German-nationalistic educated middle class had already begun to construct liberals, Marxists and feminists alike as 'non-humans'. The 'cultural' argument of lacking sexual morality, grounded in Gobineau's race idea, thus became the basis for constructing women (feminists), Jewish people, 'minor races' and classes altogether as a 'unity' of alterity and hostility (Fuchs 2005:11). Those Jewish women who were educated and politically engaged in emancipatory issues and the socialist movement were thus considered as a 'special danger' (cf. Ottenbacher 1999).

Disciplines and power: Fights to establish anthropologies

Anthropology was a new and striving field when Eugenie Goldstern and Marianne Schmidl began their studies. Like every rising field, many students were attracted to it (Mayer 1991). Michael Haberlandt was the first *Privatdozent* (Extra-Ordinary Professor) for 'ethnography' at the University of Vienna.[17] He gave lectures on ethnology and comparative ethnography at the university and also at the Natural History Museum where he was employed in a tenured position, as well as at the Folklore Museum,[18] which he founded with a colleague in 1885. He had previously also founded the society *Verein für Volkskunde* (Society for Folklore Studies), and the journal *Zeitschrift für Österreichische Volkskunde* (Journal for Austrian Folklore). Despite his earlier cross-cultural ethnography, in the first decade of the twentieth century, he increasingly concentrated his work on his passion for collecting folk art objects. However, he was not successful in his efforts to establish *Volkskunde* as a discipline (Jacobeit, Lixfeld and Bockhorn 1994; Dow and Bockhorn 2004).

While anthropology in its current disciplinary divisions – namely, social and cultural anthropology, European ethnology, physical anthropology and prehistory – was not established at that time, its distinct fields, organisations and research activities crossed in various ways inside and outside the university. 'Ethnography' comprised the study of extra-European and European regions and societies alike but was mainly Slavic, Germanic, historic-geographic and linguistic ethnology. However, the field of ethnology was definitely divided into *Völkerkunde* (now social and cultural anthropology) and *Volkskunde* (now European ethnology) with the establishment of the former at the first Institute for Anthropology and Ethnography[19] in 1913, and finally with the foundation of the Institute for *Völkerkunde* in 1929. Whereas the first institute was initially led by a physical anthropologist, Rudolf Pöch, the second was epistemologically[20] and socially dominated – though not led – by one of Haberlandt's opponents, Wilhelm Schmidt, until 1938. He was a member of a Catholic order, and became a victim of Nazism when he was forced into Swiss exile in 1938. His writings, however, are characterised by explicitly anti-Semitic ideas (Conte 1987; Dostal 1994; Linimayr 1994).[21] Nevertheless, or perhaps because he did not know about her Jewish background, he supported and promoted Marianne Schmidl in her job search in Vienna in the 1920s.

In the end, *Völkerkunde* proved to have the more powerful agents for promoting its establishment as a discipline in the inter-war period. *Volkskunde,* on the contrary, was only able to establish itself as a discipline in conjunction with the takeover of Austria by the Nazis in 1938. For various reasons, *Volkskunde*, the discipline Eugenie Goldstern had subscribed to until the early 1930s, became crucial to the Nazi regime (Heiß *et al.*1989; Dow and Bockhorn 2004). In fact, in Vienna, as in Germany in 1933, 'there was no lack of candidates for a professorship who were committed to the concept of "pure German-Germanic cultural studies"' (Dow and Bockhorn 2004: 128; original quotation in English), which significantly contributed to the race and *völkische* ideology. Arthur Haberlandt, who was appointed as an adjunct professor and succeeded his father, Michael, as head of the museum in 1924, was among them.

In contrast to many other disciplines, which present the National Socialist takeover as an assault from the outside, *Volkskunde*, in particular, continually emphasised and strengthened the main ideas of a pan-German nationalism, overt anti-Semitism and racism.[22] In the same vein, it promoted membership of the National Socialist Party and its 'key persons' worked for Heinrich Himmler's scholary organisation 'Ancestral Inheritance' [in German *Ahnenerbe;* in English also 'Ancestral Legacy'– HN], on the one hand, and, on the other (for example, Arthur Haberlandt) for Alfred Rosenberg, Commissioner for the Supervision of all Intellectual and World View Schooling and Education of the NSDAP (Dow and Bockhorn 2004:108).

The Research and Teaching Community 'Ancestral Inheritance' was devoted to the study of pre- and early Germanic history whereby the political nature of this society was always at its centre. Among others, this society supported experiments on concentration camp inmates and the transportation of Jews to those same camps (Bockhorn and Dow 2004: 125). In this respect it should be added that the majority of *Volkskunde* anthropologists who collaborated with 'Ancestral Inheritance' mainly occupied regular university positions, in Vienna and elsewhere. Those, however, who worked for the Rosenberg Bureau failed to gain regular university positions (ibid.: 124). Among the latter a group of 'key male persons' founded a Working Community that was supported by the Rosenberg Bureau and was intended to become the primary *Volkskunde* institution of the NSDAP. It decided to 'develop German *Volkskunde* scholarship into a fortress for the NS world-view' (Bockhorn and Dow 2004: 127; original quotation in English). When creating outposts for this 'Advanced School', departments such as the Institute for Research on the Jewish Question, the Institute for Biology and Racial Studies, the Institute for German Folklore were included (ibid.).

Entering anthropology: Between professional passion, networking and exclusion

In choosing anthropology in 1910 and 1913 respectively, Eugenie Goldstern and Marianne Schmidl entered a field entirely dominated by male teachers who were probably not anti-women per se vis-à-vis their female students. But both women certainly had to – and I suppose did – find clever strategies within a field dominated by competing 'key male teachers', and the methods, branches and 'schools' they represented. Both had a remarkable network of male teachers and mentors. While Goldstern established her professional relations mainly in Austria, Switzerland and France, Schmidl's networks were mainly located in Austria and Germany.[23]

But Goldstern and Schmidl not only faced gender hierarchies in academia; at the same time, they entered a field that was – and still is – marked by hierarchical differences in ethnic, religious and other socio-culturally relevant backgrounds.[24] With regard to these, none of their 'key' male teachers in their Viennese context was Jewish or with a background other than Catholic or Protestant. This is not to say that there were no Jewish male anthropologists, for there were; however, they had less well-established positions inside the Austrian anthropological institutions at that time.[25] Those professors who did have powerful positions mainly had Catholic and to a lesser extent Protestant backgrounds before and until 1938. Nevertheless, both women were able to find a first teacher and mentor who was not anti-women and who would be very important for their careers: Michael Haberlandt, who was of Protestant and initially liberal background.

During her studies, Eugenie Goldstern attended Michael Haberlandt's lectures and was fascinated by the variety of topics he introduced, including issues related to women. In particular, she became influenced by his comparative approach to researching the roots of European cultures. Both also shared a deep passion for studying and collecting folk art and popular material culture (cf. Haberlandt 1900), a passion that led Goldstern to donate a great number of objects to the Folklore Museum (cf. Ottenbacher 1999).[26] The museum and the journal were important sites for Goldstern's anthropological representation. Collecting and then displaying material culture was indeed very significant for an anthropologist's reputation and identity. But instead of focusing on the Balkan region, as would have been expected of her according to 'Austrian ethnographic tradition', Eugenie focused on the Western Alps. In spite of this different regional focus, Michael Haberlandt remained without doubt a significant teacher for her for several years before he let her fall for 'racial' reasons. However, the previously more or less liberal ethnographer Michael Haberlandt became more and more of a folklorist, and right after the downfall of Austria-Hungary in 1918 turned to a nationalistic, pan-Germanic and racial ideology (cf. Dow and Bockhorn 2004). This ideological and political turn had a serious impact on Eugenie Goldstern, as she was subsequently ignored and excluded by the Viennese scientific *Volkskunde* community.

Interested in the lives of small communities in villages of the Western Alps, Eugenie's first journey led her to the Wallis region in Switzerland in 1912 and to her first publication (Goldstern 1912). In Switzerland, she met two ethnographers who would influence her greatly: Leopold Rütimayer and Arnold van Gennep. Not only did some of Goldstern's family members live in Switzerland, but from then on she also had an 'extended scientific family'. It was especially van Gennep, with his modern ideas, who proposed and supported her research in Bessans, a village, at an altitude of nearly 1800 m, in the region of Savoyen in the French Alps. One year later, Goldstern went there to work on one of the first monographs on a mountain village and its economy. Working with the methods of participant observation, she got close to the people and their lifestyle and became acquainted with the rough, brutally cold Alpine climate. Eugenie lived with the people in underground dwellings that also served as stables and were warm in the freezing wintertime. The rural people respected this urban researcher and Eugenie Goldstern is remembered in Bessans even today. There she found two distinct communities living a traditional and a modern life respectively. In one, people lived without electricity and modern conveniences and used dung for heating; they baked their bread in communal ovens and had democratically organised communal structures. The other community was completely modern and lived close to the railway line to Turin. This detailed and insightful investigation of Bessans became Eugenie Goldstern's dissertation (Goldstern 1922). She was indeed an innovative researcher for several reasons: she was one of the first anthropologists of *Volkskunde* to study not only folk art but mainly the tools of everyday life, and popular material culture. In addition to that, she had a modern approach to interdisciplinary and comparative research.

Before Eugenie Goldstern left for Bessans, however, she met Marianne Schmidl. This was the year Schmidl moved to anthropology. Perhaps they had already known each other from Haberlandt's courses, but their paths certainly crossed in the Folklore Museum in 1913. Both were engaged as hard-working volunteers in an exhibition project about a large ethnographic collection from the Basque Country. Goldstern's colleague and mentor Rudolf Trebitsch (see note 24) had dedicated the collection to the museum (cf. Geisenhainer 2002).

As noted, changing to the newly established institute in 1913 enabled Marianne Schmidl to graduate in ethnology. Prior to the disciplinary change to the new institute she had become a member of the Verein für Volkskunde – like Goldstern before her – and had already published her first article in the *Zeitschrift für Österreichische Volkskunde* after she had conducted her initial ethnographic study in Austria's Ötztal. Marianne Schmidl became the very first female ethnologist (*Völkerkunde*) in Austria with a Ph.D. in 1916. She had even published her dissertation the previous year (Schmidl 1915; Kossek and Habinger 1993). By combining her previous study of mathematics and African ethnography she graduated on the topic of *Zahl und Zählen in Afrika* ('Numbers and Counting in Africa') (Schmidl 1915). Based on a remarkable bibliography, Marianne Schmidl studied the history of African counting systems and their socio-culturally diverse changes. Her dissertation was reviewed in two journals and also found full recognition in the journal *History of Mathematics* in 1923 as 'the standard authority on the number systems in Africa, together with a full bibliography' (Geisenhainer 2002: 275, quotes E. Smith 1923: 14fn.). As recently as 1999 an expert in ethnomathematics has praised Schmidl's work: 'I have found no later work equal to it' (Geisenhainer 2002: 275, quotes Zaslavsky 1999: 14). As a student of Michael Haberlandt who previously had a more dynamic cultural approach and was a critic of the 'Culture Circle' theory, she was even successful in garnering praise from representatives of the latter 'school' of ethnology (Geisenhainer 2002: 275). Notwithstanding her new disciplinary identity as an ethnologist, Marianne Schmidl always remained closely connected to *Volkskunde* as represented by the Folklore Museum.

While Marianne Schmidl graduated in Vienna during the First World War, Eugenie Goldstern faced the obstacles of war and nationalism during her fieldwork in the Western Alps. The outbreak of the First World War forced her to flee Bessans. When Austria-Hungary declared war on France, the Austro-Hungarian researcher photographing and documenting in the French-Italian border area was suddenly regarded with suspicion as a political spy. Political violence once again led to a rupture in her life and the war brought an abrupt interruption to her career. Back in Vienna things were no better as the nationalist climate had also seeped into academia. She tried to forget by travelling and working. Under the wartime circumstances, her research, however, was limited to Austria and Germany. Only after the end of the First World War could she continue with her Ph.D. in Switzerland. She graduated *summa cum laude* in 1920 at the Institute for Geography. Both of her teachers, Girardin in Switzerland and van Gennep in France, were enthusiastic about her monograph on Bessans (Ottenbacher 1999).

In brief, the political climate became considerably more charged after the war. Nationalism, chauvinism, anti-Semitism and race ideology were increasingly supported by the population and also by scientists. Anthropologists positioned themselves either on the side of the ideology of nationalism and race or against it. Eugenie Goldstern and Marianne Schmidl belonged to the latter group. Whereas Goldstern's anti-nationalistic teacher and mentor Arnold van Gennep was dismissed from his professorship in Neuchatel and expelled from Switzerland for political reasons in 1915, Michael Haberlandt – like his son Arthur – opted for a politically opportunistic alternative and positioned himself in support of the ideology of nationalism, race and Nazism as did most anthropologists in Austria and Germany in *Völkerkunde* and *Volkskunde* alike (Gerndt 1987; Fischer 1990; Mayer 1991; Pusman 1991; Kossek and Habinger 1993; Dostal 1994; Dow and Lixfeld 1994; Jacobeit, Lixfeld and Bockhorn 1994; Linimayer 1994; Byer 1999; Ottenbacher 1999; Geisenhainer 2002; Dow and Bockhorn 2004; Gingrich 2005; Gingrich forthcoming).

Gender and 'race' at work: Anthropological dimensions of 'triple death'

'Institutional death'

As has already been emphasised, Goldstern's and Schmidl's 'institutional death' comprises their being 'forgotten', neglected and ignored in their professional field of anthropology for an extended period. The reason for their 'institutional death', I specifically argue, largely corresponds with the organisation of academia and anthropology, areas that require more critical reflection. As has already been implied and demonstrated, the organisation of these areas is characterised by racialised, gendered and other dominant structures related to social practices of institutional inclusion and exclusion. In other words, those social groups and representatives who are not institutionally integrated are considered 'less significant' and are correspondingly rendered less visible or even invisible. Women and ethnic and religious minorities were historically (and to a considerable extent still remain today) non-integrated in Austrian universities. Studying academia's organisation and, namely, its socio-cultural 'composition' may thus reveal how historical representation constructs and reproduces national hegemony and a national elite.

While only a very few female researchers belonging to the Austrian majority society had, exceptionally, been integrated into academia by achieving university positions and jobs as anthropologists[27], none of the pioneering female-Jewish anthropologists had been integrated as such before the tragic rupture caused by Nazism in Austria in 1938, nor after the Holocaust/the Second World War. Anthropology, the discipline that predominantly studies 'others', historically has not integrated people with distinct socio-cultural backgrounds into university positions and it still continues to exclude them today. In the past and in the present it only exceptionally opens its hegemonic borders for men, but not for women, with different minority backgrounds.

Despite women's exclusion from anthropological jobs and university positions, there are studies that focus on women in academia from a different perspective. Feminist anthropologists have shown the historical continuity of women's generations – including the pioneering roles of women with Jewish backgrounds – especially for today's socio-cultural anthropology in Vienna (Kossek and Habinger 1993; Smetschka 1997; Fuchs, Nöbauer and Zuckerhut 1999; Grubner and Zuckerhut 2004).[28] However, these studies and others (like Geisenhainer 2002; Ottenbacher 1999) demonstrating the different roles of female anthropologists and their contributions to anthropology's history in the context of Nazism are only marginally incorporated into mainstream anthropological knowledge. This is because, I argue, most such anthropological studies are characterised by a male-biased approach which informs the concept of 'key (male) persons' and its variations and critics.

Such foci, however, signify a dominant bias, which only takes into account particular agents within organisations, who, for the most part, are represented by politically, ethnically and confessionally dominant males in established positions of power. This not only represents a *his*tory of anthropology based on a hierarchy between men and women, but at the same time a hierarchy among women and men. Additionally, the mainstream focus is even more astonishing when one considers that anthropologists derive their identity from being strongly informed by studies carried out 'from below', and by critically reflecting on structures of dominance.

It may be concluded that it is Goldstern's and Schmidl's Jewish background in combination with their gender that led to their 'institutional death'. Compared to other female anthropologists, however, it is their Jewish background alongside their status as murdered victims of Nazism that probably led a few researchers to study their lives and work more intensively (Kossek and Habinger 1993; Ottenbacher 1999; Geisenhainer 2002) than the lives and work of female researchers who contributed to the racist and Nazi ideology (cf. Kossek and Habinger 1993) or of women who remained hidden for other reasons, to name a few different perspectives. However, it must be mentioned that there is also a difference between today's social anthropology and European ethnology in terms of studying their own history during Nazism. Without doubt the latter has begun to study its history earlier and in a more systematic way than the former due to its specific involvement with Nazism during its establishment as an academic discipline. This has certainly had an impact on getting more detailed insight into the lives and work of its institutionally exceptional women but less so in the case of non-integrated women, be they Jewish or not.

After this 'institutional death', the same influential aspects of anti-Semitism, 'race' and gender will be examined in more detail in relation to our pioneers' 'social-professional death'.

'Social-professional death'

The process of Goldstern's and Schmidl's social-professional death is informed by gender, as it is a fundamental category structuring not only society in general but also academic everyday life, organisation and knowledge in particular. At the same time, anti-Semitism and 'racialised' ascriptions become increasingly and even more relevant in these two women's lives from the late 1920s on (in the case of Goldstern) and especially in the 1930s (for both women). Nazism did not introduce either gender or 'race' as 'new' concepts. On the contrary, both present a continuation of previously existing ideas that were appropriated and modified by Nazism in a specific manner. Based on gender concepts of the Western European middle-class ideal from the nineteenth century, the constructions of female and male gender culminated in Nazism because they were strongly tied to the race ideology. According to this intersection of gender, 'race' and anti-Semitism before 1938, our two anthropologists were excluded from university positions for their Jewish background and their gender. After the Nazis took over power in Austria in 1938, however, all Jewish people were immediately dismissed from their jobs in the Civil Service for 'racial' reasons regardless of their gender.

The notion of 'race' itself also implies a gendered structure. As already mentioned in the definition of 'race' (see fn 15), it involves constructions of sexuality and gender differences that imply a naturalised opposition of female 'sensuality'/sexuality ('hybridity') and male 'culture' ('purity') (Fuchs 2003; 2005). According to this, Jewish and all non-German women of 'minor races' were 'impure' (like Jewish men) because of their association with compulsive sexuality and transgression of the boundaries of 'culture' as constructed by Nazi ideology; meanwhile the ideal for German women was constructed around 'motherhood', which would guarantee the reproduction of the German *Volk* and German soldiers who were considered fundamental in constructing German masculinity (Mosse 1985; Gehmacher 1998; Amesberger, Auer and Halbmayr 2004). To conclude, the gendered construction of 'race' was strongly based on ascribing 'too much' masculinity and 'too little' femininity to Jewish women and 'too much' femininity and 'too little' masculinity to Jewish men. Such constructions legitimised the hierarchies within genders, on the one hand, and between women and men, on the other hand (Rommelspacher 1996; Kossek 1999; Fuchs 2003; 2005; Amesberger, Auer and Halbmayr 2004).

Several anthropologists, among them teachers and previous mentors of Eugenie Goldstern and Marianne Schmidl, contributed to this race ideology to different degrees as will be shown.

Social exclusion from the 1920s through 1938

In the following section I will illustrate in more detail some aspects of Eugenie Goldstern's and Marianne Schmidl's social-professional death. Within the greater context of National Socialist jurisprudence, particular emphasis is given to the racialisation they experienced in their immediate professional environment. Specifically,

I examine those occasions when anthropology professors discriminated against and racialised Goldstern and Schmidl. In other words, I focus here on the reproduction of anti-Semitism and race ideology within the daily practices of academics.

As demonstrated earlier, the Viennese Folklore Museum, which was a site of illegal Nazi activities long before 1938 (Ottenbacher 1999), was one of the most important institutional sites for Eugenie Goldstern's anthropological work in the Austrian context. Goldstern as a modern and liberal female-Jewish researcher made considerable contributions to the reputation of the Viennese Folklore Museum collections that she had acquired during her travels through Europe and to the Near East. Being a modern anthropologist of *Volkskunde* with international recognition, she made a clear and innovative mark on the museum. She also supported the museum with a generous donation when its finances were drained after the end of the First World War. In spite of her innovative approach and the international reputation she achieved, she did not succeed in obtaining a (tenured) position in Austria or abroad. While she was finishing her studies abroad, her teacher, Michael Haberlandt, as we have seen, opportunistically turned to a nationalist and race ideology (cf. Dow and Bockhorn 2004) and Arthur Haberlandt declared that in Judaism he saw 'a racial-physiological degeneration of the female sex, in particular' and an expression of 'the wild effusiveness of sexual life' (Ottenbacher 1999: 86, quotes *Sitzungsbericht der Anthropologischen Gesellschaft 1921-1922, 1922*).[29]

This statement made by an anthropologist clearly demonstrates the gendered and sexualised construction of the race ideology by ascribing to Jewish men and women – but women in particular (cf. Fuchs 2005) – uncontrolled sexuality. As the latter would be directed towards non-Jewish people it would threaten the 'purity' of the 'German race' (Mosse 1985).

At about the same time, in 1922, Lily (Elisabeth) Weiser, a *Volkskunde* anthropologist and student of Haberlandt's rival Rudolf Much,[30] also promoted her Ph.D. on Germanic Christmas customs (Weiser 1923). In contrast to Goldstern, her dissertation was very favourably reviewed by Michael Haberlandt (Bockhorn 1994: 480). She received her *venia legendi* in 1927 for her work on Ancient Germanic men's unions (*Altgermanische Männerbünde*) (Weiser 1927) and was indeed one of the 'token' female anthropologists of *Volkskunde* with a *Habilitation* (see also fn 28), whereas it seems that the first woman in *Völkerkunde* was promoted with a *Habilitation* only in 1997. After her marriage to the Norwegian professor A. Aall, Weiser migrated to Oslo in the early 1930s. Like the 'ritualists' camp' of early *Volkskunde* she came from, she actively worked for the Nazi scientific organisation *Ahnenerbe* during the Second World War (Bockhorn 1994; Dow and Bockhorn 2004).

Experiencing the personal and political impact of the First World War and especially of increasing anti-Semitism in her job situation, Eugenie Goldstern became seriously concerned about her future, and also depressed. In her letters to M. Haberlandt (cf. Ottenbacher 1999; Catalogue of the Österreichisches Museum für Volkskunde 2004) she expressed her hopes for a job in Vienna and even apologised for her 'not being well'. The following quotation from a letter she wrote from Paris to M. Haberlandt in Vienna in July1921 illustrates her troubled situation, which sharply contrasts with that of her opportunistic teacher:

> Dear *Hofrat!*[31] Please be not angry with me for only today sending you the missing parts of my manuscript of the Münster study.[32] I have felt so constantly miserable psychologically that I was completely unable to bring myself to write. Only recently has the realisation of the absolute necessity of completing this work strengthened my willpower to do so… I hope, Sir *Hofrat*, that despite the disturbance which I have now caused, your holidays have been otherwise quiet and comfortable and that you and your wife have recovered and built up your strength well… With best regards to you and your wife, your most obedient, Eugenie Goldstern. (Copy from a letter from Eugenie Goldstern to Michael Haberlandt, in: Ottenbacher 1999: 88).

This letter represents a clear hierarchy between an established male anthropologist – who already had an anti-Semitic attitude – and a female junior researcher with no job, who is Jewish and dependent on him. Given this structural dependency the woman's language may be considered not only as polite but also as a 'language of adaption'. As such it also implies a symbolic heterosexual hierarchy between a partly weak yet busy woman acquainted with will power, and a strong man who needs to recover and to strengthen himself during his holidays. As a second symbolic gendered asymmetry, this letter represents the construction of 'a woman making trouble for a man', which is frequently used by men in everyday situations that are 'uncomfortable' for them.

While Eugenie Goldstern published her last article on children's toys in the journal edited by Michael Haberlandt in 1924 (Goldstern 1924), as we have seen, Arthur Haberlandt was not only appointed adjunct professor but also became director of the Folklore Museum. He immediately buried Goldstern's collection in a dusty storage room. This act also seems surprising insofar as Goldstern's and Trebitsch's large collections strengthened his position vis-à-vis the great pressure coming from the neighbouring discipline of *Völkerkunde* and its 'culture circles' (cf. Dow and Bockhorn 2004).

Although previously committed to comparative ethnography and then to cultural scientific research, Arthur Haberlandt also moved closer and closer to pan-Germanistic and race ideology from the 1920s onwards. In fact, he vigorously supported Austria's 'Return to the Reich' in 1938. He 'had become a *Mitläufer* [a hanger-on], an accomplice who hoped to gain advantages, at least for himself, the *Verein* [the society; HN] and the Museum. He became a member of the NSDAP and… later received assignments in the Implementation Staff Rosenberg and belonged to its Working Community for German Folklore' (Dow and Bockhorn 2004: 107; original quotation in English).

In 1924, however, Arthur Haberlandt supported an excursion to Bulgaria in which Marianne Schmidl participated together with Michael Haberlandt. Having succeeded in obtaining a tenured position at the Austrian National Library in January 1924 with the fervent support of Catholic Father Wilhelm Schmidt, Marianne Schmidl was approved a six-week holiday in order to travel to Sophia. One year later, she published two articles on this research (Schmidl 1925; 1926) and in 1926 she, too, offered a contribution to the journal. On the whole, Marianne Schmidl was very active throughout the 1920s as anthropologist of both *Völkerkunde* and *Volkskunde* in Austria and Germany alike. However, when she was nominated for a position as assistant in the ethnographic department of the renewed Viennese Natural History Museum in 1926, the director of the department rejected her because she was a woman (Geisenhainer 2002).

Eugenie Goldstern made her last donation, of three toy animals, to the museum in 1930 (Ottenbacher 1999). In the same year she wrote yet another friendly letter (Catalogue of the Österreichisches Museum für Volkskunde 2004: 41) to her teacher on the occasion of an honour that he had received. Yet he did not even respond to her letter. Not even a request for a loan of her collection for an exhibition in France in 1926 nor her international reputation could prevent her full exclusion from the academic field by her previous teachers who had become Nazi accomplices (Ottenbacher 1999).

How must she have felt when writing those friendly letters to M. Haberlandt, her professor, who had opportunistically turned to embrace nationalistic and racist ideology? How must she have felt about his 'betrayal' when she donated a considerable sum to the society one month prior to the letter quoted above? How did she, committed to a democratically based view as she was, deal with his ideology? Were her letters to M. Haberlandt an expression of her state of denial (Cohen 2001)?[33]

Fleeing social and physical death: Anne Marie Jolles and Ilona Löwy

While anti-Semitism and racism were increasing in Austria, two other female-Jewish students graduated in anthropology in Vienna. After Marianne Schmidl had graduated in 1916, another female-Jewish pioneer, Anne Marie Jolles, enrolled as a student. She was the second female anthropologist at the new institute to graduate with a Ph.D., on education in Australia (Jolles 1919). Referring to psychology and Freud, her dissertation represents a remarkably independent work. It is no less remarkable that she professed to Judaism in a historical period that was already characterised by increasing anti-Semitism. However, after only one further publication (Jolles-Kulka 1928), she very probably emigrated with her husband, Dr Emil Kulka, to New York in 1933 (Kossek and Habinger 1993).

Before 1938, a third female-Jewish anthropologist graduated as the first female student at the new Institute for *Völkerkunde* in 1932: Ilona Löwy. She was the only female anthropology student who professed to Judaism in the 1930s when the political climate was severely anti-Semitic. Löwy was the very first ethnologist to put women at the centre of her dissertation by examining girls' education in Assam and Burma (Löwy 1932). Her study is even more remarkable in that she criticised the male bias of anthropological knowledge. However, like Jolles-Kulka, she married after her Ph.D. and very probably emigrated with her husband, Dr Josef Reizes, to Palestine in 1938 (Kossek and Habinger 1993).

Immediately after the *Anschluss* ('annexation') of Austria in 1938, all Jewish students and academics were banished from the University of Vienna.

Approaching physical death: 1938 and after

I have shown that Eugenie Goldstern was increasingly excluded from the scientific community in Vienna from the mid-1920s. While her public social-professional life was fully disturbed, her personal social network was not, for she was socially integrated into her extended family and into the social life of her brother's sanatorium. In this difficult situation, as we have noted, she seems not to have been very well respected by her brothers because of her unmarried status and joblessness (Ottenbacher 1999). Her social death intensified in the 1930s and in particular from 1938 on, when the National Socialist terror against the Jewish population was turned into systematic exclusion, deprivation, banishment and deportation. After the pogrom of 10 November 1938, most of her family members fled Vienna for different countries. Eugenie Goldstern and her elder brother Sima remained in Vienna.

Whereas Marianne Schmidl had received much support and gained a solid reputation in the scientific community during the previous years, she experienced a rupture immediately after the *Anschluss*. A few weeks after her promotion at the National Library in 1938, Schmidl required six months sick leave. She suffered from severe digestive problems and this had a serious impact on her health. Only a few days prior to the approval of her sick leave, on March 12, Austria was also formally 'annexed' to the German Reich. Like all Austrians, she had to prove her Aryan descent immediately.[34] However, as Marianne Schmidl was Jewish on her father's side, a letter arrived to inform her that 'she was no longer allowed to work in the National Library' and the demand was made that she 'request to be permanently retired' (Geisenhainer 2002: 289). According to this demand she was granted an annual retirement benefit (*Ruhegenuß*) of half of her earlier income (Kossek and Habinger 1993; Geisenhainer 2002).

Like the rest of the Jewish population, Marianne Schmidl also began to suffer under the Nazi race laws at the time. Her economic situation rapidly deteriorated and she became dependent on her brother-in-law's support.

Schmidl also fell victim to a long-standing hate campaign initiated by a German anthropology professor, Otto Reche. Reche was head of the Institute for Anthropology and Ethnography at the University of Vienna from 1924 to 1927. He gave racist lectures and promoted racist dissertations. Under his chair, women also graduated with clearly racial/racist topics (Kossek and Habinger 1993). As a convinced Nazi, he founded a racist society entitled *Wiener Gesellschaft für Rassenpflege* (literally: Viennese Society for Racial Hygiene; HN) in 1925 in Vienna (cf. Kossek and Habinger 1993; Linimayr 1994; Geisenhainer 2002).[35] In 1927 he was appointed professor at the University of Leipzig, where he changed the name of the institute and thus became director of the *Institut für Rassen- und Völkerkunde* (Institute for Racial and Ethnological Studies).

Reche was the professor chosen as newly appointed director of the research institute titled *Staatlich-Sächsisches Forschungsinstitut für Völkerkunde* in Leipzig where Schmidl had previously been granted funding. The funding was for completing her wide-ranging study of African basket weaving. She had begun to compare techniques of African basket weaving in the late 1920s and did research in several Western European ethnology museums. Her work had already been presented at a conference in 1926 and was published in an article in 1927 (Schmidl 1927). However, because she was an extreme perfectionist, Schmidl was again late with her research results just as she had been in previous years. Especially because she was a woman, she had to be that much better to obtain approval within male academia. Additionally, this particular research project was so immense that it was difficult to complete (Geisenhainer 2002). Consequently, she asked Reche, whom she probably knew from Vienna, for an extension for the submission of her research results. Reche rejected her plea and tried to institute legal proceedings against her in 1934 in order to force her to refund the money. He obviously knew about her Jewish background as he referred to her as 'the Jew Schmidl'. At the same time, Reche had meanwhile shown his satisfaction with the new formal opportunity in Germany 'to reject an author because of his/her Jewishness' (Gaisenhainer 2002: 287). However, due to the resistance of the University Council, he was unable to institute legal proceedings against her in 1934. Finally, Reche intensified his hate campaign from 1938 onwards and started legal proceedings against Schmidl who was sick and had been fired from her position in the National Library. She deliberately proposed to Reche that he accept her research material 'into which she had put great effort and work' because she was not able to refund the money (Geisenhainer 2002: 292). She sent her manuscript to him in 1939. At the same time, she asked another professor, Bernd Ankermann, for support. Ankermann attempted to make Reche more conciliatory. The latter, however, vehemently refused. In his letter to Ankermann from May 1939 he wrote:

> [I]t goes without saying that it is impossible for the very strongly Jewish Schmidl to publish her material in a German journal; in the same vein, publication in a foreign journal is also unacceptable because then the lady could write anything she pleased, which would be beyond our control and thus damage the German reputation; and she would negate her responsibility by moving her place of residence… (Geisenhainer 2002: 293).

Reche asked two male professors, Martin Heydrich from Dresden and Johannes Lehmann from Frankfurt, to 'improve' and publish Schmidl's research material. Heydrich declined because he did not have enough time. He responded to Reche in July 1939 that he had never seen Marianne Schmidl nor had he known that she was Jewish, and then concluded 'yet the business acumen needed to win such an enviable grant for museum visits very much confirms the race diagnosis' (Geisenhainer 2002: 294). Also the other anthropologist, a rival of Schmidl, was quick to ascribe racial 'abilities' to Schmidl. Accordingly, Lehmann responded to Reche in February 1940: 'At that time I did not know that she was Jewish... But she was accused rather bluntly by Germann [a colleague from the Leipzig museum, HN] of her Jewish behaviour during her studies at the Leipzig museum. She had made demands of the attendants in an improperly heavy-handed manner...' (Geisenhainer 2002: 294).

1942: Deportation and murder

The racist terror outside academia and the hate campaign within led Schmidl's family and her friends to advise her to emigrate. However, like Eugenie Goldstern, she did not. After having spent much of her money on the museum, like Goldstern, and after having been deprived of most of their wealth by the 'race laws', unfavourable economic circumstances prevented both women from leaving; but this was probably not their only reason for staying (cf. Geisenhainer 2002). After the expansion of the Nazi regime in Austria's neighbouring countries, Goldstern's and Schmidl's chances of emigrating diminished greatly from 1940 onwards. Both researchers were not famous enough to receive support from abroad as was the case with some other Jewish and dissident intellectuals. Having been cut off from all-important social-professional ties, Eugenie Goldstern and Marianne Schmidl had to face and suffer the systematic terror of Nazism like so many other Jewish people and other victims of Nazism. After the Jewish population had been systematically forced to restrict their living space and movements to the open ghetto of the Viennese Ninth District, the next step, to its deportation, was already rather close. Jewish people had to buy and wear the yellow Star of David, which Eugenie Goldstern bought on 19 September 1941 from the *Israelitische Kultusgemeinde* (Ottenbacher 1999: 108). Jewish people were ordered to give notice in their place of residence and to 'apply for a permit for travel'. Leaflets were handed out with notes on a few personal things for travelling. In addition they were issued with a sort of identity card carrying their fingerprints and a stamp of the letter 'J' signifying 'transport' of Jews. Their homes and possessions were confiscated before they were carried off to 'transit camps' in Vienna. Members of the Rosenberg Bureau in which Goldstern's and Schmidl's former colleagues participated examined the confiscated Jewish possessions for possible use by Nazis. After having been forced into 'transit camps', Jewish men, women and children were taken to railway stations from where they were deported to various concentration camps.

Between April and June 1942, about 6,000 Viennese Jews were deported to Izbica in eastern Poland. It was an *Auffanglager* (intermediate camp) where the deportees were deprived of their last valuables before being sent to the extermination camps of Belzec and Sobibor. Marianne Schmidl and Eugenie Goldstern were among these people. On 9 April 1942, at the age of fifty-two, Marianne Schmidl was deported with 998 others to Izbica. Schmidl sent three messages from there to her brother-in-law's family. They were the last signs of her still being alive before she was murdered by the Nazis (Kossek and Habinger 1993; Geisenhainer 2002).

Only two months later, on 14 June, Eugenie Goldstern, fifty-eight years old, was deported with 1,000 others also to Izbica or Sobibor.[36] There she was 'murdered by those henchmen who had converted what folklorists worked up as the primacy of the Aryans into a deadly practice'(Dow and Bockhorn 2004: 100, quote Ottenbacher 1999: 111).

Having been built for expelled Jews in the eighteenth century, Izbica was a small town in the southwest of Lublin. In spring 1942, however, its inhabitants were forced to 'resettle' and were subsequently murdered in Sobibor. It became a huge ghetto and 'intermediate camp' for the deported. About 4,000 older Jewish people were immediately killed and buried in mass graves by the Nazis in Izbica while many other Jews were 'selected' to work in the camps for German enterprises (cf. Ottenbacher 1999).

Even without knowing more personal details about Goldstern's and Schmidl's assassination it may be concluded that from their arrival in the 'intermediate' and concentration camps onwards they had to endure violent experiences informed and shaped by their gender and the National Socialist hierarchisation of 'races' and prisoners. According to the Nazi race ideology Jewish people were ascribed to the 'lowest' categories of prisoners along with homosexuals, Roma and Sinti people. As Amesberger, Auer and Halbmayr (2004) have carefully and convincingly shown in their study of female survivors of concentration camps, all these women had experienced a broad range of 'sexualised violence'. Goldstern and Schmidl may also be assumed to have experienced diverse forms of direct/personal violence as well as indirect/structural violence. It must be emphasized, however, that their experiences of 'sexualised violence' had already begun before arrival in the concentration camp: their integrity and privacy[37] were already significantly compromised when they were carried off to 'transit camps' in Vienna as well as during their deportation to Poland.

In Lemberg, on 1 August 1942, Governor General Dr Hans Frank publicly announced the collective murder of Jewish people by stating: 'The Jew is no longer a problem in this country but at best he [in German: male expression; HN] is suitable for racial [in German: *artgemäß*; HN] interest on our part' (Ottenbacher 1999: 114).

It is to be hoped that the 'interest' expressed in this sentence, which points to the tragedy of the physical death of these two pioneering anthropologists and the collective murder of many Jews and others will not be supported by future anthropologists in any way as it has been in the past.

Conclusion

In this chapter I have demonstrated Eugenie Goldstern's and Marianne Schmidl's multiple positionings and experiences as Jewish women who were passionate and innovative anthropologists. At particular stages of their biographies, I have highlighted the similarities and differences in their ties to family, academic organisations, the scientific community and nation. In particular, I have analysed how 'race' and gender have informed and defined the stages of their 'triple death'. I have also demonstrated how anthroplogy and politics had an effect on both women, leading to the disintegration of their lives and, in particular, to their 'triple deaths'.

Acknowledgements

My warmest thanks go to Michaela Aloni, Esther Hertzog, Sabine Strasser and to anonymous reviewers for their enriching comments on an earlier draft of this essay and to Andre Gingrich and Gertraud Seiser for their most helpful discussions about the history of anthropology in the German-speaking area. I am most grateful also to Julene Knox and Lisa Rosenblatt for their professional and careful editing.

Notes

1   'Austria is free!' was famously said by Foreign Minister Leopold Figl to the Austrian population from the balcony of the Belvedere Castle in Vienna after the signing of the State Treaty in 1955. This proclamation and the picture of the scene on the balcony are part of a persisting national memory, for instance, in schoolbooks and on TV. Historically it is strongly connected to state neutrality. Therefore, it also implies the commitment to work actively towards peace both nationally and internationally. Significant background for this is also the political identification with the status of first victim of Nazism. This reduced status has indeed been contested on an ongoing basis, for it denies Austria's active role in Nazism.

2   For instance, the refusal of formal acknowledgement of the left resistance movement and the *Wehrmacht* deserters.

3   The civil protests also included the so-called 'Thursday marches': for over a year, and still continuing to a lesser extent today, protesters gathered every Thursday in Vienna and also in other parts of Austria to march against the People's Party's coalition with the Freedom Party. A remarkable number of academics, among them socio-cultural anthropologists, supported and initiated protest letters against the coalition.

4   Although the boundaries between the distinct approaches of feminist anthropology are certainly not strict and are informing each other my argumentation is based upon Moore's (1988) distinction between women's studies, gender studies and studies of differences among women. With regard to this distinction it must be acknowledged that a few women anthropologists are mentioned or even honored in one way or the other by male researchers writing anthropology's history in the context of Vienna (like for instance Linimayr 1994 and Gingrich 2000/01 with regard to Anna Hohenwart-Gerlachstein, Bockhorn 1994 to

Lily Weiser, and Dow and Bockhorn 2004 to Eugenie Goldstern). Nevertheless only a very small number of anthropologists put an analysis of gender into the center of their research of anthropology's history. However, Eugenie Goldstern's biographer, Albert Ottenbacher, who is a historian, must be emphazised in this respect as an exception.

5 For ethnologists who were persecuted and forced to emigrate see Hauschild (1995). Anthropology's history/herstory in the German-speaking area, however, especially lacks studies on female-Jewish anthropologists who emigrated/went to exile.

6 For Kaplan, who analysed everyday life experiences of Jewish women in Germany, social death, that is, the loss of Jewish people's social networks, is a crucial precondition for their physical death.

7 According to Fischer (1990) 'key persons' are those few who determine the relevant theories of a historical period, and shape the scientific community and a discipline more significantly than others. 'Without doubt not all persons have *the same influence, significance and recognition* within the (every) scientific community. *If statements about "the" ethnology can be made*, at all, then mainly so, based on the examples of key persons' (Fischer 1990: 5; translation and emphasis by HN).
All subsequent translations of quotations are the author's unless otherwise stated.

8 The theory of the intersection of gender with race, class, ethnicity, religion, sexual identity and so forth was introduced into anthropology by Women of Colour mainly in the late 1980s and early 1990s.

9 In this biographical introduction, I refer mainly to Eugenie Goldstern's biography by Ottenbacher (1999) and to Kossek and Habinger (1993) and Geisenhainer (2002) regarding Marianne Schmidl.

10 Therefore many female anthropologists had other jobs, often as teachers in primary and secondary schools and in the Civil Service. In other cases they relied financially on their families or husbands (cf. Kossek and Habinger 1993).

11 Founded in 1365, the University of Vienna only allowed women to study in 1897. After serious struggles within 'male-only academia' Austria was, after Prussia, the last European country to allow women's entry into the university (Heindl and Tichy 1990).

12 This percentage of female-Jewish students was rather high considering that people of Jewish confession represented 5 percent of the Austrian population. Compared to this, the relation between Austria's Catholic majority of 80 percent and the 69 percent of Catholic female students at the Faculty of Philosophy may be seen to be rather low (Kossek and Habinger 1993 [no page no.], quote Heindl and Wytek 1988).

13 In 1933/34, for instance, only 12.6 percent were female-Jewish students (Kossek and Habinger 1993 [no page no.], quote Heindl and Wytek 1988). Unfortunately, there seem to be no statistics on female students of anthropology in the first three decades of the twentieth century (cf. Kossek and Habinger 1993).

14 A prominent book of that time, written by a Dr Möbius and entitled *Über den physiologischen Schwachsinn des Weibes* ('On the physiological *deficiency* of the Woman'), was extensively republished in the first two decades of the twentieth century (Kullik 1990).

15 Signifying 'gendered deviation', the German word *Mannweib* (sgl./pl. *Mannweiber*) has a strongly negative meaning even today; it is used to describe a woman who does not behave as society expects of women, but rather, behaves in ways expected of men.

16 There is a broad and diverse anthropological body of knowledge on the notion of 'race' and racism (cf. Anthias and Yuval-Davis 1992; Brah 1992; Frankenberg 1993; 1996; Stolcke 1995; Fuchs and Habinger 1996; Kossek 1999; Fuchs 2003; Gingrich 2004; Strasser, forthcoming). This chapter, however, refers to 'race' as defined by French ethnologist Gobineau in the mid-nineteenth century in order to justify the social inequality of his age. According to Gobineau's doctrine, 'the different races of humankind are innately unequal in talent, worth and ability to absorb and create culture, and change their innate character only through crossing with alien strains... Only the white race', according to him, 'is creative of culture, but it was exhausted because its racial composition was no longer pure' (Dostal 1994: 253, quoting Encyclopedia Britannica, X 1962: 459). With this idea Gobineau constructed an opposition between 'culture' and 'racial fusion', whereby only the 'Aryan race' represented 'culture' (Hannaford 1996: 265f.; Fuchs 2005: 11).

When claiming precedence in the formulations of nation and state from the late nineteenth century on, this idea of race became crucial not only for intellectuals in Europe, the United States and Australia alike but also for Hitler and Nazism (cf. Hannaford 1996). As a consequence, Hitler's ideological fabrication of state 'was based on the idea that there was a difference in the respective *natures* of the Jewish and German races' (Hannaford 1996: 365; emphasis HN). In accordance with this 'naturalisation' of difference, the German Ministry of the Interior and the Ministry of Education and Science defined race 'as a human group distinguished from other groups by physical, moral and intellectual characteristics sui generis resulting from consanguineous relations between its members' (Hannaford 1996: 367). While 'race' had a purely biological base, nation had a historical one. It described 'a group unified by ties of blood, common destiny, and common ties of migration, language, and tradition. It followed, therefore, that nobody could be considered to belong to a national community if he or she belonged to a race with no consanguineous relations, cultural or otherwise' (Hannaford ibid.). In a similar vein, the programme of the National Socialist Party in Germany of February 1920 already defined a 'citizen' as a member of the German race; a person of German blood and descent without any other references. Thus no Jews could be members of the German race (Hannaford 1996: 363ff.).

As Fuchs (2003; 2005) has convincingly demonstrated, this idea of race simultaneously and clearly involves constructions of sexuality and gender differences. According to her, it implies a naturalised opposition of female 'sensuality'/sexuality ('hybridity') and male 'culture' ('purity').

In using 'racialised' I therefore address the historical process of ascribing racial 'qualities' to Jewish people according to this complex construction of differences.

Additional comment, however, is necessary in this respect: the term 'race' has been used very differently in the German and English languages after the Second World War. In German-speaking realms, the academic and political usage of 'race'/*Rasse* became completely unacceptable after 1945, as part of the efforts to leave Nazism behind. The fact that 'race' became a non-word, however, does not result in the disappearance of racism or xenophobia. Rather it is necessary to study empirically local and global forms of contemporary concepts of 'race vanishing/racism rising' (Gingrich 2004: 158ff.).

17 The title Extra-Ordinary Professor (or *Extraordinarius* or Adjunct Docent) must be distinguished from Full Professor (or *Ordinarius*) in German-speaking academic spheres. While for both titles a *Habilitation* (postdoctoral/second thesis) is required, the latter position is characterised by more rights and privileges. However, Michael Haberlandt had no licence to take the oral doctoral examinations. Only his son and successor Arthur Haberlandt succeeded in getting it (Jacobeit, Lixfeld and Bockhorn 1994; Dow and Bockhorn 2004).

18 Known today, in English, as the Austrian Museum of Folk Life and Folk Art (http://www.volkskundemuseum.at/sprachen/english.htm [accessed 15-11-2004]).

19 It comprised physical anthropology and ethnology. Graduation was possible in *Völkerkunde*/ethnology at that time but not in *Volkskunde,* which was included with specific lectures in Ethnology.

20 In particular, this was the 'Viennese school' of *Kulturkreise* ('Culture Circles').

21 Schmidt's anti-Semitism is analysed by Conte (1987) and Dostal (1994) in detail. Parts of his anti-Semitic writings were used by the Nazi propagandists who left out the Catholic elements and focused on the anti-Semitic and pan-Germanistic ones (Conte 1987: 269f.).

22 It must be emphasised, however, that *Volkskunde* in the German-language spheres and also in Vienna was more heterogeneous than represented within this context considering Goldstern and Schmidl.

23 Eugenie's teachers and mentors included Michael Haberlandt and Rudolf Trebitsch (both in Austria), Paul Girardin (Switzerland) and Arnold van Gennep (Switzerland and later France). Marianne's teachers and mentors included Michael Haberlandt, Wilhelm Koppers, Rudolf Pöch, Wilhelm Schmidt (all in Austria), and Fritz Krause (Germany). From the perspective of methodological and theoretical orientation, both women may be ascribed to have been critical though distinct parts of the secular diffusionists of that time.

24 See the feminist study on differences of gender, class, 'race', ethnicity, religion and social obligations in academia by Nöbauer and Zuckerhut 2002.

25 For instance, Eugenie Goldstern had a close professional relationship with the Jewish ethnologist Rudolf Trebitsch, who committed suicide in 1918 after his tragic experiences during the First World War.
    Another Jewish ethnologist of that time with whom the two female anthropologists seemed to have had no relation was Friedrich Salomon Krauss. Studying sexualities and eroticism, he was attacked by several of his ethnology colleagues. His intense exchange with Sigmund Freud characterised a close relationship between ethnology and psychoanalysis at that time (Daxelmüller 1994a). Yet another Jewish anthropologist with a particularly Austrian aristocratic bacgound was Robert Heine-Geldern, a Professor/ *Dozent* at the newly founded Institute for *Völkerkunde*; he remained in exile during his

visit to the U.S. in 1938 and returned to Vienna in 1946 (Linimayer 1994).

Apart from these scholars mentioned here, there was also a *Gesellschaft für Jüdische Volkskunde* (Society for Jewish Folklore Studies) founded by Rabbi Dr Max Grunbaum. However, both of our female anthropologists maintained their distance from it, and F.S. Krauss who was also against nationalist ideologies overtly criticised this society (cf. Daxelmüller 1989; 1994a; 1994b).

26 An exhibition held from August 2004 to February 2005 at the Austrian Museum of Folk Life and Folk Art presented the ethnographic collection of Eugenie Goldstern. It was entitled 'Ur-Ethnographie. Auf der Suche nach dem Elementaren in der Kultur. Die Sammlung Eugenie Goldstern'.

27 While *Volkskunde* offered lectures held by a woman with a *Habilitation*, namely Lily Weiser, already in the late 1920s *Völkerkunde* had only two non-graduated women as part of its staff from the 1940s on: Anna Hohenwart-Gerlachstein and Erika Sulzmann. The latter followed Annemarie Hefel who was a graduated assistant for only a very short period. Hohenwart-Gerlachstein must be particularly respectfully mentioned here for she saved the institute's valuable materials and could graduate only later in 1951 on the topic of women in Ancient Egypt. Her graduation remained prevented during the years of Hermann Baumann as head of the department and who was a member of the NSDAP (Hohenwart-Gerlachstein 1951; Kossek and Habinger 1993; Linimayr 1994; Smetschka 1997; Gingrich 2000/01).

28 A dictionary on women of the first generation of academics in Austria (Keintzel/Korotin 2002) contributes to a alternative representation of academia's history.

29 Another professor, Robert Stigler, ascribed to Jewish women a 'masculinisation' of their gender, which, according to him, was a reason why Jewish women represented a majority among female political revolutionaries and leaders. Jewish women, he said, would 'blur their psychological femininity... in particular, a withdrawal of their specifically female instincts, of female passivity and of inhibitions of those psycho-motor stimuli typical for women (for instance a shyness in public performance)...' (Ottenbacher 1999: 86). According to Fuchs' (2005) analysis this is clearly informed by the race idea based on Gobineau and adopted by the Nazi ideology.

30 The so-called 'ritualists' around Much focused on Germanic and Nordic studies of rituals and men's unions (*Männerbünde*) and became regular University of Vienna faculty (Bockhorn and Dow 2004).

31 The Austrian term *Hofrat* (Court Councillor) is an honorary title conferred on senior tenured staff in the Civil Service. It is still used today.

32 The study on Münstertal was published in Goldstern 1922.

33 Cohen (2001) emphasises that not only perpetrators and observers but also victims practice denial. He states that denial connotes a belief that suffering is always happening elsewhere but not to oneself, on the one hand, and to the fact that suffering is not publicly acknowledged in most societies on a macro- and micro-level. He emphasises that Jewish communities in Germany and the rest of Europe – in spite of clear warning signals and explicit warnings – refused to believe what was about to happen to them, or was already

happening to their fellow Jews (2001: 14).

34 In Austria in 1938, as in 1933 in Germany, the Law for the Reconstruction of the Body of Public Functionaries dismissed all Communists and Jews, all the inefficient and the untrained (cf. Hannaford 1996: 366).

35 Despite his ideological position, Reche was honoured by the Austrian Republic as recently as 1965 (Kossek and Habinger 1993).

36 According to Ottenbacher (1999) and Bockhorn and Dow (2004) it is not clear if Eugenie Goldstern was deported to Izbica or further to Sobibor. While the first assumes that she was deported to Izbica, Bockhorn and Dow assume that it was Sobibor.

37 As Amesberger, Auer and Halbmayr (2004) point out in detail, the loss of integrity and privacy was powerfully experienced due to reduced and missed opportunities for hygiene, lack of clothes and especially due to being forced to get all hair cut off, being naked in front of Nazi soldiers and due to menstruation (whilst menstruation ceased for many women after their arrival in the concentration camps, others had to make do with makeshift sanitary protection).

References

Amesberger, Helga, Katrin Auer and Brigitte Halbmayr (2004). *Sexualisierte Gewalt Weibliche Erfahrungen in NS-Konzentrationslagern*. Wien: Mandelbaum Verlag.

Anthias, Floya and Nira Yuval-Davis (1992). *Racialized boundaries. Race, nation, gender, colour and class and the anti-racist struggle*. London and New York: Routledge.

Bandhauer-Schöffmann, Irene (1990). Frauenbewegung und Studentinnen. Zum Engagement der österreichischen Frauenvereine für das Frauenstudium, in: Heindl, Waltraud/Tichy, Marina (Eds.), *Durch Erkenntnis zu Freiheit und Glück...': Frauen an der Universität Wien (ab 1897)*. Wien: WUV-Verlag.

Bockhorn, Olaf (1994). Von Ritualen, Mythen und Lebenskreisen: Volkskunde im Umfeld der Universität Wien. In: Jacobeit, Wolfgang, Hannjost Lixfeld and Olaf Bockhorn (Eds.), *Völkische Wissenschaft. Gestalten und Tendenzen der deutschen und österreichischen Volkskunde in der ersten Hälfte des 20. Jahrhunderts*. Wien, Köln, Weimar: Böhlau Verlag, pp. 477-526.

Brah, Avtar (1992). Difference, Diversity and Differentiation. In: James Donald/Ali Rattansi (Eds.), *"Race", Culture and Society*. London et al.

Byer, Doris (1999). *Der Fall Hugo A. Bernatzik. Ein Leben zwischen Ethnologie und Öffentlichkeit 1897-1953*. Wien, Köln, Weimar: Böhlau.

Cohen, Stanley (2002). *States of Denial. Knowing about Atrocities and Suffering*. Cambridge: Polity Press.

Conte, Edouard (1987). Wilhelm Schmidt: Des letzten Kaisers Beichtvater und das ‚neudeutsche Heidentum'. In: Gerndt, Helge (Ed.), *Volkskunde und Nationalsozialismus*. Münchner Beiträge zur Volkskunde. Band 7. München:

Münchner Vereinigung für Volkskunde, pp. 261-278.

Daxelmüller, Christoph (1989). Nationalsozialistisches Kulturverständnis und das Ende der jüdischen Volkskunde. In: Gerndt, Helge (Ed.), *Volkskunde und Nationalsozialismus*. Münchner Beiträge zur Volkskunde. Band 7. München: Münchner Vereinigung für Volkskunde, pp. 149-167.

Daxelmüller, Christoph (1994a). Friedrich Salomo Krauss (Salomon Friedrich Kraus[s]) (1859-1938). In: Jacobeit, Wolfgang, Hannjost Lixfeld and Olaf Bockhorn (Eds.), *Völkische Wissenschaft. Gestalten und Tendenzen der deutschen und österreichischen Volkskunde in der ersten Hälfte des 20. Jahrhunderts.* Wien, Köln, Weimar: Böhlau Verlag, pp. 463-476.

Daxelmüller, Christoph (1994b). Jüdische Volkskunde in Deutschland zwischen Assimilation und neuer Identität. Anmerkungen zum gesellschaftlichen Bezug einer vergessenen Wissenschaft. In: Jacobeit, Wolfgang, Hannjost Lixfeld and Olaf Bockhorn (Eds.), *Völkische Wissenschaft. Gestalten und Tendenzen der deutschen und österreichischen Volkskunde in der ersten Hälfte des 20. Jahrhunderts.* Wien, Köln, Weimar: Böhlau Verlag, pp. 87-114.

Dow, James R. and Hannsjost Lixfeld (Eds.) (1994). *The Nazification of an Academic Discipline. German Volkskunde of the Third Reich. Folklore Studies in Translation.* Bloomington: Indiana.

Dow, James R. and Olaf Bockhorn (2004). *The Study of European Ethnology in Austria.* Aldershot: Ashgate.

Dostal, Walter (1994). Silence in the darkness: German ethnology during the National Socialist Period. *Social Anthropology* 2(3), pp. 251-262.

Fischer, Hans (1990). *Völkerkunde im Nationalsozialismus. Aspekte der Anpassung, Affinität und Behauptung einer wissenschaftlichen Disziplin.* Berlin: Reimer.

Fuchs, Brigitte (2003). *‚Rasse', ‚Volk', Geschlecht. Anthropologische Diskurse in Österreich 1850-1960.* Frankfurt am Main/New York: Campus Verlag.

Fuchs, Brigitte (2005). ‚Kultur' und ‚Hybridität': Diskurse über ‚Rasse', Sexualität und ‚Mischung' in Österreich 1867 bis 1914. *Austrian Studies in Social Anthropology* 1/2005, http://www.univie.ac.at/alumni.ethnologie/journal

Fuchs; Brigitte and Gabriele Habinger (Eds.) (1996). *Rassismen und Feminismen. Differenzen, Machtverhältnisse und Solidarität zwischen Frauen.* Wien Promedia Verlag.

Fuchs, Brigitte, Herta Nöbauer and Patricia Zuckerhut (1999). *‚Das Fremde im Eigenen'. Eine Ethnographie der feministischen Forschung im deutschsprachigen Raum.* Research Report, Vienna. Funded by the Austrian National Bank and the City of Vienna.

Gehmacher, Johanna (1998). Mutter/Beruf. Deutschnationale und nationalsozialistische Debatten um Mutterpflichten und Frauenberufe. Ein Vortrag und zwei Textversionen. In: Perko, Gudrun (Ed.), *Mutterwitz. Das Phänomen Mutter – eine Gestaltung zwischen Ohnmacht und Allmacht.* Wien: Milena, pp. 117-139.

Geisenhainer, Katja (2002). Marianne Schmidl (1890-1942). *Zeitschrift für Ethnologie* 127 (2), pp. 269-300.

Gerndt, Helge (Ed.) (1987). *Volkskunde und Nationalsozialismus. Referate und Diskussionen einer Tagung.* Münchner Beiträge zur Volkskunde. München: Münchner Vereinigung für Volkskunde.

Gingrich, Andre (2000/01). Anna Hohenwart-Gerlachstein zum 90. Geburtstag. *Mitteilungen der Anthropologischen Gesellschaft in Wien* 130/31, pp. 215-217.

Gingrich, Andre (2004). Concepts of Race Vanishing, Movements of Racism Rising? Global Issues and Austrian Ethnography. *Ethnos* 69(2), pp. 156-176.

Gingrich, Andre (2005). The German-speaking Countries. In: Barth, Fredrik, Andre Gingrich, Robert Parkin and Sydel Silverman, *One Discipline, Four Ways: British, German, French and American Anthropology – The Halle Lectures.* Chicago: Chicago University Press, pp.61-153.

Gingrich, Andre (in press). Anthropology under Hitler. Exploring an academic past and implications for the present. The Eleventh Annual Sidney W. Mintz Lecture in Anthropology, John Hopkins University, Baltimore, November 10th 2004.

Goldstern, Eugenie (1912). Twardowski, der polnische Faust. *Zeitschrift für österreichische Volkskunde* XVIII, pp. 36-46.

Goldstern, Eugenie (1918). Beiträge zur Volkskunde des Lammertals, mit besonderer Berücksichtigung von Abtenau (Tännengau). *Zeitschrift für österreichische Volkskunde* XXIV, pp. 1-29.

Goldstern, Eugenie (1921). Das Haus in Bessans (Savoyen). *Wiener Zeitschrift für Volkskunde* XXVII, pp.33-56.

Goldstern, Eugenie (1922a). Hochgebirgsvolk in Savoyen und Graubünden. Ein Beitrag zur romanischen Volkskunde. I. Bessans. Volkskundliche monographische Studie über eine savoyische Hochgebigsgemeinde (Frankreich); II. Beiträge zur Volkskunde des bündnerischen Münstertales (Schweiz). (= Ergänzungsband XIV zur *Wiener Zeitschrift für Volkskunde* 1921).

Goldstern, Eugenie (1922b). Bessans. Volkskundliche monographische Studie über eine savoyische Hochgebirgsgemeinde. Ph.D. thesis: University of Fribourg. (Ergänzungsband VIV zum XXVII. Jg. *Wiener Zeitschrift für Volkskunde*).

Goldstern, Eugenie (1922c). Beiträge zur Volkskunde des bündnerischen Münstertales (Schweiz). (Ergänzungsband XIV zum XXVII. Jg. *Wiener Zeitschrift für Volkskunde*).

Goldstern, Eugenie (1923). Eine volkskundliche Erkundungsreise im Aostatale (Piemont). Vorläufige Mitteilung. *Wiener Zeitschrift für Volkskunde* 28. Jg., pp. 55-57.

Goldstern, Eugenie (1924). Alpine Spielzeugtiere. Ein Beitrag zur Erforschung des primitiven Spielzeuges. *Wiener Zeitschrift für Volkskunde* 29. Jg., pp. 3-4; 45-71.

Haberlandt, Michael (1900). *Cultur im Alltag.* Wien.

Hannaford, Ivan (1996). *Race. The History of an Idea in the West.* Washington, D.C.: The Woodrow Wilson Center Press and Baltimore, London: The John Hopkins University Press.

Hauschild, Thomas (1987). Völkerkunde im ‚Dritten Reich'. In: Gerndt, Helge (Ed.), *Volkskunde und Nationalsozialismus.* München: Münchner Vereinigung für Volkskunde, pp. 245-259.

Hauschild, Thomas (Ed.) (1995). *Lebenslust und Fremdenfurcht. Ethnologie im Dritten Reich.* Frankfurt a.M.: Suhrkamp.

Heindl, Waltraud and Tichy, Marina (Eds.) (1990). ‚*Durch Erkenntnis zu Freiheit und* Glück...': Frauen an der Universität Wien (ab 1897). Wien: WUV-Verlag.

Heiß, Gernot et al. (Eds.) (1989). *Willfährige Wissenschaft. Die Universität Wien 1938-1945.* Österreichische Texte zur Gesellschaftskritik. Band 43. Wien: Verlag für Gesellschaftskritik.

Hohenwart-Gerlachstein, Anna (1951). *Die Stellung der Frau im Alten Ägypten. Eine ägyptologisch-ethnologische Studie.* PhD thesis: University of Vienna.

Jacobeit, Wolfgang, Hannjost Lixfeld and Olaf Bockhorn (Eds.) (1994). *Völkische* Wissenschaft. Gestalten und Tendenzen der deutschen und österreichischen *Volkskunde in der ersten Hälfte des 20. Jahrhunderts.* Wien, Köln, Weimar: Böhlau Verlag.

Jolles, Annemarie (1919). *Die Erziehung bei den Australiern. Eine Untersuchung über die ersten Anfangs- und Entstehungsgründe der Erziehung.* PhD thesis: University of Vienna.

Jolles-Kulke, Annemarie (1928). Über das Feuer. Ein volkskundliches Stundenbild in 2 Teilen. *Völkerkunde* IV, pp. 81ff and 176-180.

Kaplan, Marion (2001). *Der Mut zum Überleben. Jüdische Frauen und ihre Familien in Deutschland.* Berlin: Aufbau Verlag.

Keintzel, Brigitta and Ilse Korotin (Eds.) (2002). *Wissenschafterinnen in und aus Österreich. Leben-Werk-Wirken.* Wien, Köln, Weimar: Böhlau Verlag.

Kossek, Brigitte (Ed.) (1999). *Gegen-Rassismen. Konstruktionen, Interaktionen, Interventionen.* Hamburg, Berlin: Argument Verlag.

Kossek, Brigitte and Gabriele Habinger (1993). *Ausblendungen – Zur Geschichte der Wiener Ethnologinnen von 1913 bis 1945 und ihrer Vorgängerinnen.* Research Report, Vienna.

Kullik, Rosemarie (1990). *Frauen ‚gehen fremd'. Eine Wissenschaftsgeschichte der Wegbereiterinnen der deutschen Ethnologie.* Bonn: Holos.

Linimayr, Peter (1994). *Wiener Völkerkunde im Nationalsozialismus. Ansätze zu einer NS-Wissenschaft.* : Frankfurt am Main, Wien: Peter Lang.

Löwy, Illona (1932). *Die Erziehung der Mädchen in Assam und Birma.* Ph.D. thesis: University of Vienna.

Mayer, Adelheid (1991). *Die Völkerkunde an der Universität Wien bis 1938.* MA thesis: University of Vienna.

Moore, Henrietta (1988). *Feminism and Anthropology.* Cambridge: Polity Press.

Mosse, George (1985). *Nationalismus und Sexualität. Bürgerliche Moral und sexuelle Normen.* München, Wien: Rowohlt.

Neugebauer, Wolfgang and Peter Schwarz (2005). *Der Wille zum aufrechten Gang. Offenlegung der Rolle des BSA bei der gesellschaftlichen Reintegration ehemaliger Nationalsozialisten.* Herausgegeben vom Bund sozialdemokratischer AkademikerInnen, Intellektueller und KünstlerInnen (BSA). Wien: Czernin Verlag.

Nöbauer, Herta and Patricia Zuckerhut (2002). *Differenzen. Einschlüsse und Ausschlüsse – Innen und Außen - Universität und freie Wissenschaft.* Materialien zur Förderung von Frauen in der Wissenschaft. Band 12. Wien: Bundesministerium für Bildung, Wissenschaft und Kultur.

Österreichisches Museum für Volkskunde (Ed.) (2004). *"Ur-Ethnographie". Auf der Suche nach dem Elementaren in der Kultur. Die Sammlung Eugenie Goldstern.* Catalogue of the Österreichisches Museum für Volkskunde, Vol. 85.

Ottenbacher, Albert (1999). *Eugenie Goldstern. Eine Biographie.* Wien: Mandelbaum Verlag.

Pusman, Karl (1991). *Die Wiener Anthropologische Gesellschaft in der ersten Hälfte des 20.* Jahrhunderts. Ein Beitrag zur Wissenschaftsgeschichte auf Wiener Boden unter *Besonderer Berücksichtigung der Ethnologie.* PhD thesis: University of Vienna.

Schmidl, Marianne (1913). Flachs-Bau und Flachs-Bereitung in Umhausen. *Zeitschrift für österreichische Volkskunde* 19, pp. 122-125.

Schmidl, Marianne (1915). Zahl und Zählen in Afrika. *Mitteilungen der Anthropologischen Gesellschaft Wien* 45, pp. 165-209.

Schmidl, Marianne (1925). Beiträge zur Kenntnis der Trachten von Südwestbulgarien. Verein für Volkskunde in Wien (Ed.), *Festschrift für Michael Haberlandt.* Wien: Vlg. Des Vereins für Volkskunde.

Schmidl, Marianne (1926). Volkskundliche Studien in der Ebene von Sofia. *Festschrift der Nationalbibliothek in Wien.* Wien: Österreichische Staatsdruckerei, pp.723-736.

Schmidl, Marianne (1927). Das Verhältnis von Form und Technik bei der Übertragung afrikanischer Flechtarbeiten. *Sitzungsberichte der Anthropologischen Gesellschaft in Wien,* 1926-1927, pp. 101-104.

Schmidl, Marianne (1928). Altägyptische Techniken in afrikanischen Spiralwulstkörben. In: Wilhelm Koppers (Ed.), *Festschrift für Wilhelm Schmidt.* Wien: Mechitharisten-Congregations-Buchdruckerei, pp. 645-654.

Schmidl, Marianne (1935). Die Grundlagen der Nilotenkultur. *Mitteilungen der Anthropologischen Gesellschaft in Wien* 65, pp. 86-125.

Smetschka, Barbara (1997). *Frauen- Fremde-Forscherinnen: Leben und Werk der Absolventinnen des Wiener Instituts für Völkerkunde von 1945-1975; ein Beitrag zur Wissenschafts- und Frauengeschichte.* Frankfurt am Main, Wien: Peter Lang.

Stolcke, Verena (1995). Talking Culture: New Boundaries, New Rhetorics of Exclusion in Europe. *Current Anthropology* 36(1): 1-24.

Strasser, Sabine (in press). I am not a politicized migrant! Transnational relations and transversal tactics among political activists in Vienna, Austria. *The Journal of Economic and Social Research.*

Weiser, Lily (1923). *Jul. Weihnachtsgeschenke und Weihnachtsbaum. Eine volkskundliche Untersuchung ihrer Geschichte.* Stuttgart and Gotha.

Weiser, Lily (1927*). Altgermanische Jünglingsweihen und Männerbünde. Ein Beitrag zur deutschen und nordischen Altertums- und Volkskunde.* Bausteine zur Volkskunde und Religionswissenschaft. Band 1. Bühl.

(Re)-Interpreting Stories of Sexual Violence: The Multiple Testimonies of Lucille Eichengreen [1]

Kirsty Chatwood

In the light of the stories of rape and other forms of sexual violence that are a part of the larger narratives of genocide in Darfur, Rwanda and the former Yugoslavia, it is virtually a truism to suggest that sexual violence is an intrinsic feature of genocide. In the realms of Holocaust history and studies, however, it is still a subject that has not attracted a great deal of attention. Certainly scholars such as Myrna Goldenberg and Joan Ringelheim, whose work considers the specificity of female experience, have always acknowledged the existence of these stories in Holocaust testimonies, but they have focused on the specific sexual vulnerability of women due to pregnancy, motherhood, or amenorrhea, so mention only small numbers of testimonies by women who claimed to have been sexually assaulted or raped, or even to have witnessed sexual assaults or rapes, partly because of the paucity of material. But although there may only be a small number of women who have explicitly described such events in their testimonies, these scholars seem to be overlooking a significant number of male testimonies that discuss the sexual violence experienced by female prisoners, while stories of male sexual violence are considered even less frequently.[2] Such scholars' research has also been sidelined in traditional histories of the Holocaust, leading to what Joan Ringelheim conceptualizes as a split in memory between genocide and gender (notwithstanding other categories of difference); that is to say "memory is split between traditional versions of Holocaust history and… [the] experience" of individual survivor-witnesses.[3] This split has allowed the stories of sexual violence to be elided from mainstream research.

My own (feminist) readings of the testimonies of witnesses Lucille Eichengreen, Sarah Magyar Isaacson, Thaddeus Stabholz, Weislaw Kieler, Thomas Geve and Ruth Elias, however, lead me to believe that there are more stories of sexual violence than have been acknowledged or explored.[4] Furthermore, if one accepts that sexual violence is not only a common part of genocide but can also be genocidal, then it needs to be explored within the context of the Holocaust and the murder of the Jewish people, the Soviet POWs, the Sinti and the Roma, the mentally ill and differently-abled, and the exploitation of 'Slavic' slave-labour during the course of Nazi Germany. Furthermore this new history of sexual violence under the Third Reich needs to include not only that which was perpetrated by the German SS, the Wehrmacht, and other Aryan administrators, but also the Soviet mass rapes of women at the end of the war and during liberation, and the acts of sexual violence committed by all other militaries, Allied or Axis, as well as those perpetrated by 'victims' of Nazism. Moreover, as Ringelheim insists, these personal experiences need to be " … connect[ed] to the broader systematic persecution and murder that is the Holocaust".[5] It must also be acknowledged that within the Holocaust, sexual violence was not an intrinsic part of the genocidal process, as defined in Rwanda and the former Yugoslavia, but part of the continuum of violence that involved genocide. That is to say that rape was not a tool to commit genocide but a by-product of the dehumanisation process of genocide.

However, in suggesting that there is a need for a new history of the Holocaust that includes and acknowledges these events, I am not claiming that sexual violence was especially widespread or that particular acts of violence that now appear to have had a sexual component should be reinterpreted as sexual violence, but simply that we need to acknowledge those stories which do describe it, as well as examining why some stories are/were not perceived in these terms. This involves (re)reading witness testimonies to understand the relationship between the lived experience, which may or may not have interpreted an event as sexual violence at that time, and the socially and historically contingent representation of that lived experience, which is situated within a particular time and place and shaped by the particular practices and preconceptions of this situation. As such, these representations of lived experiences may well involve the (re)writing/(re)interpretation of an event to include sexual violence.

For example, the past twenty years has seen an expansion in the number of stories interpreted and represented as sexual violence in testimonies, partly due to new feminist research into rape, pornography, prostitution, and sexual trafficking, which casts some testimonies in a new light, but due also to the fact that the number of Holocaust testimonies (re)published has increased exponentially since the genocides in the former Yugoslavia and Rwanda.[6] These new testimonies include more stories of sexual violence and interpret more events as having a sexual component rather than simply an act of violence or humiliation, and it is thus tempting to conclude that contemporary events and discourse have led Holocaust survivors to reinterpret the violence they experienced as having a sexual component. However, it is important to acknowledge that a number of testimonies published in the 1940s, such as Mary Berg's *Warsaw Ghetto: A Diary*,[7] discussed rape and other forms of sexual violence. Thus, while new interpretations may consider particular aspects of violence as sexual, the existence of early testimonies which recognize rape and sexual violence demonstrate that the emergence of scholarly interest in the issue of sexual violence as a facet of Holocaust studies is not simply due to changes in feminist research, an insight that has a direct relevance to those "difficult interpretative questions as to the relationship between actuality and representation":[8] current research into sexual violence in Bosnia and Darfur might call for a re-examination of testimony, but the testimony already existed.

In the context of this paper, I use the term 'sexual violence' to encompass a continuum of sexual violence where 'heterosexual' rape is but one extreme.[9] Other forms of sexual violence include forced abortions, forced pregnancies through denying access to birth control or abortion, "sex for survival" (that is, requiring sex as a payment for food, documents, or employment within the ghettos and camps, as evinced by survivors Helen Lewis, Thomas Geve, Hedi Fried and others),[10] forced sterilizations and other medical experiments which are understood as sexual violence by some witnesses,[11] and sexual slavery (meaning the use of women within the slave-labour, concentration and death camps to work in the camp brothels 'servicing' both the guards and certain privileged prisoners).[12] Moreover, it includes complicated constructions of homosexuality, which bear no relevance to the lived experience of men and women who would define themselves as homosexuals, such as the trade in young boys, referred to as *Pielpels* or dolly-boys, in Auschwitz.[13] Since, perforce, I can only examine the representation of sexual violence through witness testimonies and not the actuality of the lived experience, I am particularly interested in events for which there are multiple witnesses but which are not represented by all witnesses as stories of sexual violence, since this raises important questions and suggests useful insights as to why they are represented this way by some witnesses but not by others, but also of witnesses who have multiple testimonies and how the relationship between the lived experience and the representation are contextualised.

For instance, in women's testimony the forced shaving of inmates upon entry into the Auschwitz camp system is often represented differentially, with survivor Livia Bitton-Jackson describing it as a trauma of sexual violence, while for Nadine Heftler it is a story of sexual vulnerability in that it involves forced nudity in front of men.[14] Furthermore, male survivors rarely described forced shaving as entailing the same level of trauma or destruction of one's identity.[15] Another question is what purpose the shaving of all body hair assumed within the slave-labour and concentration camps? Was it intended to be another way of humiliating the inmates? Was it for use by the Nazi regime (hair collected was certainly exported to Germany for use in mattresses) or was it even more mundane and simply a way of controlling the diseases, spread by lice, which were endemic in the camps?[16] More likely, it was a combination of the three, but its differential representation in witness testimonies exemplifies the complexities in using witness testimonies as the basis of evidence.

As the example of forced shaving on entry to the camp illustrates, examine what the witnesses themselves represent as sexual vulnerability or violence, what witnesses do not perceive to be sexual violence, and what part gender identity and gender *narrative* play in the representation of an act as sexual violence.[17] The experiences of witnesses need to be differentiated in gendered terms because gendered self-concepts lead individuals to perceive their experiences differentially and to be targeted as victims differently.[18] The issue becomes even more complex when one acknowledges that many stories of sexual violence were recorded by others than those directly involved, all of which only serves to emphasize that, since I am examining how witnesses represent sexual violence and vulnerability, it is important that I endeavour not to impose definitions that do not necessarily correspond to those of the witnesses to these events, although the inherent conflict between my own perception and that of the witness will always be present.

With all this in mind, I will examine the numerous testimonies of survivor-witness Lucille Eichengreen and the multiple and diverse definitions of sexual violence that occur in her two published testimonies, *From Ashes to Life: My Memories of the Holocaust* and *Rumkowski and the Orphans of Lodz*,[19] which together form an appropriate basis for the following analysis. I also consider the testimony Eichengreen has recorded for two online archives, *Telling Their Stories: Oral History Archives Project* and *Remember.org*, as well as the online archive of Laurence Rees' PBS documentary special, *Auschwitz: Inside the Nazi State*. Focusing on such English-language testimonies and online resources has, however, a secondary purpose—since through the utilization of sources such as these that are accessible to the general reader, I mean to acknowledge the importance of collective memory in representing Holocaust testimonies.[20]

Lucille Eichengreen was born Cecilia Landau in Hamburg in 1925. Her father Benjamin was originally arrested as a Polish Jew in 1938 and was eventually murdered in Dachau, after being rearrested following the outbreak of war. Eichengreen, her mother and sister were deported to the Lodz ghetto where Eichengreen survived three years. Her mother Sala perished from hunger in the ghetto and her sister Karin disappeared there during the *KinderAktion*. Eichengreen was then deported, first to Auschwitz, then to two further slave-labour camps, before finally being liberated from Bergen-Belsen.[21] The mediation of the lived experience through the identity she constructs in her two written texts are different, while the representation of sexual violence, those events Eichengreen chooses to record as sexual violence and why she interprets them as such, also changes between them. Moreover, her second text emphasizes stories of sexual violence, many of which do not appear in the first text.

Why, in the second text, does Eichengreen feel she needs to witness sexual violence that she did not record in her first text? Why did she not choose to bear witness to this violence in her first text? Does her failure to include it in the first text cast doubt upon her second? Are these differential retellings the effect of the influences of co-authors—in 1994 she worked with Harriet Hyman Chamberlain, in 2000 with Rebecca Camhi Fromer—changing contexts, or the vagaries of memory? Obviously, these are questions that cannot be answered through simple readings of her testimony, especially when we consider that the self recounted in recollection is actually mediated through a present, authorial self, but while an understanding of testifying as a form of self-portraiture, but also of agency, may explain the differences in the selves presented in 1994 or 2000, it does little to help solve the problems outlined above. Perhaps, however, these are not the right questions, and I would suggest that a more profitable approach to her texts is an exploration of the differences between them and of how these differences change how we approach each of the testimonies recorded by Eichengreen and of what possibilities they open for the (re)interpretation and (re)reading of 'rape' stories in both her and other survivors' testimonies.

There are several stories of sexual violence in Eichengreen's first text, *From Ashes to Life: My Memories of the Holocaust*. The first typifies "sex for survival", that process whereby sex is understood as a commodity to be traded for another commodity such as documents or food. After the death of her mother Sala in the Lodz ghetto, Eichengreen becomes responsible for her younger sister Karin. In attempting to secure a job for Karin, Eichengreen is introduced to yet another type of black market commodity: "One manager asked what I would give him in return if he found a place for my sister. When I explained that I had neither money nor valuables, he laughed and said that that was not what he had in mind. I was stunned. The realization was sudden and painful: there were favors to be bought, but they had to be paid for one way or another—even among our own".[22]

Eichengreen does not record this as a 'rape' story, but it does imply the existence of coercive sexual acts ('sex for survival') which, at the very least, can be interpreted as sexual violence: the factory manager would not be in a position to offer this type of trade if he did not perceive Eichengreen as being vulnerable to sexual predation.

But this is a complicated story. After all, Eichengreen herself does not participate in the trade. She acknowledges the existence of a trade in sexual favours in which she was clearly participating from a weaker vantage point. Eichengreen was vulnerable to exploitation, or at least the factory manager assumed she should be, and this exploitation involved a sexual 'favour'. In this we can see the negotiation of individual agency, for Eichengreen had a 'choice' to participate or not participate. But given the fact that Eichengreen was desperate to secure a work permit for her sister—without it her sister's chance of surviving an *Aktion* was small—the extent of such 'choice' was limited. The fact that Eichengreen does not agree to the exchange does not negate the fact that this was an attempt at sexual exploitation and that Eichengreen was shocked that another Jewish person could require that type of favour in exchange for a document that could increase the chances of Karin's survival. Moreover, Eichengreen compounds the emotional and psychological effect of this story by going on to tell her readers that Karin disappeared during the *KinderAktion* in the fall of 1942, partly because she lacked the protection of a valid work permit, knowledge which thus affords us—her audience—the benefit of hindsight and effectively shapes the way that we perceive the story: perhaps if Eichengreen had made a different 'choice' her sister might also have survived. The juxtaposition of the two stories is an intentional narrative device by which Eichengreen places responsibility for Karin's death at the nameless Jewish factory manager's door; however, whether we, as readers, are prepared to engage with this tenuous teleological construction of blame is a separate issue. We also know from survivors Trudi Birger, in her testimony, *A Daughter's Gift of Love: A Holocaust Memoir* and Mary Berg in *Warsaw Ghetto: A Diary,* that trading sex for food or documents within the ghettos was not uncommon.[23] What is relevant here is that Eichengreen herself feels that this story, in relation to other stories she could have told of her experience, is important. It implies the sexual vulnerability of young women in the Lodz ghetto, and by extension in other ghettos, but also of a sexual vulnerability now intimately tied in with the murder of Eichengreen's little sister.

A second story of sexual violence in *From Ashes to Life* is the attempted rape of Eichengreen by an SS officer after she was transferred from Auschwitz to *Arbeitslager* Dessauer Ufer near Hamburg in November 1944.[24] The attempted rape happens moments after she had stolen material to make a headscarf: "His left hand moved swiftly down my body. I no longer doubted that he knew my secret. My absurd vanity would be my death. My head was still in his viselike grip as his hand came to a stop between my legs. He fingered the scarf. I stopped breathing, convinced that my life was over. Suddenly he shouted in my ear, 'You filthy, useless bitch! Pfui! Menstruating!' He pushed me away in disgust".[25]

We are able only to infer that the intention of the soldier was to further sexually assault Eichengreen. Specifically, Eichengreen herself interprets it as an (sexual) attack on her person. She interprets this as the beginning of her death and the beginning of her death will be rape. Menstruating, yet another thing that made women vulnerable, particularly since there was no way to deal with it hygienically, may have saved Eichengreen from rape but it could also have caused her death. When asked how she felt about this incident in an interview for the *Telling Stories* online archive, Eichengreen replied: "I put it out of my mind because I knew it was a possibility any time, anywhere. It had happened before to other people, and there was nothing you really could do. Incidents happened. Some were talked about, some were not".[26]

For Eichengreen, then, sexual violence was not an anomaly but simply part of her personal lived experience of the Holocaust, just as the previous story is evidence that some people in positions of power used 'coercive prostitution' (or 'sex for survival') to gain sexual favours, even if both were victims of Nazism. This returns us to Ringelheim's point about the split between genocide and gender where the personal experience of rape is subsumed under the collective experience of all.

A third story of sexual vulnerability and violence in this first text concerns a chance meeting between Eichengreen and her former Auschwitz *Kapo*, Maja, in New York. The encounter is the catalyst for what is possibly the most difficult to interpret story of (sexual) violence within Eichengreen's testimonies. Eichengreen attempts to reconstruct the conversation between the two women, a conversation, which demonstrates the difficulties involved in defining 'sexual violence' within the camps. Eichengreen was disturbed by the meeting; she remembers the physical abuse and the beatings she had received from Maja and raises the rumours about Maja in Auschwitz:

> "I remember you were well fed. And there were rumors about an SS man who came to visit you at night in your private, privileged cubicle. He must have been the blond, tall one who returned during the day to beat us and laugh with sadistic pleasure at our suffering. We nicknamed him 'Siegfried'".[27]

At first glance, this appears to be another example of "sex for survival"; the clear implication is that Maja engaged in sexual acts with an SS man for special privileges, which, no doubt, included extra food and a 'good' job. Eichengreen's personal feelings for Maja's way of survival are mixed: "I had loathed Maja even more than the SS and had often wondered about the price she was paying to survive. But I could not condemn her for her will to live—what would I have done in her place"?[28]

What makes this story different from other stories of "sex for survival", such as that of the 'privileged' orchestra member's sexual relations with male *Kapos* and members of the SS in Fania Fénelon's *Playing for Time,*[29] is that the Jewish Maja apparently married the SS officer after the war. This marriage raises many questions about the placement of this story within a paradigm of sexual violence. We have only Eichengreen's remembrance of Maja's words mediated through Eichengreen, and her incredulousness that Maja, who could also be identified as a perpetrator of violence against Eichengreen, married a perpetrator. What we lack is the actuality of Maja's lived experience, or at least Maja's representation of her lived experience. Maja's explanation (which is, of course, also mediated through Eichengreen's memory), is nonetheless disturbing:

> "Let me explain", Maja started again. "You are judging me by the past, and you have no right to do so. Circumstances were not normal then. I didn't care"! she sounded very angry and self-righteous. "Now I'm considered an outcast, a criminal by those who knew me then. There were others who were far worse than I during those years!
>
> "Your memory is accurate", she went on, still angry and abrupt. "A nameless, faceless SS man came every night. I feared for my life and thought it would ensure my survival in Auschwitz. I loathed him then; I knew he was a criminal and a killer. But as months went by, I got used to him. He kept me out of the gas chamber. He gave me food. I didn't think of the future then. I lived one day at a time. Whatever I did was my way of surviving".
>
> She paused, and then, with great effort, she continued. "After the war I spent two years in Germany in a Displaced Persons camp. He found me there, but I refused to see him or talk to him. Then I came to New York. He followed me again. He kept coming back into my life. I knew his past, and he knew mine. I was tired of running and hiding. We decided to start a new life together. Can you understand? I didn't do anything wrong!"[30]

The story of Maja and the SS guard appears to be a story of a rape victim who is also a victim of genocide, and questionably also a perpetrator of violence, who marries both the perpetrator of her rape and a perpetrator of genocide. Maja's definition of her SS officer is at first as a killer and a rapist, but then his status changes. He becomes somehow normalized. He is no longer a rapist but a husband, and a husband who is not a rapist or a murderer but rather one who understands the present Maja through the Maja incarcerated in Auschwitz, in a way that no other husband could. The SS officer is Maja's normality. Of course, this change in identification is still mediated through Eichengreen; I cannot 'know' what Maja's 'normality' was, as I have no testimony recorded by Maja. I can only interpret her story as it is mediated and represented in the testimony of Eichengreen, a testimony that resonates with a condemnatory representation of Maja as perpetrator, a prejudice that must be kept in the forefront of one's mind when (re)reading this complicated story of sexual violence. But of course Eichengreen does not use the word 'rapist'; I infer that he was Maja's rapist through her construction of the "nameless, faceless SS man [that] came every night".

Moreover, this clearly involved "sex for survival" in that the SS officer was exploiting Maja's sexual vulnerability by force (raping her) and is apparent from her description of the exchange: "I feared for my life and thought it would ensure my survival in Auschwitz. I loathed him then; I knew he was a criminal and a killer". At the same time, however, 'rapist' seems too ordinary a term to describe the behaviour of this SS officer. Certainly Maja had no choice in his nightly visits at first, but then, apparently, the frequency of his visits changed her understanding of the situation. She began to depend upon him in a way she would not have if he were just an SS guard who had repeatedly raped her. Furthermore, it is a valid assumption that rape was not the only (war) crime the officer committed, even though the officer lacks an identity other than that given by Eichengreen, or Maja through Eichengreen, and thus the identity of the officer is the important question when defining this story. Is he a rapist and a husband who, we assume, does not rape his wife after he marries her (although this might itself be a highly dubious assumption)? Does Eichengreen see him as a rapist even if she does not use the term, or simply as yet another vicious SS officer whose other activities in Auschwitz supersede any identification as rapist? If he is both, then does he remain a rapist after marrying the victim of the rape? Or is rape simply the wrong term to be using? Is the sexual violation of women, and by correlation children and men, so common in situations of genocide as to render the discussion of rape and sexual violence less significant than the other conditions of genocide? There are no clear-cut answers to these questions, I simply raise them as another way of (re)reading Holocaust witness testimonies.

A completely separate question, but one which is no less significant, is whether or not the SS officer would himself have identified himself as Maja's rapist in the camps. The fact that he repeatedly tracks Maja down after the war could lead to the assumption that he did not see himself as Maja's rapist, but rather her protector. In fact, one could use the word 'love' to describe this relationship, or, at least, that the behaviour of the SS officer can be described in terms of 'love', however complicated the application of this term may be. The SS officer followed Maja around after the war, not because he felt he had no other 'choice' but rather because he wanted to and needed to, as he 'loved' her. Another interpretation, suggested to me by Rochelle Saidel at the 2005 *Gender and the Holocaust* conference in Israel, is that perhaps this SS officer is actually stalking Maja; that is to say, that he follows her from a Displaced Persons camp to New York because he needed to be in control and Maja became the object of this control. He revictimizes her every time he follows her. In this scenario, the abuse that started in Auschwitz continues throughout the life of Maja as every act of sex becomes a repeat of the rape experienced in the camp, while in her inability to formulate a positive self-image, she only feels 'secure' married to her abuser. Again, the complexities of this cannot be fully understood because we have no witness testimony from Maja herself, or even the SS officer. The existence of either testimony would allow us another layer of textual evidence for the representation of the lived experience of rape in Auschwitz. In its absence, however, we must return to Eichengreen—for despite the fact that her mediation must certainly colour our understanding of this complex situation, her testimony nonetheless brings to light the ways in which, within the context of a genocide, a single 'sexual' event can become the site of multiple meanings.

From Ashes to Life is dominated by Eichengreen's recollections of personal relationships. In the Lodz ghetto the most significant of these were with her mother Sala, her sister Karin, and her boyfriend Szaja, and then in the camps with her friend Elli. Notably, however, while Szaja was an influential character in *From Ashes to Life*, his presence is almost negligible in her second memoir, *Rumkowski and the Orphans of Lodz*. This is a more difficult text, as it is not really Eichengreen's memoir—it does not read as her testimony—but rather Eichengreen's retellings of the life-stories of several people she met in the Lodz ghetto who were all either sexually abused by Mordechai Chaim Rumkowski, Chairman of the Lodz ghetto Council, or intimately knowledgeable about the abuse.[31] Thus it is actually the story of three orphans, Luba, Bronia and Julek, all of who were apparently sexually abused by Rumkowski in the orphanage where he worked prior to the war. To further complicate matters, the question of a different co-author also changes the representation of sexual violence and it is difficult to know where Eichengreen's story is elided by the presence of a second different author. There are also a number of questions of narrative emplotment and literary devices that are difficult to ascribe to either Eichengreen or Rebecca Camhi Fromer (or, for that matter, between Eichengreen and Harriet Hyman Chamberlain).[32] The complications created by co-authors aside, *Rumkowski and the Orphans of Lodz* is a very different text to *From Ashes to Life,* and their relationship to one another is worth exploring.

In *From Ashes to Life*, Eichengreen's knowledge of Rumkowski is mediated through Szaja. In *Rumkowski and the Orphans of Lodz*, the knowledge of Rumkowski is, at first, mediated second-hand through Shlomo Berkowicz, a man she meets on the streets in the ghetto while searching for a needle and black thread.[33] Berkowicz recounts the stories of abuse perpetrated by Rumkowski that Berkowicz learned via his friend Sergei, who came across the children in the orphanage. In the first instance, then, the knowledge of the abuse is second-hand, but it is then confirmed when Eichengreen meets the three orphans, Luba and Bronia in the Lodz ghetto and Julek after the war. The second confirmation of Rumkowski's sexual deviancy, and we are speaking here of pedophilia but also of 'heterosexual' rape, is from Eichengreen herself as she also testifies to her own sexual abuse perpetrated by Rumkowski.

There are also other variances between the two texts. In *Rumkowski and the Orphans of Lodz*, Eichengreen basically writes a catalogue of the sexual violence committed by Rumkowski, including against Eichengreen herself. There is, however, no real mention of Rumkowski and the sexual violences in the first text. In *From Ashes to Life*, Eichengreen writes of meeting Rumkowski while working in a ghetto kitchen. He only speaks to her twice, although the second of these incidents makes clear his consciousness of her sexual vulnerability, but also her knowledge of his sexual deviancy:

> Every evening, he came to inspect our work. Some he praised, some he scolded, and those who displeased him he beat with his cane. One evening while I was working alone in the office, Rumkowski entered, pulled up a chair, and sat down.
> "Do you have family in Palestine"?
> "My father's two brothers", I replied.
> "I want your promise", he continued. "After the war, you have to ask them to help me".
> I was confused. Rumkowski needing help? Why was he worried about the future? Was it fear of possible revenge from his fellow Jews or fear of the Germans?
> The following evening, he sat down again next to my desk. "I want you to move", he said sharply. "There is a nice room above the kitchen, and I will be able to come see you there". Once again Szaja's warning came to mind, and I started to cry. "Please, let me stay where I am, please, please …".
> His cane came down brutally on my shoulder, "After all I have done for you, how dare you refuse?" he yelled furiously.
> Luck was on my side: three days later, the kitchens were closed on orders from the Germans.[34]

Yet, in her second text, *Rumkowski and the Orphans of Lodz*, the meeting in the kitchen is much longer and follows Rumkowski's disappearance into a storeroom with another woman, Salka Meyerowicz, where Eichengreen infers that Rumkowski sexually assaulted Meyerowicz.[35] The discussion over Eichengreen's two uncles in Palestine is present but ends with a kiss, not Rumkowski's fury. The kitchen is not immediately disbanded, and Rumkowski returns several days later and sexually assaults Eichengreen. After Rumkowski forces Eichengreen to manually masturbate him, he then offers her a new room near the kitchen. She does not want to move but is given no choice. The abuse continues for several weeks, creating a time and detail discrepancy between the two texts. Because of the complicated authorial relationship, we cannot tell if the abuse of Eichengreen is in actual fact a plot device used to confirm the previously second-hand stories of sexual violence, which would not invalidate the historical authenticity of the text but merely creates another layer for textual analysis. It is not unusual for Holocaust witness testimonies to include stories that would be prohibited from a court of law due to rules of hearsay. Regardless of the 'factual truths' of the lived experiences of Meyerowicz and Eichengreen, Eichengreen is clearly placing Rumkowski not only as an agent of genocide—particularly since her sister Karin was deported after the infamous 'Give me your children' speech—but also as a sexual predator.[36] This complicated relationship between actuality and representation is at the heart of understanding Holocaust witness testimonies.

We now have two stories of the same event written by the same person, although with two different co-authors, that contains factual differences. I can only hypothesize the reasons for this. The first is the time between the publications of each text. *From Ashes to Life* was published in 1994 and the second in 2000. The difference of six years includes two well-documented genocides where rape was a standard tactic, and an increased awareness of rape in 'normal' society. It is possible that Eichengreen simply did not want to document her abuse at the time she wrote *From Ashes to Life*. Alternatively, one might hypothesize that Eichengreen, after garnering a public persona based on her original memoirs, feels more confident about witnessing the stories of abuse, or that she feels she is in a position to incorporate other people's stories, stories that Eichengreen may not have personally witnessed but stories she feels need to be told; stories that are second-, third- and sometimes fourth-hand. As such, the discrepancies between the two texts do not create a hierarchy of truth but rather create another space in which to discuss sexual violence and its reality within the Holocaust. Such inferences are, of course, only speculative, yet they are based upon readings of other Holocaust memoirs, which incorporate second-hand rape stories, such as the testimonies of Mary Berg and Moshe Avital.[37] While we can question the motivation for Eichengreen writing the stories of sexual violence, at the most basic level we also have to acknowledge that Eichengreen clearly felt it necessary to testify to the existence of the sexual abuse.

The questions raised in this paper are further complicated when we consider the problems of defining sex acts of a coercive nature. Even in so-called 'normal' societies, there is a differentiation across a spectrum from preying on sexual vulnerability, to sexual exploitation, to actual rape, and in any case the definitions of what is rape or what is sexual violence, and what is simply an act with a sexual component, differ across cultures, legal systems, and personal beliefs—differences which depend on how we define sexual vulnerability and choice. Furthermore, they frequently differ between victim and witness, writer and reader. However 'choice' in the context of sexual behaviour is defined, though, it is indisputable that an individual's choices are drastically reduced while living within a ghetto, concentration camp, or in hiding, and their vulnerability is increased. This does not discount the possibility of individual agency, for as we have seen in Eichengreen's first testimony concerning 'sex for survival', agency did exist, but it does place agency within the context of genocide where perhaps the agency is in the representation of the lived experience in the writing of the testimony rather than the lived experience itself.[38]

But before I get too bogged down in debating semantics, perhaps there is some solid ground here. If one accepts that coercive sex can be rape, then being put in a situation where the choice is between slowly starving to death or engaging in 'consensual' sexual acts for food renders the consensual coercive, even if, in the case of Eichengreen, the 'victim' does not participate. Furthermore, contemporary (legal) definitions of rape include instances where the choice not to engage in a sex act is available but that the choice is one made in a situation where coercion is present. This is not regarded as prostitution but as a form of sexual violence. Prostitution, sexual slavery and trafficking are very difficult terms to discuss, differentiate and define outwith genocide, but once in a situation where the intent to commit genocide is evident, trading sex for food moves outside the definitions of prostitution (although one could argue that a street prostitute who is working to feed her children in non-combat zones is also placed in a position where choice is so curtailed as to appear non-existent).

The divergences between Eichengreen's two written texts, and the multiple and varied number of sexual violence stories in them, open up many new areas of research. They question what stories we can define as sexual violence and who has the authority to define these stories. If a survivor does not interpret an event as sexual violence, can we do so? How do we include stories as sexual violence if they were not actually intended as such? Whose self-representation do we interpret as dominant when there are a myriad of selves presented in a variety of sources or even within one witness testimony itself? These questions are further complicated if, instead of assuming a female victim of male aggression, we include children and men as victims and consider a wider spectrum of perpetrators, which includes same-sex assaults on people, both perpetrators and victims, who define themselves as homosexual as opposed to those who do not. These are only a few of the problems that still need to be addressed when interpreting sexual violence stories from the Holocaust. What I hope I have demonstrated, however, is that although tackling these questions may be hard given the lack of direct evidence, the complexity of the issues and the sensitivity of the subject, it is possible and productive to do so.

Notes

1   Earlier drafts of this paper were presented at two conferences, *The Legacy of the Holocaust: Women and the Holocaust,* (Jagiellonian University: Krakow, May 2005), and *The Third International Conference: Women and the Holocaust: Gender Issues in Holocaust Studies,* (Beit Berl College, Beit Terezin, & Beit Lohamei Haghetaot, Israel, September 2005). I am grateful to delegates at both for their comments and questions

which have enabled me to develop it further, especially Esther Hertzog, Jay Leese, Rochelle Saidel and Myrna Goldenberg.

2   This is not a criticism of their research but rather an acknowledgment of the research required. See Myrna Goldenberg. "Different Horrors, Same Hell: Women Remembering the Holocaust." In *Thinking the Unthinkable: Meanings of the Holocaust,* edited by Roger Gottlieb, pp.150-166. New York: Paulist Press, 1990; Joan Ringelheim. "Women and the Holocaust: A Reconsideration of Research." In *Signs: A Journal of Women in Culture and Society*, vol. 10, no. 4, pp. 741-761, (1984-1985); Other examples of this type of scholarship include Judith Tydor Baumel. *Double Jeopardy: Gender and the Holocaust.* London: Vallentine Mitchell, 1998; Renate Bridenthal et al., eds., *When Biology Became Destiny: Women in Weimar and Nazi Germany*. New York: Monthly Review Press, 1984; Anna Hardman. *Women and Holocaust*. U.K: Holocaust Educational Trust Papers, 1999–2000; Marlene E. Heinemann. *Gender and Destiny: Women Writers and the Holocaust.* New York: Greenwood Press, 1986; Sara R. Horowitz. "Memory and Testimony of Women Survivors of Nazi Genocide." In *Women of the Word: Jewish Women and Jewish Writing*, edited by Judith R. Baskin, pp. 258-282. Detroit: Wayne University Press, 1994. Both Goldenberg and Ringelheim have recently published articles dealing with the issues of rape: Myrna Goldenberg. "Sex, Rape, and Survival: Jewish Women and the Holocaust." In *Women and the Holocaust: A Cyberspace of their Own,* edited by Judy Cohen. (www.theverylongview.com/WATH/) and Joan Ringelheim "Genocide and Gender: A Split Memory." In *Gender and Catastrophe*, edited by Ronit Lentin, pp. 18-33. London: Zed Books, 1997.

3   Joan Ringelheim. "Genocide and Gender: A Split Memory." p. 20.

4   Lucille Eichengreen with Harriet Hyman Chamberlain. *From Ashes to Life: My Memories of the Holocaust*. San Francisco: Mercury House, 1994; Ruth Elias. *Triumph of Hope: From Theresienstadt and Auschwitz to Israel*. Translated from the German by Margot Bettauer Dembo. New York: John Wiley & Sons, Inc. published in association with the United States Holocaust Memorial Museum, 1998, 1988; Judith Magyar Isaacson. *Seed of Sarah: Memoirs of a Survivor*, 2nd ed. Chicago: University of Illinois Press, 1991; Wieslaw Kielar, *Anus Mundi: Five Years in Auschwitz*. Translated from the German by Susanne Flatauer. London: Penguin Books, 1982, 1972; Thaddeus Stabholz, *Seven Hells*. Translated from the Polish by Jacques Grunblatt & Hilda R. Grunblatt. New York: Holocaust Library, 1990; Thomas Geve. *Youth in Chains*. Jerusalem: Rubin Mass. Pub. 1981, 1958.

5   Joan Ringelheim, 'Genocide and Gender', p. 20

6   Much of this research has grown in relation to the wars in the former Yugoslavia. See, for instance, Beverly Allen. *Rape Warfare: The Hidden Genocide in Bosnia-Hercegovina and Croatia*. Minnesota: The University of Minnesota Press, 1986; Alexandra Stiglmayer. *Mass Rape: The War against Women in Bosnia-Herzegovina*. Bison Books, 1984; Anne Llewellyn Barstow. *War's Dirty Secret: Rape, Prostitution, and Other Crimes against Women*. Ohio: The Cleveland Press, 2000; Euan Hague. "Rape, Power and Masculinity: The Construction of Gender and National Identities in the War in Bosnia-Herzegovina."

In *Gender and Catastrophe*, edited by Ronit Lentin, pp.50-63. London: Zed Books, 1997; Rose Lindsey. "From Atrocity to Data: Historiographies of Rape in Former Yugoslavia and the Gendering of Genocide." In *Patterns of Prejudice.* (vol. 36, no. 4, October 2002).

7   Mary Berg. *Warsaw Ghetto: A Diary*. New York: LB Fischer, 1945.

8   Anna Hardman. *Women and Holocaust*. U.K: Holocaust Educational Trust Papers, 1999–2000.

9   The idea of a continuum of sexual violence is taken from Liz Kelly, *Surviving Sexual Violence.* Cambridge: Polity Press, 1988. p.76

10 The label "sex for survival" is Myrna Goldenberg's as outlined in her paper 'Rape and the Holocaust.' Presented at *Legacies of the Holocaust: Women and the Holocaust* Conference, Krakow, Poland. May 2005. I have termed this 'coercive prostitution' in "Gendering Memory: Perceptions of Sexual Assault in Holocaust Witness Narratives", a paper presented at the same conference. Elizabeth Heinemann names this 'hunger prositution' in "Sexuality and Nazism: The Doubly Unspeakable?" *Journal of the History of Sexuality* p. 22 –46, (vol. 11, no. 1/2, Jan/April 2002). For examples of this kind of behaviour see, for instance, Helen Lewis. *A Time to Speak*. New York: Carroll & Graf Pub. Inc., 1992; Hedi Fried. *The Road to Auschwitz: Fragments of a Life*. Edited and translated from the Swedish by Michael Meyer. Lincoln: University of Nebraska Press, 1990; Thomas Geve. *Youth in Chains*; Wieslaw Kielar. *Anus Mundi*; Gisella Perl. *I was a Doctor in Auschwitz*. New Hampshire: Ayer Co., 1992, c1948.

11 Le Matricule 55.310. *Birkenau: Bagne de Femmes*. Fernand Nathan, 1945; Gene Church. *"80629" A Mengele Experiment*. Albuquerque New Mexico: Route 66 Publishing Ltd., 1986; Moshe Ha-Elion. *The Straits of Hell: The Chronicles of a Salonikan Jew in the Nazi Extermination Camps, Auschwitz, Mauthausen, Melk, Ebensee*. Revised by Ralph H. Herolzer. Cincinnati: Bowman & Cody Academic Pub., 2005.

12 Pelagia Lewinska. *Vingt Mois a Auschwitz*. Paris: Editions Nagel, 1945; Helen Farkas. *Remember the Holocaust: A Memoir of Survival*; Louis J. Micheels, M.D., *Doctor # 117641: A Holocaust Memoir.* New Haven: Yale University Press, 1989; Eva Tichauer. *I was # 20832 at Auschwitz.* Translated from the French by Colette Lévy & Nicki Rensten. London: Vallentine Mitchell, 2000.

13 Léon Arditti. *The Will to Live: Two Brothers in Auschwitz*. Translated from the French by Nanette Guinta. New York: Shengold Pub., 1996; Fania Fénelon with Marcelle Routier, *Playing For Time.* Translated from the French by Judith Landry. Syracuse: Syracuse University Press, 1997, 1976; Thomas Geve. *Youth in Chains*; Wieslaw Kielar, *Anus Mundi: Five Years in Auschwitz*; Louis J. Micheels, M.D., *Doctor # 117641: A Holocaust Memoir*; Herman Sachnowitz as told to Arnold Jacoby. *The Story of 'Herman der Norweger' Auschwitz Prisoner #79235.* Translated by Thor Hall, (Lanham: University of America Press, 2002).

14 Livia Bitton-Jackson. *I Have Lived a Thousand Years: Growing Up in the Holocaust*. New York: Aladdin Paperbacks, 1999, 1997; Nadine Heftler. *Si tu t"en sors... Auschwitz, 1944-1945*. Paris: Éditions La Découverte, 1992. p. 34.

15 See Zoë Waxman. "Unheard Testimony, Untold Stories: the representation of women's Holocaust experiences." *Women's History Review.*(vol. 12., no. 4, 2003), for further discussion of this point.

16 For further discussion of this point see: Pascale Rachel Bos. "Women and the Holocaust: Analyzing Gender Difference." In *Experience and Expression: Women, the Nazis, and the Holocaust*, edited by Elizabeth R. Baer & Myrna Goldenberg, pp.23-50, Detroit: Wayne State University Press, 2003. footnotes 55 & 56; Zoë Waxman. "Unheard Testimony, Untold Stories: the representation of women's Holocaust experiences." *Women's History Review.* (vol. 12. no. 4, 2003).

17 The idea of a *gendered narrative* is from Zoe Waxman. *Writing the Holocaust: Identity, Testimony, Representation.* Oxford: Oxford University Press, 2006, p. 128. The italics are Waxman's.

18 See Marion Kaplan. *Between Dignity and Despair: Jewish Life in Nazi Germany.* New York: Oxford University Press, 1998. & Myrna Goldenberg. "Different Horrors, Same Hell: Women Remembering the Holocaust." In *Thinking the Unthinkable: Meanings of the Holocaust*, edited by Roger Gottlieb, pp.150-166. New York: Paulist Press, 1990.

19 Lucille Eichengreen. *From Ashes to Life*; Lucille Eichengreen with Rebecca Camhi Fromer. *Rumkowski and the Orphans of Lodz.* San Francisco: Mercury House, 2000.

20 Zoë Waxman. *Writing the Holocaust: Identity, Testimony, Representation.* Oxford University Press, 2006; Peter Novick. *The Holocaust and Collective Memory: The American Experience.* London: Bloomsbury Press, 2000; Christopher Browning. *Collected Memories: Holocaust History and Postwar Testimony.* Madison, 2003. for further discussion on representation of testimony and collective memory.

21 Lucille Eichengreen. *From Ashes to Life.* pp. 18-31, 34-46, 47-53.

22 Lucille Eichengreen. *From Ashes to Life.* p. 49.

23 Trudi Birger written with Jeffrey M. Green. *A Daughter's Gift of Love: A Holocaust Memoir.* Philadelphia: The Jewish Publication Society, 1990; Mary Berg, *Warsaw Ghetto: A Diary.*

24 Lucille Eichengreen, *From Ashes to Life*, p. 107

25 Lucille Eichengreen, *From Ashes to Life.*, p. 107.

26 Lucille Eichengreen, *Telling Stories*, 2002-2003, (2005)

27 Lucille Eichengreen. *From Ashes to Life.* p. 189.

28 Lucille Eichengreen. *From Ashes to Life* p. 189.

29 Fania Fénelon. *Playing for Time.* pp. 105, 115, 229, 252.

30 Lucille Eichengreen. *From Ashes to Life.* p. 190.

31 Mordechai Chaim Rumkowski was murdered either during the deportation to Auschwitz or at Auschwitz itself with all the members of his family. Testimony on this subject varies widely. Jonathon C. Friedman in *Speaking the Unspeakable: Essays on Sexuality, Gender, and Holocaust Survivor Memory (*Lanham: University Press of America 2002) claims there is testimony of the sexual predation of Rumkowski held at the Survivors of the Shoah Visual History Foundation in Los Angeles, although the cataloguing of the testimonies was not complete at the time of his publication. He does list the testimony of

survivor-witness Gina L., which appears to include evidence of the sexual predation of Rumkowski. P.57

32 I am a aware of a second Holocaust witness testimony co-authored by Rebecca Camhi Fromer: *The Holocaust Odyssey of Daniel Bennahmias, Sonderkommando*. Tuscaloosa: The University of Alabama Press, 1993, which is a more difficult text to contextualise. Daniel Bennahmias was a Greek Jew of Italian citizenship, who was originally incarcerated in the spring of 1944 in the Haidari Camp in Athens before being transported to Birkenau. He also survived the Death Marches before being liberated near Ebensee. Bennahmias was the only surviving member of his family. The text is purportedly based on a series of interviews between Camhi Fromer and Daniel Bennahmias, however there are no existing transcripts of these interview and many of the interviews were rewritten from memory over a period of three years. Because of this the text does not read as the memoir of Daniel Bennahmias but rather Camhi Fromer's relationship with Bennahmias, which makes it more difficult to contextualise.

33 Lucille Eichengreen. *Rumkowski*. pp. 6-27

34 Lucille Eichengreen. *From Ashes to Life*. p. 84.

35 Lucille Eichengreen. *Rumkowski and the Orphans of Lodz*. pp. 77-84.

36 Rumkowski made this speech in the fall of 1942. There is debate over Rumkowski's exact knowledge of the fate of those deported East, however he asked for the ghetto population to hand over their children, elderly, and the ill to make the quota of deportees required by the Nazi administrators. While there is debate over Rumkowski's exact knowledge of the fate of the deportees and his personal responsibility as an agent of the genocide, I do not want to enter this debate. What I want to acknowledge is that Eichengreen is clearly representing Rumkowski as a perpetrator of genocide but also of sexual violence, which includes pedophilia.

37 Mary Berg. *Warsaw Ghetto: A Diary*; Moshe Avital. *Not to Forget: Impossible to Forgive*. Jerusalem: Mazo Publishers, 2004.

38 Pascale Rachel Bos. "Women and the Holocaust: Analyzing Gender Difference." *p.29*

References

Le Matricule 55.310. *Birkenau: Bagne de Femmes*. Fernand Nathan, 1945.

Adelsberger, Lucie. *Auschwitz: A Doctor's Story*. Boston: Northeastern University Press, 1995.

Allen, Beverly. *Rape Warfare: The Hidden Genocide in Bosnia-Herzegovina and Croatia*. Minnesota: The University of Minnesota Press, 1986.

Arditti, Léon. *The Will to Live: Two Brothers in Auschwitz*. Translated from the French by Nanette Guinta. New York: Shengold Pub., 1996.

Avital, Moshe. *Not to Forget: Impossible to Forgive*. Jerusalem: Mazo Publishers, 2004.

Barstow, Anne Llewellyn. *War's Dirty Secret: Rape, Prostitution, and Other Crimes against Women*. Ohio: The Cleveland Press, 2000.

Baumel, Judith Tydor. *Double Jeopardy: Gender and the Holocaust*. London:

Vallentine Mitchell, 1998.

Ben-Sefer, Ellen. "Women and Reproductive Issues in Westerbork." Presented at the *Legacies of the Holocaust: Women and the Holocaust Conference*, Krakow, Poland, May 2005.

Berg, Mary. *Warsaw Ghetto: A Diary*. New York: LB Fischer, 1945.

Birger, Trudi with Jeffrey M. Green. *A Daughter's Gift of Love: A Holocaust Memoir*. Philadelphia: The Jewish Publication Society, 1990.

Bitton-Jackson, Livia. *I Have Lived a Thousand Years: Growing Up in the Holocaust*. New York: Aladdin Books, 1999.

Bridenthal, Renate et al. eds., *When Biology Became Destiny: Women in Weimar and Nazi Germany*. New York: Monthly Review Press, 1984.

Browning, Christopher. *Collected Memories: Holocaust History and Postwar Testimony*. Madison: University of Wisconsin Press, 2003.

Bos, Pascale Rachel. "Women and the Holocaust: Analyzing Gender Difference." In *Experience and Expression: Women, the Nazis, and the Holocaust*, edited by Elizabeth R. Baer & Myrna Goldenberg, pp.23-50.Detroit: Wayne State University Press, 2003.

Chatwood, Kirsty. "Gendering Memory: Perceptions of Sexual Assault in Holocaust Witness Narratives." Presented at the *Legacies of the Holocaust: Women and the Holocaust Conference*, Krakow, Poland, May 2005.

Chatwood, Kirsty. "Gendering Memory: Categories of Sexual Violence in Holocaust Testimonies. Presented at *The Third International Conference: Women and the Holocaust: Gender Issues in Holocaust Studies,* Beit Berl College, Beit Terezin, & Beit Lohamei Haghetaot, Israel, September 2005.

Church, Gene. *"80629" A Mengele Experiment*. Albuquerque New Mexico: Route 66 Publishing Ltd., 1986.

Cohen, Anthony P. *Self Consciousness: An Alternative Anthropology of Identity*. Oxford: Routledge, 1994.

Eichengreen, Lucille with Harriet Hyman Chamberlain, *From Ashes to Life: My Memories of the Holocaust*, (San Francisco: Mercury House, 1994)

Eichengreen, Lucille with Rebecca Camhi Fromer. *Rumkowski and the Orphans of Lodz*. San Francisco: Mercury House, 2000.

Eichengreen, Lucille. *Telling Their Stories: Oral Histories Archive Project*. (www.tellingstories.org). 2002-2003, March 2005.

Eichengreen, Lucille, *"Lucille E. Testimony."* (http://remember.org/witness). April 2005.

Elias, Ruth. *Triumph of Hope: From Theresienstadt and Auschwitz to Israel*. Translated from the German by Margot Bettauer Dembo. New York: John Wiley & Sons, Inc. Published in association with the United States Holocaust Memorial Museum, 1998, 1988.

Farkas, Helen. *Remember the Holocaust: A Memoir of Survival*. Santa Barbara: Fithian Press, 1995.

Fénelon, Fania with Marcelle Routier. *Playing For Time*. Translated from the French by Judith Landry, Syracuse: Syracuse University Press, 1997, 1976.

Fried, Hedi. *The Road to Auschwitz: Fragments of a Life*. Edited and translated from the Swedish by Michael Meyer. Lincoln: University of Nebraska Press, 1990.

Fromer, Rebecca Camhi. *The Holocaust Odyssey of Daniel Bennahmias, Sonderkommando*. Tuscaloosa: The University of Alabama Press, 1993.

Geve, Thomas. *Youth in Chains*. Jerusalem: Rubin Mass. Pub. 1981, 1958.

Goldenberg, Myrna. "Different Horrors, Same Hell: Women Remembering the Holocaust." In *Thinking the Unthinkable: Meanings of the Holocaust*, edited by Roger Gottlieb, pp.150-166. New York: Paulist Press, 1990.

Goldenberg, Myrna. "Rape and the Holocaust" Presented at *Legacies of the Holocaust: Women and the Holocaust Conference*. Krakow, Poland: May 2005.

Goldenberg, Myrna. "Sex, Rape, and Survival: Jewish Women and the Holocaust." *Women and the Holocaust: A Cyberspace of their Own*, edited by Judy Cohen. (www.theverylongview.com/WATH).

Greenman, Leon. *An Englishman in Auschwitz*. London: Vallentine Mitchell, 2001.

Ha-Elion, Moshe. *The Straits of Hell: The Chronicles of a Salonikan Jew in the Nazi Extermination Camps, Auschwitz, Mauthausen, Melk, Ebensee*. Revised for American edition by Ralph H. Herolzer. Cincinnati: Bowman & Cody Academic Pub., 2005.

Hague, Euan. "Rape, Power and Masculinity: The Construction of Gender and National Identities in the War in Bosnia-Herzegovina." In *Gender and Catastrophe*, edited by Ronit Lentin, pp.50-63. London: Zed Books, 1997.

Hardman, Anna. *Women and Holocaust*. U.K: Holocaust Educational Trust Papers, 1999–2000.

Heftler, Nadine. *Si tu t'en sors... Auschwitz, 1944-1945*. Paris: Éditions La Découverte, 1992.

Heinemann, Marlene E. *Gender and Destiny: Women Writers and the Holocaust*. New York: Greenwood Press, 1986.

Herzberger, Magda. *Survival*. Austin: First World Publishers, 2005.

Horowitz, Sarah H. "Memory and Testimony of Women Survivors of Nazi Genocide." In *Women of the Word: Jewish Women and Jewish Writing*, edited by Judith R. Baskin, pp.258-282. Detroit: Wayne University Press, 1994.

Isaacson, Judith Magyar. *Seed of Sarah: Memoirs of a Survivor*. 2nd ed. Chicago: University of Illinois Press, 1991.

Kaplan, Marion. *Between Dignity and Despair: Jewish Life in Nazi Germany*. New York: Oxford University Press, 1998.

Kielar, Wieslaw. *Anus Mundi: Five Years in Auschwitz*. Translated from the German by Susanne Flatauer. London: Penguin Books, 1982, 1972.

Klein, Aranka Ari. *My Life Story*. Unpublished testimony in Yad Vashem archives. 2001.

Lentin, Ronit. "Introduction: (En)gendering Genocides." In *Gender and Catastrophe*, edited by Ronit Lentin, pp. 2-17. London: Zed Books, 1997.

Lewis, Helen. *A Time to Speak*. New York: Carroll & Graf Pub. Inc., 1992.

Levy, Ernest. *Just One More Dance: A Story of Degradation and Fear, Faith and Compassion from a Survivor of the Nazi Death Camps*. Edinburgh: Mainstream Publishing Press, 1998.

Lewinska, Pelagia. *Vingt Mois a Auschwitz*. Paris: Editions Nagel, 1945.

Rose Lindsey. "From Atrocity to data: historiographies of rape in Former Yugoslavia and the gendering of genocide." In *Patterns of Prejudice.* (vol.36, no. 4, October 2002).

Micheels, Louis J. M.D. *Doctor # 117641: A Holocaust Memoir.* New Haven: Yale University Press, 1989.

Novick, Peter. *The Holocaust and Collective Memory: The American Experience.* London: Bloomsbury Press, 2000.

Perl, Gisella. *I was a Doctor in Auschwitz*. New Hampshire: Ayer Co., 1992, 1948.

Ringelheim, Joan. "Women and the Holocaust: A Reconsideration of Research." In *Signs: A Journal of Women in Culture and Society*, vol. 10, no. 4. (1984-1985). pp. 741-761.

Ringelheim, Joan. "Genocide and Gender: A Split Memory." In *Gender and Catastrophe* edited by Ronit Lentin, pp. 18-35. London: Zed Books, 1997.

Rees, Laurence. (writer/producer) *Auschwitz: Inside the Nazi State: Online Resource to complement PBS documentary Auschwitz: Inside the Nazi State*. (www.pbs. org/auschwitz/). 2004-2005. April 2005.

Rosenberg, Otto as told to Ulrich Enzenberger. *A Gypsy in Auschwitz*. Translated by Helmut Bögler. London: London House, 1999, 1988.

Sachnowitz, Herman as told to Arnold Jacoby. *The Story of 'Herman der Norweger' Auschwitz Prisoner #79235*. Translated by Thor Hall. Lanham: University of America Press, 2002.

Stabholz, Thaddeus. *Seven Hells*. Translated from the Polish by Jacques Grunblatt & Hilda R. Grunblatt. New York: Holocaust Library, 1990.

Stiglmayer, Alexandra. *Mass Rape: The War against Women in Bosnia-Herzegovina*. Bison Books, 1984.

Tanenbaum, Roy D. as told to him by Sigmund Sobolewski. *Prisoner 88: The Man in Stripes*. Alberta: University of Calgary Press, 1998.

Tichauer, Eva. *I was # 20832 at Auschwitz*. Translated from the French by Colette Lévy & Nicki Rensten. London: Vallentine Mitchell, 2000.

Waxman, Zoë. "Unheard Testimony, Untold Stories: The Representation of Women's Holocaust experiences." *Women's History Review*, (vol. 12. no. 4, 2003).

Waxman, Zoë. *Writing the Holocaust: Identity, Testimony, Representation*. Oxford: Oxford University Press, 2006.

Zur, Judith. "Reconstructing the Self through Memories of Violence among Mayan Indian War Widows." In *Gender and Catastrophe,* edited by Ronit Lentin, pp. 64-76 London: Zed Books, 1997.

Nazi Differentiations Mattered: Ideological Intersections of Sexualized Violence during National Socialist Persecution

Helga Amesberger, Brigitte Halbmayr

Introduction

In no other ideology has sexuality played such an important role as in National Socialism. The enforcement of its racist goals made it necessary to control the sexual behaviour of the population of the German *Reich*, especially that of women. Women's sexuality and their reproductive ability were subjected to the racist paradigm of generating and preserving the 'Aryan race' and the 'German national community' (*Deutsche Volksgemeinschaft*). The German 'Aryan' woman was meant to back the project of the 'Thousand-Year Empire'. Those women who did not want to perform this task, or could not accomplish it because of racial laws, were subjected to persecution. Belonging to the 'German *Volk*' was determined predominantly by one's ethnic heritage or 'blood'.[1]

With this, all Jews and Roma/Sinti were excluded from the German community. But even those with 'German blood' had to submit to the standardization and control of their way of life, so as not to be seen as 'un-German' (*undeutsch*). For being 'un-German', women could be persecuted, arrested and murdered: either because of their way of life (under the accusation of being 'antisocial') or because of 'high treason' and so on; these ideological and legal structures made possible the cruel treatment of women in concentration camps. The persecution of women as well as forced abortions, forced sterilisations, and forced sex work seem to contradict the idealization of women and motherhood in NS propaganda. But indeed, these outrages were the logical consequences in pursuing the political goal to build an 'Aryan nation', to create the so-called *Herrenmenschen*.

Both women and men were subjected to the control of their sexuality, and both genders were punished for disobedience of the various laws; both had to suffer from sexualized violence during persecution. Nevertheless, we focus in this article on women, dealing with two main topics. The first is women who were persecuted because of non-compliance with the so-called 'Blood Protection Law' ('*Blutschutzgesetze*'). This group consisted of women having, or suspected of having, relationships with Jews, an offence called '*Rassenschande*', meaning 'racial disgrace'; or with forced labourers and prisoners of war, an offence called '*Verbotener Umgang*', 'forbidden contact'. Nazi state terrorism destroyed many families and loving relationships by enforcing this law. The second topic is that of pregnancy and motherhood during persecution. The Nazis ignored the fact that many of the persecuted women were pregnant or already mothers; they didn't flinch from sending them to concentration camps. Despite the commonality of persecution, the punishment of women – according to our hypotheses – was determined by various factors. The Nazi laws, the judges and the SS made distinctions among women in persecuting them, which we would like to present, discussing the two aforementioned 'crimes' from the *'Blutschutzgesetz'* and the treatment of pregnant women and mothers. We therefore ask, which laws and decrees were relevant; how were they applied; and what consequences did they have for the various groups of women? And for whom and to what extent was motherhood possible?

It took a long time in the field of contemporary history to see gender as a crucial criterion for National Socialist analysis. In the last three decades, the feminist focus on Nazism and the Holocaust brought new insights and explanations. Nevertheless, gender is still a contested category in the field of mainstream history, and is often misunderstood as research on women, with the consequence that the male experience – seemingly neutral – is still the norm or standard experience from which other/ female experiences deviate.

Focusing specifically on women's experiences is not meant to imply that all persecuted women shared the same or similar experiences. We are well aware of the danger of essentialising gender, and we do not argue that gender can explain all difference in the 'universe of the camp society'. 'Race', ethnicity, nationality, class, sexual orientation, and religion play important roles in explicating differences among women. Therefore we apply 'intersectionality', developed by Kimberlé W. Crenshaw (1994), as a theoretical feminist approach regarding simultaneous and multiple suppressions.

Our data bases are life story interviews with Austrian survivors of the Ravensbrück concentration camp which were conducted by the authors between 1998 and 2002 (Amesberger/Halbmayr 2001; Amesberger/Auer/Halbmayr 2004), plus a data bank of Austrian women and men imprisoned in Ravensbrück,[2] and other studies of the topics and other historical documents. From this, it follows that we deal primarily with the situation in the *Ostmark* (Austria) which differs in some cases from the *Altreich* (Germany), and with the structural conditions of Ravensbrück as well as with Austrian inmates of Ravensbrück. 'Blood' ruled the Nazi world – the offences of *'Rassenschande'* and *'Verbotener Umgang'* and their effects.

The regulation of sexuality was not an invention of the National Socialist regime. The various rules of exogamy and endogamy as well as religious regulations are examples of this elsewhere and in other eras. In Austria, civil marriage was only introduced by the National Socialists on 1 August 1938.[3] Until then, the Catholic Church had regulated marriage partnerships, forbidding religious intermarriages. The maintenance of power through the building of homogenous religious communities was accompanied by notions of 'purity'.

However, the church's position offered the possibility of conversion to overcome such prohibitions, whereas the later NS regulations did not; it was impossible to escape one's 'racial' designation set in the Nuremberg Racial Laws of 1935.[4] Under the Nazis, civil marriage offered the legalization of relationships between people of different religions, or without religion, but still judged other relationships illegitimate because of the accompanying Blood Protection Law.[5] Not only intermarriages, but even friendships between Jewish and 'Aryan' people were forbidden; relationships with other 'non-Aryan' people stood under rigorous scrutiny of the Nazi authorities. Such offences against the *'Blutschutzgesetz'* were termed *'Rassenschande'* in the case of relationships between Jewish and non-Jewish people, and *'GV Delikte'* (sexual intercourse offences), *Umgang mit Kriegsgefangenen* (contact with prisoners of war), *'Verbotener Umgang'* ('forbidden contact') in the case of relationships with forced labourers and prisoners of war.

'Rassenschande'

According to the Statistical Yearbook of Vienna, 185 lawsuits concerning *'Rassenschande'* took place between 1938 and 1943 in Vienna (Saurer 2005, 349).[6] In the following we refer to the findings of Edith Saurer's study of the *Eidesstattlichen Erklärungen der KZ-Verbände* (declarations in lieu of an oath at the associations for former inmates of concentration camps) and our own findings in the framework of the Registration by Name research project concerning Austrian inmates in the Ravensbrück concentration camp.[7]

The 31 couples accused of *'Rassenschande'* whom Saurer (2005, 354ff.) studied came mainly from petit bourgeois backgrounds or the urban working class. Three of them married abroad to circumvent the laws and a great majority of the others lived together without a marriage certificate. Ten of the couples had children, of whom half were born after 1939. Most of these relationships were destroyed by the Nazis; only seven out of 31 couples together survived the Holocaust, and only 38 persons – 61 percent of the total, but including only 21 percent of the Jews – were still alive after the defeat of National Socialism.

The Ravensbrück data base details 26 cases of *'Rassenschande'*. 13 of the women were Jewish, 13 non-Jewish. The majority of them lived in Vienna at the time of imprisonment and belonged, as in Saurer's case study, to the urban working class. The women were accused of living together with Jewish partners, of hiding Jews, of helping Jews to escape from the grasp of the Gestapo, or of just being 'friendly' to Jewish people.[8] The analysis of the data shows major differences between the Jewish and the non-Jewish group in two respects. Firstly, they differ in respect to the time of persecution. The Jewish women were imprisoned in the first years of the war (1939-1942), whereas the majority of the non-Jewish women were imprisoned from 1943 on. An explanation for this is that by 1943, the majority of the Austrian Jewish population had already either emigrated or been deported to ghettos and concentration camps (Moser 1999).

The question remains why the non-Jewish women charged with *'Rassenschande'* were not prosecuted earlier; it seems that the Nazis were, in this case, less vigorous against perpetrators of 'their own race', whereas the 'Jewish race' was condemned anyway. The second difference concerns the death rate. More than 80 percent of the

Jewish women did not survive. All of them fell victim to the NS policy of 'freeing' the concentration camps on German territory of Jews. These Ravensbrück inmates were deported to Bernburg or Auschwitz where they were murdered. In contrast, about 90 percent of the non-Jewish women did survive; [9] the vast majority of them were released from Ravensbrück before it was liberated. This difference in death rates can only be attributed to the racist and anti-Semitic policy of the National Socialists. Even when one correlates the data with factors like age and length of imprisonment (which had an important influence on the chances of survival), the huge gap between the death rates still exists. These results confirm our hypothesis that 'race' determined the chances of survival.

'Verbotener Umgang'

The NS regime regulated the contact with 'foreigners' in Paragraph 4 of the *Wehrkraftschutzverordnung* ('Soldier Protection Law'), a decree supplementary to the Penal Provisions for the Protection of the Defence of the German People (*Strafvorschriften zum Schutz der Wehrkraft des Deutschen Volkes*).[10] Under the terms of this law, everyone who acted against the rules concerning the contact with prisoners of war, or maintained contact with other prisoners which violated the so-called *gesunde Volksempfinden* (roughly, 'healthy common sense of the people') had to be punished with imprisonment. This *gesunde Volksempfinden* was already violated when people talked with forced labourers or prisoners of war, or gave them cigarettes or bread. A sexual relationship was not necessary to be turned in to the authorities and sentenced. It is obvious that such 'crimes' could only be traced with the help of the population; most of the 'criminals' were denounced by civilians.

The number of persons who were persecuted because of *'Verbotener Umgang'* was very high. There are no overall figures for Austria or Germany, but according to Strebel, in the spring of 1942, every sixth newly registered inmate of the Ravensbrück concentration camp was imprisoned because of this offence; by the end of the year 1944 these had totalled about 3,500 women. In other words, approximately 15 percent of all 'German' inmates in Ravensbrück were accused of this 'crime'. The number then was as high as that of the other 'German non-Jewish political' prisoners (Strebel 2003, 117f.).

The duration and location of imprisonment varied. According to Gabriella Hauch's findings,[11] the convicted Upper Austrian women were imprisoned for between four months and three years (Hauch 2006, 267). Our secondary analysis of criminal procedures in Tyrol (Austria) listed by Josef Waldner (1994, 47ff.) yielded similar results:[12] The duration of imprisonment was from six weeks to two years and six months. Most of the women were put into prison[13] and – as with the Upper Austrian cases – the penalties sometimes were suspended. The reasons for suspension included pregnancy or giving birth and the need for the female 'manpower' in the home (Hauch 2006, 267); but also – as the Tyrolian cases indicate – because of the lack of manpower in industries important for the war, because the husband was on front-relief, or because of successful petitions for mercy. According to Hauch only few women (seven) were deported to concentration camps after having served the sentence. All of them were released from the concentration camp in question after one to one-and-a-half years. For Tyrol, no case of deportation to a concentration camp is reported in Waldner's list. A reason for that could be that most of the women in Tyrol had contact with French 'civil workers', whereas the contact alleged for the Upper Austrian women was with Polish forced labourers.[14]

Our Ravensbrück data base contains far more cases, as the above mentioned studies would suggest. Despite a high congruence between the aforementioned data and our findings concerning social background, age, and length of imprisonment, one important difference has to be stressed: all these 56 women and one man were imprisoned in the Ravensbrück concentration camp. The charge was 'friendliness to foreigners' or *'Verbotener Umgang'*. 19 months was the average time of imprisonment (prisons and concentration camps together); five women did not survive the concentration camp.[15] The penalties for the accused persons differed greatly according to the hierarchy of people made by the Nazis (Hauch 2006, 250f.): Polish forced labourers and Soviet prisoners of war of both sexes who were alleged to have had sexual intercourse with a 'German' were sentenced to death[16] or to deportation to a concentration camp. Others besides Polish or Soviet men were sentenced to jail. The punishment of 'German' women depended on their marital status, the intensity of the relationship, the 'degree of indignity', and if the accused was the wife or mother of a soldier (Hauch 2006, 249). 'German' women were sentenced to imprisonment in jails or concentration camps, while 'German' soldiers at the front were not prosecuted for having sexual intercourse or raping women (Hauch 2006, 251).

Mostly the females came from a rural and sub-proletarian background, working as maids at farmyards or in enterprises where they worked along with forced labourers. Many of them were young, unmarried, and had already children at the time of imprisonment. In that, this group of victims differs from the one imprisoned for *'Rassenschande'*. The latter primarily lived in urban areas and were older.[17] Their higher age is an incidence for their more longstanding relationships and marriages

Remembrance of humiliation and enduring shame

Statistics give an impression of the dimensions of persecution and the number of affected people, but at the same time they veil individual sufferings and experiences. Therefore in this section we follow some testimonies to get an idea of what lies behind the figures mentioned above. Apart from the judicial penalties, our knowledge about the treatment of persecuted persons by the Gestapo, SS and the guards in the concentration camps derives mainly from personal testimonies. That is, we know much more about the sufferings of the survivors than about the sufferings of the ones who perished. Unfortunately this also is true for the Jewish people discussed here, about whom we therefore know nearly nothing. One has to keep this fact in mind when talking about treatment experienced during persecution. Additionally, shame often makes the survivors hesitate to speak about certain experiences.[18] For example, when we were doing the documentation on Austrian inmates of the Ravensbrück concentration camp, it was very difficult to convince women convicted of *'Verbotener Umgang'* to give us an interview, and all but one of them chose a pseudonym for the publication of their story (Amesberger/Halbmayr 2001, vol. 2).

The aforementioned different effects of the laws foreshadowed the legal proceedings and the accompanying treatments by the perpetrators (neighbours, Gestapo, SS and guards in the concentration camps), as well as the different conditions of survival for various groups of inmates.[19] From the very beginning of persecution, women had to endure humiliating acts by police, Gestapo, and SS men. These quite common tortures had specific characteristics in the case of women accused of *'Rassenschande'* and *'Verbotener Umgang'*. One of these specific treatments, reported by our interviewees, was public derision and humiliation. Maria S., a former inmate of the concentration camps Auschwitz-Birkenau and Ravensbrück, imprisoned for 'forbidden contact' (she had a daughter with a Czech man) and work sabotage, remembered:[20]

> They shaved my hair. And then they hung a board around my neck on which was written: 'While our men shed their blood at the front, I defiled my German blood with a Czech.' With that board around the neck we had to sit in a tramway so everyone could see. (*IKF-Rav-Int._12/1, 49*)[21]

The Nazis used various means for humiliation and stigmatizing, including hair shaving and additional marking through the use of hanging a signboard, as in the above quotation. Verbal abuse, such as calling the victims 'whores', and physical abuse, were further means.

A. Huber, a maid at a farmyard in Upper Austria, was denounced for having a relationship with a Polish forced labourer. Imprisoned in December 1943 in Linz, she was forced to listen to the torturing of her beloved, and had to repulse sexual advances by a Gestapo man.

> I had to wait outside and he [the Pole] was inside the small room and I had to listen how they [the Gestapo] beat him and how he screamed. The Gestapo man wanted me to go with him in a dark room. The next day I would be free, if I did what he wanted. But I told him: 'See, you imprisoned me as a whore and I will stay in prison as a whore'. (*IKF-Rav-Int._14/1, 15f.*).

Aloisia Hofinger, a maid at a farmhouse, fell in love with a Polish forced labourer, Jozef. Denounced by another maid, she and Jozef were imprisoned by the Gestapo in Linz in 1942, but after some weeks she was released so she could give birth. In the following interview sequence she remembers the humiliating interrogation procedures:

During imprisonment, at the interrogations, they were so humiliating. Oh God! What they said to one's face! (*IKF-Rav_13/1, 21*).

In this interview she also spoke about what happened during her second imprisonment (after giving birth to a daughter), when by chance she met Jozef. He was ravaged by SS torture. It would be their last meeting.

> Suddenly Jozef was standing next to me, and he made like this [*Aloisia Hofinger made a hand gesture*]. Oh God, when I saw, I could have cried so much! But I was not allowed to do so. He signalled that he would be hanged. (*IKF-Rav-Int._13/1, 4*).

It was nearly unbearable for the women to witness the tortures of their friends, and to know about their executions (one was hanged, the other was shot). It caused heavy trauma which often had long-lasting consequences. The way the women spoke reveals that sixty years later, the memories are still burdensome.

> Once I saw him. They had beaten him so heavily that he was not able to walk any more. They carried him out on a stretcher… Eight days later I was told that he had been shot. [*silence for 8 seconds*] This was very difficult. (*IKF-Rav_14/1, 2*).

In the concentration camps there waited further torments for these groups of women. Non-Jewish women who were imprisoned for '*Rassenschande*' and '*Verbotener Umgang*' had to endure – like their Jewish fellows in misery – repeated hair shaving for the sake of stigmatization. Not only were they insulted as 'whores', they were checked for sexually transmitted diseases, and the non-Jewish women were 'offered' labour as sex workers in a concentration camp, SS or military brothel. Mrs. Huber had to undergo such a recruitment procedure:

> We once came into the *Krankenrevier* [camp hospital] and there we were selected. They stuck hot iron bars into the abdomen. They would have chosen us for the SS, for the brothel. And I refused to do so. I did not go there. Because, they told us, one would go free after half a year. But no one came back. (*IKF-Rav_14/1, 17*).

This interview sequence reveals the double moral standards of the SS. Many women were on the one hand persecuted because of prostitution or their sexual lives, and on the other hand they were forced into sex work.[22] A very painful and humiliating torture with sexual connotations was public whippings, up to 70 lashes on the naked buttocks.[23] Anneliese Bach reported in 1960 at the administration of the city of Linz that she had had to witness the whipping of her fellow inmate A.L. in the Ravensbrück concentration camp:

> Mrs. L. told me then that she was alleged having had contact with a Pole and that she was imprisoned for that reason. Once together with many others I had to watch her lashing by a female SS guard at the *Lagerplatz* [camp place]. (*OF-Akt Magistrat Salzburg*).

These brief sketches give only a glimpse of, and nevertheless a horrible insight into, the reality of the camp. We can hardly imagine what happened to the ones who were murdered – who did not have the luck to survive, as in the case of most of the Jewish women in our data base convicted of *'Rassenschande'*. But humiliation and stigmatization did not end even when the women were set free, which sometimes was delayed by local authorities, as they didn't support petitions for mercy from relatives and employers (see IKF-Rav_ 13/1, 12). The stories about returning home indicate the ongoing shame, humiliation and stigmatization which continued after being freed. The women waited until night and took side roads so as not to be seen. Later on, they hesitated to go to church or even walk through the village; always they had the feeling of being watched. Two quotations, the first one by A. Huber, the second by Aloisia Hofinger, give an idea of the anxieties of the survivors and the atmosphere in the villages.

> When I arrived in Attnang-Puchheim, I stood there, considering whether to go home or what else to do. It was a one and half hour walk to my home. I walked across the fields and meadows… The first way was to the grave of my grandmother… And then through the village, I took the side roads because I felt so embarrassed. Because all the people shouted, 'Someone should cut her hair! Put her in chains! Beat her!'… My father cried, 'My God! A.!' And I knelt down, I tell you the truth [*A.H. cries calmly*], and then I asked pardon, I asked to be allowed to come home. My reputation was so bad, and the people held my parents responsible for it. (*IKF-Rav_14/1, 5*).
> I did not go through the village for ten years, because I always was afraid that people were watching me… I always had the feeling that they despised me. The feeling! They talked nicely with me, were not mean or cross. But I had this feeling. Behind my back they talked, nevertheless. (*IKF-Rav_13/1, 35*).

These small villages where most of the women lived gave no protection from libel and slander: one could not hide in the anonymity of the city. So it is not surprising that some of these women left their home villages for places where no one knew their stories. Others fled into marriage to escape from gossip and from being stigmatized as 'whores' (Amesberger/Halbmayr 2001, vol. 2, 222ff.; see also Hauch 2006, 269f.).

Pregnancy and motherhood

The National Socialist conceptions of gender display continuities of bourgeois attitudes of appropriate behaviours and roles. The ideals of bourgeois morals determined the gender-specific division of labour, the standardization of sexuality, of masculinity and femininity. They experienced a critical development in National Socialism insofar as the gender conceptions were informed and reinforced by an anti-Semitic and racist ideology. Masculinity was the fundament of the nation and society, while at the same time the 'German' woman was idealized as keeper of the societal morals and the public as well as private order (Mosse 1985, 23). In the attribution of these functions and roles the control of women's sexuality and reproductive abilities already was set; indeed, it was a precondition. The idealization of women, therefore, only seems to contradict National Socialist practices of forced abortion, forced sterilization, the killing of newborns and the removal of children from their parents. These practices were intended to help to create a 'healthy, racially pure body of the *Volk*'. Sexual behaviour therefore became a state affair, an affair of the whole society (Foucault 1983, 95ff.).

The Nazis financially supported marriages and births, provided they concerned 'racially pure Germans'. Until 1933, abortion and sterilization were forbidden by law (Schulz 1994, 136); in Germany in January 1934, the 'Law for the Protection of Hereditary Health' (*Gesetz zum Schutz der Erbgesundheit*) was enacted, whose aim was the forced sterilization of certain groups like people with handicaps, Jews, Romas, and people who were labelled 'antisocial' (*gemeinschaftsfremd*).[24] The situation of pregnant women and mothers therefore depended heavily on the racist and anti-Semitic classification, but also – as we have already seen in the cases of women accused of *'Rassenschande'* and *'Verbotener Umgang'* – on whether a woman met the morals of the Nazi regime.

Pregnant women and mothers were confronted with additional psychic as well as physical burdens, and threatened with being killed (Embacher 1996, 145f.), which often had severe effects on the ones who survived.

These agonizing memories describe the penetration of cruelties into the most intimate corners of life, and how mothers were made incapable of being mothers. In that, the NS system played off the well-being of the mother against the well-being of her child; it made the mother [a party] to the means of her own torture. As an answer to this merciless system ... the infinite multifaceted life stories by female survivors of the Holocaust reveal a split of the personality of the protagonists. (Horowitz 1997, 133; translation by the authors).

But here again we have to distinguish between different groups of women. The National Socialists treated pregnant women and mothers also according to their primary goal of the creation of a 'master race', a *Herrenrasse*. Thus pregnant women and mothers who were classified as Jews or Roma/Sinti were deported to the concentration camps despite their status. The Nazis did not care about their condition. These women and their young children had nearly no chance to survive (Embacher 1996, 146). Whereas 'Aryan' women, insofar as they were not handicapped or classified as antisocial, were not exposed to forced abortion or deported to concentration camps with their children. As already stated above, many (but not all) pregnant 'Aryan' prisoners were released for the time of giving birth, even when the father of the child was a Slav. This was mainly due to the lack of facilities in the prisons, but also to the National Socialist population policy.

Unfortunately we do not know anything about the fate of the children of those women who were deported because of *'Rassenschande'*. According to Saurer's case study, 10 of 31 couples had children (Saurer 2005, 356). In most cases, our Ravensbrück data base does not give any indication about the number of children the women had, but we can deduct from the average age of the persecuted women, and the figures given by Saurer, that at least one-third must have had children. It can be assumed that the children, if they were classified as 'half-breeds', were not imprisoned. Nevertheless, the separation would have been dreadful for many women. The two groups of women studied here share the fate of separation from their children. Even though it might have been a relief to know that the children were safe, the separation caused sorrow, as our interviewee Aloisia Hofinger remembered:

> When the police came for me, I ran quickly to the grandma who took care of her [*her daughter Anneliese*]. I *had*, I had to say good bye to her! The police thought I wanted to flee. They ran after me. ... I told them: 'I'm not running away!' I just had to see her once more. She was a very pretty girl. (*IKF-Rav-Int. 13/2, 52*).

We do not know if some women of the *'Rassenschande'* group were pregnant at that time either. The penalties of pregnant women of the *'Verbotener Umgang'* group were often suspended for giving birth, but being a young mother did not protect them for further persecution, as Mrs. Hofinger's fate among many others proves. In these cases the NS authorities seem to have followed a decree from the year 1943, which forbade deporting pregnant women to concentration camps.[25] Before deportation women were to be examined for possible pregnancy, and it was to be verified if a postponement of the penalty was possible. The decree indicates that pregnant women were nevertheless deported. Survivors reported that pregnant women who were brought to the Ravensbrück concentration camp before 1944 were taken to a nearby hospital in Templin to give birth; but they also tell of childbirths in the camp and forced terminations of pregnancies even when well-advanced.[26]

Newborns were killed with injections of gasoline or air. In September 1944, a *Geburtenblock*, a barrack for births, was installed. Between September 1944 and April 1945, over 560 babies were born in Ravensbrück. The women in childbed had to work soon after giving birth and therefore were not able to take care of their babies. Most of the babies were actively killed or allowed to starve.[27] Only few of them (the estimated number is 100) survived, thanks to the solidarity of fellow inmates and/or because they were born in the last weeks before liberation. These traumatic experiences – whether separation from their children, being pregnant and giving birth under inhuman conditions, or to seeing their newborn killed – sometimes alienated the survivors from their children. Some hesitated to have children at all and/or to marry (Amesberger/Auer/Halbmayr 2004, 288ff; Horowitz 1997, 133).

Conclusions

The penal legislation and its implementations show the intersections of patriarchal and racist ideology. Patriarchal, because in the case of soldiers, the authorities tolerated sexual intercourse with women of 'non-German blood' outside the so-called *Heimatfront* (home front), justifying it with the different male character. The latter has to be seen as a war strategy, too, which fulfils two purposes at once, as Ruth Seifert (1994, 181f.) has stated: Sexual abuse harms the individual male identity of the enemy and the national masculinity at the same time. In any case, the legislation and its implementations were built upon and enforced basic gender-specific norms, values and notions. The female role model was constructed primarily in a dichotomous way – the mother and the whore. But the patriarchal-sexist impetus alone is insufficient for explaining the different treatment of the victims. The offences of *'Rassenschande'* and *'Verbotener Umgang'* reveal strongly social-Darwinist thinking and the racist aim of the National Socialists to create a master race, a pure breed of 'Aryan' mankind. Jewish people and Slavs convicted of these 'crimes' were more likely to die or be killed then their 'Aryan' counterparts.

As we have elaborated above, the treatment of these women by the Nazis was accompanied by sexualized violence.[28] Differentiating forms of sexualized violence according to their ideological layers shows that violence against women cannot be seen exclusively as an expression of misogyny, as violent acts against women or symbols of femininity would seem to indicate. The fact that specific forms of violent acts were executed only against specific groups of women, refers to ideological intersections of misogyny with racism, anti-Semitism, hetero-sexism etc. Concerning the intersection of sexism and anti-Semitism/racism we therefore can differentiate various forms of violence: *Sexualized misogynistic violence* was directed against one's identity as a woman, against one's sexual integrity, against one's identity as a mother and against the self-determination of one's own body. The main goals of sexualized-misogynistic violence were to humiliate the victim and to strengthen the patriarchal system. *Sexualized anti-Semitic* or *sexualized racist violence* was directed against a woman as a representative and a symbol of a persecuted group, against women who offered resistance to the racist population policy, and against the female body defined in a racist way. Sexualized violence was directed towards her as a woman *and* as a Jewish person, as a woman *and* as a Roma or a Sinti, etc. Repeated hair shaving, forced sterilization and abortions were forms of this kind of violence. The goal of the Nazis was the meta-level 'race'. They pursued a strongly racist and anti-Semitic population policy that aimed to eliminate people who were categorised as 'non-Aryan'. The examples of *'Verbotener Umgang'* and

'Rassenschande' discussed above, as well as the different treatment of Jewish and non-Jewish women, make obvious how interwoven ideological aspects affected the persecution of women, and how strongly this interdependence determined the extent of sexualized violence.

Notes

1 The 'Blood Protection Law' went into effect on 15 September 1935 in Germany; in Austria this law was inaugurated 20 May 1938, only two months after the so-called *Anschluss.*

2 The project 'Registration by Name: Austrian inmates of the Ravensbrück concentration camp' is an ongoing research project by the authors and Kerstin Lercher at the Institute of Conflict Research in Vienna. So far the data base consists of approximately 2,150 names.

3 In Germany, interdictions of marriages by the Catholic Church had been overturned in 1874 (see Saurer 2005, 342).

4 Ibid., 342f. Saurer stresses that these religious regulations had contributed significantly to the notion of 'mixture' as evil without referring to 'race'. She does not consider, in her reflections on the continuities of ideas, that in the late fifteenth century the Catholic Church had already introduced the imperative of the *limpieza de sangre* ('purity of blood'): descent, and not religious affiliation, became the ultimate borderline (Amesberger/Halbmayr 2007).

5 Paragraphs 1 and 2 of this law say: '§ 1 (1) Eheschließungen zwischen Juden und Staatsangehörigen deutschen oder artverwandten Blutes sind verboten. Trotzdem geschlossene Ehen sind nichtig, auch wenn sie zur Umgehung dieses Gesetzes im Ausland geschlossen sind. ... § 2 Außerehelicher Verkehr zwischen Juden und Staatsangehörigen deutschen oder artverwandten Blutes ist verboten.'

6 Figures are available only for Vienna; no research has been done so far for the other Austrian federal states. In Germany (*Altreich*) 2,211 lawsuits concerning *'Rassenschande'* were filed in the years 1935-1945 (Przyrembel 2003, 499).

7 In the following, this is called 'Ravensbrück data base'. The two data bases slightly overlap because we too studied the 'declarations in lieu of an oath' at the Documentation Centre of Austrian Resistance. On the one hand our data are broader, insofar as we did not constrict our research to the region of Vienna; on the other hand it is narrower, because we only were interested in cases where the woman or man was imprisoned in the Ravensbrück concentration camp.

8 About the fate of the partners or the hidden persons, we do not know anything. Nor do we know how many children they had or what happened with them.

9 The exact figures: nine Jewish women were murdered, two survived, and the fate of the other two is unknown. Out of the 13 non-Jewish women, only one died, the fate of one is unknown, and 11 survived.

10 The law 'Verordnung zur Ergänzung der Strafvorschriften zum Schutz der

Wehrkraft des Deutschen Volkes' was enacted on 25 November 1939 (RGBl. I, 2319). It says: '(1) Wer vorsätzlich gegen eine zur Regelung des Umgangs mit Kriegsgefangenen erlassene Vorschrift verstößt oder sonst mit einem Gefangenen in einer Weise Umgang pflegt, die das gesunde Volksempfinden gröblich verletzt, wird mit Gefängnis, in schweren Fällen mit Zuchthaus bestraft. (2) Bei fahrlässigem Verstoß gegen die zur Regelung des Umgangs mit Kriegsgefangenen erlassenen Vorschriften ist die Strafe Haft oder Geldstrafe bis zu einhundertfünfzig Reichsmark.'

11 Hauch studied 453 criminal procedures of the *Sondergericht* at the *Landesgericht Linz* (at that time *Oberdonau*, now Upper Austria) from 1940-1943.

12 Waldner listed a total of 76 cases of *'Verbotener Umgang'*. 61 of the alleged lawbreakers were women, 15 were men. A comparison of the penalties according to gender showed no differences, but a male foreigner got the highest penalty; he was sentenced to eight years of aggravated punishment camp.

13 Such as the women's jail in Aichach, Upper Bavaria; the Munich-Stadelheim women's prison; the police prison in Linz; and the youth prison in Frankfurt/Main-Preungesheim.

14 In our Ravensbrück data base there is only one exception. Gritta Kral-Baumgartner met with French civil workers but also violated the law concerning listening to the radio. This double infraction could be an explanation for her deportation to the Ravensbrück concentration camp.

15 In 29 cases we do not know whether the victims survived or not.

16 Usually they were executed at the local police station or in the village where they lived for the purpose of deterrence.

17 Nearly two-thirds of the *'Rassenschande'* group were over 30, whereas two-thirds of the *'Verbotener Umgang'* group were younger than 30. The youngest was 16 when imprisoned.

18 Amesberger 2003; Amesberger/Auer/Halbmayr 2004, 43ff.; Rosenthal 1999.

19 As the statistics above have shown, the social hierarchy created by the SS within the prisoners' society was essential for survival. Jewish people along with Roma, Sinti, homosexuals and Soviet inmates were ranked at the bottom of the hierarchy and had to endure the worst conditions. For the social structure and power relations within concentration camps see Sofsky 1999, 152ff.

20 The quotations that follow are from interviews conducted in 1999; the interviews are archived at the Institute of Conflict Research (IKF) in Vienna. For the biographies of Maria S., A. Huber and Aloisia Hofinger, see Amesberger/Halbmayr 2001, vol. 2, 211-215, 76-81, 99-103. In respect to this kind of public abuse, see also Hauch 2006, 258ff.

21 All translations of IKF-Rav-Int. quotations are done by the authors.

22 For a more thorough discussion of forced sex work, the legal basis, the motives of the SS, the recruiting procedures and so on, see Halbmayr 2005.

23 See collections MGR/StBG. – RA I/6-7-6; collections MGR/StBG. – F.7.Kie; interview no. 12/1, 13/1 and 14/2 with survivors of the Ravensbrück concentration camp archived

at the Institute of Conflict Research, Vienna.

24 In Austria, similar laws (the 'Gesetz zur Verhütung erbkranken Nachwuchses' and the 'Gesetz zum Schutze der Gesundheit des deutschen Volkes') were enacted on 1 January 1940 (Treiber 2004).

25 Decree on the 'Verbot der Einweisung schwangerer Häftlinge in das Frauenkonzentratio nslager Ravensbrück bzw. in die Frauenabteilungen der Konzentrationslager Auschwitz und Lublin', 6 May 1943 (Sammlungen MGR/StBG. – RA II/3-1-16, copy).

26 Pawelke 1994, 158; see also IKF-Rav-Int. 20_1-3; Sammlungen MGR/StGB. – Bd. 15/3, 11.

27 We have elaborated the topic of pregnancy and births during persecution more thoroughly in Amesberger/Auer/Halbmayr 2004, 245ff.

28 We prefer the term *sexualised violence* to the term *sexual violence* as we do not only mean direct, physical violence against women (and men) referring to their sexuality but also violent acts beyond these physical forms, such as: infringement on the sense of shame, verbal humiliation, psychical constraint to sexual actions, medical intervention or experiments etc. The term *sexualised violence* refers to the dimension *direct/physical violence* as well as to the dimension *indirect/structural violence*. Directly acting perpetrators are, in any context, transgressing the physic and psychic borders of the victims. Indirect violence includes suppression by an institution or system. For a more detailed definition of sexualized violence, see Amesberger/Auer/Halbmayr 2004, 26ff. and 326ff.

Sources and References
Sources
Ravensbrück Memorial Museum

Collections MGR/StGB. – Bd. 15/3, ,Helmstedt, Stahlwerke Braunschweig, Behrndorf, Lebensborn (…)', p.11, 13 and 14.

Collections MGR/StBG. – F.7.Kie; Kiedrzynska, Wanda: Ravensbrück: kobiecy oboz koncentrcyjny/Polska Akademia Nauk. – Warszawa: Ksiazka i Wiedza, 1961. – 379 S., Abb.

Collections MGR/StBG. – RA I/6-7-6; Überblick über die Reviertätigkeit von März 1942 bis Ende April 45, S. 1-16.

Collections MGR/StBG. – RA II/3-1-16 (copy). – RdErl. Des ChdSPudSD vom 6.5.1943 – IV C 2 Nr. 43 076.

Institute of Conflict Research (Vienna)
Life story interviews with survivors of the Ravensbrück concentration: IKF-Rav-Int. 12/1; IKF-Rav-Int._13/1-2; IKF-Rav-Int._14/1-2; IKF-Rav-Int._20_1-3.
Others
OF-Akt des Magistrat Salzburg von A.L. (administration file of the city of Salzburg).

References

Amesberger Helga, 'Die Schwierigkeit zu reden. Die Thematisierung von Zwangssexarbeit in der Lebensgeschichte', in *kunst – kommunikation – macht. Sechster Österreichischer Zeitgeschichtetag 2003*, eds Bauer Ingrid, Embacher Helga, Hanisch Ernst, Lichtblau Albert and Sprengnagel Gerald, Innsbruck et al., 2004, 310-314.

Amesberger Helga, Auer Katrin and Halbmayr Brigitte, *Sexualisierte Gewalt. Weibliche Erfahrungen in NS-Konzentrationslagern*, Vienna, 2004.

Amesberger Helga and Halbmayr Brigitte, *Das Privileg der Unsichtbarkeit. Rassismus unter dem Blickwinkel von Weißsein und Dominanzkultur*, Vienna, 2008 (in print).

Amesberger Helga and Halbmayr Brigitte, *Vom Leben und Überleben – Wege nach Ravensbrück. Das Frauenkonzentrationslager in der Erinnerung*, 2 vols, Vienna, 2001, vol. 1: Dokumentation und Analyse, vol. 2: Lebensgeschichten.

Crenshaw Kimberlé W., 'Demarginalizing the Intersection of Race and Sex: A Black Feminist Critique of Antidiscrimination Doctrine, Feminist Theory, and Antiracist Politics', in *Living with Contradictions. Controversies in Feminist Social Ethics*, ed Jaggar Alison M., Boulder/San Francisco/Oxford, 1994, 39-52.

Embacher Helga, 'Frauen in Konzentrations- und Vernichtungslagern – weibliche Überlebensstrategien in Extremsituationen', in *Strategie des Überlebens*, eds Streibel Robert and Schafranek Hans, Vienna, 1996, 145-167.

Foucault Michel, *Sexualität und Wahrheit. Der Wille zum Wissen*, Frankfurt/Main, 1983.

Halbmayr Brigitte, 'Arbeitskommando „Sonderbau". Zur Bedeutung und Funktion von Bordellen im KZ', *Dachauer Hefte 21*, no. 21, (2005), 217-236.

Hauch Gabriella, '"... das gesunde Volksempfinden gröblich verletzt". Verbotener Geschlechtsverkehr mit „Anderen" während des Nationalsozialismus', in *Frauen in Oberdonau*, ed Hauch Gabriella, Linz, 2006, 245-270.

Horowitz Sara R., 'Geschlechtsspezifische Erinnerungen an den Holocaust', in *Forschungsschwerpunkt Ravensbrück. Beiträge zur Geschichte des Frauen-Konzentrationslagers*, eds Jacobeit Sigrid and Philipp Grit, Schriftenreihe der Stiftung Brandenburgische Gedenkstätten, vol. 9, Berlin, 1997, 131-135.

Moser Jonny, *Demographie der jüdischen Bevölkerung Österreichs 1938-1945*, Vienna, 1999.

Mosse George L., *Nationalsozialismus und Sexualität. Bürgerliche Moral und sexuelle Normen*, Munich/Vienna, 1985.

Pawelke Britta, 'Als Häftling geboren – Kinder in Ravensbrück', in *Frauen in Konzentrationslagern. Bergen-Belsen, Ravensbrück*, eds Füllberg-Stolberg Klaus, Jung Martina, Riebe Renate and Scheitenberger Martina, Bremen, 1994, 157-166.

Przyrembel Alexandra, *„Rassenschande". Reinheitsmythos und ernichtungslegitimation im Nationalsozialismus*, Göttingen, 2003.

Rosenthal Gabriele, 'Sexuelle Gewalt in Kriegs- und Verfolgungszeiten: Biographische und transgenerationelle Spätfolgen bei Überlebenden der Shoah, ihren Kindern und EnkelInnen', in *Krieg, Geschlecht und Traumatisierung. Erfahrungen und Reflexionen in der Arbeit mit traumatisierten Frauen in Kriegs- und Krisengebieten*, eds Medica mondiale e.V., Fröse Marlies W. and Volpp-Teuscher Ina, Frankfurt/Main, 1999, 25-56.

Saurer Edith, 'Verbotene Vermischungen. "Rassenschande", Liebe und Wiedergutmachung', in *Liebe und Widerstand. Ambivalenzen historischer Geschlechterbeziehungen*, eds Bauer Ingrid, Hämmerle Christa and Hauch Gabriella, L'homme Schriften 10 (Reihe zur Feministischen Geschichtswissenschaft), Vienna, Cologne, Weimar, 2005, 341-361.

Seifert Ruth, 'Weiblichkeit, kriegerische Gewalt und männliche Macht. Zur Funktion von sexueller Gewalt im Krieg und im Frieden', in *Gewalt gegen Frauen, Frauen gegen Gewalt. Tagungsdokumentation*, ed. Dohnal Johanna, vol. 2, Vienna, 1994, 175-185.

Schulz Christa, 'Weibliche Häftlinge aus Ravensbrück in Bordellen der Männerkonzentrationslager', in *Frauen in Konzentrationslagern. Bergen-Belsen, Ravensbrück*, eds Füllberg-Stolberg Klaus, Jung Martina, Riebe Renate and Scheitenberger Martina, Bremen, 1994, 135-146.

Sofsky Wolfgang, *Die Ordnung des Terrors: Das Konzentrationslager*, 3rd edn, Frankfurt am Main, 1999.

Strebel Bernhard, *Das KZ Ravensbrück. Zur Geschichte eines Lagerkomplexes*, Paderborn et al., 2003.

Treiber Isa, *Menschenrechte trotz Behinderung: Zur Sexualität, Partnerschaft, und Sterilisationsproblematik geistig behinderter Menschen*, (diploma thesis University of Klagenfurt, 2004), http://bidok.uibk.ac.at/library/treiber-menschenrechte.html#id2849921, download 17 April 2006.

Waldner Josef, *"Verbotener Umgang mit Kriegsgefangenen"* in Tirol. Die Akten des Sondergerichts beim Landgericht Innsbruck 1939-1945, diploma thesis, University of Innsbruck, 1994.

Social Base of Racial Othering in Nazi Society: The Racial Community and Women's Agency in Denunciatory Practices

Vandana Joshi

This essay explores the social process of 'racial othering' in Nazi Germany, which culminated in the Holocaust known to the entire humanity for its notoriously organised, bureaucratised, impersonalised and industrial mass murder of the Jews carried out as a 'state enterprise'. This unimaginable reality, however, had a very personal, individual and intimate side to it that expressed itself in spontaneous forms of willing participation in the perpetration of crimes on the part of its ordinary citizens. Racial othering in Nazi Germany, therefore, was a dynamic process in which both the state and its citizens participated actively. Although 'Aryan' men's agency has been a subject of scrutiny in their various capacities as state functionaries, policemen, army men, doctors, ordinary people, and so on, women perpetrators have almost been entirely absent from this discourse, mainly because they were a minority in official positions of any kind.

My concern in this essay is to probe human agency in acts of denunciation carried out in an entirely voluntary manner on the part of ordinary Germans, especially women. Women's agency in the power structure unfolds here in its most intimate, private and informal settings of the family, community and society. For it is here that they are found in their masses. What I write here is social history of the intimate and the personal, the trivial and the mundane, which acquired a dangerously political colouring in Nazi Germany. And the Gestapo files seem to be an appropriate source to dig out stories of compliance and collaboration.

These Gestapo files pertain to persecuted Jewish individuals whose cases came to the notice of the Gestapo functionaries as a result of denunciations from ordinary Germans. Since the 1990s, important work on the Gestapo by Gellately and others has shown how the Third Reich's feared political police force was not an all-pervasive, omnipotent network of surveillance and control, as previously thought, but it was, rather, a relatively small organisation that depended heavily for its information on unsolicited denunciations of deviants and dissenters by ordinary people.[1] Ordinary women sent in a substantial number of these denunciations. So far no one has thought to ask why. This paper attempts to seek an answer by looking beneath the skin of these denouncers and thereby recreating their life-world situations, which tied them to the 'big politics' of the racial state.

Denunciations, as they are generally understood, were reports filed by ordinary citizens in their individual capacities, of infractions on the part of the so-called 'enemies of the Reich' with an intention of punishing the offender. Denouncers were different from informers who were regularly in touch with the political police and who were rewarded in cash or kind for their deeds. Denunciations, on the other hand, were completely spontaneous acts understood as an event-based participation in the terror apparatus. This illustrates how longstanding neighbors suddenly became aliens overnight, how relations accused each other of anti-state activity for helping the Jews, how conspiracies were hatched in closed circles, and how a highly assimilated community was marginalized, stigmatized and excluded at a societal level.

The study is based on an intensive treatment of individual case files categorised as Jewry in the Gestapo Archives Düsseldorf. It situates the problematic of denunciation in its quotidian context of ordinary citizens in order to find out who the formal denouncers were, and who the instigators. How did women denouncers use it to root out those 'aliens to the community'?

Let me first talk briefly about the nature of the Gestapo files. These files were minimalistic in their content some times, and quite detailed at others. The Gestapo functionary relied more on oral communication where dangerous enemies like the Communists were concerned, and indoctrination certainly played no minor role here. On the other hand, detailed enquiries into the crime were made where unorganized, spontaneous infractions were concerned. They presented a sanitized version of the events as they unfolded. There are, for example, no traces of torture and third degree interrogation that the Gestapo became so notorious for. Nevertheless, certain clues betrayed the sense of brutalization and intimidation that the victims suffered in statements like, "after being warned to tell the truth I now confess…" Similarly, the duration of the stay in the Gestapo torture cells, during which victims were interrogated repeatedly – which itself was harrowing enough for people with no criminal record – communicated a sense of how different crimes were treated differently. As the atrocity visited upon the Jews intensified with time, so did the treatment of the Gestapo. The Gestapo files can be juxtaposed with oral testimonies – to which I shall turn later – of the victims that appeared mostly after the fall of the Reich. It is in these accounts that the full horrors of the Gestapo brutalities come alive in telling details. Social history writing, however, moves beyond the experiential and the subjective realities of these stigmatized individuals as enemies of the Reich, and yet problematizes political denunciations as stories of envy, jealousy, human pettiness and hatred and provides insights into a radically altered moral universe. It shows how definitions of 'threat', 'ethics' and 'security' changed beyond imagination as normal relations were criminalized.

The qualitative analysis, among other things, deals with the power relations between denouncers, denounced and the Gestapo. This entails analysing popular perceptions of the terror state whereby the discrepancies between the original intention of the state in declaring something an offence and its appropriation by ordinary citizens become visible. Out of the 20 categories listing various crimes of Jews, I have selected four, which hinted at some interaction between 'Aryans' and Jews. These were *Rassenschande* or race defilement, *Judenfreundlich* or friendly behaviour towards the Jews, *Staatsfeindlich* or anti-state activities of the Jews, and *Kennkartebestimmung* or verification of identity cards.

Quantitative participation of the *Volksgenossen* in denouncing the Jews

In total I studied some 138 case files. Sixty-one (about 45%) of them resulted from denunciations. From these 29 came from male denouncers, 8 were anonymous and 20 came from women, while in 4 cases women acted as accomplices. By women accomplices, I mean those women who did not surface at the first look in the file, but ended up playing a more important role as witnesses. Let me give an example: this is a case of 'race defilement' filed against one Leo, a Jew, who was charged of having sexual relations with various German women. Leo's neighbour Peter, a businessman, denounced him in 1938. He stated that he was informed by the Reichmann couple that last year an 'Aryan' maid, Bertha, stayed in Leo's house in an advanced state of pregnancy. Leo's wife was not there at that time. When Bertha started bleeding, Leo accompanied her to the doctor. The treatment cost to the tune of RM. 200. After the birth of the child Leo went around telling the neighbours that he was the grandfather of the child.[2]

The denouncer Peter then suggested the Gestapo to get in touch with the Reichmanns to get exact information. First, Herr Reichmann was contacted. He could not be of much help. He just aired his suspicion that from the behaviour of Leo towards his maid anybody could gauge that there was more between the two than a mere acquaintance, and suggested turning to his wife for inside information. Now the main witness entered the scene. Frau Reichmann had worked in Leo's house after Bertha left. She told the Gestapo that Leo brought Bertha home the previous year in an advanced state of pregnancy. Later, Bertha was shifted to another place at Leo's wife's insistence, who wanted Bertha to be sent away, before she started on her journey to the south. But as soon as she left, Bertha was again in Leo's house and they both visited the doctor regularly. Having finished with her story, Frau Reichmann told the Gestapo to contact Frau Neumann to get more information. She also said that Leo had made advances towards her, but she had turned a cold shoulder and later left the job. Frau Neumann again had a thing or two to say about the whole matter. She suggested names of a few more women who could help the Gestapo in this matter. The point of narrating the whole episode is what seemed like a case and initiated by a male denouncer at the first sight was actually substantiated by a chain of women denouncers. Their statements clearly carried more weight than that of the original denouncer!

Out of the total 24 cases reported by women denouncers and accomplices, the majority of cases (i.e. 16) were against their neighbours, while 3 were against relations, 4 against colleagues, and one against a stranger. Out of 28 male denouncers 12 were neighbours, 2 relations, 5 colleagues and 9 strangers. The faceless data hide tragic destinies of Jewish victims, which will be unveiled in the subsequent parts of the paper by citing profiles of victims. My effort here would be to recreate the cosmos of women denouncers by giving an in-depth analysis of some representative cases.

While both men and women denounced their neighbours and relations to the Gestapo, their motives varied at times, as did the number. Women, especially housewives, expressed more vehemently and openly their desire to make the community free of Jews, especially in families and neighbourhoods. They virtually acted as *self-appointed neighbourhood watchdogs* and *social mothers* of the racial community and denounced Jewish neighbours, Jewish passersby or inconspicuous fellow shoppers in the supermarkets, groceries and provision stores, to the control organisations. These areas were, so to say, the niche areas of female 'racial comrades'.

Further, a tendency was found in 'Aryan' women to gang up against Jews, typically a neighbour or sometimes even an employer. We have already seen in Leo's case how a male neighbour along with several maids in Leo's employ gave testimonies against the accused. Similarly, an 'Aryan' soldier's Jewish wife, Frau Müller, was denounced by her neighbours, two women and one man, of having illicit relations with a German, Herr Mann, while her husband was at the front.[3] The letter sent to the Gestapo on 23 July 1942, was full of moralistic overtones, charging Frau Müller of indulging in the 'shameless act' of race defilement and treating her six children callously. The neighbours were 'rightly' enraged about this immoral act and felt compelled to report the matter to the Gestapo.

The Gestapo took the accusation very seriously and enquired about the character of the involved 'Aryan', Herr Mann, as well as the concerned Jewish woman. Herr Mann's employer gave a very positive report about the accused, and the neighbours could not give any eyewitness account of the race defilement. It was also found that both the accused had been colleagues in the same firm earlier and Frau Müller had to leave her job upon becoming pregnant. It was in fact Frau Müller's husband who had requested Herr Mann to help his wife in need. The Gestapo report concluded that the charges of the race defilement were baseless. However, the Müllers did not go scot-free. A new enquiry started into Frau Müller's racial origins and religious background. It was discovered that her parents were 'full Jews'. She was, therefore, to be treated as a Jew. It was mandatory for her to have a Jewish identity card and add 'Sara' to her name, which she had not done. She was charged with hiding her racial identity and fined RM. 80. Her husband was expelled from the army in January 1943 for being married to a Jew. Had she not been denounced she would probably have been freed from wearing the star and enjoyed the privilege of mixed marriage. Even a false accusation made in 1942 could have serious consequences! Living in a privileged marriage with six children could not shield the victim.

Our next example goes on to show how various women neighbours first fought their own battles with a Jew living in privileged marriage, a fact not hidden from the Gestapo, and then eventually joined together in 1943 to persecute her. The file of the fifty-three-year-old Jewess Frau Schade, married to an 'Aryan', opened with accusations from her neighbour women for regularly abusing them and creating nuisance in the neighbourhood apart from issuing anti-regime statements.[4] The denunciation letter informed the Gestapo that Frau Schade had regularly been cursing the Rosenthal couple living in the same house. During these fights, which had had a disturbing impact in the neighbourhood, the local police had to intervene on some occasions.

The Schade couple was characterised by the complainant, as 'asocial' and opponents of the regime. The party leader took up the cause of the denouncers and requested the Gestapo to take appropriate action in the matter. The Gestapo's efforts to meet the couple failed thrice as they were not available at their residence for about two months. Eventually they were traced and interrogated. The enquiry revealed that it was just an enmity between two neighbours. Frau Rosenthal called Frau Schade names, who on her part was forced to defend herself. The real reason for the denunciation was the eviction notice, which the Schades had served the Rosenthals. Besides, Frau Schade had filed a defamation and damages suit against Frau Rosenthal. The enquiry report concluded by saying that the state police had no interest in the matter as there was nothing more to it than just trivial domestic gossip. According to neighbours' testimonies the fighting couples had lived in perfect harmony for years. They used to visit each other quite often. The Schades were summoned in any case by the Gestapo, who instructed Frau Schade to exercise restraint as a 'Jewess'.

The case file opened again in September 1943 with a letter from the Security Service (SD) to the Gestapo regarding the 'indecent behaviour of the Jewess'. It stated that for years the Nazi party functionaries *(Ortsgruppenleiter)* had been involved in this case particularly, due to the provocative behaviour of the full Jewess Frau Schade. The local party leader reported that all warnings had gone unheeded, as the Jewess knew that the police were powerless in this matter. A denunciation letter signed by Frau Rosenthal, Frau Eberwald and Frau Jochum was enclosed with the SD letter, which in turn had arrived there from an Army welfare officer.

The most interesting part of the case file was the enclosed letter of denunciation written by Schades' neighbours, all women from middle class backgrounds, who were determined to get rid of her and her 'Aryan' husband at a time when deportation and killings operations were in full swing. It was written on Herr Eberwald's stationery with a stamp: Diploma in management W. E. The letter was written in Frau Eberwald's handwriting and signed by two other women. It was not addresses to any particular office or person so it could be assumed that it was posted to various authorities for taking action, among whom an Army welfare officer took the initiative. The letter read:

> *As a soldier's wife (a prolific mother with six children) I hereby make a request to sternly warn my neighbour, a full Jewess, at once. It has been observed that the Jewess has adopted a particularly provocative stance in the last few months of the war, in spite of the fact that I have already put up with it for so long. Ever since my husband has become a soldier (he was earlier block warden), the situation has become unbearable. The Jewess pours two barrels of liquid*

manure on the hedge on hot days so that one cannot sit outside. I work a lot outside and even eat there. She continuously belches loudly with open mouth, making me feel sick. This goes on the whole day. But she does not do this while talking to others, which she does rather pleasantly. She does not do it either when she sits for hours in the bunker or when she queues up to get the milk. It is only towards us that she turns provocative in every way.

In these times one is happy if one got an hour of relaxation, but one does not get it and boils in rage. I have been patient for many years, but it has become too much now and I cannot bear it any longer. On top of this comes the preferential treatment that the Jewess enjoys when the firewood is being distributed in the nearby bunker. Another neighbouring woman whose forty-five-year-old husband has been a soldier for the past four years asked the building site foreman for some firewood. She did not get it, and the Jewess got two cartfuls. This foreman even told Mr. Schade, who gives himself out as a war invalid, that if he required things like roofing felt, cement, etc. he would get it from him. Thereafter, roofing felt and cement got stolen and were recovered from Schades' house, hidden under the plants. I can tell you that these are only some glimpses of what goes on here. I plead to you to help the parties in this matter urgently. You will also get to know that Schade is a cheat. One should revoke his card for the severely wounded, which has been obtained through unfair means. Even the party knows that he was expelled from the army for insulting His Majesty. If something is not done fast we, soldiers' wives of the neighbourhood, would resort to self-help and take action against the Schades. There is no other way out.

Heil Hitler,
Frau Eberwald
Frau Rosenthal
Frau Jochum

Note: Frau Rosenthal is a war widow from 1914. She lost her son-in-law in Russia who left three children behind. Her own son is at the front. The party has warned Schade three times. The fourth time she was not there and we have no idea about what followed... Frau Jochum is the soldier's wife I mentioned in connection with the firewood.

This was a crafty, well-thought-out letter of a highly aware and literate 'Aryan' housewife who knew what kind of ingredients a denunciation letter should have to make a palatable recipe for evoking a sympathetic response from the authorities. She consciously conjured up black-and-white images of the denouncers and the denounced, projecting all evil onto the Jewish woman and her husband and all good and virtuousness onto the denouncers. Presenting herself as a prolific mother and a soldier's wife, who had sacrificed immensely for the fatherland and so on, were obvious efforts in this direction. Men of successive generations of their families were presented as brave soldiers of the Fatherland, and so on.

Their Jewish neighbor, on the other hand, was a mischiefmaker, a matchmaker, and a quarrelsome woman. While the denouncers were deprived of essential items like firewood, Frau Schade was apparently living in abundance and luxury. Herr Schade was accused of procuring his card for severely wounded war veterans through fraudulent means. Equally interesting in the letter were some realities that remained hidden. Repeated mention was made of the war years and resultant hardships for ordinary 'Aryan' women like the denouncers, but the letter was silent about any knowledge that the denouncers may have had as to what the war years meant for the Jews. Considering that they were all soldiers' wives, who were themselves quite aware of the realities of the Third Reich, they certainly could not have been totally oblivious of it. Despite this, they constantly addressed Frau Schade as 'the Jewess'.

The letter demanded that the Jewess be 'warned sternly', even though the denouncers were aware that the couple had already been warned thrice. It was clear that they were not satisfied with mere warnings. While Frau Eberwald wrote with much pride that all complainants were soldiers' wives, she completely ignored the fact that she was herself complaining against a soldier's wife. It is from the Gestapo's record that we learn that Herr Schade was a war veteran who sustained major injuries in the First World War that left him a physically challenged person for the rest of his life. The denouncers did not just disregard his sacrifices for the Fatherland, they even projected him as a cheat who procured his card for the severely wounded war veterans through fraudulent means.

Silence also prevailed upon the serious illnesses that the denounced couple suffered from. Frau Schade was a diabetic who was under medical observation when the Gestapo came to her house for investigations. Similarly, Herr Schade suffered from heart problems and epileptic fits in addition to being physically challenged. One wonders how such politically vulnerable and physically ailing people could afford to be provocative towards their neighbours all the time? No mention was made in the letter of the fact that Frau Rosenthal turned vicious towards the Schades only after the latter filed an eviction suit against her.

In the whole case, the Gestapo seemed to be more considerate towards the denounced couple than the denouncers. They had to be so, tied as they were to do their obligation towards a severely injured invalid war veteran. If Frau Schade survived the Third Reich, which we cannot say with certainty as the file closed in 1943, it was because her invalid 'Aryan' husband supported her to the bitter end.

'Aryan' neighbors friendly to the Jews were not spared either. Two neighboring women, Frau Möser and Frau Berg denounced another 'Aryan' woman, Frau Frei, for interacting with two Jewish men.[5] The enquiry revealed that there were no objectionable personal relations between the Jews and Frau Frei. However, Frau

Frei had to confess that she took up sewing tasks for them once in a while. She was warned strictly. She had to give a written apology and assurance of compliance in the future, otherwise she would have to reckon with stern state police measures.

There were various motives at work, social jealously being a major one. Frau Lambach, for example, wrote a letter to the district leader (*Gauleiter*) denouncing an 'Aryan' woman living next door for having suddenly become rich and possessing things that did not go with her status as a saleswoman.[6] The denunciation took place in 1940, and the reason for this sudden wealth was given as her friendship with a Jew from Cologne, who had emigrated long before and with whom she had travelled to Brussels and Spain in 1935. The letter ended with the comment that by reporting this she was "responding to the wishes of the *Führer*, who had called upon his comrades to fight for the community in the same spirit as in the days of struggle". The victim had to reckon with postal surveillance, but this did not render any results as the Jew had migrated long ago.

Our next case would demonstrate how social jealousy towards a better-off Jewish neighbour mixed with racial hatred made this denouncer come out in her true colours. Even though the denouncer tried to give an ideological garb to her denunciation, she failed to hide her jealousy and meanness. The denunciation letter was written on 15 September 1941 and was addressed to the Black Corps (*Schwarzes Korps*), the SS mouthpiece. It read as follows:[7]

> *Dear Black Corps,*
> *After much thought, I have decided to write to you, to inform you of a matter relating to the Jewish question and in strict confidence. Before this, I must point it out that it is not now that my 'Aryan' consciousness has awakened. In 1903, as a young woman, I lived with a teacher's family to learn Italian. Once a gentleman came to visit them and asked me if I had heard the beach concert. I said, 'I did not go there'.*
> *He said, 'How sad! There was German music there'.*
> *'What was that', I said.*
> *'Pieces by Meyerbeer'.*
> *I replied, 'Since when has Meyerbeer become a German? He is a 'Jud' [sic; a derogatory term used for Jews]. And then I gave a piece of my mind to them on the question of race...Now back to the point. I want to know who is obliged to wear a star? Is a Jewish woman married to an 'Aryan', and converted since her childhood, freed from wearing the star?*

[The Gestapo remark in the margin of the letter said, "Yes!"]

> *I find that disgraceful! I feel that she should wear the star and her husband too, should do the same. For me, an 'Aryan' who marries a Jew is to be condemned a thousand times more than the Jewish spouse. In our neighbourhood there are*

two rich Jewish sisters living with their 'Aryan' partners. One of these Jewesses has often been seen without a star, the other one is not seen in public at all. The 'Aryan' husbands had to give up their jobs as conductors after the Jewish laws were passed. One of these couples travels a lot and the Jewish woman lives in 'Aryan' hotels. Is it allowed? Is the race of only the husband taken into account? Then an 'Aryan' woman with a Jewish husband must be suffering more under the race law, when she has her husband marked as a Jew.

The family in our neighbourhood owns a house with 32 rooms. They have two 'Aryan' maids and other helpers, two central heating systems. My daughter and I, (on the contrary) are both widows. We have a small house and not even enough coal to heat our house properly and we have to manage with that".
Heil Hitler
Frau Wunder

The cases of social jealousies resulting in denunciations demonstrate how the newly acquired political power was utilised by the ordinary Germans (*Volksgenossen*) to attack the economic superiority of Jews. Pure anti-Semitic hatred could also be the cause of denunciation. The people who were close to the party or those who did believe in the racist doctrines of the regime mostly did this.

Her male neighbour Langmann who, however, named his wife as the main witness, denounced Frau Kohl, a Jewish woman living in a mixed marriage. Frau Langmann told the Gestapo that ever since she had come to know that Frau Kohl was Jewish, she had kept her distance from her. Frau Kohl did not like this and looked for reasons to pick up a fight. Every time she saw Frau Langmann or her children she started abusing them. On one occasion Frau Langmann warned her that if she continued this, she would report her to the public prosecutor. Frau Kohl maligned both the public prosecutor and Frau Langmann in a fit of rage and even tried to hit her with the floor scrubber.

Frau Kohl in her defence told the Gestapo that the complaint was lodged out of pure hatred of the Jews. Frau Langmann regularly harassed and insulted the Jewish women in the building using derogatory terms. On one such occasion she confronted Frau Langmann for using abusive language. She blew the whole thing out of proportion and fabricated a story. Frau Kohl never tried to hit her with a scrubber, as she never possessed one. However, to sound trustworthy to the Gestapo, Frau Kohl had to prove her racial credentials. She managed to convince the Gestapo with documents, which established her as a half Jew married to an 'Aryan'. Her birth certificate stated that she had been born out of wedlock to a Jewish mother, and the father was an 'Aryan'. Her eldest son from the first marriage was an SA member and her husband was also a Party member. To prove further that Frau Langmann was by nature a troublemaker in the building, she named a few other neighbourwomen as witnesses. Among them figured one other Jewish woman, who characterised Frau

Langmann as a Jew-hater who had insulted her on several occasions. The statements of Frau Kohl were found to be trustworthy as all records regarding her origins and the political leanings of the family were found to be genuine.[8]

Jewish people who were related to 'Aryans' through matrimonial alliances had a particularly tough time. A mother-in-law or a sister-in-law of Jewish origins fell prey to daughters-in-law. Sibling rivalry, generation conflict and so on were played out making the Jewish relative a scapegoat.

Male denouncers who reported their neighbours mostly did it with the intention of grabbing their properties. Their wives obviously cooperated with them, and there was one example where 18 tenants, men and women alike, signed a signature campaign to bar a Jew from renting his premises to other Jews. This was a classic example of the racial community (*Volksgemeinschaft*), irrespective of their class and gender, coming together to make their surroundings free of Jews. This also demonstrated openly the greed and envy of some of his neighbours (*Volksgenossen*) who could not swallow the fact that a Jew even in such times of anti-Semitism continued to possess a big house with more than twenty tenants and a firm. They all ganged up and tried their best to dispossess him of his belongings and throw him in a camp, but he came out unscathed as his wife stood by him through thick and thin.

Separate spheres, slanderous gossip and its function in Nazi Germany

Let me now go a little deeper into the tendency in women to target people within their 'separate sphere', mostly their neighbours and relations. I would like to place this problematic of 'separate sphere' within the broader context of gossip and its function in a racial society, and the role and responsibility of women in their traditional sphere of motherhood and housewifery, issues that came up during what came to be called 'the women historians' dispute' (*Historikerinnenstreit*), which ensued between Claudia Koonz and Gisela Bock in the late 1980s.

Bock launched a scathing attack on Claudia Koonz for locating women's guilt in the Nazi crimes in their separate sphere', in their function as dutiful wives and nurturing mothers. She found Koonz's concept of the separate sphere as ill-conceived, ambiguous and contradictory.[9] Bock, on her part, exonerated all housewives and mothers from the Nazi crimes, arguing that Koonz's diagnosis of women's roles and responsibilities was wrong and that her search for women criminals was misplaced.

According to Bock, it was women's role as unmarried, paid workers-outside-the-home employed in the destructive state machinery, and working within the evil-male-world where women's guilt should be probed and found.[10] What disturbed Bock, therefore, was not the quantitative participation, which was comparatively low, but the qualitative attitudinal change in women, which she ascribed to the brutalisation of the female sex as part of their socialisation in the Nazi public, non-domestic, domain. Unfortunately, she found no traces of this brutalisation in women's role as housewives and home keepers. In what follows, I intend to argue that this brutalization of the female sex extended to their domestic sphere as well, and that it was in this sphere that they were even numerically in larger numbers compared to their professional counterparts.

What does Bock herself mean by the traditional separate sphere? Isn't she herself defining it in very narrow terms of household activity, the daily routine of housekeeping, feeding and rearing the children and taking care of the husband? Such narrowly defined role of the housewives and mothers ignores vital roles that they played in the Third Reich. The Third Reich bestowed upon women the responsibility of guarding the purity of 'Aryan' blood and honour, which many women carried out religiously as has been cited through individual examples in this study. Most of our denouncers here were housewives and mothers working in the capacity of self-appointed neighbourhood watchdogs of the racial community.

Secondly, when one talks about housewifery and motherhood as professions, one only takes into consideration the work that it entails and leaves out the leisure activities of the housewives that were part and parcel of the everyday lives of these housewives. Gossip was an important component of it. Gossip usually involved those who were either not present, or not included in these informal interactive sessions. They are in effect declared strangers. These strangers, in a racial context, were none other than one's racially unfit neighbours, conveniently branded as aliens to the community of people. They were consciously cast outside the web of informal gossip sessions of the *Volksgemeinschaft* of men and women alike, but especially of women in the neighbourhoods. And the gossip that was traded there turned discriminatory, malicious, slanderous and venomous towards these 'racial enemies' (*Volksfeinde*). This gossip, this slanderous gossip, was not just an exercise in character assassination, but could mean the end of life for a Jew.

This tendency manifested itself, for example, in the exchange of notes between maids about the employer Leo and his sexual exploits; cooking up stories of race defilement (*Rassenschande*) between Frau Müller and Herr Mann by her neighbour women; Frau Lambach's spying on an 'Aryan' neighbour who suddenly became rich courtesy of her Jewish boyfriend, Frau Langmann's calling her Jewish neighbours names, picking fights and provoking them while cleaning the staircase and later charging them of anti-regime activities, pointing out to the Gestapo how she kept her distance from the Jews when she got to know about her racial origins. This entailed conniving with other anti-Semitic neighbours and converging all material and personal interest together. This became visible in Frauen Eberfeld, Rosenthal and Jochum's repeated acts of denouncing a Jewish landlady Frau Schade on frivolous grounds and in spewing hatred and venom against her. This entailed exchanging glances and passing snide remarks at 'Aryans' friendly to the Jews, talking about and observing visitors who frequented a Jewish neighbour, or a 'Jewish-looking' visitor to an 'Aryan' neighbour.

This informal power of housewives and mothers, which was elevated to the level of state and politics as it reached the Gestapo office; this variant of the politicization of the private and the privatization of the political,[11] needs to be taken into account when dealing with the question of the roles and responsibilities of housewives and mothers. The separate sphere did not just involve housekeeping, cooking and looking after the children, it also involved keeping a watch on the neighbor, cooking up malicious stories, eavesdropping, guarding the morality and sexuality of the neighbor, things which housewives and mothers seemed to be doing with much relish in the Third Reich. This activity required no formal gathering at the fixed place. Shop floors, house floors, doorsteps, staircases and bunkers provided space enough for this gossip to go around. Coffee-table conversations and idle gossip (*Kaffeeklatsch* and *Haustratsch*) took on an anti-Semitic color just as living rooms turned into venues for drafting letters of denunciation signed by groups of 'disgruntled 'Aryan' women'.

The act of denunciation in itself has broader implications regarding issues of women's consent and dissent in Nazi Germany. Denunciatory behavior provides a yardstick to measure ordinary people's willingness to collaborate and make the system work. Denunciation provided women the possibility to alleviate their personal, civil, moral, sexual and racial conflicts to the level of state politics. They could coat these so-called private motives with their loyalty for the regime. This had a deeper meaning for the womanpower in the system. Such acts of pseudo-politics, where the actual motives wore the garb of a workable one, activated many apolitical, apathetic to the goings-on and politics-shy women. Their testimonies and denunciation reports indicated how much the politicization and criminalization of interpersonal relations opened them to things from which they would have kept away in normal times. Also to note is the liberty they took with the most notorious secret police in history, clearly because they knew they would not face any sanctions even if their allegations were wrong. This also helped the regime in expanding its consensual spaces. The female population was thereby effectively co-opted in the system of terror. The state police were actively helped by these denouncing women especially in private realms of family networks and neighborhoods, and in areas of morality, sexuality and race mixing, areas otherwise difficult to reach.

Notes

1   See Robert Gellately, and Sheila Fitzpatrick, Introduction to the Practices of Denunciation in Modern European History", *Journal of Modern History* 68 (December 1996), pp. 747-767; Robert Gellately, *German Society and the Gestapo: Enforcing Racial Policy 1933-45* (Oxford, 1990); Eric Johnson, *Nazi Terror: the Gestapo, Jews and Ordinary Germans* (New York, 1999); K. M. Mallmann and Gerhard Paul (eds.), *Die Gestapo: Mythos und Realität* (Darmstadt, 1995).
2   Hauptstaatsarchiv Düsseldorf, hereafter, HstAD RW/ 58 – 58403.
3   HStAD RW /58 – 60074
4   HStAD RW /58 22416
5   HStAD RW /58 – 66498

6   HStAD RW /58 - 46589
7   HStAD RW/ 58 - 2908
8   HStAD RW/ 58 - 4635
9   Gisela Bock, 'Ein Historikerrinenstreit?' in *Geschichte und Gesellschaft*, 18 (1992), pp. 400-404, here p. 400-401; Gisela Bock, 'Die Fauen und der Nationalsozialismus: Bemerkungen zu einem Buch von Claudia Koonz' in *Geschichte und Gesellschaft*, 15 (1989) pp. 563-79, here p. 576-578.
10 Gisela Bock, *Ein Historikerinnenstreit*, p. 401.
11 cf. Alf Lüdtke, "Formierunf der Massen" in: Mitmachen and Hinnehmen. *Alltagsgeschichte*, and Faschismusanalyse, in Heide Gerstenberger und Dorothea Schmidt (eds.) *Normalität und Normalisierung* (Münster, 1987), p. 26.

Part 3

Gendered Altruism and Women's Leadership

Sophie Scholl
An Exploration of a Young Woman's Courage in Nazi Germany

Annette Dumbach

The full story of German Resistance in the Third Reich has never been told, and probably never will be. Much of the evidence has been annihilated, and statistics are mere guesswork. The role of women cannot even be truly estimated; the genders melt away in the horror. However, even saying that, we can state with some conviction that hundreds, perhaps thousands of German women took part in some act of resistance, of kindness, of decency amid existential perils. Many were tortured and killed. A large number of these women were Social Democrats, Communists, some Catholic nuns, and many who remain unnamed and unknown.

It is in this context that Sophie Scholl, a young woman who, as a member of a student group called the White Rose, knowingly took part in activities that led to her capture and execution. Her story has become more and more significant over the decades to an ever-growing number of people all over the world. She, like all those who resisted, women and men, is unique. Her story is uniquely her own; there are no generalizations to be made. In her case, we can dimly sense the enormity of her acts and the terror that engulfed her world. Finding out about her and trying to understand what made her so unlike the overwhelming majority of her fellow countrymen has been a dominant feature of much of my life.

The summer when I was nineteen, I visited my uncle and his family in Munich. He was in the Foreign Service, working at the American Consulate. It was all very exciting for a nineteen-year-old girl from the Bronx who had always dreamed of a Europe both terrifying and beautiful. I enrolled in a basic German course for foreigners at the university, not having the slightest knowledge of the language. Every day was fascinating beyond my expectations: the city was in Technicolor, not black-and-white as in the war movies; the Occupation currency we used resembled Monopoly money and that was fun; I was awed by the presence of a driver and maid at the family home; and I enjoyed the very idea of paying with Mickey Mouse money for hamburgers and cokes that were served by haughty waiters in the enormous hall of the *Haus der Kunst*, the "House of German Art", built by Hitler and now transformed into a U.S. Officers Club.

The University of Munich itself was still pretty much a shell, a facade, part of the bombed-out cityscape that was Munich in the mid-1950s. One day after class I sat on a bench on the university plaza and noticed the street sign near the splashing fountain that read *'Geschwister-Scholl-Platz'*, or Hans and Sophie Scholl Plaza.

"Who are they?" I pointed to the sign, asking a German student also sitting on the bench.

"They were students here", he said. "They passed out leaflets calling on the people to rise up against Hitler and the Nazis. They were executed by the Gestapo".

I was nineteen, the time was the mid-1950s – and I was stunned. Finally I asked: "Were they Jewish?"

"No", he said. "They were German students who felt they had to stand up and fight the Nazis".

I was dumbfounded. I could not imagine any non-Jewish German doing anything except cheering Hitler and his marching phalanxes. Thinking back to that moment, I see it as the beginning. Since that time, many decades ago, Sophie and Hans Scholl and the other members of the group that called itself 'The White Rose' have never let me go, or perhaps I should say, have never left me.

Oddly, though – even after years of research, examining trial records, doing interviews, watching films, and then writing a book on the subject with co-author Jud Newborn – only one member of the original White Rose remains elusive and unclear to me, and that is the only woman in the group, Sophie Scholl. At the same time, in the Germany of media and mainstream opinion, Sophie has gradually been transformed into an icon, a symbol, not only of the White Rose but of the miniscule but tragically significant German Resistance as a whole. The various streams of the German Resistance, from Left to Right, flow together into a unified essence that Sophie seems to embody. Sensitive and moving films about her last days of life and her death have been made in Germany, and several years ago her bust was placed in the Hall of Great Germans at Valhalla. This gradual shift of attitude over the years – moving from disdain, silence, and even hostility toward the idea of resistance – to one of appreciation and deep admiration for this young woman has occurred in virtually all strata of German society.

This surge of interest and admiration is a counterpoint to my own readings and efforts to get inside the skin of Sophie Scholl. In spite of all the information we have acquired over the years, Sophie has remained somewhat blurred in contour. I know her less well than I know Hans Scholl, Alexander Schmorell (called Shurik, his Russian nickname), Willi Graf, Christoph Probst and Professor Kurt Huber –the nucleus of the White Rose.

Sophie's life was short; she was beheaded by the Nazis when she was twenty-one years old. Her life can be summarized fairly briefly. She was one of five children raised in Swabia, the province in southern Germany; she was born in 1921, one of three girls and two boys. Her father was a municipal accountant and executive, and was *Bürgermeister* in several small towns while she was growing up. Her mother, a former Protestant nursing-sister in the First World War, kept house and raised the children. Their life was simple and unpretentious; it was a fairly contented home, relatively untouched by larger issues and problems – until the Nazis took power in 1933. Her father, Robert Scholl, was passionately opposed to Hitler and his values, but the encroachments by the new regime on all levels of life – public and private – soon had its impact.

All the Scholl children joined the Hitler Youth, in spite of their father's vociferous opposition. Hans was temperamentally most like his father, but unlike his father, he spoke out vehemently for the New Order. Quickly he was promoted to a Hitler Youth leader. Sophie became a member of the BDM, the girls' youth movement, going on hikes and leading a girl-scout kind of life, but also quietly listening to the stormy arguments at home between her older brother and her father. Till one day after the 1936 Nuremberg Party Rally in which Hans had led his troop of boys, he abruptly changed his views without explanation, and began expressing opposition to the Nazis. Gradually the other children followed suit; the injustices and outrages of the regime became more and more visible and clear to all the children.

Sophie reluctantly went through the usual compulsory Labor Front assignments after completing her *Abitur,* her high school diploma. Those months were difficult and unpleasant for her, but she was determined to get to university somehow, even though few girls were admitted and even though the war was raging. She was finally accepted at the University of Munich for the summer semester, in May 1942, to study philosophy and biology. The acceptance was one of the most exciting days of her life. Hans was studying medicine at the university in Munich while still a medic in the Wehrmacht – medical students were furloughed during the school year to study, and then were shipped off to the war front in the long semester breaks to work as medics.

Sophie joined her brother and his friends in Munich the week of her twenty-first birthday, a moment of celebration, of coming of age, and the excitement of the intellectual, open life that she had dreamed of for years. The war was at its height at that time; Germany was winning on all fronts. Sophie was not privy at first to the clandestine operations being undertaken by Hans and his friends, but early on, she found one of the leaflets in the University and brought it to Hans' rooms; she wanted to show her brother that some opposition to the hated regime still existed. She saw that the leaflet she brought matched passages from classical texts that were underlined in books on Hans's desk; she knew instantly who was behind it, who constituted 'The White Rose'. She confronted Hans and his friends when they came home; they told her someone had to stand up and fight back, especially since the moral spine of the academic and intellectual elite of Germany had been broken. Their leaflets were aimed at intellectuals, students, and eventually the general population of Munich – and later Germany as a whole.

Sophie was shocked and terribly dismayed: her father had been found guilty of making anti-Hitler remarks and was due at any time to go to prison; her younger brother Werner was in combat on the Russian front; her mother suffered from a weak heart – how could Hans do this to their family? His reply was: There is no choice; we have to fight back. The young men explained to her their painstaking efforts to be cautious, the use of a cellar in an atelier owned by a sympathizer at night for their printing operation, and that in fact there was no way to link them to the clandestine activities.

Sophie did not react to this revelation at first; Hans had wanted desperately to keep her out of it. But several days later, she told him and his friends that she wanted to take part in the White Rose activities, that she would do her share in making sure the leaflets were disseminated wherever possible. There was no dissuading her. For me, here is the moment of mystery, the moment of courage. The moment where a person "crosses the line" between what was called "inner emigration" – the withdrawal into oneself to evade the miseries of present-day life – and go over to active opposition, to resistance. Fear, rationality, anxiety for one's family and oneself – all are tossed overboard in that existential decision. How it happened varied from individual to individual: for some, spontaneous rage exploded after a decade of tension and frustration, as was the case with Professor Huber, or for others, the agonizing reflection went on over a period of days or weeks, as with Sophie Scholl.

There seems no evidence, no diary entries available about her thoughts as she agonized before making her decision to join her brother. Some Germans have airily explained her decision as "the loyal act of a young sister for an admired older brother", which may explain it partially, but which is utterly insufficient. In effect it trivializes her decision. An act of courage, or rather a decision of courage, I have come to believe, is rarely accessible in hard evidence to historians. That crucial moment of decision occurs in the unmeasured recesses of the mind and spirit, and not usually while sitting at a desk and writing about it – with an eye to posterity. Ultimately that act or decision remains a mystery.

Once, however, the decision is made, it seems there is no going back. There are no rear exits as one's complicity in "acts of treason" against a tyrannical and ruthless state grows more and more complex. Sophie did not write the leaflets, but under extremely dangerous conditions she printed them, mailed them, procured special paper for duplicating them, bought large amounts of envelopes and stamps under watchful eyes searching out suspicious behavior. She organized the finances, however scanty, of the Group, took dangerous trips at night on trains, carrying suitcases filled with leaflets to stuff in a mailbox in another city, posted to yet a third city. Her participation in the White Rose was total and so she said later when the Gestapo offered to "lighten" her sentence because she only "had followed" her brother. She was as "guilty" as he, she told her interrogator, and if Hans was to die, then so was she. From a state of fear, anxiety and passivity, a mysterious energy seems to emerge: to use the image Willi Graf employed to describe the major expanding of the White Rose activities, "a stone begins to roll" in a descent that goes faster and faster: the growing confidence – or new awareness – or depth of truth – or liberation – grows stronger and stronger. It is an amazing process to observe and it can't be stopped; it is exhilarating and frightening.

These activities of the White Rose went on over a period of nine or ten months; the Gestapo was aware of the leaflets, but had no idea who led this opposition or where it came from. The Group expanded after the medics – Hans, Shurik and Willi – returned from the Russian front with renewed determination to fight the Nazis, after what they had seen. They began reaching out to other cities, other universities, other like-minded individuals. Hans had the idea of joining up with the 'All-German

Resistance', his optimistic belief that scattered people and groups all over the nation were trying to unify into one hard fist of resistance in order to stop the insane killing. After the shattering German defeat at Stalingrad in early 1943, Professor Huber, their major inspiration as a lecturer in philosophy at the University, threw his natural caution to the winds and joined them; his act of writing the sixth leaflet of the White Rose was spontaneous and it was desperate. The Group convinced itself that the war would end soon and the Allies would defeat Germany, even in that very year, 1943. But they were wrong.

No one is quite sure why Sophie and Hans carried a large suitcase one day to the university; the date was February 18, 1943. While everyone was in classes and the halls were silent, they quietly and quickly placed leaflets – the one written by Professor Huber about Stalingrad and the loss of young life – around doorsteps, windowsills, staircase landings, and finally threw a batch of leaflets down into the great vaulted hall. They were spotted by a janitor, arrested and taken away to Gestapo headquarters; the entire university premises were locked and people stood frozen in terror.

Sophie and Hans, after many hours of separate relentless interrogation, confessed to the acts, claiming to be the only ones responsible. Of course the Gestapo searched their home and found much incriminating evidence. Now the Gestapo interrogations of all their friends and contacts began. Sophie was asked to reject "her brother's views" and say that she was only a "tool" in the project. It was made clear to her that if not, she would also be executed for treason. She nodded, indeed she demanded that she die like her brother if he was a traitor. The Gestapo and prison guards regarded her with disbelief; this young girl who appeared even younger than her age: slender, with brown eyes, brown hair, unextraordinary features, unadorned – a reserved middle-class well-brought-up girl, not silly, not vain, an 'ordinary and decent German girl' – how could she be associated with 'treason' and 'criminal acts'?

But their astonishment, of course, did not stop the course of events. A trial was held on February 22, 1943 at the Palace of Justice in Munich. Roland Freisler, the hanging judge of the regime, was flown in from Berlin, at Hitler's request, to preside over the spectacle in his scarlet robes. The other judges presiding were from the Bavarian Ministry of Justice, the SS and the SA. The families of the three arrested were not informed, but the Scholls in Ulm found out about the trial and dashed to Munich by train.

The trial of Sophie, Hans and Christoph was a series of shrieks, insults, vituperations and swirling arms in red cloaks: there was no defense to speak of. But once in all the tirades, Sophie had the strength to call out – after seventeen hours of interrogation – "Somebody had to make a start", she shouted at Freisler "What we said and wrote is what people are thinking!"

This brought on another seizure of shrieking. Then, as the moment of the verdict was drawing near, there was a stirring in the courtroom. Robert Scholl, with his wife and their son Werner on leave, pushed into the guarded courtroom. "Tell the President of the Court that the father is here and he will defend his children!" Scholl shouted.

Freisler heard this and with a great swoop of his arm, ordered the family thrown out. Guards surrounded them; Frau Scholl almost fainted but managed to go on. Robert Scholl shouted at the top of his lungs: "There is a higher justice! They will go down in history!" The doors slammed shut behind them.

The verdict came shortly thereafter; the family saw it in the faces of those leaving the courtroom: the verdict was death. It ended the same day; the execution took place the afternoon of the trial, a rare occurrence in the Nazi procedures for eliminating "troublemakers". All three candidates for death were permitted to write farewell letters to their families. They thanked their parents for their love and warmth, and asked forgiveness for the pain they had caused. They could not have done otherwise, and were sure their families would understand and that the future would justify their actions. The letters were never sent.

One at a time, first Sophie, then Hans and Christoph, walked across the small courtyard at Stadelheim Prison to the small building housing the guillotine. Sophie was the first to go. She went with her head held high and her spine erect as she crossed that courtyard.

* * *

Perhaps one way to try and know Sophie better is to examine some of her writings. She turned to diaries to record thoughts and reflections. Some of the diaries and letters she wrote in her teenage years are still in existence. They are filled with descriptions of nature and her delight in the outdoors, a kind of *Wandervogel*-worship of nature that was fashionable among young people in Germany since the early twentieth century. The people who trekked through the forests and steppes of Europe were mostly groups of young men, but Sophie felt a deep kinship with them. Her feelings about nature were often lyrical, perhaps too sweet for our taste today. Here is one of the effusive comments she made in her diary about the natural world around her:

> *Just as I can't see a clear brook without stopping to dangle my feet in it, I can't just pass by a meadow in May. Nothing is more appealing than that fragrant earth, the clover blossoms that sway over it like a light foam... When I turn my head, my cheek grazes the rough trunk of the apple tree... without ceasing the sap rises from its roots, nurturing even the smallest leaves. Do I hear, perhaps, a secret heartbeat? How protectively it spreads its good branches over me... I press my face against its dark, warm bark and think to myself: Homeland – and am so indescribably happy in this moment.*

Without attempting an inept foray into psychoanalysis, it seems to me that there is something else beyond adolescent rapture, something very sensual in Sophie's relationship to nature, a kind of sensuality that does not come through in most of her diary entries. Here is an example:

> *I could shout with joy that I am so alone, with the wild rough wind drenching my body. I'd like to be on a raft, standing upright on the gray river... The sun comes out and kisses me tenderly. I'd like to kiss it back, but I forget that instantly because now the wind leaps on me. I sense the wonderful firmness of my body: I laugh out loud with joy because I can offer the wind such resistance. I feel such strength in me.*

This is one of the few passages by Sophie that refers to her body, her strength, and her sheer pleasure in challenging or joining nature. Perhaps in a world dominated by male power and obediently accepted by women, this was the only way for her to express the changing needs and feelings in her body and mind. The rules were hard and rigorous, and the demand for conformity, especially for middle-class women, was absolute.

Some historians have referred to Sophie's friendship with Fritz Hartnagel, a young Wehrmacht officer whom she had known since she was sixteen, as 'unofficially engaged". That is not an impression that I share. From their correspondence it is clear that she was deeply fond of him, enjoyed challenging his views on the military and the regime, made trips with him and saw him as an intrinsic part of her life – perhaps more so than any of her female friends.

> *It is true, isn't it, she wrote him in a letter, that sometimes in the evening you think of me? You dream occasionally of our vacations together. But don't just think of me as I am: think of me also as I would like to become. Only then if you still care for me, will we truly understand one another... I've always been aware subconsciously of the career to which you are committed. I can't imagine how two people with such differing perspectives ... could live together.*

On September 1, 1939, the day that Germany invaded Poland and unleashed the war, Sophie wrote Fritz: "*I can't grasp that now human beings will constantly be put in mortal danger by other human beings. I can never grasp it and I find it horrible. Don't say it's for the Fatherland*".

In June, 1940 as France collapsed, she wrote him in a depressed and bitter state:

> *I'm sure you find what I am writing very unfeminine. It's ridiculous for a girl to involve herself in politics. She should let her feminine feelings dominate her thoughts. Especially compassion. But I believe that first comes thinking, and that feelings....maybe about your own body, deflect you so that you can hardly*

see the big things any more.

She loathed the giggling girls at the Labor Front camps where she was assigned, their endless whispering and sighing about boys and sex; she felt like a snob but she couldn't help it, and once wrote: *We live like prisoners; not only work but free time is turned into duty-hours. Sometimes I want to scream: 'My name is Sophie Scholl! Don't you forget it!'*

The choices seem clear: either adolescent giggling or silent 'serious' withdrawal: Sophie often chose the latter. But there was a conflict going on inside her – between body and mind; she wanted terribly for her mind to win out. To have both – 'soft' feminine feelings and serious ideals and determination – seemed out of the question.

To fall in love, to feel so deeply that little else matters, was something that Sophie dreamed of – and rejected. There is one significant entry into her diary, written October 10, 1942, while the male White Rose members were medics on the Russian front, that speaks volumes, if only in a coded way – as if even her diary could not be trusted with the truth:

> *This morning I was at the Schmorells' (in Munich) in Shurik's room, looking for books. What false dreams people can create for themselves! Months ago I was still thinking my feelings for Shurik were stronger than for anyone else. But this was such a false delusion! It was only my vanity that wanted to possess a person who had value in the eyes of others. I distort my own self-image in a ridiculous way.*

In the time of the White Rose, it is apparent that Sophie was infatuated by Alex Schmorell; regarding Sophie and Alex from a distance, it seems a natural attraction. Alex was the kind of person that Sophie – with all her contradictions – could love. Alex was dynamic, good-looking, half-Russian and determined to appear exotic in his Cossack blouses, relaxed, artistic and somewhat bohemian in his tastes and attitudes, deeply anti-Nazi and ready, like Hans, to put his life on the line. It was Hans, with Alex, who actually wrote the leaflets. Sophie's feelings for him, however, do not seem reciprocated and for a while at least, it appears that Sophie suffered from his implicit rejection or indifference.

She threw herself into the expansion of the White Rose with all her energy when the men returned from the front. A diary entry at the time:

> *Many people think of our times as being the last before the end of the world. The evidence of horror all around us makes this seem possible. But isn't that an idea of minor importance? Doesn't every human being, no matter which era he lives in, always have to reckon with being accountable to God at any moment? A bomb could destroy all of us tonight. And then*

my guilt would not be one bit less if I perished together with the earth and the stars.

Her determination and anger seemed to swell in the few months before the end. In the only reference I have found about her thoughts on the use of violence was a comment she made, reported by her hometown friend, Susanne Hirzel:

If I had a gun, I'd shoot him [Hitler].
If the men don't do it, then a woman will have to. You have to do something so avoid being guilty yourself.

Why it was, on February 18, 1943, that Sophie and Hans Scholl chose to place leaflets in broad daylight in the university atrium, remains something of a mystery. They had not informed the other members about this plan, and much speculation abounds. As they were tossing the last batch down from the highest balustrade, they were spotted by a dedicated Nazi janitor who immediately arrested them. In Gestapo headquarters, in nonstop interrogation, both denied any involvement in the White Rose leaflets, but finally, after Hans saw the incriminating evidence, he took the guilt solely upon himself. Sophie, when she learned of it during her interrogation, said she and Hans were the sole perpetrators. Throughout the interrogation she remained calm and composed, and even argued with the Gestapo official who showed some sympathy for her; he could not believe these middle-class educated students could be enmeshed in such a 'criminal' plot.

She shared a special cell with a woman prisoner; the lights burned day and night in the cell, a sign that she was a candidate for death. Falling on her bed in total exhaustion after hours of being grilled, she reported with relief to the woman sharing her cell, Else Gebel, that she had not broken, and that even if others were being picked up, there was no evidence that they were involved. Soon, she said defiantly, the Allies would liberate them. Robert Mohr, her investigating officer, tried to convince her that admitting Hans had led her 'astray' was the only way to save her life. That was out of the question: *I would do it all over again,* she said to Mohr.

There was only one moment at which she was close to breaking. Sunday, the last full day of her life, was a warm spring like day in February. Sophie stood at the barred window and looked out for a long time. She murmured: *Such a beautiful sunny day and I have to go....*

She talked about her mother and how unbearable her suffering must be, about her father who also was suffering but he would understand. Reason, not feeling, strength, not giving in was all that mattered.

On Monday morning they took her away; Else Gebel had tears streaming down her cheeks, Sophie was dry-eyed as they said goodbye. Later the cellmate found Sophie's indictment lying on her bed. On the back of the sheet of paper, Sophie had written: *Freiheit!*

The trial, the verdict of guilt, and the last hours need not be related again here; Sophie, Hans and Christoph maintained their strength and dignity through the horror; indeed, both Sophie and Hans shouted out at the trial, arguing with the fanatic judge and shocking the invited spectators, all eminent members of the Nazi-elite. The strength of all the "accused" held till the very end.

Every member of the original White Rose group was executed on the guillotine after similar trials; by the end of 1943, all of them were dead and many members of their families had been imprisoned – a warning to other students who were ready to defy the regime of terror.

It seems as if a short and minor episode was over, an incident that would go down in history as part of the German legacy of failure – of failed coups and assassination attempts. Resistance that failed.

But surprisingly it has not happened that way. Perhaps the meaning of the White Rose is best summed up in a description of the impact of their death on those who were still waiting to be taken away, waiting in the fortress of death that was Europe, waiting to be tortured and killed. Ilse Aichinger, a young poet in Vienna was one of those; she was categorized as a *Mischlinge,* or 'half-Jewish'. She wrote later about her reaction after seeing a wall poster proclaiming the death of the Scholls and Christoph Probst:

> *I read the names of the White Rose. I had never heard of any of them. But as I read those names, an inexpressible hope leaped up in me... I was not the only who felt that way...This hope – which made it possible for us to go on living – was not just the hope of our survival...It helped so many that still had to die: even they could die with hope...It was like a secret light that spread over the land: it was joy. I remember one day I went out on the street to meet a friend and he said, "Don't look so radiant –they'll arrest you!"*
> *We didn't have much of a chance to survive, but that was not what it was about. It wasn't survival. It was life itself that was speaking to us through the death of the Scholls and their friends...You can live without owning anything. But you can't live without something ahead of you, ahead of you in the sense of something inside of you. You can't live without hope.*

Hope. The mysterious essence of Sophie Scholl is hope: she gives it to all of us and that is why we can't forget her.

Jewish Political Prisoners in Ravensbrück Concentration Camp

Rochelle G. Saidel

From the time that the Ravensbrück concentration camp opened in the spring of 1939 until it was liberated by the Soviet Army at the end of April 1945, there were almost always Jewish political prisoners in the camp. With the exception of prisoners arrested while posing as non-Jews, the Jewish political prisoners were designated as both Jewish and political and targeted for especially harsh treatment. The story of Jewish political prisoners in Ravensbrück is not and may never be complete. Not only did some Jewish political prisoners conceal their true identity, but the Nazis destroyed many records and some testimonies from the former Soviet Union and elsewhere are still unknown. The stories presented here are those of Jewish political prisoners who were at the camp at different times during its six years of existence.

Background on the camp

Ravensbrück, a concentration camp originally constructed for female political prisoners, was located about 90 kilometers north of Berlin (in an area that became part of the German Democratic Republic). The camp held Jewish prisoners as well as political prisoners (a category that included dissidents, resistance fighters, and prisoners of war), Jehovah's Witnesses, "asocials" (a category that included lesbians and Gypsies), and criminals. The female prisoners came from twenty-three countries. Each category was identified by way of a distinctive color-coded triangle: yellow for Jews, red for political prisoners, purple for Jehovah's Witnesses, black for asocials, and green for criminals. The Jewish prisoners who were also classified as political wore both a red and a yellow triangle, arranged as a Star of David. Jewish women were always set apart by their "race" on camp lists, even when they were also in another category.

An unknown number of Jewish women (an estimated 12,000 – 18,000) died of illness in this camp or its satellites, or were murdered by means of slave labor, torture, starvation, shooting, lethal injection, "medical" experiments, or gassing. Others were transferred and exterminated at death camps such as Auschwitz-Birkenau. Among the some 132,000 women in the camp, about twenty percent were Jewish, and an unknown but small number of Jewish prisoners were also designated as political prisoners.

Political prisoners included those arrested for such activities as spying for the Allies, helping Jews, publishing illegal materials, participating in outlawed political parties (such as Communists or Social Democrats), or carrying out other forms of organized or individual resistance. The Jewish political prisoners were part of a much larger mix of red-triangle prisoners. Those women arrested as political prisoners ranged from Jewish and non-Jewish confirmed atheists to Roman Catholic nuns and Orthodox Jews, and came from many countries in Europe. The largest groups of political prisoners were from Poland, France, Germany, and Russia.

Olga Benário prestes: A Jewish political prisoner on the first transport

Olga Benário Prestes, a German Communist, was on the first transport to Ravensbrück in the spring of 1939. She was born in Munich on 12 February 1908 to Eugenie and Leo Benário, a family that was considered upper middle class.[1] Her father, a Social Democrat, was a prestigious lawyer who volunteered to represent poor factory workers fighting for fair working conditions. He taught Olga concern for the poor and oppressed. She became more radical than her father, joining the Communist youth organization in Munich at age fifteen. Soon afterward she became romantically involved with Communist leader Otto Braun and left home to carry out her revolutionary activities.

When she was eighteen years old in 1926, she was imprisoned for the first time, along with Braun. She was released after three months of solitary confinement in Moabit Prison, and then in April 1928 she organized Braun's jailbreak. Her role in this mission made her famous—or infamous—and she and Braun fled to Moscow. While there, Olga was elected to the Central Committee of the Communist Youth International. She eventually broke off her relationship with Braun and was sent to Paris on a mission. When she returned to Moscow, Olga was given military training and named as a member of the Presidium of the Communist Youth International, the highest level in any Communist organization.

In 1934, at the age of twenty-six, she was chosen by the Comintern to accompany the Brazilian Communist leader Luis Carlos Prestes from Moscow to Brazil. Her mission was to help him in his revolutionary activities there, but his November 1935 revolution failed. They and other Communist revolutionaries were captured and imprisoned in Rio de Janeiro. In the meantime, she and Prestes had fallen in love, and she was pregnant.

At the time of the Prestes revolution, the Brazilian President Getúlio Vargas had a friendly relationship with the Hitler regime. To retaliate against Prestes, in September 1936 Vargas had the pregnant Olga snatched from her prison cell and brought to the port in Rio de Janeiro. She—a pregnant Jewish German member of the Communist Party—was placed on a German ship and sent back to Nazi Germany under armed guard. Upon arrival in Germany in October, Olga was brought to the Berlin prison for women on Barnimstrasse, and her daughter, Anita, was born there on November 27.

After the Prestes family miraculously rescued Anita, in February 1938 Olga was transferred to Lichtenburg. In this medieval fortress that predated Ravensbrück as the main women's concentration camp, Olga was first placed in solitary confinement. According to an account by fellow prisoner Erika Buchmann, Olga was in a solitary dark cell in the basement for several months, with a cement bed, a straw mattress, and wood for a pillow. Her diet was bread and water, with warm food every third day. "The Gestapo had then not yet given up trying to get information from Olga on the activities of the International Communists in South America". Erika Buchmann wrote. "For every interrogation she was brought to Berlin to Prinz-Albrecht Street. She was kicked, tortured, threatened with being shot, but she remained mute. The Nazis withheld information on the whereabouts of her daughter to pressure her".[2]

Later, in a collective cell, she was reunited with some comrades she had known in Berlin, as well as her beloved friend and comrade Sabo, Elisabeth Saborowski Ewert, who had also been part of the failed 1935 revolution in Brazil. Olga was on the first transport from Lichtenburg to Ravensbrück, and she became a great heroine at both camps. She carried out many acts of resistance and worked to better the conditions of the other women, despite her own suffering. She was assigned as a *Blockälteste,* in charge of an unruly group of women whom she organized and taught the necessity of personal hygiene. Olga reportedly told her charges: "If we don't take care of our bodies, the Nazis can do with us whatever they want. We are all in the same boat, and if we want to be treated with dignity we need to keep ourselves as human beings and not as animals. I was instructed to be responsible for this block and therefore some things will be changing as of tomorrow". Olga was rapidly accepted as the authority, and after two weeks the block was as clean as the circumstances allowed it to be. The women paid attention, took care of their hygiene, and every day more women took part in the morning gymnastics that Olga arranged. She also organized secret classes, including Russian and French lessons, and literature evenings.[3]

Olga even made a small secret atlas to teach other prisoners about geography and the war, and this amazingly detailed atlas is today in the Ravensbrück archives. In addition to her other work assignments, she was a slave laborer for the Siemens electric company at Ravensbrück. In January 1940, along with seventy-nine other women, Olga was sent to the prison bunker and remained there for thirty days. She had been among the six thousand prisoners kept for "security reasons" in closed in barracks when *Reichsführer* Heinrich Himmler visited the camp. After one of the women in the barracks called out, "Heinrich Himmler, you are nothing more than a pederast and a murderer", Olga and the other women were selected for the punishment bunker. She was whipped and on the verge of death, but when she was released she had to immediately return to forced labor at the Siemens factory.[4] Thirty-four-year-old Olga was among those Jewish political prisoners gassed at Bernburg in the winter and early spring of 1942.[5] Her last act of resistance was a letter to her husband and daughter, which they received many years later. Writing on her last night at Ravensbrück, knowing she would be sent to her death the next day, she told them:

> It is utterly impossible for me to imagine, my dear daughter, that I will never see you again, never squeeze you in my eager arms. I wanted so to be able to comb your hair, to braid your braids... Above all else, I'm going to make you strong... I've already gone back to dreaming, as I do every night, forgetting

that this is to say goodbye. And now, when I'm reminded of this, the idea that I will never again be able to hold your warm little body is like death to me.

Brave and concerned about others until the end, Olga ended her letter: "I promise you now, as I say farewell, that until the last instant I will give you no reason to be ashamed of me". [6]

Dr. Käthe Pick Leichter: An Austrian Jewish heroine

Käthe Leichter was born in Vienna on 18 August 1895, the daughter of Josef Pick, a member of the Viennese cultural elite, and Charlotte Rubinstein Pick, the daughter of a banker from Bucharest, Romania.[7] Käthe's "belief in socialism and her dedication to the cause was the strongest moving force in her life", according to her oldest son, Henry Leichter. "She was brought up under the strong influence of an immensely well-read father, a true liberal of the second half of the nineteenth century, with an unlimited faith in the forces of progress and justice".[8] Even as a youngster Käthe had a strong sense of social justice, siding with the servants against her mother and at family gatherings.

With her father's support, Käthe was admitted to the University of Vienna. However, women were not allowed to enter the Faculty of Political Science there, so she obtained her degree by transferring in her last year to the University of Heidelberg, Germany. She studied under sociologist Max Weber in Heidelberg and was deeply influenced by him. Together with other students, she organized discussion groups at the university on the topic of women's rights.

She became a leading member of a leftist student antiwar group during her studies in Germany in 1917; the military authorities expelled her from the country and forced her to return to Vienna. Her father managed to negotiate her return to Heidelberg for forty-eight hours to take her final exams, and she was granted a Ph.D. *magna cum laude* in Social Sciences from the University of Heidelberg. After receiving her degree, Käthe became deeply involved in the growing Austrian student socialist movement and through it met Otto Leichter, another activist. They were married in 1921, and in 1925 Otto joined the staff of the *Arbeiter-Zeitung*, the official paper of the Social Democratic party.

"In the early twenties there was a great movement, particularly among socialists, to shed the affiliation with the Catholic Church, to which some 90 percent of the Austrian population belonged, at least on paper", Henry Leichter wrote. "This was conceived as a protest against the dominant role which that church played through its close affiliation with the Christian Social Party. The movement also spread to other religions, and shortly before my birth, my parents formally left the Jewish faith".[9] Despite this renunciation and assimilation, the Nazis considered Käthe Jewish.

By the time Henry (then called Heinz), was born in March 1924, Käthe had already held a number of important positions. She had been secretary to Otto Bauer, the leader of the Austrian Social Democratic Party and, briefly, Foreign Minister of the new Austrian Republic. After the Social Democrats left the government, she went to work for the Chamber of Labor, where she founded and became head of the Department of Women's Affairs. She was instrumental in organizing a union of domestic employees, and was an activist, speaker, and writer for the party. She wrote articles for the party's theoretical journal, which were among the first to call for militant action against the advance of Fascism. In 1929 she published a major study based on interviews with female workers, and the following year her *Handbook of Woman's Labor* was issued. In addition to her political and sociological work, she was also an accomplished pianist and violinist. Amid all of these activities, her second son, Franz, was born in 1930.

Meanwhile, the political situation had become dangerous for the Leichters and their associates. In February 1934, at the insistence of Mussolini, the Austrian Fascist government banned the Social Democratic Party. A civil war broke out, and Käthe and her husband were forced to go into hiding. By the beginning of March they had escaped to Switzerland but then returned to Vienna and became deeply involved in the political underground. A year later, in March 1935, Käthe was jailed for four days and Otto was imprisoned for a longer time. In 1937 she took over the weekly *Information and News* publication of the "Revolutionary Socialists", and continued until 7 March 1938. She also wrote two illegal pamphlets, one entitled "*Was den Proletarierfrauen droht!*" (What is in store for the proletarian women!), and the other, "*Muttertag?*" (Mother's Day?), both of which focused on the rights of women.[10] Then on 11 March 1938, Austria became part of the German Reich. The next day the SA came to arrest Otto Leichter, who was not at home.[11] A few days later he escaped to Czechoslovakia using a false passport.

"Why didn't my mother leave with him?" her son Henry asks. Answering his own question, he writes:

> Part of the reason was probably that arrangements had to be made for us children, either to go with them or to follow them in short order. Another strong argument was that my father really was the more endangered of the two, was better known, and the Nazis had already come to look for him. But the main reason was that she had strong nerves and an unquenchable optimism which simply did not permit her to be scared, and, rather, led her not to recognize the danger she was in... Thus she determined to apply formally for an exit permit and to make arrangements for furniture and personal belongings to be packed in order to accompany us.[12]

After some threats that included being forced to paint the word *Jude* on her window and hints of her imminent arrest, she finally accepted a false Czech passport that Otto had smuggled into Vienna through his contacts. Preparations were made for the housekeeper to take Franz, her younger son, out of the country, and Käthe and Henry left the apartment by climbing over the garden fence, expecting to take the train to Czechoslovakia the next day.

On 30 May 1938, the day of the planned departure, Käthe called her mother from a public phone to say goodbye. A strange male voice answered, informing her that unless she turned herself in at her mother's apartment, her mother would be arrested. After sending Henry back to her friends, she went to her mother's apartment, was arrested, and sent to prison.

On 7 August 1938, Henry visited his mother in Gestapo headquarters, the Hotel Metropole. "I have always been grateful to my mother for making this last visit with her so friendly and pleasant", he wrote. "I have the memory of great confidence, even cheerfulness, when she told me that, in three months at the latest, she would be free again and would join us abroad".[13] That evening he left for Switzerland by train and then joined his father and brother in Paris.

In the fall of 1938, Käthe was transferred to the *Landesgericht* jail and endured several months of solitary confinement. To survive the terrible loneliness, she began to write her memoir. After a trial in the summer of 1939, she was sent to Ravensbrück in January 1940.

Käthe Leichter's political resistance in Ravensbrück

Rosa Jochmann, a non-Jewish Social Democratic resistance leader and friend who arrived at the camp a short time later and was with Käthe, tells of their encounters:

> Then I saw Käthe again in the camp. She knew I would hold the post of *Blockälteste* in the political block, and she immediately told me three things on the first day: "Don't forget that you are not a shop steward here, you always have to pretend to be following all commands because the SS is always right, but you also have to do everything to sabotage their work and to protect the inmates. You always have to pretend to be more stupid than our tormentors, because most of them are more than primitive..."
> We were not allowed to talk to the Jewish prisoners [such as Käthe] and were not allowed any contact with them, either, but we never obeyed that rule and were just careful not to get caught. On Sunday afternoons, when we had the least trouble with the SS, Käthe organized literary afternoons in Block Eleven, the Jewish block. Of course we had posted our friends outside the block. Old freedom poems and songs were sung, and we had many unforgettable hours that allowed us to forget our terrible hell at least for a short time. Together with Communist comrade Dr Herta Breuer, Käthe created a play titled *Schum Schum*. It was about two Jewish prisoners who escaped to a deserted island, and were shipwrecked.[14]

The play mocked the Nazis, but Käthe destroyed the written version and kept a fake innocuous play in her closet, in case of discovery by the camp authorities. Käthe organized all sorts of celebrations, according to her friend Rosa:

When we walked along the camp street on Sundays, we always asked Käthe to tell us something, for example about the French Revolution. "But I don't know any more than you do", she would say, and then proceed to give lectures on many Sundays about the things she didn't know "very well". She was self-confident, yet very modest and warm. She was always interested in what was considered the "lowest of the low", the prostitutes, thieves, murderers. Unfortunately, we had to destroy her sociological research into these topics when a block search was about to take place. She proved that these people were doomed to failure because of their circumstances: "It is not the fault of these people, it is the fault of society", she said again and again, and she was right.

Käthe was forced to carry out hard physical labor, loading bricks onto ships on the Havel River. Political prisoner Erika Buchmann later gave an eyewitness account of the brutality of this work assignment, which she said was designated to the Jewish women:

> They were forced to do the most difficult jobs and the tragic images of them when they left work, mostly weak, many of them old and sick, were unforgettable. Outside boats arrived fully loaded with bricks and building blocks, and the strictest supervisor of the camp would receive the order to go to the boat with the Jewish commandos. Uninterruptedly, the exhausted and nervous women felt the beating. Gloves were not distributed and in a period of a few hours their hands were injured from the stones and the coal, and bleeding from uncountable small wounds".[15] Among the poems that Käthe wrote at the camp, one was about her bloody hands. Her friends finally managed to have her transferred so she could stay inside the block and knit socks. Since she never learned to knit, other women would knit for her while she told them about the world, and how she thought it should be. They were all political Jewish prisoners who loved her and tried to help her. For example, they straightened her closet and made sure her bed was tightly made.[16]

The gassings of Jewish political prisoners in 1942

Rosa Jochmann was an eyewitness to the beginning of the end for Käthe and some fifteen hundred women, mostly Jewish:

> In January 1942, a group of doctors entered the camp, and all Jewish comrades had to appear naked in the first row in front of the doctors. One of the doctors asked Käthe about her degree, and then said: "Oh, that is nice, they'll be able to use you at the new camp". Three times the trucks came in the middle of winter, and twice they had to turn around because the snow was too deep. Käthe said, "I am starting to get embarrassed. I feel like someone who always claims to go

on a trip and never actually leaves". But then finally the trucks got through. On the evening before, Helene Potetz and I had been with our friends in the Jewish block, as usual. You can't imagine what that was like. It was as if they were aware of their fate. Only Käthe stayed calm and reminded everyone to pull herself together. We had worked with some friends in the clothing department to obtain warm clothes, so we could give them to Käthe and the other women. And we had agreed that Käthe would use another woman's identification number to get news to us, if at all possible. The number belonged to a Viennese Jewish woman named Bukowitz, who was not known politically.

Then in the morning, as the *Blockälteste*, I was allowed out on the camp street, and Helene Potetz came along. We walked hand in hand, a silent mass, as we had walked twice before. I will never know if she understood that this was the end. She was so smart that I would rather think she pretended not to know, so we would feel better, to give us courage. She must have known she wasn't ever going to come back. Still today I see Käthe sitting on the truck, in the bitter cold, her eyes steadily set on us. Waving, she disappeared forever.

Fourteen days later, all the prisoners' clothes came back, all the warm clothes we had organized for them, wool socks, a scarf, canes, glasses, dentures, just everything. And with the number for the Austrian woman named Bukowitz, we found a note: "Everything fine so far, treated well everywhere, traveling through Dessau…." And that was where the words ended. The inmates working in the "Care Department" (*Fürsorgeabteilung*) walked in, as white as sheets. They had just sent fifteen hundred letters to relatives of the women. The entire transport had supposedly died of "circulatory debility".[17]

Herta Mehl Soswinski, the only Jewish political prisoner I know of who arrived at Ravensbrück before October 1942 and survived, remembered Käthe Leichter at the camp. Käthe had helped to make Herta's punishment order "disappear" when she fainted during a snow shoveling detail. Herta recalled the transport of Jewish prisoners who were sent out of the camp in March 1942:

We did not know their destination, but it was strange that their prison uniforms, they had received new clothing before leaving, was returned to camp a few days later. We had arranged with Ruth, our table-elder, to send us some news, if possible, under the star of her jacket. She did so, and the girls from the clothing detail, informed by us, gave us the note. She wrote that she did not know where she was, but that they had been received by a group of physicians which even comprised a dentist. She could not write us any more because it was her turn to get undressed. Thus, we knew just as much as before. Today, however, we know that the women were sent to Bernburg and were all gassed.

The dentist was present in order to ascertain how much dental gold could be expected from the transport.[18]

Like Olga Benário Prestes, in mid-March of 1942 Käthe Pick Leichter was gassed at the Bernburg euthanasia facility. She is now honored as a heroine in Austria.[19] While we may never know the full stories of Olga, Käthe, and other early Jewish political prisoners who were sent from Ravensbrück to be gassed in 1942, Olga and Käthe left a legacy of intelligence, political integrity, and a sense of justice, as well as their altruistic concern for the suffering of the other women at the camp. Although they had different nationalities and political affiliations, they sometimes worked together for the benefit of the other prisoners. For example, they collaborated on a clandestine newspaper and organized extra bread and margarine for women in the infirmary. Both of them were from well-off, assimilated, Central European Jewish families, became politically active at a young age, and served in high-level positions in their respective parties.

The murders by gassing of Olga Benário Prestes, Dr. Käthe Pick Leichter, and hundreds of other Jewish political prisoners during 1942 were part of the Nazis' organized extermination called 14f13. The first selections in Ravensbrück began in December 1941 and January 1942, and those selected were predominantly Jewish. Beginning in February 1942, as part of the euthanasia programs in the concentration camp under the code 14f13, they were sent to the Bernburg mental asylum, where they were killed in the gas chamber. A large number of Jewish women (some of whom were not even subjected to a perfunctory physical examination) were selected to be gassed at Bernburg, along with those prisoners who were considered insane, weak, or incapable of work, women who had tuberculosis or asthma, healthy "asocial" women and "criminals". According to inmates, about fifteen hundred to sixteen hundred female prisoners were taken to the gas chamber of the asylum in Bernburg after 3 February 1942.[20] Between that date and the construction of a gas chamber in Ravensbrück in December 1944, so-called "black transports" left Ravensbrück for the gas chambers of Auschwitz, Majdanek, Bernburg, or Hartheim. In this way, Ravensbrück was integrated into the "Final Solution", the mass genocidal murder of Jews, as well as that of the Sinti and Roma, or Gypsies.[21] On 29 September 1942 Himmler ordered the remaining Jewish prisoners in Ravensbrück to be sent to Auschwitz, in order to make Ravensbrück *Judenrein* (cleared of Jews). However, new transports soon brought other Jewish women to the camp. Herta Mehl Soswinski, (who reported on Käthe Leichter's departure to Bernburg) is the only Jewish woman I have come across who was in Ravensbrück before Himmler's fall 1942 order and survived to write an account.[22]

Stella Kugelman Nikiforova: The Smallest Jewish Political Prisoner

Stella Kugelman Nikiforova was one of the youngest Jewish political prisoners in Ravensbrück. She was only four years old when she arrived with her mother.[23] Stella was born 1939 in Antwerp, the only child of Luis Gustavo Kugelman Griez, a Spanish Jew from Barcelona, and Rosa Klionski, a British Jew from London. They met while they were studying in Belgium, fell in love, married, and then Stella was born there.

Not only were Stella's parents Jewish but they were also members of the resistance in Antwerp after the Nazi occupation of Belgium in May 1940. They were arrested in 1943, along with sixty other families that had been carrying out acts of sabotage. Even though Stella was so young when she was transported to Ravensbrück with her mother, her documents listed her as a political prisoner. Along with her mother, she had to wear a red triangle in the camp. This preschool political prisoner even had a number: 25,622. She said she was dark and looked Spanish, and was taught to say in German at the camp: "I am Spanish". She was told never to tell anyone she was Jewish.[24]

Stella's mother died of tuberculosis within three months of their arrival at the camp. Stella was then cared for by a series of substitute mothers. The women hid her where the Nazis were afraid to enter, the barrack that housed women with tuberculosis or typhus. She remembers that after her mother died, a succession of women, one at a time, always took care of her. Whenever the woman who cared for her died, another took over. "It was always one woman, but the woman changed", she said. "It was a form of resistance; they were called the 'camp mothers'".

Stella was at Ravensbrück until its evacuation, when she was six years old. Her most vivid memories of camp life are of the last few days of April 1945. When the women were driven out of the camp on a death march on 28 April 1945, some of them were permitted to push Stella and other small children in a wheelbarrow. She remembers hearing shooting as the women marched. During the night of either 28 or 29 April, there was terrible noise from bombing or shooting, and then the Nazis fled in the dark. The women found themselves free and disappeared into the woods. In the morning Stella woke up and saw that she and two other children were alone in the cart. There were no German soldiers or guards, nor any prisoners to care for the children. "It was horrible—I remember it well," she told me. "We all thought we would die. This was a moment when we thought there was no help. The women had all disappeared into the forest, and we three children were all alone, belonging to no one".

Stella was with the Russian women prisoners in the chaos of the forced march, and just as she was expecting to die in the wheelbarrow that morning, one of them suddenly returned from the woods. She was a doctor in the Soviet Army who had been a prisoner of war at Ravensbrück, and her actions prove that not all women were nurturing and altruistic. Fifty years later, Stella was still bitter about what happened next.

"If the woman had taken me back to the camp, my father would have found me", she explained. However, this doctor took Stella to the Soviet Union, and not until twelve years later did Stella have the opportunity to discover that her father had survived Buchenwald concentration camp. The doctor returned to the Soviet Union with Stella and another child in order to be "rehabilitated" as a heroic rescuer of children, rather than risking the possibility of being accused of treason for divulging secrets as a prisoner-of-war.

Because of this Soviet military doctor's action, Stella was liberated at the end of April 1945 but was soon incarcerated again in a different way. After clearing her own name with the authorities, the woman placed Stella in a cruel orphanage in an isolated area about five hundred kilometers south of Moscow. Although some of the survivors evidently made inquiries about Stella, she was never found and remained "lost" and alone until she was allowed to leave the orphanage at the age of eighteen.

After this second liberation, she looked for the woman doctor who had saved her and then abandoned her, and forced her to live twelve more years of misery. "I told her she ruined my life. She saved my life, and also ruined it", Stella said. "I found out that I had a father, and I could have been with him during those years. She told the truth and said she saved my life so she could be reinstated and have her papers back".

Stella had always thought that her father might be alive, and after her 1957 release from the orphanage, she started looking for him. She did not even remember her family name but found a camp survivor who knew it. This woman found a man in Antwerp who had been her father's friend, and through him Stella discovered that her father had immigrated to Brazil in 1952. He had remarried there and started a new life in São Paulo. When Stella visited her father for the first time in 1963, she was a twenty-four-year-old woman, and they had no language in common. Stella felt uncomfortable with his new wife and constrained by the unfamiliar language, climate, and culture. After six months she went back to the Soviet Union.

When I met her in 1994, she had returned briefly to São Paulo to take care of legal matters after her father's death. In the meantime, she had married the son of another doctor from the Soviet Army who had been imprisoned in Ravensbrück. At the time of our meeting, Stella had been married for thirty years but was planning to divorce. She had a son, then age twenty-five, and a daughter, twenty-one. Stella never recovered from the tragedies of her life that began in Ravensbrück. She lives in St. Petersburg, Russia, and has health problems that she said are the result of the severe beatings she received in Ravensbrück. She was officially declared an invalid and exempted from holding a job in the Soviet Union, because of serious headaches resulting from pressure on her brain.

Ginette Kahn-Bernheim: A Jewish member of the French resistance

Ginette Kahn-Bernheim, a heroic member of the French Resistance, was born in Paris on April 13, 1920.[25] She was the daughter of Marcel Kahn, an attorney in a prominent law firm, and Edmée Mayer. Ginette's father died in 1933, and in 1940 her mother moved with her and her younger sister Jacqueline to Marseille. Ginette completed her law degree in Aix-en-Provence, became a member of the Marseille Bar in November 1940, and several months later began working in the law firm of Gaston Defferre.

Defferre, a leader of the Socialist Party in Marseille, was the best friend of another attorney, André Boyer, who soon became the head of a resistance network called Brutus. Defferre became Boyer's deputy, and Ginette joined the network. When she was formally disbarred in March 1942 under the *numerus clausus* established by the Vichy government against the Jews, Defferre allowed her to continue to work in his law firm. After the occupation of the southern zone of France in November of that year, she began working full-time for the network. Even though she carried false identification papers with the name Ginette Calas (a French Protestant name), her situation as a Jewish woman in the network was especially dangerous.

In early 1943 the Brutus network, already established in several French cities, transferred its headquarters to Lyon. Ginette moved there in the fall of 1943, along with her mother and sister. After the network was infiltrated by an informant, a wave of arrests started in November 1943 and many of its members were caught within days. Ginette herself was arrested in Lyon with one of her comrades on December 7, 1943, but she was able to get rid of the documents she was carrying.

She was incarcerated in the Montluc prison in Lyon for more than four months, suffering through five days of interrogation by the Gestapo. She was told that both Boyer and Defferre had been arrested (Boyer was arrested in Paris on December 8, 1943, but Defferre never was), and that she was going to be executed within twenty-four hours. She never revealed any information. One day, a German female supervisor of the cleaning unit she was assigned to pulled her off the crew. When Ginette asked why, she responded: "Because, you are Jewish". Ginette replied, incredulously: "Why, are you Jewish?" She was transferred to the Romainville camp on the first of May 1944, and deported to Germany on 13 May 1944.

Ginette arrived in Ravensbrück soon afterward. She stayed in the camp for about 40 days and was then sent on to camps in the Sudetenland, including Zwodau and Graslitz. For eight months she did not leave the building that housed a military parts factory operated by a subsidiary of Siemens, except for three weeks spent in the hospital in March 1945. In mid-April, while the camp was being evacuated ahead of the advance of the U.S. Army, she escaped with three other women and hid for three weeks in the barracks of the French workers of Graslitz. The Germans never found out that she was Jewish.

Ginette was repatriated to Paris on 19 May 1945, and married attorney Jacques Bernheim on 28 March 1946. They had two sons, Olivier and Antoine. She practiced law until 1994, initially on her own and during the last fifteen years of her career, as a partner of her husband and older son, Olivier. She was diagnosed with cancer in 1989, and again in 1997. After a long and courageous battle against the disease, she died on 30 July 2000. Her husband died on 7 January 2004.

Ginette was honored for her bravery and her role in the Resistance with an Army Citation on August 20, 1946, the *Croix de Guerre*, and the *Médaille de la Résistance*. In 1986 she was awarded the *Chevalier de la Legion d'Honneur* medal with a second

Army Citation by Gaston Defferre (who had been the long-term mayor of Marseille and at the time was the Minister for Planning). In 1992 she was promoted to the rank of *Officier de la Legion d'Honneur* in a ceremony presided over by the head of the Paris Bar Association.

Doris Fuks greenberg: A "Christian" caught in the Warsaw uprising

Doris Fuks Greenberg arrived at Ravensbrück as a political prisoner directly from Warsaw in the fall of 1944.[26] More than a year after the liquidation of the Warsaw Ghetto, Doris was living as a Christian with false papers. She was rounded up as a non-Jew with thousands of Polish Christian women after the Warsaw revolt in August 1944.

The daughter of Henryk and Gucia Rosenfarb Fuks, Doris was born in Warsaw on 4 March 1930. Doris's parents and sister were deported from the ghetto, but she remained with her aunt, a grandmother, and two uncles. One of the uncles had a non-Jewish wife who managed to rent an apartment outside the ghetto, and Doris and her remaining family members were smuggled out of the ghetto, one by one, before the Warsaw Ghetto uprising in April 1943. "But it was also a short-lived thing, because somebody must have noticed and told on us", she said. "One night some agents came in, Polish agents, and they found us". They stole the family's possessions and made them promise to disappear by morning.

Afterward the family members went their separate ways. Alone at age thirteen and a half, Doris secured false documents and at first worked as a maid near Warsaw. "Then one day I had to leave", she said. "Apparently some news leaked out, and the priest saw me in church and he invited me to talk to him. He gave me a pocketful of nuts and candy, and told me that he knows who I am and that it would be nice for me to leave for a couple of days, because he feels we're going to have some guests, uninvited guests. So I understood, and I left".

Doris had become friends with another Jewish young woman who was passing as a non-Jewish Pole in Warsaw. "She got a job as a cook in a restaurant in a suburb of Warsaw", Doris said. "So she invited me because her bosses needed a helper for her. So she suggested that I come, and I got a job being the cook's helper". At the end of the Polish revolt, in September 1944, Doris and her friend were rounded up with the other local residents and put on a train headed for Ravensbrück. "The whole population was evacuated", she said. "We were running in the middle of the streets and we could see that the buildings were still smoldering. Some stones, some bricks were falling. That's how we came together to the concentration camp. We traveled together".

Doris recalled her arrival at Ravensbrück, which must have been in early October 1944:

> We were separated before we entered the gates, into different groups. There were some tables with papers where I think somebody put your name and gave

you a number.[27] This was the part—we couldn't see that until we got close to it, because the lines were enormous. We could see where the people walk in, like straight ahead to the building, quite a lengthy building. People were walking in there. But we were in the line, and when we got closer to that table, somebody was putting our name and then giving us numbers, I think. Or the numbers, we got them after the bath. But we gave our names. I think that at that time they would put the number on and then later give them out. It was only somebody writing our name and then next to it probably a number, because when we got out, we got the numbers.

Doris remembers that her friend had poison, and said to her, "Look, we see people go in, we don't see anybody that we know coming out, maybe it's time to take the poison". However, Doris, who described herself as "such a chicken", responded, "Look, if we're going to die, so another few minutes. Maybe the Germans will find a poison and test it, try themselves. Why hurry up?" After the women had their hair clipped, they were given a shower.

"That was a relief", Doris said. "We came out of the shower. The clothes that were left, any belongings or whatever we had, we don't see it anymore. We get handed the stripes. I got a dress that you could put a refrigerator in it, and I was a kid, and some tall women got a dress that I couldn't fit in". Like others who resolved this problem in the same way, Doris switched her dress with another woman. "That dress that I got was just barely covering", she said. "But they gave us also a jacket. The jacket for me was almost as long as the dress. Better than nothing. Then they gave us underwear, a pair of underpants. You should have seen that. They reached to my knees. You know, if it wouldn't be so sad, it would be very funny", she remarked. "But we were given those clothes and wooden shoes, just a sole with one stripe. We never saw our things again".

"And they gave us a red triangle with the letter *P* on it", she continued. "We had to put here the white strip with a number, and above it the red triangle with the letter *P*. That was our name. From then on it was the number". Doris's number was 74073. Although she recalls that many women's heads were shaved, she was spared this trauma. "They seemed to say that they were checking, and whoever had no lice wasn't shaved, but I don't believe that all those people had lice. No, I don't believe that. If anybody would have, it would have been us, because we had no place to wash or no... So I don't know why".

Doris recalled what happened next. "Then we came out from that building and we then understood what's happening", she said.

We didn't see people coming out, those people who came in, because they looked different. When they came in, they are people wearing clothes, having their hair and holding a pocketbook or something or some of their belongings. We were underway maybe a week or ten days, but in the train, everybody had whatever everybody had. So when we walked in, we looked like human people. When they walked out from the building we just saw people in those striped dresses, no hair. You couldn't recognize a face. Somebody came to us when we're in the line and says, 'Hi'. We didn't know who it was.

Once Doris arrived at her assigned barrack, she saw Yiddish writing on the walls. Her friend, who could read Yiddish, read the names of people and messages such as, "Tell others what they did to us". "Don't let the world forget". Another vivid memory of Doris's short stay at the camp was the day she saw "a truckload of dead bodies, skin and bones". She also remembers hearing screams. Doris and her friend stayed at the camp for a very short time, perhaps no more than a week. They were then transported to a subcamp called Neubrandenburg, where they worked in a factory that made airplane parts.

On 8 March 1945, Doris was sent from Neubrandenburg to Kühlungsborn, a small town in the north of Germany near the North Sea. As she and her friend were still posing as non-Jewish Poles, she was assigned to work for a German family and her friend was sent to a nearby farm. When Soviet Army troops arrived at the beginning of May, they assumed that Doris was a Nazi collaborator. She ran away to the farm where her friend was working, and when a group of Russians arrived at the farm, they used her friend as a translator. The two young women obtained forged Russian papers that enabled them to reach Berlin. Once there, Doris finally convinced the Jewish communal organization that she was Jewish, and then was sent to the Bergen-Belsen Displaced Persons camp in the British Zone. Afterward she immigrated to the United States, and lives in Stamford, Connecticut.

Rachel Rozenbaum Hocherman: A Polish jewish woman posing as a Christian

Rachel Rozenbaum Hocherman was born in the small town of Kurow (near Lublin) on 14 October 1927, the daughter of Golda Korenblitt Rozenbaum and Mendel Rozenbaum.[28] She was living in Warsaw with her aunts in September 1939 when the war began, and she returned to Kurow when the bombing stopped four weeks later. Rachel returned to Warsaw in January 1940, and by the end of that year or the beginning of 1941, she was required to wear an armband with a Star of David.[29]

> While she was in Warsaw, in the spring of 1942, her family was taken from Kurow and probably gassed at Chelmno. When she returned to Kurow from Warsaw soon afterward, no one from her family was left (except for a brother hiding on a farm). Polish friends gave her an unsophisticated document with a false identity. Rachel looked for her brother, and then returned to Warsaw, to her aunts. They aunts lived in the area that became the ghetto, and Rachel, then fifteen, did not want to stay there.

She again returned to Kurow, where she found Jews who had fled Czechoslovakia. She met Mikolasz Weisz, a twenty-seven-year-old Czech Jew from Bratislava who had contact with the Polish underground. She helped him with the Polish language, and he gave her an authentic-looking identity card from someone two years older who had died. She thus became Anna Janina Dolczewska. She obtained train tickets for Mikolasz and his family, and carried false identity cards for him. Rachel assisted Weisz in his flight from Poland by going on the train with him and staying in the dining car to serve as his cover. Afterward, he sent her some money and tried to help her.

Rachel also aided two other Jews from Slovakia, by taking them on the train. Ukrainian guards caught them and took them to the police. She, with her Polish identity, was free, but she bravely went to the police to try to save these people. Although she had Polish papers, there was a death penalty for helping Jews. She was placed in a prison near the Carpathian Mountains, probably in late November 1942, and remained in jail for two months, supposedly awaiting trial. She was then placed in another cell with people who had been picked up from the street for forced labor, and was sent with them directly to Auschwitz-Birkenau. As a "non-Jew", Rachel did not have to face a selection but nevertheless received a tattooed number, 35673. She wore the red triangle of the political prisoners. Her transport arrived in Auschwitz around 20 January 1943. Of this transport of non-Jewish Poles, only twenty percent survived the two-day train ride, she said.

Rachel worked in Birkenau for five months. Then she was moved to Rajsko, a work camp near Birkenau, and became an *Aufseherin*, a work supervisor. However, she wanted a simple job like the other women. She got permission to relinquish her supervisory job and did vegetable farming instead. At the beginning of 1945, Rachel was given the new job of cleaning the SS headquarters, and there she received extra food that helped her to survive the imminent evacuation and forced march.

She said she was told the women left the camp on 18 January 1945, but she was not sure of the exact date. They walked and walked, throwing away everything in order to walk without any extra weight. She saw many women who had been shot because they were unable to walk and were lying dead on the road. She felt she was walking toward freedom, but in fact she was walking toward Ravensbrück. She thought about running away, but there was no place to run. She was not even sure whether she was in Poland or Germany.

The women walked for two days or more until they reached the German border, guarded by Nazis with dogs. When they reached Germany, they were put into a closed train and continued to travel. She didn't know how long the trip took, but they finally reached Ravensbrück at night. They were put into a large barrack and had to place their belongings on the floor. A friend offered her food, but she was too sick to eat anything. Like others who arrived at that time from Auschwitz, she recalled that the camp was "a horror". "There was no place to sleep—nothing. Thousands arrived and there was no preparation for us. We were sleeping in corridors, on the floor", she said. After one month, Rachel was sent to the Malchow satellite camp, which Count Bernadotte of the Swedish Red Cross included in his "white bus" rescue mission.[30]

Rachel was rescued to Sweden and stayed there until she decided to go to Rio de Janeiro, Brazil, to find her father's brother in July or August 1946. While visiting a friend in São Paulo in 1947, she met her future husband, Moyses Hocherman. They were married on 16 November of that year, and their four daughters were born in Brazil. In 1969, after twenty-three years in Brazil, Rachel, a lifelong Zionist, moved to Israel with her husband and family. Rachel's husband died of a stroke in January 1995, after forty-seven years of marriage; Rachel died of cancer in Israel in June 2000.

Conclusions

The women whose stories were told here were of different ages, nationalities, and political beliefs, and they arrived in Ravensbrück at different times from the beginning to the end of the camp's six-year history. However, they all have in common the fact that they were Jewish women, designated as political prisoners in Ravensbrück. The category of "political" was extremely broad, encompassing a variety of Nazi-defined crimes, and the seven women whose experiences were recounted here were arrested for different reasons. German Communist Olga Benário Prestes and Austrian Social Democrat Dr. Käthe Pick Leichter were political prisoners in the true sense of the term, because they were arrested while members of outlawed political parties and carrying out political activities considered subversive by the Nazi regime. However, it is a fact that most of the non-Jewish political prisoners placed in Ravensbrück in the early years survived, while Jewish political prisoners such as Olga and Käthe were gassed in Bernburg in 1942. Thus they were doubly targeted by the Nazis, as political activists and as Jews. Herta Mehl Soswinski survived only because she had the luck to fall through a crack of the Nazis' genocidal plans. She was shipped to Auschwitz to be exterminated, but instead was assigned to harsh slave labor that ultimately saved her life.

Stella Kugelman Nikiforova's mother, like Ginette Kahn-Bernheim, was arrested as part of a resistance movement, the former in Belgium and the latter in France. These two women were among the resistance fighters brought to Ravensbrück from many countries. Stella's mother died of disease after a short time at the camp, while Ginette survived. It is unlikely that the life of little Stella or Ginette would have been spared if they had been known to be Jewish. For this reason, Stella, who herself was designated as a political prisoner, was warned at age four never to say she was Jewish.

The two Polish Jewish women also managed to deceive the Nazis, and they passed as Christian Poles until liberation. It is paradoxical that Doris Fuks Greenberg was caught in a roundup of Warsaw non-Jewish citizens after the Warsaw uprising, and even more so that Rachel Rozenbaum Hocherman, posing as the Christian Anna Janina Dolczewska, was arrested for helping Jews. While these women's stories present an idea of the wide scope of backgrounds of the Jewish political prisoners held in Ravensbrück at various times, this is a subject that has been generally overlooked and needs further exploration.

Notes

1   Information on Olga Benário Prestes is from Rochelle G. Saidel, *The Jewish Women of Ravensbrück Concentration Camp* (Madison: University of Wisconsin Press, 2004), pp.41-45 and *passim*.

2   Erika Buchmann, quoted in Jutta von Freyberg and Ursula Krause-Schmitt. *Moringen-Lichtenburg-Ravensbrück: Frauen im Konzentrationslager 1933–1945.* (Moringen-Lichtenburg-Ravensbrück: Women in concentration camps). Frankfurt: Lesebuch zur Ausstellung. VAS–Verlag für Akademische Schriften, 1997, 133.

3   Ibid.

4   Ibid.

5   Anita Leocádia Prestes dates her mother's death as April 1942, but most other sources say February or March.

6   Fernando Morais, *Olga: Revolutionary and Martyr* (New York: Grove Weidenfeld, 1990), pp. 241–42.

7   Information on Käthe Leichter is from Rochelle G. Saidel, *The Jewish Women of Ravensbrück Concentration Camp*, pp. 45-52 and *passim*.

8   Henry O. Leichter, *Childhood Memories* (unpublished English manuscript, 1995), p. 38.

9   Ibid., 59.

10 Herbert Steiner, *Käthe Leichter: Leben und Werk* (Vienna: Europa Verlag-AG, 1973), 8–9.

11 SA is the abbreviation used for *Sturmabteilungen*, the stormtroopers or Brownshirts, founded in 1921 as the Nazi Party's private army. They were later eclipsed by the SS *(Schutzstaffel)*.

12 Henry Leichter, *Childhood Memories,* 122–23.

13 Ibid., 136.

14 Herbert Steiner, *Käthe Leichter: Leben und Werk,* interview with Rosa Jochmann, April 1970, p. 262.

15 Jutta von Freyberg and Ursula Krause-Schmitt, *Moringen-Lichtenburg-Ravensbrück: Frauen im Konzentrationslager 1933–1945*, p. 132.

16 Herbert Steiner, *Käthe Leichter: Leben und Werk,* p. 262.

17 Ibid.

18 Herta Soswinski, "Why We Have to Tell about It", in *Auschwitz: The Nazi Civilization*, edited by Lore Shelley. (Lanham: University Press of America, 1992), pp. 129–130.

19 On the hundredth anniversary of her birth in 1995, the Austrian government issued a postage stamp in her honor.

20 See Bernhard Strebel. "Ravensbrück-das zentrale Frauenkonzentrationslager" ("Ravensbrück, the central women's concentration camp"), in *Die nationalsozialistischen*

Konzentrationslager. Entwicklung und Struktur. (The National Socialist concentration camps—development and structure), edited by Ulrich Herbert, Karin Orth, and Christoph Dieckmann (Göttingen: Wallstein Verlag, 1998), p. 235.

21 See Monika Herzog and Bernhard Strebel, "Das Frauenkonzentrationslager Ravensbrück," in *Frauen in Konzentrationslagern: Bergen-Belsen Ravensbrück*, edited by Claus Füllberg-Stolberg, Martina Jung, Renate Riebe, and Martina Scheitenberger (Bremen: Edition Temmen, 1994), pp. 20–21.

22 Herta Soswinski, "Why We Have to Tell about It", in *Auschwitz: The Nazi Civilization*, edited by Lore Shelley, pp.125–144. Herta was arrested in Prague on 27 August 1940 because of her underground activities, and on 14 January 1942 she was transported to Ravensbrück. At the beginning of October 1942, in compliance with Himmler's order, Herta was transported to Auschwitz. She continued working with the resistance there, managing to escape at the time of the January 1945 evacuations. Has she not escaped, there is a strong possibility that she would have been transported back to Ravensbrück, the fate of so many Jewish women evacuated from Auschwitz. She settled in Vienna and married a comrade from the Auschwitz underground.

23 Information on Stella Kugelman Nikiforova is from Rochelle G. Saidel, *The Jewish Women of Ravensbrück Concentration Camp*, pp. 69-72.

24 Evidently Stella's mother was not identified as a Jew by the Nazis when she was arrested, or she and Stella would have been forced to wear a yellow triangle along with the red one.

25 The information on Ginette Kahn Bernheim is based on e-mail correspondence from her son, Antoine Bernheim, to the author, August 24, 2004 and October 15 and 17, 2004.

26 Information on Doris Greenberg is from Rochelle G. Saidel, *The Jewish Women of Ravensbrück Concentration Camp*, pp. 88-92.

27 The numbers were on pieces of cloth that prisoners sewed onto their clothing; tattoos were not used in Ravensbrück.

28 Information on Rachel Hocherman is from Rochelle G. Saidel, *The Jewish Women of Ravensbrück Concentration Camp*, pp. 168, 178, 182-85, 206-208.

29 The Warsaw Ghetto was created over a period of six weeks in October–November 1940. As early as November 1939, *Generalgouveneur* Hans Frank ordered Jews over the age of twelve to wear white armbands bearing a blue Star of David. See Raul Hilberg, *The Destruction of the European Jews* (New York: Holmes & Meier, 1985), Vol. 2, pp. 216, 221, 226.

30 See Rochelle G. Saidel, *The Jewish Women of Ravensbrück Concentration Camp*, pp. 178-188 for the story of the rescue to Sweden.

Gender as a Factor in Rescuers of Jews during the Holocaust

Eva Fogelman

At the end of the twentieth century, popular culture in America was bombarded with emphasis on the psychological makeup of men and women as essentially different one from the other. Theories have gone as far as to say that men's and women's patterns of speaking are so different that they belong to different linguistic communities or cultures. When it comes to gender and helping, social-role theory stated that the male gender role fosters helping that is heroic and chivalrous, whereas the female gender role fosters helping that is nurturing and caring. A meta-analytic review essay in 1986 by Alice Eagly and Maureen Crowley concluded that women and men helped differently. Running throughout the various psychological literature, they described the assumption that women were more likely to help than men unless the situation was dangerous. In those cases, the presumption was that men were more likely to have the skills necessary to undertake risky rescues. It was also thought that masculinity and accompanying notions of chivalry led men to offer help more readily to strangers. The female gender role, on the other hand, motivated women to acts of caring for others.[1]

In 2004, the psychological literature shows a theoretical shift towards a gender similarities hypothesis.[2] And in fact, Alice Eagly, writing a review essay with Selwyn Becker, has reformulated her earlier understanding of helping. This time Eagly studied heroic behavior, including an analysis of rescuers of Jews during the Holocaust based on existing data. Becker and Eagly conclude that there are almost a similar number of men and women who were involved in risking their lives to save Jews. Thus, the notion that men are more readily involved in dangerous helping behavior was not substantiated.[3]

The rescuer project

My own research on rescuers of Jews during the Holocaust concurs with the gender similarities hypothesis. In the early 1980s I embarked on an international social-psychological study of why non-Jews risked their lives to save Jews during the Third Reich in German-occupied Europe. I interviewed more than three hundred *Chasidei Umot Haolam,* Righteous Among the Nations of the World, non-Jews who were designated by Yad Vashem, Israel's Holocaust museum and archives, as individuals who did not take any rewards, monetary or otherwise, for risking their lives to save Jews. I also interviewed Jewish adults and children who were rescued; in some cases the victim-rescuer pairs participated in the study.

I found rescuing behavior to be infinitely more complex and varied than these stereotypical, gender-based assumptions with men as risk-takers and women as nurturing and caring helpers. A number of factors increased the likelihood that an individual—male or female—would help: having a personality that is independent, a heightened sense of trust in one's competency, an inclination toward risk-taking, emotional involvement with Jews, special abilities, available resources, various situational elements, ability to confront complex moral questions, and ultimately a supportive social milieu. In fact, my research leads away from the traditional thinking. As social psychologist Carol Tavris has said: "We can think about the influence of gender without resorting to false polarities".[4]

Moral reasoning based on gender

Freud recognized that "character traits which critics of every epoch have brought up against women—that they show less sense of justice than men…that they are more often influenced in their judgments by feelings of affection or hostility—all these would be amply accounted for by the modification in the formation of their super-ego." But "as a result of their bisexual disposition and of cross-inheritance, they combine in themselves both masculinity and femininity which remain theoretical constructions of uncertain content".[5] Nevertheless, distinctions have been made.

Piaget, using hypothetical dilemmas to measure moral judgment in children, found that boys, unlike girls, tended toward organized games with elaborate rules. Therefore he concluded that boys were more concerned with justice than girls. It was the fairness and impartial, abstract justice of rules that Freud, Piaget, and others believed was the essence of an individual's morality.

In the 1960s, Harvard University psychologist Lawrence Kohlberg, refined Piaget's early work by charting moral development through six distinct stages, each one more advanced and mature than the one before. Kohlberg created hypothetical moral judgment stories. For example, your wife is very sick and will die unless she gets a very expensive medicine that you cannot afford. Should you rob the drugstore? From the answers, Kohlberg concluded that individuals at Stage Six, the highest level of moral reasoning, were those who had the ability to consult their conscience and act on universal ethical principles. At that level, an individual was motivated by abstract, ideological beliefs of justice. He asks himself, "What should I consider fair if I were in the other person's place?" and proceeded from there. Later Kohlberg backed away from this strict hierarchy, acknowledging that Stages Four, Five and Six are also "alternative types of mature responses".[6]

In the 1970s, psychologist Carol Gilligan challenged the prevailing views of psychological development, which up to that time had been based almost entirely on research with men. Gilligan agreed with Freud that women and men differ in what they regard as "clinically normal", but she maintained that women's moral reasoning was not faulty; it was simply different.[7]

Gilligan argued that there are two kinds of morality that stem from two different kinds of motivation. One is a morality based on impartial idea of justice, and the other is a morality based on compassion and care. Gilligan believed that the value of caring in human relationships, which coincides with Kohlberg's Stage Three, is as important as justice (Stage Six). What matters ultimately to women, Gilligan found, is being responsive to human feelings—that is, judging by "hearing a human voice". A woman's need to make and maintain interpersonal connections plays as important a role in moral decision-making as fairness does in the understanding of rights and rules. When facing a moral decision, women do not think about what is fair so much as "who will be hurt the least". According to Gilligan, compassion for others is not a sign of weakness or a symptom of neurotic dependency but another dimension of moral development.

Gilligan was the first theorist to place caring and justice on an equal footing. To her, morality was not an abstract concept of right and wrong to be charted in a classroom setting. Justice and mercy, responsibility and care, were learned through human interaction. This morality of care implied empathizing with another's distress and actively offering support and aid.

Female and male morality applied to Holocaust rescuers

Gilligan's notions of "female" morality as contrasted with "male" morality would lead one to expect that emotional-moral rescuers (morality based on compassion for Jews) and Judeophiles (morality based on emotional attachment to Jews) would be mostly women, and network rescuers (motivated by anti-Nazi ideology) would be male. This is not what I found in my discussions with rescuers from all walks of life. Despite their different motivations, men and women were equally represented in various groups based on why these non-Jews risked their lives to save Jews during the Shoah.[8]

Rescuers were unable to articulate all the reasons they participated in altruistic acts. Motivations were complex and real situations may have changed motivation over time of the rescuing relationship, many of which lasted years. In tracking an individual's initial rescue effort, five distinct patterns emerged: *moral*—people who were prompted to rescue Jews by thoughts or feelings of conscience; *Judeophiles*— people who felt a special relationship to individual Jews or who felt a closeness to the Jewish people as a whole; *network*—people fueled by anti-Nazi ideology, joining others who were politically opposed to the Third Reich; *concerned professionals*— people such as doctors or social workers who held jobs in which helping was a natural and logical extension; and *children*—who started helping rescue Jews at the behest of their families.

Rescuers' morality was of three types: ideological, religious, and emotional. *Ideological* morality was based on rescuers' ethical beliefs and notions of justice. A congruence between moral beliefs and actions had always been a part of their lives. They stood up for their beliefs; and so when they were asked to help, they did. They were more likely than any other moral type to be politically involved. *Religious-moral* rescuers described their sense of right and wrong in religious rather than ethical terms. Their morality was based on tenets of "Do unto others as you would have them do unto you". *Emotional-moral* rescuers felt a compassion for victims of Nazi persecution that compelled them to help. Emotional-moral rescuers were the rarest of the moral rescuers. They responded to the helping situation out of compassion and pity, not just from an ideological sense of right and wrong. Theirs was a morality based on caring and responsibility, the same morality that now New York University psychologist Carol Gilligan celebrated in her groundbreaking book, *In a Different Voice*. Gilligan proposed that a morality based on compassion and concern for others was more prevalent among women than among men.

I saw, in my research, the two kinds of moral reasoning Gilligan describes. But the link between gender and reasoning style was not as strong as Gilligan's analysis suggested it would be. Both men and women showed morality based on caring and attachment. Both men and women had emotional responses to the plight of the Jews. Both men and women came to the aid of victims through an outraged sense of justice

Women undertook dangerous missions. Women were involved in high-risk activities like slipping Jews past German patrols and guiding them safely across the border. On the other hand, men were motivated by feelings of compassion and pity, with some still emotionally shaken by their experiences, weeping unashamedly as they relived that time.

In the course of my research and work at the Anti-Defamation League's Jewish Foundation for Christian Rescuers,[9] which I founded along with Rabbi Harold Schulweis (1986), I talked with men who were so emotionally affected by what they saw that they turned their lives upside down, jeopardizing everything in order to save Jews. The story of Alexander Roslan was certainly the most dramatic example of this. The sight of the bodies of children in the Warsaw ghetto so affected Roslan that he risked his life, fortune, and emotional stability to save Jacob, Sholom, and David. Roslan characterized those scenes he witnessed in the ghetto as the most difficult moments for him during the war. "You can't eat", he remembered. "You can't sleep. If you see things like that, you can get sick". It was this emotional reaction that transformed Roslan into a rescuer.

Roslan's love for Jacob, Sholom, and David transcended any cognitive moral imperatives of fairness or justice. He nurtured three youngsters even more than his wife did, who could never completely overcome her fears of discovery and death. Similarly, the responsibility for the emotional care and welfare of the two Jewish children sheltered with the Stenekeses fell on John Stenekes rather than his wife Berta. Even at the start, when the children were staying with Stenekes' sister, John kept a paternal eye on Jack and Anna and gave them bakery treats when they came around. It was he who offered to hide the children when his sister lost her nerve and planned to put them into a hotel. John Stenekes empathized with their situation, took to heart their need, and felt compelled to act. He was the one who broke the news to his wife that the two children who played with their baby were Jewish and that unless they took them in, the children would be killed. Berta Stenekes agreed to shelter them, but John shouldered the responsibility for looking after them.[10]

The work of University of Massachusetts social psychologist Ervin Staub shows similar findings.[11] Staub found that gender did not necessarily predispose a person to be caring. Staub, who as a six-year-old child was rescued in Budapest by Raoul Wallenberg, developed a scale to identify people with altruistic natures. Those who scored high on his scale were more concerned with the welfare of others. Staub found both men and women who scored high. Staub concluded that while there may be a tendency for women to be compassionate and caring, this was largely due to early socialization, and men were just as capable of having such feelings and acting on them. It is the development of caring and responsibility in boys that enables them to be just as kind as women.

While male rescuers sometimes used Gilligan's "female voice", women frequently displayed temperaments and attitudes that Freud attributed to his model of "moral man". In women such as Marion van Binsbergen Pritchard and Louisa Streenstra, Hitler's philosophy and Nazi policies triggered deep-seated revulsion. They were outraged by seeing justice so perverted. Witnessing German soldiers carelessly tossing Jewish children into trucks and watching as two passerby tried to stop them left Dutch rescuer Marion van Binsbergen Pritchard shaking with anger. Louisa Steenstra's anger at the German bombing of Rotterdam and the unjust killing of 30,000 people in one day shocked her into action. "When you hear that, how can you not act?" she said. "I couldn't stand it. I hated the Germans". This anger consumed her and consumes her still. Anti-Nazi anger and rage at the human race for its proclivity for cruelty were themes to which she returned time and again in her conversation with me.

Recent research has further undermined the notion that men and women differ appreciably in their moral reasoning, or that women have a permanently different voice because of their early closeness to their mothers. Anne Colby and William Damon found little scientific support for Gilligan's claims for general gender-based distinctions. They concluded that "to the extent that differences of this sort do exist, there is no evidence whatsoever that they are due to early and irreversible emotional experiences between mother and child.[12]

But Gilligan's research was not the only body of work which led me to believe that there might be differences in the way men and women reacted to Hitler's war against the Jews. Philip Friedman, one of the first historians to write about the Holocaust rescuers, suggested that non-Jewish women may have been more sensitive than non-Jewish men to the plight of Jews. Friedman hypothesized that women's nurturing and caring natures might have made them a soft touch, especially when those in danger were children. Women might have been "more easily moved by their emotions and thought less of the consequences".[13]

Frances Henry, a Canadian anthropologist who studied a Bavarian community whose pseudonym is Sonderburg, reported that in her study more women than men helped. Henry, whose grandparents and ten other Jews living in Sonderburg were helped by locals for three years until their eventual discovery and deportation, felt that this was because most of the help involved giving the fugitives housing and food. Unlike the administrative tasks of obtaining forged documents or lining up escape routes, food and domestic arrangements were the traditional province of women. This same point was made by Pierre Sauvage, the filmmaker who as a boy was saved by rescuers in Le Chambon. Sauvage noted that most often it was the women, who were at home most of the day and were in charge of the domestic arrangements, who were the first ones to be approached to take a stranger into their homes. That first important critical decision, to help or not, was theirs to make. In Sauvage's mind, the women of Le Chambon were the "backbone" of that community's rescue effort.[14]

Yet an early study by German political scientist Manfred Wolfson contradicts Henry's findings and Sauvage's observations. In 1966, Wolfson who was working in the United States, solicited letters and other documents from seventy Germans who helped Jews between 1938 and 1945. He concluded that more men than women helped.[15]

Female rescuers defy stereotype

Running through all these various inquiries was the assumption, sometimes implicit, sometimes overt, that in dangerous situations men would be more likely to help. I too assumed that women would undertake less physically taxing or hazardous tasks and leave the heroics to men.

Time and again I was proven wrong. Women told of how they had acted as decoys, couriers, double agents, and border runners. Women such as Czechoslovakian historian Vera Laska were an integral part of both resistance and rescue work. Laska was a Czech resistance fighter who also led Jews and other fugitive to safety in Yugoslavia. German patrols made these border crossings extremely dangerous. Nonetheless, men and women such as Laska and John Weidner gambled that their wits and luck would see them through.

Polish resister and rescuer Jan Karski felt that women were better suited for undercover or conspiratorial work because they were quicker to perceive danger, less inclined to risky bluffing, and more optimistic of the outcome. In particular, he praised the role of the network liaison woman or courier, whose job it was to warn of impeding raids, move the hunted from house to house, and carry information from one network member to another. Marc Donadille, the French Protestant minister who led the Cévennes escape network, years later paid public tribute to such women:

> I want to praise the operator in the post office in Saint-Privat, whose name I don't remember. She was Catholic, but shared our feelings and our concerns. One day she said, "The phone calls between the police at Florac and the brigade at Saint-Germain come through me. I can pass that information on to you".
> Then, rather than relay information, she simply hooked my line into these conversations so I could listen directly... Then she told me that she had orders

to intercept my mail. "I'll put your mail aside and you can get it at night from my house. Then you can remove the compromising letters and I will send [the rest] on". This we did regularly.[16]

The telephone operator was playing a very risky and dangerous game. Had the Nazis caught her, she would have faced the same possibility of imprisonment, torture, or execution as Donadille or any other male resistance worker. She did have, however, one advantage: officials in some countries, particularly the Netherlands, were sometimes loath to pronounce a death sentence on a woman. A woman who was caught often stood a better chance of being sent to a concentration camp than being summarily executed. Hetty Dutihl Voûte, who was caught for her illegal Utrecht children's rescue work and sent to Ravensbrück, thought that had she been a man, the Nazis would have shot her.

Given the opportunity, women proved to be good spies, smugglers, and saboteurs. Yet their deeds were largely overlooked. In the postwar celebration of men's daring deeds, the quiet bravery of women was ignored. The traditional hero was a swashbuckling male. And heroes who did not fit that model were ignored. Movies and made-for-television features portrayed male heroes. Women, if they had any rescue or military role at all, were cast in minor roles.

In building a new, postwar national identity, heroes needed to be larger than life, and so military leaders such as Charles de Gaulle and those active in armed resistance were glorified. The medals and ceremonies recognized military heroes, not the milkman who left an extra bottle of milk for a family sheltering Jews, or the nurse who put a sign in a hospital room "Quarantine" "Do Not Enter" so that the SS would think twice about entering the room to deport a Jewish patient.

World War II represented an opportunity for women to escape their normal domestic concerns and express their anti-Nazi outrage by taking action in behalf of a just cause. "We think of war as a male activity and value", social psychologist Carol Tarvis noted, "but war has always given even noncombatant women an escape from domestic confinement—the exhilaration of a public identity—and a chance to play a heroic role usually denied them in their private lives".[17]

The chance to escape normal boundaries and become an important part of a larger cause sometimes gave women the courage they needed to undertake risky ventures. Certainly this was the case with Anje Roos, a woman whose implacable opposition to Nazism grew from small acts of kindness.

In 1940, when the Germans took over Holland, Anje Roos had nearly completed her training as a psychiatric nurse. Roos had no illusions about Hitler's intentions. Her parents, who lived in Alkmaar, a town twenty miles north of Amsterdam, had told her and her seven brothers and sisters often enough that the *Führer* meant what he said. He aimed to rid the world of the infirm and the racially impure and rule the world. With the Germans now in charge, Roos knew psychiatric nursing did not have much of a future. She changed directions and began to study to be a midwife.

Soon after the Germans took over, they banned Jews from professional employment. Jewish doctors and nurses were no longer permitted to work at the hospital. Roos, who in addition to taking courses at the hospital worked in the tuberculosis ward, was outraged. The patients were too. Together with the head nurse, Roos wrote a petition asking that the order be withdrawn. All the patients signed it, and it was sent off to the Austrian governor in charge of the occupation. It proved to be a futile effort, but for Roos and the patients it was, nonetheless, a healthy tonic. "It didn't help; no reply ever came. But there was a kind of elevation around the ward that they did something", Roos explained. "It was important for them as well as for us to do something—to demonstrate—to tell them we didn't like it and we were angry".

In the spring of 1941, Roos completed her training and rented a house in Amsterdam with three other nurses. Her roommates had many Jewish friends, and on Fridays it became the custom for Roos and her roommates to buy goods for them that they were not permitted to purchase. Through these new friends and through the Jewish family she worked for as a baby nurse, Roos's awareness of the plight of the Jews increased. She felt close to her employers and knew the dangerousness of their situation. The precariousness of their position became evident one day when she answered a knock on the door. It was the Gestapo hunting for Jews to deport. With the family safely out of sight, she faced the Gestapo and told them no Jews were there. They had already been arrested. "You do *such wonderful* work", she told them sarcastically.

With little time to lose, Roos arranged for the family to travel to Utrecht and be hidden in a home there. Later she learned the family had been captured by the Germans when they naively went for a walk in town. Roos returned to work at the hospital, but it was clear to her and her friends that the Jewish situation in Amsterdam was rapidly deteriorating. When Jewish friends who belonged to the Palestine Pioneer movement asked her for help, she was ready, even eager. Her anti-Nazi rage needed an outlet.

By day, Roos bicycled around town hiding Jewish children and delivering documents, food, and money to those in hiding. By night she worked at the hospital, where, along with her nurse friends, she stole as many drugs and hospital supplies for the underground as she could. Her duties for the Palestine Pioneers, a network affiliated with the Dutch underground Westerweel Group, were arduous and not always predictable. She was frequently late for work or absent altogether. Her nursing supervisor told her to shape up or she would be fired. Roos did not know what to do. Both jobs were important to her, but she did not know how she could manage both. So she turned to her parents for advice. As she recalled, her parents told her, "If you want to help the Jews—and you should—then do that and don't work with the nurses anymore. They don't need you there. They need you with the Pioneers".

Her parents' blessings broke Roos's last restraints. A new persona, free of the ordinary expectations of female behavior, was born. She immersed herself in rescue work. She involved her whole family. Roos picked up Jews and transported them to her parents' house. From there she would find safe houses for them in other parts of northern Holland. Through friends and Christian religious circles, she found safe places for all her charges.

The Palestine Pioneers was only one of several networks for whom Roos worked. Along with one of her brothers, who was a police officer, Roos joined the Arondius Group, an underground sabotage organization. Members of the group, Jews and non-Jews were on the Germans' most-wanted list. In March 1943, the Arondius Group decided to raid the Nazi registration office to burn the files that held the names and addresses of all the Jews in Amsterdam. They thought that without such information the Nazis would find it more difficult to round up and deport the Jews.

Dressed like police officers, the saboteurs overpowered the night watchman and set the place on fire. The mission was a success, but their victory was short-lived. Careless talk among network members gave them away, and a month later Roos, her brother, and the others involved in the raid were arrested. Roos's brother and twelve other Arondius members were tried and shot. Roos was sentenced to serve one year of hard labor in Ravensbrück.

After a year and a month, Roos came home. She was weak, painfully thin, and ill with tuberculosis. That slowed but did not stop her. As soon as she was physically able, she rejoined her friends and the Amsterdam resistance. She worked as a courier for an underground newspaper, distributing news and false identification papers as needed.

Roos does not fit the implicit social-gender role of a female rescuer. Her rescuer self was not that of a resourceful, home-based caretaker. While she and her roommates hid fugitives in their house, most of her rescue activities took place outside the home. Her rescuer self was adventurous, daring, and bold. This kind of rescue is alleged to describe a male social-gender role. While many women in networks were called upon to help in domestic chores, Roos had many other women in her network and in others whose rescue activities ignore social-gender roles.

The existence of heroic women seemingly contradicts other social-psychological research, which suggests that daredevil women would be rare. In experimental situations requiring one-time heroic actions (such as jumping into a river to save a drowning person), researchers have found that men tend to be more responsive. Women are more apt to size up the situation as too dangerous to attempt to do anything.

During the Shoah, women confronted a myriad of situations—not a one-time experience—that required heroic interventions. By "heroic" I mean deliberate actions, which place the person in sharp danger. Without question, rescuers who hid Jews in their homes were heroic people; their actions, however, were not. They had all the comforts and familiarity of home and neighborhood. They did not repeatedly seek dangerous missions. Heroic rescues did. From one night to the next, Roos never knew where she would sleep. Laska did not even know what country she would be in the following day.

The work of Kay Deaux, social psychologist at the Graduate Center of the City University of New York, helps explain the apparent gap between my findings and the work of others. Deaux found that skill level matters in moral acts as well as in more commonplace ones. For instance, a woman who was a good swimmer would be just as likely to jump into a river to save a drowning person as a man who was a good swimmer. The key variable is swimming ability, not gender or morality. Women did not avoid danger or hang back from risk per se. If women felt they had the skills useful in a particular situation, they helped.[18]

Much of the time skills are divided along stereotypical gender lines. Fifty years ago, most women were full-time housewives and mothers. If they worked outside the home, they were most likely to be factory workers and farmers or to hold jobs in traditional women's fields of teaching, nursing, or social work. Very few women were printers, mechanics, or captains of industry. In wartime resistance activities these distinctions between men and women were not absolute. There were women forgers, saboteurs, and money launderers. But for the most part, women undertook or were assigned rescue tasks that centered on their household and child-rearing skills.

Stereotypical women's role in rescue

At home, women took responsibility for the people they were hiding. It was difficult work. Quarters were often cramped, nerves frayed, and hunger constant. Each simple task, from hanging out laundry to emptying chamber pots, contained the possibility that someone would spot something suspicious and report it to the authorities. It was left to one member of the household to keep things running and to keep people's spirits up in the process. That job usually, but not always, fell to the woman of the house.

The Voses, for example, divided up the chores. Aart Vos was responsible for the house's outside liaisons with the underground and obtaining food, while Johtje was in charge of the household. Each of them had a dangerous task. Aart traveled all over the countryside on his motorbike, calling on his dairy-farm contacts to scrape up supplies to feed his burgeoning household. He knew that anyone caught transporting food over a road was subject to arrest.

Johtje Vos oversaw the domestic arrangements of the household. She acted as a combination traffic controller, cook, arbitrator, psychoanalyst, and entertainer. She hosted candlelit parties for which the fugitives dressed up in clothes borrowed from one another. She led the children in games, such as "Who remembers what a banana looks like?" Johtje did anything she could think of to distract them from dwelling on their discomfort and fears. Aart Vos realized how demanding a job his wife had:

> We had thirty-six people hiding in our house at one time. When you have a home, not a big one, and you have it filled up with Jewish people coming in and out the whole day, every day, not for a week but for four or five years, you

can't understand what that takes out of a woman. I was out on my bicycle, but she had to keep everyone together.

When the Nazis suspected the Voses of possessing the stamps to forge illegal documents, it was Johtje who was left to deal with the Gestapo and connive a way out of a lethal situation. Her ability to act took charge, bluffing, stalling, and finally strategizing their charges' according to sociologist Cynthia Fuchs Epstein, show that "behavior that we link to gender depends more on what an individual is doing and needs to do than on his or her biological sex".[19]

At times, however, the roles of men and women in rescue activities were determined by gender stereotypes. For example, when children needed to be transported, hidden, and cared for, women usually saw to it. Many of the networks that were engaged primarily in the rescue of children were headed by women. Irena Sendlerowa in Poland, Anje Roos Geerling and Hetty Dutihl Voûte in Holland, and Andree Guelen Herscovici in Belgium led their country's efforts to save children. Those children's rescue networks not headed by women, like NV (short for *Naamloze Venootschap*, the Dutch equivalent of "limited company", or "Ltd.") and the Piet Meerburg, boasted an overwhelmingly female membership.

But for the most part, it was women who led or rallied behind efforts to save children. There were a number of reasons for this. To some extent, women were more actively called upon than men to rescue children because women's efforts were perceived as having a greater probability of a safe outcome. Networks assigned tasks according to skills, and most male network leaders assumed women were better suited to care for children. Jewish parents made the same association. They were more likely to trust the safekeeping of their children to a Christian woman than to a Christian man. Among Jewish parents, nannies were the rescuers of choice. When that was not an option, parents looked for the next-best thing, a single young woman. A couple was not desirable. Jewish parents feared a couple would try to convert their children and that a couple, who represented a ready-made family, would be more reluctant to return their children to them after the war.

Network leaders knew that and assigned the job of prying Jewish children from their parents to women. Belgian schoolteacher Andree Guelen Herscovici, for example, was recruited by the *Comite de Defense des Juifs* (CDJ) to call on Jewish parents and lead their children to safe houses. The Gestapo had a list of all the Jews who still lived at their official addresses, and the CDJ had the same list. It became a race between Herscovici and the Gestapo over who would get there first.

Clark University historian Deborah Dwork, who interviewed rescuers of children in the NV and Piet Meerburg networks, found that women couriers were the mainstays of both operations. The groups, most of whose members were university students, specialized in saving children because they felt their age would undermine their authority and effectiveness with older victims. Piet Meerburg, the student who formed the network, told Dwork why 90 percent of his members were women: "It was much more suspicious for a boy of twenty to travel with a child than a girl. It was absolutely a big difference. We went to fetch the children from the crèche [nursery] together, but then the woman student accompanied them on the train to Friesland and Limburg".[20]

There was still one other role that women, and only women, played in the rescue efforts, and that was the role of "single mother". Nannies, friends of the family, and even strangers—often found through network contacts—were asked by Jewish parents or by intermediaries to shelter a child. Those who agreed needed to make up a story to cover the sudden arrival of a baby or a child. Exactly what the cover story was and how believable it was depended on the individual and the circumstances. Many young women moved to other villages and posed as married women whose husbands were at the front. Still others claimed the child was a relative whose parents had been killed in a bombing raid. Whatever cover the rescuer self-scripted, the person had to act it convincingly. Husbands, wedding days, tragic war events—a whole family album of lies—had to be fabricated to lend an air of authenticity. No man could ever get too close. Secrets kept them on their guard at all times. These "mothers" did not want to place their own family and friends in danger. The other, they dared not trust.

Single mothers created stories that were inventive, daring, and frequently unbelievable. Relatives and old friends doubted the existence of a husband they had never heard of or seen. The suspicion among neighbors, the gossip around town, labeled them unwed mothers. All of a sudden, they were young women of uncertain reputations who were no longer desirable as potential wives. In a Catholic country like Poland, such whisperings were devastating. These women were considered social outcasts. To escape the gossip and any suspicions of the truth, they moved to another village. When the whisperings and suspicions started up again, they moved on.

These women willingly paid a huge personal price. Their reasons were no different from anyone else's. Like men and other women rescuers, they faced danger and gambled their lives to alleviate suffering and satisfy their sense of justice. What they did and how they did it reflected their individual personalities, talents, and social roles. Women helped in typical social-gender roles, such as taking care of children, as well as in roles that defied or ignored social-gender expectations of others. In the extreme situation, one never knows how he or she will react in a particular moment in time. In the end, Carol Gilligan's "different voice" can be a motivating force for both men and women. What is expressed is a shared voice of common decency and humanity.

Notes

1 Eagly, A. H., & Crowley, M. 1986. Gender and helping behavior: A meta-analytic review of the social psychological literature. *Psychological Bulletin*, 100 (3), 283-308. The review article also mentioned that there was a slight tendency for women to help women more than men to help women.

2   Shibley H.J. 2005. The gender similarities hypothesis. *American Psychologist,* 60 (6), 581-592.

3   Becker, S.W., & Eagly, A. H. 2004. The heroism of women and men. *American Psychologist,* 5, 163-178.

4   Tavris, C. 1992. *The Mismeasure of Women: Why women are not the better sex or the opposite sex.* New York: Simon and Schuster. p. 289.

5   Freud, S. 1925. Some psychical consequences of the anatomical distinctions between the sexes. *Standard Edition,* 19:257.

6   Kohlberg, l. 1969. The cognitive-developmental approach to socialization. In D.A. Goslin (ed.), *Handbook of Socialization Theory and Research.* Chicago: Rand McNally. pp. 347-480.

7   Gilligan, C. 1981. *In a different voice: Psychological theory and women's development.* Cambridge, MA: Harvard University Press.

8   Fogelman, E. 1987. The rescuers: A socio-psychological study of altruistic behavior during the Nazi era. Unpublished doctoral dissertation, Graduate Center of the City University of New York.
Fogelman, E. 1990. What motivated the rescuers? *Dimensions: A Journal of Holocaust Studies,* 5 (3), 8-11.
Fogelman, E. 1994. *Conscience and Courage: Rescuers of Jews during the Holocaust.* New York: Anchor Books, Doubleday.

9   The ADL's Jewish Foundation for Christian Rescuers, now the Jewish Foundation for the Righteous. More than 1,700 rescuers are receiving monthly financial stipends to assist them in their waning years in 26 different countries.

10   My findings mirror those of sociologist Barbara Risman and Lenard Kaye and Jeffrey Applegate. Risman compared the personality traits of single fathers, single mothers, and married parents. She found that single men who had custody exhibited personality traits—specifically nurturing and caring –that were much more like mothers than married fathers. Similarly, in 1990 psychologists Lenard Kaye and Jeffrey Applegate, who studied 150 men who were spending sixty hours a week caring for their ailing parents or spouses, found that these men provided just as much emotional support as women traditionally do. The obligation of providing care customarily falls to women, but when men do it, they do it just as well and lovingly. Risman, B.J. 1987. Intimate relationships from a microstructural perspective: Men who mother. *Gender and Society,* 1, 6-32. Kay, L. W., & Applegate, J.S. 1990. Men as Elder Caregivers: A response to changing families. *American Journal of Orthopsychiatry,* 60, 86-95.

11   Staub, E. 1978. *Positive Social Behavior and Morality.* New York: Academic Press. vol. 1, pp. 39-73.

12   Colby, A., & Damon, W. 1987. Listening in a different voice: A review of Gilligan's *In a Different Voice.* In: M.R, Walsh (ed.), *The Psychology of Women: Ongoing Debates.* New Haven: Yale University Press. p. 327

13   Friedman, P. 1955. Righteous Gentiles in the Nazi era. In A. J. Friedman (ed.),

Roads to Extinction: Essays on the Holocaust. Philadelphia: Jewish Publication Society. pp. 409-421

14 Sauvage, P. 1986. Ten questions. In: C. Rittner and S. Meyers (eds.). *The Courage to Care*. New York: New York University Press. p. 137.

15 Wolfson, M. 1970, April. *The subculture of freedom: Some people will not*. Paper presented at the regional meeting of the Western Political Science Association, Sacramento, CA.

16 Joutard, P., Poujol, J., & Cabanel, P. (eds.). 1987. *Cevennes: Terre de refuge 1940-1944*. Montpellier: Presses du Languedoc/Club Cevenol. pp.257-258.

17 Tarvis, p. 68.

18 Deaux, K. 1976. *The Behavior of Women and Men*. Monterey: Brooks/Cole Publishing Compant.

19 Fuchs E.C. 1988. *Deceptive distinctions*. New Haven, London and New York: Yale University Press, Russell Sage Foundation. p. 99.

20 Dwork, D. 1991. *Children with a Star*. New Haven: Yale University Press. p. 53.

Part 4

Gender and Womanhood in Holocaust Representations

Past and Present in my Mother's Holocaust Memories

Esther Hertzog

Introduction

Although both of my parents were Holocaust survivors, I was quite detached from the subject for many years. I knew of the Holocaust from films, school, and so on, but at home it was not discussed. My father actually wanted to talk, but my mother would stop him. Even after many conversations with her in recent years, I am still not sure whether she did this because she wanted to protect me and my sister, or herself, or perhaps all three of us. Only in the summer of 2000, when I came to Oxford University and happened upon an international conference on the Holocaust being held there, did I open up to the subject. This was mainly thanks to my exposure to studies conducted by feminist researchers notably Dalia Ofer, Esther Fuchs and Myrna Goldenberg,[1] who presented their papers at the conference.[2]

At the time, my mother, Eva Ben-Tal (née Viteles) was urging me to write down her story of the Holocaust. This change in her approach—from silencing talk about those memories to yearning for them to be documented—apparently reflected an emerging, broader phenomenon among many Holocaust survivors. For years, they preferred silence, until the stirring awareness that their lives were drawing to a close, the need increased to leave behind them a personal testimony of their experiences. The need to tell their story also seems to entail the urge to serve as a voice for their dear ones who died, thereby to assure memorializing them and conveying their personal Holocaust heritage to the coming generations. It is also probable that as the harsh memories were fading away with the passage of time, and the pain they brought was becoming more bearable, the survivors' experiences could be openly unfolded. Indeed, the changing attitude in Israel toward the Holocaust survivors, from silencing them to embracing their narratives, must have had a crucial impact as well.

This article was written out of love and appreciation of my mother,[3] from my desire to articulate her unique experiences during the Holocaust and her observation of events past, to the way in which she connects and interprets them relative to other episodes in her life and to later events in Israel. In this article, I also examine my role in these conversations with my mother, how I channel the questions from my world and my own needs, and burrow into the past and its connections relevant for me now.

Gender differences and similarities regarding Holocaust experiences

One of the prominent issues of the Holocaust research done by feminist scholars is the uniqueness of women's experiences during the Holocaust. Designating the experiences of women as a separate domain within Holocaust research emerges from the claim that women, as women, had unique experiences, different from men's. I would like to further this discussion and explore it through my mother's eyes and memories, as I understand them. Having examined my conversations with her, I find, as anticipated, that the way women coped with the living conditions and camp procedures is unique from the biological perspective. However, the gendered social aspects of their lives as women, both their upbringing and the way they coped with daily life in the camps, shaped their experiences, as different from men's. Following conversations with my mother, I contend that even the thinking now about that past, the ways of recollecting and of dealing with it, reflect the divergent social-gender behavior of men and women.

Notwithstanding the above, the analysis of the conversations with my mother raises key social issues that have relevance and meaning that transcend gender differences. Issues linking Holocaust recollections to the manifestations of suppressed groups are a clear example of this. The conversations with my mother will, therefore, afford the basis for discussing the gender differences connected to remembering Holocaust experiences on the one hand, and aspects of 'non-gendered' memory under conditions of collective suppression, on the other. Nevertheless, when one considers that the reaction to suppression is also affected by the individual's upbringing according to his/her sex, then their memory may well also be examined in gender terms.

My initial hypothesis was that the Holocaust survivors' hatred towards all those who were directly or indirectly connected to the Nazi regime would be inclusive and absolute. However, to my astonishment, my mother's statements in relating to Nazis in general and to individuals in the camps where she was interned, were repeatedly forgiving, understanding and even compassionate. Attempting to understand these reactions led me to think about people's behavior in conditions of helplessness in which others almost totally control their lives and death. The analogy to kidnap victims and to prisoners evokes a broad spectrum of situations, ranging from complete alienation and distancing between the inmates and staff, reported by Goffman,[4] to essential cooperation and even friendship between prisoners and warders, according to Greenberg,[5] who discusses the shared dependency dictated by the common framework.

Cooperation between the murderers and their victims existed in the death camps, even if from a lack of choice. My mother's 'compassionate' and 'understanding' recall can be interpreted as an expression of the prisoners' absolute dependence on the warders, creating a negation of self before the strong, and sometimes even admiring them in their recollections many years later. My mother's statements should also be viewed within the current context of her reminiscences. I propose that the humanization of the representatives of 'absolute evil', that she evinces when thinking about the past, is not connected to what she felt or experienced in the event, but rather to her way of coping in the present with the distanced memories of the past, and perhaps also with the emotional price she pays today for remembering.

The victim's forgiveness – An expression of survivor behavior?

Research into the Holocaust raises in full force the issue of suppression. The tendency of the oppressed to 'understand' their oppressors affords them, perhaps, a sense of relative power. If they 'understand' those who hurt them in so total and destructive a manner, they are better than they, stronger than they (in terms of the human quality wherein 'wo/man surpasses the beast'). If the people who hurt them did so because they 'had no choice' and were thus forced, coerced to operate as they did, this clearly diminishes the reputed powers of those who performed the atrocities. In contrast, 'I, the one hurt, can allow myself to forgive'. Forgiveness comes from a position of relative strength, certainly when it is illuminated in the present light, far from the horrors of the camps. Similarly, the current need is apparently to buffer the bitter memories, with which the sense of moral superiority is likely to help. The profound difficulty would appear to lie in recognizing the fact that you have been humiliated and were helpless. Hence, the need to transform the memory of the events to one that corrects, *post factum,* the unbearable power imbalance, the sense of threat to one's individual existence, human dignity and self-esteem. Only when the vicious perpetrator is perceived as a human being does the suffering and abuse acquire a conceivable and therefore tolerable meaning. This conception links to an analysis of the ways oppressed people cope with their oppression by redeeming their sense of being a subject and negating the sense of being a helpless object. Another issue emerging from this line of argumentation relates to therapeutic treatment based on the victim's ability to forgive as stemming from the need to reconcile with the past and to carry on with one's life. The discussion, to this point, is appropriate for both genders as well as for other contexts of collective suppression.[6]

Nevertheless, observation of the behavior of women as the oppressed and as victims of abuse demonstrates patterns of female behavior that evolve from their socialization, different from those associated with males. Violence against women is a conspicuous issue in feminist research and discourse. Responses of acceptance, obedience, surrender, understanding, self-blame, through to "loving" the abusive partner, are reported among women who suffer from spousal abuse. However, Barbara Swirski's, research[7] on wife-beating in Israel rejects theories about female's "victim behavior", and biological, psychological and cultural explanations for men's violence against women. According to her the male hegemony enables, and even directly or indirectly strengthens, male dominance over women in the family array. The use of violence is one of the means of deterrence used by men to maintain control of their spouses and the latter's dependence on them.

In the context of the Nazi concentration and extermination camps, this analysis point again to issues rooted in the extreme power gaps between groups on the basis of race ('Aryan'/Jewish), thus reducing the prominence of the gender aspect. However, it is worth noting here that the Nazi regime was also based on male hegemony. To pursue this direction further, one can state that the Holocaust is an extreme case of destructive, power-domination by males across the world during that period. A variety of studies further point to the fact that non-Jewish women were also among the Nazis' victims, and even that German women were abused and murdered by that regime.[12] Extensive feminist research suggests that the differentiated gender education nurtures different patterns of behavior among men and women. Swirski, for example, suggests that the family institution "...maintains and perpetuates the status of men as possible aggressors and the status of women as possible victims" (1993:234). She states: "She learned from an early age that to be a 'good woman' means being passive and submissive... she learned to behave weakly in order to be a suitable object for 'redemption' by men. This education turned women into 'suitable victims of violent men" (ibid: 235-236). Further to this claim, one might posit that the readiness and ability to forgive are also both part of women's socialization.

In the context of the Holocaust, this argument calls for a comparative gender analysis. However, it would appear reasonable to assume that despite their own prior socialization for dominance, oppressed men also behave as 'victims' under conditions of harsh suppression and humiliation, such as those that prevailed in the Holocaust. Thus, I contend that the concrete means of coercion, operating in a given situation, foster 'supra-gendered' behavior that corresponds to the enforced conditions, rather than a differentiated social-gendered upbringing that has socialized the 'victim' and the 'aggressor' to behave as such.

What and how my mother remembers – Forgetfulness and erasure

Repeated reading of things my mother said in our conversations makes me wonder about details she notes. Sometimes they sound superficial, as if flicking through the events with a distant touch; sometimes they contain contradictions and lack clarity. Time and again, I found myself wondering—while talking to her, after saying goodbye, and when I read her words—whether she is evading me. If this is the case, when she stops talking and ends her words with remarks such as "That's it", or "It's hard", is it because she does not want to expose the pain and the hurt?

I asked my mother whether she thinks about things after our time together and she replied: "I think, regardless". "What do you think?" I insisted. "Really... Oy, this accompanies you throughout life... all the time. Sometimes you don't fall asleep at night. So there are things... mainly from the camp, when you think, they took Grandmother, what did they do with her, and the parents, and anyway, how is it you remained [alive]? It accompanies you all your life, all the time, little one, no way out. That's it". Mention of her grandmother, with whom she stayed at home for three more weeks, after her parents and her sister were taken from the village, arises in the traumatic context of the two-day journey to Auschwitz in a freight train. They put them into "... freight trains, people one on top of the other, thousands in one train... and old Grandma... something ghastly. This, this... Look, it's not good to talk about it. I'm surprised at myself for talking at all. It's hard to describe, a woman of 84, like this, without being able to get off, to drink or anything... They did their bodily functions in a vessel placed in the corner... It's impossible to think about it. A person is also incapable and d-o-e-s-n'-t w-a-n-t to. It's impossible".

Repeated reference to her grandmother being taken from her in Auschwitz made me wonder whether this recollection involves special suffering, or whether mentioning her serves as a stimulus or confirms the memory, a promise that she will not be forgotten. In other words, retaining this memory may work as a 'trigger' that assures fulfilling the obligation of those who did survive to remember those who did not.

I kept asking about her nights, "What do you mean, at night?" "At night, when you don't sleep—What happens then?" "It's night, and that's it. So what do I think? People are like that, it goes through one's head all the time". Thus she goes over, repeats and secures the meaning of the suffering and the difficulty involved in remembering throughout her life, but either does not want or is incapable of going into details. Being unsatisfied with her stubbornness over that which is obvious in the constant presence of the painful memory I challenge her: "But you never spoke about it, never said anything about it". "No. It's enough that I think. Even now. Have I got anything to say? I've already said it a million times, so it's already totally superfluous to tell, isn't it? You want to know, you're writing about it, but for me it's already... that's it".

Nonetheless I don't give up, and continue: "But that's not it. According to what you say it's with you constantly, and that's..." "Well, of course it is. If you had some sort of trauma or something like that, wouldn't you think about it all the time? Not all the time, but mainly when you're like this, when you rest, when you have the time, when you wake up at night and can't fall asleep again, so you sometimes have to really exorcise all these thoughts and because of that who wants to talk about it at all?" Here I put on my pseudo-psychotherapist's hat, hoping to help 'the client' by making her conscious of past experiences in order to achieve a release from burdensome experiences. "Don't you feel the need to talk about it?" I ask. "No, no", she replies, but I persist, "Is it better to be alone with such thoughts at night?" And on another occasion I again ask: "But perhaps talking about it with someone makes it easier and then you are not left alone with them?!" And she replies determinedly: "No, no, no, who could be interested in it? Everyone has his own burden to bear".

My mother's reluctance to go into details when describing her experiences may indicate that she cannot find words to describe those terrible experiences. Her responses to my prying questions might also reflect her great difficulty in remembering the experience in all its intensity. My mother may have also forgotten and finds it hard to admit that the details have escaped her and only a dull echo of pain persists. If it is hard for her to talk about the painful details, she may perhaps prefer to talk about them superficially, vaguely, thus avoiding the pain. Is this 'post-traumatic' behavior (as she herself suggests) that channels the attempt to interpret and explain towards the domain of mental health? Or is this 'simple', unavoidable forgetfulness over the years, that prevents remembering things in detail. For it is the details that afford meaning to the event, making it real, giving it presence. If this is forgetfulness, then why does my mother insist on talking about "bitter memories" that make her nights miserable? Could it be that a sense of obligation towards the dead, and even the feeling of guilt for remaining alive, explain her insistence on her version of suffering at night? From this point of view, mention of the grandmother from whom she was separated in Auschwitz is the most tangible way to enable my mother to hold onto, and to fulfill, her 'obligation' to remember and to be connected to the dead who did not survive.

Later, she openly attributes her difficulty in remembering events to the prosaic reason of the distancing due to the decades that have passed. She says, "It's not from today nor from yesterday. It's almost 60 years. What do you want? Exactly 59 years ago. On the contrary, all my mother's family was expelled to the Ukraine in 1941, so it's more than 60 years. One lives with it. It was Grandmother and my aunts with children, whom I find it hard to remember today, right? I was just a young girl. So, that's it". And in another context, she again admits that the passage of time affects her ability to remember details. "Today I can no longer remember so well the events of almost 60 years ago, that you come and ask me to remember. Sixty years, I was a young girl! What? Who remembers? It's impossible to remember". She explains that she can remember things through associative recollection, but "Much of it is also imagination... and also what people have already set in their minds".

The question of memory continues to trouble me, and I ask her: "And do you remember them? In your mind's eye, do you remember what they looked like?" And she replies, "No, not even my father, for I have no photo of him. I have no photos of Father, so it's hard now, even to think... Sometimes I imagine him like your father, you know? It's already..." "Confusing?" "Yes". And a picture of your mother, do you have one?" "Yes, of Mother I have. The picture with the aunt from Romania, when they weren't in the camps. They brought me the photo with Grandmother, Mother, and myself on her arm. The photo of my mother by herself has vanished. I sent to your Aunt Bobby [her sister in America – E.H.] and she returned it to me. And I hunt and turn things over and don't know where it is. It's a shame, I've taken out and checked in all the photo albums".

While my mother admits her memory is blurry, she insists on her claim that remembering presents an emotional difficulty. She explains to me that it was particularly "difficult for her" in the past, and now, to deal with memories and says, "Your father, poor thing, would talk, but I shut him up. I couldn't stand it. I really suffered. No, no, I couldn't. Now I can still talk about something here and there, but it's not good for me. It's difficult, hard to manage". "When we talk, is it hard for you to speak about it?" I ask. "Not difficult, no; I talk, but it doesn't do me any good, neither the talking nor the thinking. So it's not good at all". In order to further emphasize the meaning of the suffering involved in remembering, she employs proof of the damage this causes everyone who makes a point of exploring their memories: "People are really going crazy now, in their old age. Really. This is the reason I don't want to discuss it at all". And when I continue to push her, and wonder aloud at her reluctance to remember, I almost preach to her, saying, "But there are those..." "...

who like to talk", she continues my words, then criticizes those who do talk: "Those who talked and talked obsessively..." Then she offers triumphant proof of her claim regarding the difficulty and its dangers: "They really lost their minds. Those who are constantly involved in this really go crazy. You know? It's really an obsession for them. All the time dealing with it; it's not good. It's forbidden. One should be busy with other things, with one's children, with grandchildren". This focus on the content of her present life seems to be a means my mother employs in order to distance the threat of remembering the past.

In past times my mother avoided the threatening recollection and would also like to avoid it in the present. She was and remains absolutely convinced now that discussion of what occurred should be withheld from others, especially children. She criticizes those parents who told their children what happened to them in the Holocaust, asserting: "There were parents who destroyed their children's lives. For this reason I told your father, 'They're still young. What do you want? Why do you wreck their lives? No, they don't need to live with it. We moved on, moved on; they aren't guilty. How can they help? I don't think it helped them as children. Now it's something else. You already see they're living... But he would sit and talk wherever he was. I said to him: 'I went through no less'. He really had it tough. But we all went through it. Why should we tell the children? No, no, I didn't like it. No, no, it was too difficult. We suffered enough. In general, I wanted to forget. I didn't talk about it".

When I press her further, saying, "But you see that you haven't forgotten, it's with you all the time", she says, "It's impossible to forget. How can one forget? People lost parents there. Mother was 43. What are you talking about? Cremating my mother at such an age in Auschwitz, and Father, who was 44. Grandmother was 84, but she was healthy. I always think that she could have lived till now if she hadn't been burned to death there. And to think that they sent people as if to shower, and then opened the gas on them. Really, what do you think of that? You know, just thinking about it. For what?" "So you do think about it?" "Yes, of course—not every day; I try not to, but it comes. It's something..." Such remarks make it seem as though my mother is incapable of *not* remembering the events, and how important it is to her that she at last release them to the world. Her descriptions of her many efforts, throughout the years of opposition to my father—and in light of the burdensome nature of her thoughts, to erase, to silence and to 'bury' the bitter memories, expose the silenced presence of memory in her life, from the Holocaust to this day.

I ask whether she can single out a particularly strong recurring memory. And she responds, "No, not any memory concerning myself; I was young, I was 19. Only in connection to my parents and family". It seems that she wishes to disassociate herself from every concrete, realistic aspect of her experiences of suffering during that period, while allowing (and perhaps even forcing) herself to anchor the essence of the horror in everything pertaining to remembering her parents and family. When I persist, ask difficult questions, and wonder about what she characterizes as the bitter experiences she remembers, such as my asking whether she recalls 'fragments of humiliation', she replies with a vehement negative, "No, no, no". "Did you erase it?" And she replies: "No, no, no, they did not humiliate me particularly". When I directly inquire, "Did they shave your head?" she raises her voice slightly and says, "That was humiliating? That was something done to millions, and to me too. That was something, if you stayed alive, that was the least awful thing they could do". And I don't let up. "You stood there naked, naked in front of the..." "That was already nothing". I wonder: "Really?" And she continues: "Nothing. Right". "How could that be? They stripped you naked and you walk around there like some sort of... " "Yes, like a what? Like everyone else. That's it. You get used to it". "Yes?" "I could get used to that. So I walked around. So what? It passed. Look, it's one thing when you're stripped, when a man takes someone and does that. But when you're in a group, is it which one's standing there that matters? He's looking exactly at you? He doesn't see anyone. He sees women as animals, that's all. So it's not something that... No, it shouldn't be taken to heart. I didn't give a damn about him. As far as I'm concerned, he humiliated himself. Understand: whoever does something like that..." "Yes? Have you thought about it? So, have you thought about it?" I wondered whether this was her present view of the past or rather that it was how she had perceived the situation at that time. Obviously, she would not offer a calculated answer, for my mother certainly spoke from her current thinking. She answered confidently, offering from another context an example of a positive memory: "Yes. Always. Like I thought then. As I would say to those *Kapos* and to Peppy [her *Kapo* friend in the camp – E.H.], "Watch out. When we get out of here you'll be in real trouble".

My mother's words and resolute reactions to my questions regarding remembering the humiliating situations, indicate her determination to now perceive her past experiences as bearable rather than exceptional, unconceivable events. She insists upon interpreting things in a manner that diminishes the humiliation. She does this by reframing the social-humanitarian aspect of the situation and of the abusers not seeing the naked women before them as women, but as animals. From that perspective, the perception of humiliation is subjective. Similarly, my mother presents the memory of the situation in terms of relativity: Baldness and nakedness lose their dehumanizing significance and their power to undermine the female self-image when considered in relation to "what happened", i.e. to death vs. survival. Furthermore, as the humiliation is collective in nature, it is perceived as 'a trouble shared.' Hence the individual becomes part of a collective. All are affected and thus the harm is not individual, and accordingly felt less severely. The 'togetherness' of the humiliation reduces and mitigates its weight and impact. An intellectual process is manifested here, in retrospect, of processing the experience of nakedness, converting it into something that was "not awful" when there were many partners to the event, something that happens to "everyone".

In my mother's recollection, the situation in which these events occurred affords them their significance in her eyes today and also explains female adaptation in the past. The nakedness of women before men, which under normal circumstances is considered taboo, can be perceived as less humiliating in some situations. Just as in the hospital people come to terms with exposure and nakedness, so the significance of humiliation is diminished when naked women freeze in the cold.

My mother also employs techniques of cognitive transference: While the Germans perceived the naked women in front of them as animals lacking human consequence, their own participation in the event rendered them bestial creatures, lacking human consequence—and thus their deeds had no impact on the women's human value. This nakedness is like standing naked in the presence of non-humans: animals or inanimate objects.

Nevertheless, the ambivalence in remembering penetrates from time to time. At one point, she almost admits to the feeling of humiliation regarding the baldness and nakedness. But then, too, the humiliation is not personal but relates to a group: "They took everything from us, our hair, everything. You know, wandering around there like that, girls did not know anything about undressing before someone". And she immediately says something contradictory, and returns to grasp onto the observation that reduces and softens the bitter meaning of the events: "They shaved, and sometimes had no razor, so they used scissors. So, for me, for example, they cut my hair with scissors. So a little bit more was left. But what we looked like... Anyway, who had a mirror to see ourselves? But there were girls who were very quick and found themselves some rags [to cover their bald heads – E.H.] helped by men who worked in the railway carriages in which they'd arrived, in which they'd left their belongings".

In other words, the situation negates the import of the loss of feminine external appearance (not having a mirror in which to see the distortion) while, at least for some, quickly finding a means to hide it, also meant "pulling a fast one" on the Germans. However, in my mother's recollections of nakedness before the Germans, something more in keeping with the familiar descriptions of that ordeal was revealed in regard to the social-specific context, mainly of elderly and religious women. I asked: "What happened to someone who did not want to get undressed, and tried to object?" My mother answered, raising her voice, "There was no such thing as 'not wanting' to get undressed. My poor old grandmother—well, imagine, an 84-year-old woman, so religious all her life. She got undressed there, such shame, it was something—ghastly, even though we already saw in what trouble we were. In general, these things are difficult; what went on there was hard". In other words, there is an inconsistency in the attitude toward memory: relative to herself, it wasn't so bad, she 'got used' to it and didn't give a damn, but for her grandmother and other religious women, it was "a total disgrace, horrific".

When she talks about herself—such as in her account of Mengele separating the old women from the young, forced to parade naked in front of him—the shame vanishes. "When we arrived in Auschwitz, stripped of everything, they of course took us to be examined and to shower. He stood in the middle, and we were naked, I don't know, I was no longer embarrassed in the least, you can laugh... We went past as if there were no one present. He also looked at us as if we were sheep and not women, even though I think that sometimes he chose mistresses... but not from there". According to her, the Germans, including Mengele, would take Jewish women, but not those whom they encountered in such circumstances of viewing women as animals.

Several researchers, among them Rochelle Saidel, describe this situation of women going naked before the Nazis as one of the worst experiences women recall from their internment in Auschwitz. According to this approach, religious women suffered particularly since they came from a social world that considered nakedness as an absolute taboo. This is to say that the perception of nakedness is influenced by cultural contexts. Elaborating on my mother's words stresses adaptive coping, that drafts the ability to rationalize and come to terms with memories of the "inhuman" experiences, that are highly anomalous in comparison to "regular" life prior to the Holocaust. Furthermore, the women interviewed by Saidel may have perceived, *post factum*, this marching naked before Nazi eyes as symbolizing the experience of total humiliation that they went through, which they wished to present thus in their postwar social surroundings.

Recollecting the past in mitigating and even positive terms is prominent in my mother's comments about the cessation of menstruation. Today, she regards this result of the Nazi damage to the female physiological functioning as a positive thing, and even as 'fortunate'. in an environment lacking any suitable sanitary conditions. The issue of cessation of menstruation arises in our conversations following my question, "How did women manage while menstruating without underwear, if none was provided after they came out of the showers with only their shoes and the striped nightdress they were issued?" Her sharp response was: "We didn't menstruate. They gave us bread with bromide to eat, which burned our stomachs. It caused me, at least, such heartburn that I couldn't... Or they gave us potatoes with their peels to eat. That was the food. It was bitter... " I interrupt her to ask: "So did it immediately stop all women from menstruating?" and she replied: "Yes, yes, of course. They thought of that. It's such a demonic thing. And yet, that was luck". And I wonder aloud, "Why was that lucky?" And she replies, "Well, what would we have done there? There was nothing there. A piece of rag for one's head. If I already had one that someone had given me, someone else would have stolen it, right from under my head. There were four to six girls in a bunk, on two tiers. We may have been some 400 girls." The biological manipulation was indeed vicious, but in my mother's recollection, the results are associated with 'good luck'.

Humanizing the ultimate evil – To forgive and forget?

Reflecting on the transcripts of the conversations with my mother, I found myself surprised not only by her words that diminish the significance of the humiliation by the Nazis in the camps, particularly in Auschwitz. I was also surprised by the way in which my mother 'humanized the devil'—contrary to what I had considered as self-evident and part of my initial hypothesis. Time and again, I discovered her forgiving, understanding and even compassionate attitude towards the Germans. Consistently and stubbornly, she insisted that there is no 'they' that comprises all Germans and camp staff. In her descriptions, there are different individuals and changing situations. There is no hatred in my mother. I ask her about this: "Look, you don't talk out of hatred". And she answered: "There is no hatred in me". And when I pondered, "There is no hatred in you?" she explains, "No, no. Because I know, they also suffered, the Germans, OK? But the point is that they followed the *Führer* like idiots. Didn't some try to kill him several times? Among the officers, there were some who tried. It was impossible. They were always caught and killed".

I insist on understanding the absence of hate: "In any case, it's hard to understand that there is no hate. You know, after all they did to you, such horrific things, remove all self-respect, all the... " And she insists, "Right, but they were given orders. That's what they had to do. It didn't help them". And I explain to her: "When they took people to the gas chambers they could have not taken them, and then they would also have been killed." She again refrains from condemning all Germans collectively. She says to me, "Look, the Germans were not all animals. Hitler only made them... out of the youngest in particular... They got excited. But there were those who had no choice".

I argue with her and wonder upon what grounds does she base her assessment that there were Germans who did not become beasts, but rather were trapped without any choice. She estimates that among the youth were many more who were swept away by Hitler. I ask several times whence she draws her assessment and conviction that "They were forced". She says resolutely, "Absolutely 100%. It was known. They were forced. They were forced to be..." and when I ask whether it was discussed, if it was stated clearly, she answers, "No, why on earth? But there were some, those from the SS who said it. They, they had no choice, they were forced to go – to guard. There were some who were a bit older, who viewed us as their children. You really saw..." And I ask again if these things were said. "What are you talking about? Why on earth?... There was one who was really nice. We went once, they took us one day when we didn't work outside the camp, on a Sunday; there was a factory owner who had ice, so they took a group of us in winter to cut ice and load it on the truck and afterwards got us to take the ice down to the storage cellar. After that they prepared food, gave us some in the factory kitchen. Did we eat! We were sick. We ate cabbage. What food did the Germans eat? After all, one laughs at this; they would make 20 dishes from cabbage, all sorts. So we sat there and ate. That's why we went to work there, because we knew we would get a good meal". And she brings another good story. "But the *postens* [guards] were nice. There was a sweet one, a handsome young fellow. So he sort of always came up to me and started showing interest, asking how and what, and from where am I; I also had a *"shikse"* [non-Jewish]-looking face, round with a nose like that. And he also told how he was sent there. They were very humane and didn't lift a finger on us. Straight, like that". And when I ask if there were those who did touch them, she replies, "No, no one there touched me. No one".

She even draws on stories of good Germans from her memories. She tells of German workers on a passing produce truck who threw apples to the women who were being trucked from the brick factory back to the camp in Praust (the German name for Pruszcz Gdański, near Danzig). Those people, she believed, provide an example of the existence of good Germans who helped them. "I try to remember those things... so it's not awful. Otherwise it's impossible to live with it... There were decent people. Of course there were. What do you think, all the Germans were evil? Some of them suffered. They had no choice. Of course some were bad, really... or that they had no choice... look, well, I don't envy anyone who does bad to another. I don't believe that he can ever be at peace with himself". She almost apologizes for speaking positively about the Germans and for viewing them as people rather than as 'animals'. Weak, admittedly, but themselves controlled by a cruel master (who is the one fittingly described as 'demonic').

In my mother's perception, there were various types of Germans and locals staffing the camps, and among them, of course, were bad and even vicious individuals. One such example was a Ukrainian SS female soldier who was exceptionally cruel. She used to walk around with a stick "... like this in one hand... and with it she was a queen there. Heaven help her victims, poor things. I still remember her, just like that, with the stick in her hand walking around in the barracks where we lived. When she heard of prisoners who had gold and property she forced them to give them up and threatened to turn them in if they didn't hand over their property to her. I think they killed her after the war".

At the same time, she expresses understanding and even compassion for women recruited by the Nazis to serve as SS. She says, "But they were poor things, all of them here, suddenly you see one with such a belly, Hitler wanted them to have children, to bring children into the world... So they made babies with every soldier, so that Hitler would have... And he took the children. Just as long as they had children, so there would be future generations since maybe some 20 million Germans died in the war. So there would be soldiers. He thought of that, that Satan... So they would wander around there pregnant, then suddenly vanish. Went to give birth and returned a few weeks later. I remember them like that... *'Los, los!'*—move it, quickly, quickly, quickly... and they were sometimes worse than the men".

The memory of their evilness mingles with the understanding and forgiveness. They were 'poor things', they were forced and they had no choice. She also praises some of them. When she suffered from terrible pains in her legs after laying railway tracks in the sweltering sun near Danzig, Peppy, her *Kapo* friend, obtained medication from a member of the Czech SS who worked in the pharmacy. She most forgivingly explains how unfortunate the women SS were: "There were young girls there, most of whom went and actually left these babies with their own mothers back home, and they were brainwashed that they should give birth... were forced to do this, they went because this was their source of income, there was nothing else to live off; after all, they were in a desperate situation. Why did all this business begin? Have you understood? They came and worked there, they received a wage—it's not like real soldiers, they came to be warders. They believed. Hitler put the need for children into their heads. Nationalism is an awful thing, a terrible illness. They suffered afterwards..." And I wonder aloud, "Who suffered?" and she explains: "The Germans". And when I ask, "Do you feel sorry for them?" she answers unhesitatingly, "There were many who suffered, those who didn't do anything. Those who did things got out of there, escaped. Where did they catch Eichmann? In Argentina".

My mother's perspective in describing the Germans, both men and women, as 'poor things', 'innocent' and exploited by Hitler, as needing an income and so on, amounts to 'normalizing' them. It also bolsters her own integrity and humanity in her self-perception in the present. This recollection makes her strong and ethical.

The forgiveness approach, interwoven as a consistent thread in her memories, even includes appreciation for those who were supposed, according to my assumptions, to be the incarnation of evil for her. She tells me, "They also knew how to respect people; if they saw that someone was not lazy, who worked, didn't exploit the situation". I try to point out to her the absurdity in her statements about the inmates, as though female forced laborers could take advantage of their German employers, but she insists: "Whoever did not waste time, you know, who worked and didn't malinger by remaining in the hut when the others went out to work..." My hesitant reaction does not deter her, so she adds positive descriptions of her taskmasters, of their 'consideration', that there were some who allowed them to take jugs of water from the barracks in the morning, and when they worked at the airport allowed them to collect potatoes from field close by. The women cooked the potatoes over a fire in the work area and divided them up among themselves. "Some girls managed to get a hold of some salt, and even if we ate without salt it kept us going". She is swept up in her considerate and comprehending regard for the taskmasters' distress. "There were also Romanians. There was this man, a young fellow, poor thing, whom they took... Was he guilty? They took him and made him into an SS, to guard the girls. In the beginning he was OK and everything, but towards the end they saw they were going to lose, so they became nerve-wracked and really began to take out their nervousness on the girls. Then it was very tough".

In other words, she perceives the SS as those caught in a no-choice situation, and even then, when they were forced to pitch in and integrate into the death apparatus, some of them managed to preserve some sort of humanitarianism. Only when their own situation came under existential threat did the good ones among them become cruel. Humanizing the Germans, thinking about them in human terms and as individuals with reasonable and even positive characteristics, apparently helps my mother in her remembering while ignoring the threatening, painful memories. And perhaps this way she can forget. This analysis does not deny, of course, the humanitarianism, the consideration, the help and even the good-heartedness of the Germans and others, as arises from my mother's descriptions. My claim supports the central place held by positive thought in my mother's memories, as a means of alleviating harsh recollection and its implications for her life.

Encumbering motherhood – Another dimension of remembering suffering

Another statement made by my mother, that astonished me involves her memories from the post-WWII detention camps on Cyprus.[8] In total contrast to my assumption, she sometimes presented her memories from there as more difficult than those from the Nazi camps, including Auschwitz. Even while writing these lines, I find it hard to comprehend this. My mother's statements vary: at times she remembers events in Cyprus as having been more difficult, while at others she describes her experiences from the Nazi camps and death march as harsher. The explanation she offers for the perception of the great suffering in Cyprus is linked to the change in her human-social condition. She was unmarried and childless when she was interned in the Nazi camps, while in Cyprus she was married and the mother of a baby. This transformation had extremely meaningful implications on her situation in Cyprus and on the way that the unbearable difficulties were fixed in her memories. Thus she explains the recollection in the context of responsibility for a human creature dependent on her: "In Cyprus it was no more difficult than in the camps, where we slept one next to the other and one atop or under another, but it was just more difficult because I did not have only myself to take care of. There was you and there was your father, although Father helped and made sure there was food... I can't tell you. But I found it difficult; why I had those boils".

According to this, from my mother's descriptions, the responsibility for another, a baby in this case, is so significant for her, to the extent that it can influence the degree of suffering perceived in her memory of the past. One may further assert that in the social reality of that time (and to a great extent, today also), the social existence of women who are mothers was connected to expanding the female self. As a mother, she is no longer an entity unto herself, concentrated on her personal needs and concerns and on her own survival when under existential threat. The paramount bond to a baby, the responsibility for another, a helpless human creature, made her too, at least in her memory, helpless, dependent even more on my father who brought her food.

Although unmarried in the camps, she was also dependent on others there, particularly upon her friend Peppy, the *Kapo*, thanks to whom she survived. But the memory of the feeling of helplessness, implied by her words, is more serious with respect to Cyprus, where she, and not my father, was connected as though through the umbilical cord to her baby. More than the subjugation nurtured by the biological connection, there is room to talk of a situation of subjugation to society, to the arms embracing the individual and specifically women: The close social supervision of a woman's behavior, her clothing, her modesty. Her adopting the condemnation of sexual relationships outside marriage, the condemnation of sexual relations to obtain benefits—and in the context of the Nazi camps to increase the chances of survival, her punishment by being distanced from the "decent" public, and sometimes the threat of physical violence or even death. It transpires that these means of control and supervision do not dissipate even in conditions of existential threat, when due to external coercion both personal responsibility and control by the group weaken.[9]

The overwhelming mantle of absolute responsibility for a baby is placed on the woman and demands of her unhesitating commitment and giving precedence of its need over her own, though not over the man's needs. The socialization of women from birth onwards, encourages their development and transition towards motherhood. It shapes their personality to be cognizant of their children's needs and lives, to the point of forgoing their own. Behavior that deviates from these expectations-norms is condemned. Stories of mothers going to their death because of subjugating their existence for that of their children, especially babies, are praised—as, for example, Lea Balint suggests in her article (in the Hebrew version of this book)[10] on the heroism of mothers who saved their children at the expense of their own lives. Stories of renunciation, labeled as 'abandonment', are rarely told or documented. In other words, the historical documentation also strengthens coercive social conditioning in favor of the overpowering bond between mother and child. The film Out of the Ashes illustrates this argument. It tells the story of Dr. Gisella Perl, a Hungarian-Jewish doctor and Auschwitz survivor who sought American citizenship. It portrays the investigation in which her experiences in the Auschwitz death camp resurface. The three panel members—all male, one of them Jewish—express overt and piercing criticism of her having performed thousands of abortions in Auschwitz. Her claim—that she thereby saved the young women from certain death—fails to persuade them that her actions were ethically correct. The significance of the judgmental-moral stance they represent is that the mother's right to life is not in itself an issue, nor does it automatically preempt the right to life of their embryo or fetus. What is self-evident and expressed by the male judges of the medical deed is the protection of the embryo's or fetus' life expected of women even when their own lives are in danger. While they eventually approve Dr. Perl's citizenship application, they contend that her acts were not without blame.

The socially-determined subjugating imperative of the mother-child bond often resulted in women's deaths. My mother speaks of those who went to their deaths together with their babies and of others who went to the gas chambers with their sisters who had babes in arms. For example, she remembers her cousin, Onush, who at age 14 was in Auschwitz with Sidi, her husband's daughter. "She got her out of there alive, from the hands of Mengele. All the time they underwent selections— who for life, who for death. So she, when she was with the girl, who was so thin and little, 'So she wanted to take me', she says. 'But no, I grabbed her by the hand and pulled her to me'. That's how she tells it now... Of course she saved her. Bobby [my mother's sister] arrived in Auschwitz with Jenny [their aunt] and with their mother's sister [age 43 at the time] and her three small children. And there, mother grabbed her sister, went to help her with the children, straight to the gas chambers. Bobby went with Jenny and remained alive".

Making comparisons – An instrumental application of recollection

Another coping mechanism adopted by my mother regarding her memories of the Holocaust period is the drawing of comparisons. When speaking of what was, she shifts associatively and fluently between periods, regimes, and situations, and easily sees parallels between diverse social and historical events and the Holocaust.

She unhesitatingly compares her opinions of Nazi collaborators to collaborators in other contexts: The camps in Cyprus where my parents spent six months with me, a year-old infant, the American conquest of Iraq, and bringing foreign workers to Israel. Then in almost the same breath she'll explain to me: "There too [i.e. in Cyprus, as in the Nazi camps – E.H.] they had Jews who were in charge... now look what's happening in Iraq, who do they let govern? The Iraqis. They kill each other. Look, how many killed other Iraqis by mistake. But that's how it goes. The boss allows the other to be the bad guy. The same with the Germans. They let our girls be the bad guys. Why them? We did the work for them. Yes, that's the entire philosophy in a nutshell... Look, here in Israel, we bring over foreign workers, now we're the bosses. How can that be? Why can't we do the work on our own? Why?" My mother associates the *Häftlingen* (German: prisoners, also inmates in Nazi camps) with the period in Cyprus, where, according to her, there were "... many who dressed like I, like *Häftlingen*". And I query, "What, were you also called *Häftlingen* there" And she replies: "Of course we were *Häftlingen* there as well. What do you mean? Didn't they put us into barracks?"

In contrast, she protests the suggested comparison between the condition of the Holocaust survivors when they reached Israel and the difficulties of the Jewish immigrants from North Africa and the Arab countries of the Middle East who arrived several years later. She is highly indignant over those immigrants' complaints of deprivation, and their attempt to compare this to her deprivation as a Holocaust survivor who arrived after great suffering, having lost her family, destitute. Believe me, till today many talk out of envy, first of all. We came, a miserable lot, after the camps, without anything—and they came, lucky them, with their families, with parents, with siblings. Is that the same thing? What do you mean? We came naked. Honestly, whoever comes to tell me today, I get so angry about such things. What are you talking about? How could one compare them at all?" And I get defensive in view of her increasing anger: "We're not comparing; who's comparing?"

Later, she also draws a comparison with immigrants who came from Romania. "The Romanians too. Mady [her good friend, who died a few years ago – E.H.] came with her father, although they had went through some very tough years, in Transnistria, but they (raising her voice) were with a mother, with a father, with everyone. They weren't taken to the gas chambers. They may have died of hunger there, of illness, but they weren't taken, they weren't cremated, and they survived—Mady came with her brother and sister, with her father and mother and all the family..." And thus continues the conversation, whereas I, again, defend myself and insist that I am not comparing. Nevertheless, she stubbornly continues: "... You hear the Moroccans, going on about '... what they gave them [i.e. the Holocaust survivors]'. What did they give us? They came with families. So what was more precious than that? Have I ever asked why that one had a grandfather and grandmother and I have no one? Did you ever think about that?" She talks in the same vein about the DDT, with which the immigrants were sprayed. She perceives this as a necessary act and the complaints as unjustified. [They too were fumigated when they arrived sick with typhus from the camps in Cyprus – E.H.]. In another context, as if without any connection, she again refers to the jealousy that angers her. "They are jealous of us for receiving money from the Germans. What is this? It is impossible to pay us for what we've been through. What is this? Peanuts! It's nothing. What did we do with it? And these people..." When I try to moderate her anger she refuses to calm down and hangs onto her furor: "And I still find those who justify it, so I don't know what to say. Don't know what to say". My defense—"There's no connection, Mother!"—does not help and she continues in her anger, "There *is* a connection. All the time envious, all the time talking. What do they talk about? That I came from a home and lost everything and we lived like that with ourselves, stripped of everything? People brought us some clothes from here and there." In yet another context she says: "We didn't get anything for free. Believe me. If there are those who complain they got nothing and the Ashkenazim[11] did receive things, it's a lie. I'll bring you others who will tell you that we paid for every last penny..." And when she discerns reservation in my facial expression, she asks, "So, what?" And I say: "Apparently it disturbs you terribly. You constantly go back to this!" and she answers vehemently, "Yes, it disturbs me terribly. Awful, awful, this injustice, that they go to complain. What is it? Nobody gave me. How many difficulties did we have to endure when we moved from the one room in which we lived? There were already four of us [after the birth of my sister, Ilana – E.H.] when we moved to *Shikun Vatikim* [a new neighborhood of Netanya, inhabited by immigrants – E.H.] and we had to commit ourselves to...What do you mean? We hardly had what to eat. Believe me. But we made it alone, on our own. So I went to work as soon as we came here... I went to work in an orchard".

Thus she also criticizes the complaints against the kibbutzim—which, from her point of view contributed much to the immigrants—as motivated by envy of them. "Today they're laying into them". Moreover, she remembers with appreciation and affection the representative of the Histadrut Labor Federation who received them when they moved to Netanya and were given their '*Sochnut beds*'.[12] They didn't complain. "Do you think it was easy? And we didn't make a fuss over all this—didn't go to complain and didn't say anything. And there were those – whatever was done for them was no good..." And she goes on to complain about the behavior of the today's unemployed by comparing them to her past: "Such a healthy young woman, striking—go and work for heavens' sake. What is that? Yes, I went to work. I was pregnant already with Ilana and I left you with Rachel Engel, when we were living in Charuvi's house. [When they left the transit camp in Ra'anana, my aunt's father rented a room for us in Netanya – E.H.] So I paid her something and went to pick oranges, and your Father was drafted. What could I do?"

Connecting the present events to those of the Holocaust (and subsequently in Israel) is a further means employed by my mother to contain the past and so perhaps assure it as part of her identity and existence. For in the past she had not wanted to remember and deal with what had happened to her (including silencing my father and preventing him from telling us), she thus eventually made herself also forget details. And now, perhaps she feels guilty for her forgetfulness and her offspring's lack of knowledge and interest. She even accuses me for not wanting to hear about the Holocaust. This charge has no basis, though, and she herself admits that she prevented my father from telling us when he wanted to.

This manner of recollection presented as comparative observation makes the events relevant for one's life, and accordingly more significant or easier to relate to. This may also be true for my mother. In other words, from her point of view, too, the Holocaust was "... so long ago, how many years have passed since then? Fifty? Sixty?" And thus, the growing distance from the occurrence of the events necessitates 'codes' or 'stimuli' that would make the bits of memory more tangible, make them 'hers', things that are part of her life now, 'what she is today'. Thus, for example, she talks of her granddaughter Sharona, my sister Ilana's daughter, and her desire to avoid military service at all costs, because it is 'hard' for her. Mother is really upset about this and reminds me (and at the same time Sharona and the rest of the family) of what happened to her when she was her 'spoiled' granddaughter's age: "How cross I got with Sharona when she phoned one night, saying: 'Grandma, I can't. It's hard in the army'. Hard in the army! I told her, 'Everyone has it OK there and everything, and what—at your age?' And then I said to her: 'Do you know what happened to me at your age? I had no one to go to. Not only did I not have a grandmother, I didn't have a mother, nor father nor anyone". It really annoyed me. "You're here, a girl from the army, and you're crying to me? What on earth are you doing?' I can't stand it".

Peppy, the *Kapo* – Friend and savior or contemptible collaborator?

Peppy had been an employee in my grandfather's lumber business before the war, and had promised him she'd look after my mother. In the camp, she was my mother's friend and savior. Peppy was also a *Kapo* (an inmate put in charge of others). My mother's comments about her range from profound gratitude for having kept a devoted eye on her—and in fact saving her life—to criticism and a bitter grudge for having served as the Nazis' active partner against her friends, other Jewish women. My mother is torn, it seems, between this dichotomy. She tells me: "I withdrew from her time and again. I couldn't stand it, that she was a boss, and how she would hit people here and there". But within that sentence itself she adds, "But that was for the Germans to see that she was OK, because that way she obtained better food for our group. She tried very hard. She was a good girl, but in those conditions, it was impossible to stay sane. She was a wonderful girl. Otherwise I would not be alive". On the one hand, my mother talks of Peppy's devotion, managing to get clothes for the women, the clothes of the dead, those same clothes that the Germans did not take. "So she always took them for us to have the best, and she really cared". And on the other hand, she returns to the criticism: "But when I sometimes saw that she was like that, I would leave her, I went so as not to be with her. And once I said to her, 'Look, don't you lay a finger on anyone. We'll get out of here, and then you'll see what happens to you'. I threatened her... I said to her, 'You'd better understand, we'll get out of here. Behave properly!' And she did listen to me a lot".

Time and again, my mother describes Peppy's help in terms of gratitude for having saved her life on so many occasions. One of her bitter memories, connected to Peppy's courageous help, is from the period of about six months when my mother was in Praust. Women worked there building the airfield. Work started at 7 a.m. and ended in the evening. She raises harsh memories of the beatings the women received from their supervisor if they did not work to his satisfaction. The strong sun scorched their legs (and she maintains that she suffers from that till now). "He was responsible, the SS, for everyone. A nasty bit of *'goy'* [non-Jew]. Walked behind us row by row... This was at that time that my legs were really giving me trouble, I couldn't stand because they were sunburned. Many were afterwards taken to Stutthof and cremated there. So he sort of walked past, and I apparently really shook, and Peppy always stood in front of or behind me and he walked past and hit me on the head, so that I was not steady on my feet—and Peppy wouldn't let me fall".

My mother's ambivalent attitude in her memories of Peppy is revealed time and again. She recounts and explains: "Peppy did not befriend the Germans, in contrast to the other *Kapos,* who did. She had the good sense to make friends with the Jewish girls working in the kitchen. She had a good relationship with them. She knew how to get in, they gave her from the officers' food. She would bring back a plate of food. 'Eat...' Yes. So I simply had no other choice but to be with her. All right? I was scared of her. Afterwards she would start in, 'Come on. What's this?' And I saw then that I would either go hungry or that there would be no one for me". In other words, she would like to remember and present her friendship with Peppy, the despicable *Kapo,* as a lack of choice in a situation of helplessness that put her under Peppy's patronage. Peppy's negative image, in her eyes, is inseparable from the gratitude for having saved her life. But even this gratitude is expressed apologetically, for having accepted help from a collaborator.

Peppy's many attempts to protect my mother were connected to the commitment that linked her to my mother's family in her youth. "She knew Father. She worked there as a clerk, cleaner, everything. Cooked there, where they worked in the forest. She liked him a lot. He helped her. She ran their home. So she told me, 'I promised your father that I would return you home. I'll take care of you'". After the liberation, they were together for a year and separated in Prague, when my mother wanted to get to Budapest. Peppy met a man in Prague and married him. She returned to Romania after the war, and later also came to Netanya, like my parents. For years, my mother didn't know that Peppy was living in Israel, in Netanya, until Peppy contacted her one day when she needed someone to testify for her to receive compensation. My mother claimed that Peppy did not seek her out until then. "She wasn't interested and apparently didn't feel comfortable with me. She may have been scared always that I would go let something out, that she was a *Kapo* or something like that. D'you understand? I didn't tell, what am I? I could only think of good things... and she wasn't a bad girl. That she definitely wasn't. She helped me from start to finish".

I wondered how my mother had never met Peppy during her years in Netanya. And my mother explains, "I wouldn't have recognized her. She had changed so. She was so miserable [when she met her in Netanya – E.H.], really a poor creature, and she wasn't [i.e., before or during the war – E.H.] the least bit a poor thing." She also stresses that Peppy pretended not to notice her when she walked past her in Netanya. Mother tried to calm her fears. She said to her once, apparently, "'Just know, Peppy, I have no complaints against you. Whoever just hears about you, like my children, hears that you saved my life... " and then I hear, 'Oh, you hear, Peterke [Peppy's son – E.H.], what's Eva saying. That I saved her.' It's very important to her. Look, she thought of me as one whose father has really saved her... and after that, when she calmed down, when she saw I wasn't angry at her, have no complaints, and believed that everything she did was, in fact, only for the best, then she calmed down". When I wondered if Peppy has guilty feelings, my mother explains "Impossible...she was only scared, perhaps, that I would tell that she had been a *Kapo* there". And to my question, "So why did she have to fear that?" she replies, "No one bragged about this. You understand? There were even good *Kapos*; there was simply a need for someone to guard the group, right?... There are some who themselves feel a bit... and don't want to talk about it. Some worked in the kitchen and they lived wonderfully and everything, and they divided the food between themselves, among all their friends. They really were not bad to anyone, but nevertheless, the jealousy was enormous... Look, they had little choice there, since it wasn't so simple. You can't come today and blame them. There were those who wanted to remain alive. That's it. And whoever didn't want, sooner or later was gone...."

On another occasion she says: "Look, no one volunteered to be evil. They had no choice". When I question why Peppy didn't seek out my mother during all the years she lived in Netanya, she explains with apparent irrelevance: "She wasn't a murderer, she wasn't a bad *Kapo* but she had to act authoritarian, otherwise what would she do? I didn't like her toughness, but the others didn't care, they liked her there. She went to the kitchen and was given good food, food from the officers that was cooked separately for the officers. She would take it and bring it to me". I ask my mother if Peppy was good only to her because of her promise to my mother's father and Mother says, "She was friendly with everyone; she knew how to be. We had jugs of water in the barracks, so they let her take these jugs when we went [to work in the airport] and we gathered potatoes, they allowed her. Her group ate potatoes, cooked them in the jugs full of water. She got on with the SS and with the guard. She was OK, we ate". And as if summing up, my mother says of Peppy—who was responsible for 50 women: "She was forced to show that she did her work, otherwise they would have thrown her out. Nowadays I see things differently; some there were real garbage".

My mother's comments today, about Peppy as representative of the *Kapos* and "our little Jewboy collaborators", reveal a complex memory that includes understanding, appreciation and gratitude mixed with criticism, derision and condescension. My mother may also not like the memory of her great dependence on Peppy, who is identified as a "traitor" who helped the Nazis against the other women, and so the warm and positive aspects return every time to harsh criticism. She identifies the *Kapos'* role with particularly profound hatred and scorn towards Jews who helped the Germans to do their "dirty work". And in her words: "The German did that because he hates me. He is my enemy. But I couldn't understand how a Jewess could do it. How does a Jewish girl hit another?" At the same time, along with the expressions of sweeping hatred towards the *Kapos* and Jews who helped the Germans, she also explains the malicious method behind recruiting Jews to harm Jews. "Who was there when we arrived and undressed? Who? Our boys helped out there. The Jews. They had Jews do the dirty work. It wasn't them. Outside, everything clean and nice. That's because earlier, these German women and our *Kapos* arrived so that everything would be orderly, by the book and then came the SS, the officer, and began to count and went through this quietly. Everything was nice and neat. That was what they knew. They knew how to hide things". Though Mother admittedly despises the female *Kapos,* still she knows they were part of a 'clean' system of control, suppression, and murder, without the murderers 'dirtying their hands', as it were. Another possibility that arises in this context is that my mother's loathing of the *Kapos* reveals her feeling of extreme vulnerability as a victim, even now when she reflects on her memories.

In loathing the *Kapos*, especially in view of her surprising forgiveness towards the Germans, my mother may be projecting her tremendous, impossible hatred onto other weak people, closer by, who were only a little stronger than she and therefore a more convenient, more real, target for hatred.

Another important aspect arising from the story of Peppy's consistent and wonderful support of my mother is the mutual help and solidarity between women (which almost certainly existed among men as well) in the camps. One of the fascinating courses of debate raised by feminist research into the Holocaust is that which describes the growth of cells, groups and diverse social arrangements among women in the camps, that contributed considerably to the survival of many women. Studies such as those by Judith Buber Agassi and Irith Dublon-Knabel (in this book) dealing with the women's camp at Ravensbrück, describe the growth of close family-like relationships there that they call 'alternative families'. These studies emphasize creating alternatives to family bonds, notably for replacing the mother and sister roles. The authors differentiate between the groups according to size and to the type of support they provided their members. From my mother's comments (limited as they are in scope and as she is my sole interviewee) I cannot draw conclusions regarding the frameworks that evolved or replaced the family. The limited material in my possession relates mainly to dyadic friendships formed between individual women. This transpires not only from the description of the connection between Peppy and my mother but also from the relationship she mentions between her sister and aunt. The central place of the protector figure within the dyad in saving her and her sister emerges from her comments. She recounts: "We were two girls at home, a bit spoiled, not knowing how to take care of ourselves, so it was lucky that Bobby [her sister] was with Jenny [their aunt, close in age] and Jenny was a toughie, and I myself had already found Peppy, the family acquaintance, in the Saklanze ghetto. So she helped me. Look, everyone had someone who helped them".

It seems to me that this type of dyadic friendship between the two is compatible with the sociological and anthropological literature on the socialization of girls compared to boys. Boys are encouraged to join groups as part of their channeling to undertake leadership roles in society. Girls, rather than joining groups, prefer to develop a more intimate relationship with one friend. Thus they decline to form groups committed to attaining organized power.[13] This is, of course, a hypothesis that calls for a comparative study to analyze survival stories of males.

The more relevant point is that my mother thus remembers the value and type of friendship that saved her from death. But on this point, too, she is consistent in her ambivalent attitude toward her memories. In this context too, her memories about women's devotion and self-sacrifice when facing the threat of suffering and death are linked to her uncompromising criticism of other women: "The desire to live was so great there, that one was capable of taking a piece of bread from another. So I thought to myself, 'Of what importance is it to you? Only you need to live? What will you do when you are alive, alone?'" In her thinking today, she explains that without cooperation and all sharing among them the little there was to be had, not enough would have remained for most of them and they would not have survived. With hindsight, she is convinced that even at the time she questioned the value of survival if individuals cared only for themselves and would survive, only to remain alone.

Summary: Shaping and losing memories

The main point arising from the conversations with my mother about her Holocaust memories and experiences is her instrumentalization of memories that have been lost, forgotten and/or obliterated. Prominent in her comments are the inconsistencies and inner contradictions in the details of her recollections, in the recalled images of the events, the characters and the insights. These phenomena are apparently related to the instrumental use that she makes of her memories, so that they serve her in a mode relevant and necessary to the particular context of our conversation. From this point of view, recollection is a means that serves and is adapted in a flexible manner to the way she now conducts herself, whether during our conversations or at other times too, when she touches upon her memories.

My mother's recollection of the events, as emerges from her remarks, replies and explanations, presents them in a modified, mellower tone. There is forgiveness, understanding, and compassion for the Germans and other camp staff, and even gratitude towards those among them who helped. They are not a collective in her eyes, nor the absolute symbol of evil, bar the satanic figure of Hitler. They are people who react in a different and varying way in situations that present a challenge to the human essence of their personalities. This viewpoint supports the argument of instrumental recollection.

The expressions regarding the past employ mechanisms that enable my mother to cope with it, whether as a means of dealing with the recollection of the unbearable suffering or whether to face the commitment to remember those who did not survive. Perhaps in the positive statements about the Germans and in her words, "They were also people", my mother finds a way to alleviate the memory of the past as a total horror, inhuman and impossible to grasp. Thus she humanizes the Holocaust. Her insistence on remembering the events through positive thinking (of good-heartedness, self sacrifice, help with the weak, luck, and so on) indicates the way in which she copes with memories, organizes and processes them in the present. In this context, I was surprised to find an interesting and significant similarity to the comparison made by Esther Fuchs[14] between her father's and mother's recollections, both Holocaust survivors. His narrative is the narrative of horror while her mother's is the narrative of heroism and praise for the lost Jew. It may thus be worth researching the types of gender-influenced memory.

Acknowledgements

I am grateful to Prof. Emanuel Marx for inspiring conversations and insightful comments. I also thank Dr. Batya Brutin, Anita Tarsi and Prof. Judith Tydor Baumel who read the essay and offered some very valuable comments.

Notes

1   See for example Dalia Ofer and Lenore J. Weitzman (eds.). *Women in the Holocaust.* New Haven: Yale University Press. 1998.
    Esther Fuchs (ed.). *Women and the Holocaust: Narrative and representation.* Lanham and Oxford: University of America Press. 1999.
    Myrna Goldenberg. *Lessons Learned from Gentle Heroism: Women's Holocaust Narratives.* Thousand Oaks, California: Sage. 1996.
    Other important publications on gender research of the Holocaust include:
    Judith Tydor Baumel. *Double Jeopardy: Gender and the Holocaust.* London: Frank

Cass. 1998.

Ronit Lentin (ed.). *Gender and Catastrophe*. London: Zed Books. 1997.

Carol Rittner and John K. Roth (eds.). *Different Voices: Women and the Holocaust*. New York: Paragon House. 1993.

2   Since my return from Oxford, the issue of women and the Holocaust has become part of my feminist and academic activity. I organized, with my colleagues at Beit Berl Academic College, Beit Terezin (Theresienstadt memorial center) and Beit Lohamei Haghetaot (the Ghetto Fighters' House museum and study center) four international conferences on this subject. Following the three first conferences an anthology (Hertzog, 2006)) was published in Hebrew by Otzar Hamishpat.

3   My father, Bondi, was also a Holocaust survivor. My parents met in a refugee camp in Italy, after their liberation from the concentration camps. They married there and I was born there. We lived in the camp till I was one year old, when they tried to reach Eretz Israel on a *ma'apilim* ("illegal" immigrants) ship. We were deported to Cyprus for another six months and arrived in Israel when Prince Charles was born, as Queen Elizabeth II approved the entrance of pregnant women and couples with babies to Mandate Palestine. My father died of a heart attack in 1971, aged 48.

4   Erving Goffman. *Asylums*. New York: Anchor Books 1961.

5   Ofra Greenberg. *Women in Israeli Prisons*. Tel Aviv: Gome 1982. (Hebrew).

6   One of the prominent examples is the termination of the apartheid regime in South Africa that was enabled due to the leadership of Nelson Mandela, and the collective pardon afforded the former white government by the blacks there. A less familiar example is the actions of a group of whites in Australia who managed to persuade the government to ask forgiveness in retrospect from the Aborigines for kidnapping their children and transferring them to State institutions and adoption by whites. Finally, the bonds between the State of Israel and Germany developed due to the financial compensation to the State and to Holocaust survivors in exchange for a collective pardon.

7   Barbara Swirski. Control and Violence: Wife-beating in Israel. In: U. Ram (ed.) *Israeli Society: Critical Perspectives*. Tel Aviv: Breirot. 1993: 222-244. (Hebrew).

8   Barbara Distel's article in this anthology notes this specifically.

9   The British Mandate government often caught and deported "illegal" immigrants reaching the shores of Palestine to refugee camps on Cyprus. With the establishment of the State of Israel the camp gates were opened and the Holocaust refugees reached the fledgling State.

10 Only recently this issue has become a legitimate topic for academic and public discussions. The literature, including feminist literature, dealing with the Holocaust tended to ignore the issue of 'sex transactions' of the camp inmates. Such an open discussion was apparently perceived as undermining the status of the women's total victimization, and as something that is liable to affix an illegitimate label of cheapening by society (and researchers), as people who sold their bodies for food, for example. In response to my questions, my mother speaks of women who went to the SS living quarters and had sexual relations there. She is not clear as to how this functioned but she assumes it

was with some sort of agreement. She mentioned one such story regarding the woman in charge of the kitchen, who "…went shopping with one of the officers in his car, and everyone knew she lived with him there". In other words, she remembers the connections between the inmates and the guards and officers in social terms (so and so's girlfriend), based, to some extent, on agreement and exchange that assured the inmates a variety of needs – from clothing and food to a sexual relationship in a reality of no tomorrow. She says, "Right, they were very, very handsome men, it's true. And girls wanted-feared as 'Tomorrow we die'. So go on, at least have a good time."

11 Lea Balint. "The Heroism of Jewish Women in Saving their Children." In E. Hertzog (Ed.) *Women and Family in the Holocaust.* Beit Yitzhak: Otzar Hamishpat. 2006. pp. 183-206. (Hebrew).
12 Immigrants from Western Europe and America.
13 Simple iron-frame beds provided as basic furnishing by the Jewish Agency
14 See for example, Margaret Mead, *Coming of Age in Samoa.* New York: Morrow. 1928. Emanuel Marx on Relationships between Spouses among the Negev Bedouin. In: E. Abuhav, E. Hertzog, H. Goldberg and E. Marx (eds.) *Israel: Local Anthropology.* Tel Aviv: Tcherikover. 1998. pp. 247-270. (Hebrew).
15 In her article, "Exile, Daughterhood and Writing: Representing the Holocaust as a Personal Memory." In: Ronit Lentin (ed.). *Re-presenting the Holocaust for the 21st Century.* Oxford & New York: Berghahn, 2004: 253-268.

Gender, Identity and Family in the European Holocaust Film: The Jewess as Virgin and Whore

Esther Fuchs

Romantic narratives in European Holocaust films tend to frame the Jewess as either a femme fatale or the ultimate victim of erotic obsession. She lives for love, dies for love, and if she survives she survives thanks to love, which is sexual rather than platonic, marital, or familial. The ultimate seductress, she is the naive virgin or experienced courtesan of Christian myth.[1] As virgin, she is very young—an irresistible object of sexual desire; in her more mature versions she is an irrepressible lover, an eager sexual agent who throws all caution to the wind in pursuit of her (gentile) man (or woman). In either case, she is defined in sexual terms. Fiercely focused on self-preservation—or conversely, suicidal—she is a liability (for her lover) in her life and a source of endless grief after her death, a death she is often shown to bring upon herself. More in heat than in love, the Jewess is somehow vacuous, unaware of her (gentile) lover's self-sacrifice. The Jewess is the ultimate narcissistic and masochistic heroine, and as such she embodies the ultimate woman in love, the stereotypic feminine subjectivity of the romantic heroine.

Isolated from family and social context as required by the romantic code, the Jewess seems unable or unwilling to extend herself to victims like herself and other persecuted Jews. Oblivious to the fate of coreligionists, to political time, or collective identity, the Jewess is usually indifferent to historical context or group solidarity.[2] As violence and destruction engulf her family and community, the cinematic Jewess is fixated on sexual exploration, adventure and escape. In mostly European films produced in the 1960s and 1970s the Jewess is attracted to socialist, anti-Fascist men, while in the 1980s and 1990s she is increasingly attracted to collaborators, anti-Semites, or Nazi party affiliates of either sex.

If the gentile woman's love (for the persecuted Jewish man) at times leads to feats of rescue and survival, offering her the status of the heroine of the redemptive Holocaust narrative, the Jewess is almost inevitably the heroine of a story of atrocity, her love constituting a temporary distraction on the path to death.[3] Yet, the Jewess's death is portrayed as the result of her own reckless behavior, her youthful passion. This construction shifts the blame from perpetrator to victim. To the extent that we are justified in associating the Nazi genocide with fantasies of Aryan virility, we may say, such films also shift the blame from the male perpetrator, to the female victim of violence.

The scenario of the beautiful and powerless female victim in the clutches of a fantastic (masculine) monster creates a terrorizing titillation familiar in popular genres of the horror film.[4] It draws as well on the long tradition in classic and artistic representations of women's bodies in danger.[5] The inevitable disaster that awaits the enchanting Jewess both terrifies and reassures the viewer who is spared the end s/he watches on the screen.[6] The genre of Harlequin romance is also manipulated, as are the conventions of the suspense film as the viewers try hard to guess whether the Jewesses' sexual partner will or will not betray her at the end.[7] The Jewess who is often sacrificed or eliminated at the end of the film is more often than not shown to have brought about her own demise. Her death is naturalized and legitimized by the generic conventions of melodrama, and offers a narrative denouement and psychological relief from the complex entanglement dramatized in the film. Because her death is made to appear as the result of her own doing, her loss is mourned as largely a private affair, which more often than not illustrates the waywardness of youth and femininity as such, rather than the historical atrocity that was the Holocaust.

Kapo[8]

One of the earliest films to present the horrors of life in a Nazi concentration camp, the film is at first glance sympathetic to the plight of the Jews. A closer look at the representation of the Jewish protagonist reveals that the film tries to explain and illustrate the evolution of a Jewish inmate, Edith, an innocent young French-Jewish girl, into the redoubtable *Kapo* whore, Nicole (Susan Strasberg). Shot in black and white, the film begins with a sequence presenting Edith as a music student. The protective piano teacher is a gentile woman who dispatches the girl home with the maternal warning not to tarry, an allusion to the potential male threat on the streets rather than to a Nazi presence in Paris. The viewers are therefore all the more shocked when the initial scene of safe domesticity, middle-class normalcy and Jewish/gentile neighborliness is followed by the horrifying scene in which Edith's parents are loaded unto a truck by Nazi officers. The French neighbors who witness this forced deportation seem concerned but helpless; their facial expressions reveal consternation and horror. As she spots her daughter approaching the truck, Edith's mother tries frantically to warn her, but the girl ignores her mother's warnings. In the midst of the chaos of their arrival at the concentration camp, Edith is separated from her parents. Sofia, a Polish "criminal", dispatches Edith to the safe office of the camp's benevolent doctor. The doctor proceeds to hide Edith's Jewish identity by offering her a striped garment and replacing her yellow star with a black triangle, the uniform that belonged to a deceased girl called Nicole.

Disguised as Nicole, Edith quickly forgets her past. She is shown to be fiercer in her fight for survival, stealing food and ignoring the other women. Despite the protests of the kindly Therese, the translator who argues that the girl is too young for sexual work, Edith agrees to follow a Nazi officer into the more spacious barracks. The camera does not follow Nicole and the German officer who becomes her first "client", but the film does not fail to record the crude jokes exchanged among the staff about the new girl's loss of virginity. Nevertheless, even among this crowd Nicole finds a protector in Karl, an attractive officer who unlike his more crude and thuggish comrades is shown to have compassion for the young girl. In response to Karl's question, Nicole responds nonchalantly that the physical comforts of her new life are worth it, adding: "What else is there?"

Though most of the women in Nicole's barrack are allegedly prostitutes, thieves and other criminals, they refuse to compromise their moral values and their dignity. As the newly appointed *Kapo* she treats the women harshly, including women who have treated her kindly. She does not return Sofia's favor, as the latter falls sick and marched off to death. Unlike Sofia and Therese who engage in small personal acts of rebellion, Nicole engages in friendly conversations with other German *Kapos*. She seems to have lost all residues of mercy or compassion, unlike Therese, who breaks down crying when one of the women is hanged for having committed "sabotage". When Therese herself becomes physically and emotionally exhausted, Nicole taunts her for her high-minded idealism, and moral principles. Shortly after one such exchange, Therese rushes toward the electric fence and hurls herself up against the wires, giving up her miserable life in a heroic gesture of protest. Nicole remains undaunted. She seems to relish her brutal job. She does not hesitate to rain blows on women who confront or resist her, or to taunt women on the verge of physical and emotional collapse. The film conveys Nicole's moral bankruptcy by using long shots that focus on her determined and disciplined posture and movement, brief dialogues and by a few close-ups that reveal her expressionless face. The hardened *Kapo* seems to have suppressed all memory of her family, or her Jewish identity, of her moral obligations to the women who helped her survive. Her frozen and purposeful face begins to thaw only after the attractive Russian officer—Sasha (Laurent Terzieff) —enters the picture.

Sasha is a Russian soldier in the Red Army, captured by the Nazis months before the liberation. He is courageous and determined even in captivity, and plots with them to stage an uprising against the Germans, though they all seem to share the conviction that the Russian army is on its way to liberate the camp. When he attempts to clandestinely dispatch a letter on behalf of a woman inmate, in violation of Nazi instructions, Nicole alerts the camp guards. The result is a harsh penalty: Sasha is brutally kicked and beaten and as Nicole looks on. However, when Sasha is ordered to stand half naked through the night dangerously close to the electric fence, the camera pans to Nicole's face which for the first time betrays recognizable human expressions—in this case, empathy and interest in the victim. The two soon fall in love. That Nicole's attraction to Sasha is not merely sexual becomes clear in the scene that shows her imploring him to flee the camp. Sasha, however, refuses to leave without Nicole. A series of two-shots in a dark corner of the camp in the middle of the night reveals the couple's romantic attraction to each other, heightened by the musical score used in the first sequence that introduced Nicole as Edith the innocent Jewish girl.[9] The association of the romantic sequence with Nicole's childhood implies that love has finally brought Nicole back to her identity, penetrated through her hard shell and awakened her to moral responsibility, political solidarity, and social consciousness. Nicole's love for Sasha imbues her with the will to live differently, as well as with the willingness to relinquish her erstwhile attachment to physical survival at all costs. When asked by Sasha and his comrades to join their revolt against the Germans by turning off the electric current that feeds the fence, Nicole agrees. Nicole sheds her *Kapo* identity as she is transformed into a resistance fighter. When Sasha tries to alert her to the risk she is taking, she refuses to let him and his comrades down. Nicole is willing to sacrifice herself, and the life she fought so hard to preserve, for the sake of her love. As the inmates stampede across the fence, Sasha, fearless, keeps walking forward, oblivious to the shots and bullets that seem to hit everyone but him. He is crying out for his beloved Nicole as the close-ups of his face and body emphasize the sincerity and depth of his grief.

But while Sasha is spared, Nicole is not. Can the Jewess be pardoned? For one thing, despite her dramatic transformation into a repentant lover, it occurs when it becomes clear to the inmates as well as the Nazis that the end is near. Could Nicole have fallen in love, because this could once again save her life? Could the Jewess be trusted? The film offers Nicole spiritual salvation, the chance to revert to her Jewish faith, as it were, but it continues to encode her identity in religious terms. Her brief monologue toward the end, as her dialogues throughout the film, continues to suppress the memory of her parents and other Jews. Rather than dying in Sasha's arms, she dies in the arms of her Nazi friend, Karl. Edith recites the *"Shema"* in a French-accented Hebrew. As she prays, she lifts up her eyes to the sky. This dramatic shot of the blue expanses offers visual confirmation of religious redemption, even sanctification. Nicole has died as Edith, the whore reverts to virginity as it were, but she must pay with her life for what she has done, for not even love can redeem her from her sin of collaboration. Much as it tries to illustrate the inhumane conditions of the concentration camp, the film nevertheless upholds a moral code that suggests that even within the camp each person had a choice. Though it tries to explain Nicole's deterioration into a life of prostitution and collaboration, the film implies that Nicole initially made the wrong choice, for which she had to be punished, at least in cinematic terms.

The Garden of the Finzi-Continis [10]

Virgin or whore, saint or sinner, is the moral-sexual question and fundamental ambiguity that constructs the beautiful heroine of *The Garden of the Finzi-Continis,* Micòl (Dominique Sanda). The mysterious beauty seems on the one hand to be the loyal daughter and sister of an aristocratic, upper-class family, the Finzi-Continis of Ferrara; on the other hand, the film suggests that what drives her, even on the eve of her family's demise, is lust rather than love, irrepressible erotic passion rather than compassion for or solidarity with her people. Though she seems to have a special affection for her brother, Alberto who eventually dies shortly before the family is rounded up, she remains strangely detached from her family. Most puzzling is her rejection of Giorgio (Lino Capolicchio), the attractive and sensitive narrator who is hopelessly smitten by her. Her indifference to Giorgio is puzzling both because they were childhood "lovers", exchanging timid glances during synagogue services and because they share much in common as persecuted Jewish students, neighbors, and friends. The opening sequence reveals Micòl's fondness for Giorgio, as she shares with him her interest in American poetry and fascination with horticultural terminology. They both bicycle together through the lush green estate gardens, smiling at each other in spontaneous conversation. Micòl implicitly declares her preference for Giorgio when she coquettishly rejects Alberto's gentile friend, Malnate as "too industrious, too Communist, and too hairy", early on in the film. In a subsequent scene, Micòl entices Giorgio to sit with her in a carriage when a sudden rain leaves them both drenched and out of breath. Yet, when Giorgio reaches out to hold her hand, she jumps out of the carriage declaring impetuously that it's too late. Giorgio, who assumes that Micòl expects him to be more spontaneous and forward in his sexual advances, proceeds during their next meeting to impose a clumsy and shy kiss on her face, only to be summarily rejected again. This time, Micòl explains that she cannot possibly accept him as a suitor because he is too close to her, and because lovers are supposed to tear each other into pieces. The ultimate embodiment of the *belle dame sans merci*, Micòl's rationalizations suggest she is the deluded young reader of modern romance, despite her intellectual pursuits and academic ambitions. Both inscrutable and unknowing, she represents the innocent, irresistible virginal heartthrob of Victorian romance, until her sexual secret is finally revealed.

Because the film is fundamentally a story of unrequited love, and because the focalizer and interpreter is the male lover, the viewers are absorbed as it were into his point of view, are made to identify with his anguish and pain, while consuming the spectacle of the ravishing Jewish beauty. For above all, Micòl provides a voyeuristic spectacle. Most of the sequences display her as an object of desire, moving about in white tennis outfits, in impeccable high-fashion suits, perfect coiffure, and chic dresses that enhance her beauty and wealth.

The numerous close-ups of Nicole's face reveal both the makeup and the coverup of her perfect features, which erase any shred of Jewish difference.[11] Micòl's features embody a European notion of beauty as white unblemished skin, blond hair, full lips, calm detached expression, and innocent blue eyes.[12] During one of the most memorable scenes cross-cutting between the Seder celebrated by the Finzi-Continis and the Bassanis, the camera pans slowly between Micòl's face and the ornate chalice from Venice, objectifying her as a precious ornament along the other objects of beauty on and around the Seder table.[13] Micòl's beauty is objectified as a central luminous possession among the numerous aesthetic objects of art, furniture, sumptuous architecture, ornate and lavish bedrooms, and above all the stunning, lush, groomed garden of the Finzi-Continis. It is therefore not surprising that it is within the symbolic garden, the Garden of Eden, as it were, that Micòl—the archetypal Eve—is revealed as the seductive virgin that she is. It is in the transition from the image of innocence to the embodiment of sexual experience that the 'truth' of the

Jewess is finally revealed. During his last visit to the enchanting garden, Giorgio stumbles across a secluded hut, and as he gazes through the window he discovers Micòl lying nude in bed next to Malnate.[14]

Emotionally, the camera evokes the shattering disappointment and disillusionment of the young man with his idealized object of desire. The naked woman lying next to his best friend could no longer comply with his fantasies of love and innocence. When Micòl becomes aware of Giorgio's gaze, she calmly uncovers herself—a gesture that seems to intensify his already unbearable sense of betrayal and discouragement. The shot/reverse-shot reveals his disenchantment and her defiance. This moment of truth conflates the viewer's knowledge with that of Giorgio's for what becomes clear is that Micòl's mysterious behavior, behavior that was mistakenly idealized and romanticized by the smitten young man, was both treacherous and immoral. From Giorgio's point of view, Micòl is nothing but a tease. Beneath the virgin there was all along a courtesan. Because the film reveals little about Micòl's perspective, we are at a loss about her motivations. It is also unclear whether she prefers the more masculine Malnate because he was sexually experienced, a socialist, or a gentile? It is unclear whether Micòl was in love with Malnate, or whether she craved a sexual experience having realized that her very life was at risk. Was then Micòl's sexual relationship with Malnate another manifestation of her escapism and obliviousness to the historical disaster unfolding around her, or was it by contrast an expression of some sort of defiance? The film implies that had Micòl followed Giorgio, had she accepted his true love, she would have been spared, like him. But this was not Micòl's choice. In some measure, then, her eventual death was the result of her own choice, and she was eventually the agent of her own demise.

On the face of it, *The Garden of the Finzi-Continis* is an extended elegy for the loss of Italian Jewry. The saturated color, sharp focus and meticulous organization of stunning surfaces from the lush garden to the architectural splendor to the furniture, décor, and actors' costumes constructs in almost every frame the beauty that was the liquidated along with the Jewish aristocracy of Ferrara.[15] At the same time, however, the film suggests that the Finzi-Continis, by withdrawing into their garden and opulent estate, have colluded to some extent in their own demise. Most of the Italian gentiles are shown to object to Fascism. Malnate, Micòl's lover, is killed as a result of his resistance work. It would seem that had they tried a bit harder, some of the Jews could have escaped their bitter fate, possibly with the help of their Italian neighbors. Micòl, then, is made to symbolize the collective tragedy of Italian Jewry, a problematic proposition to say the least, for despite its idealizing features, the film also holds the Jewish victims responsible for their own fate.

Lacombe, Lucien[16]

The question of virginity versus sexual experience constructs the representation of France Horn (Aurore Clement), the Jewish girl who falls in love with the boyish French collaborator Lucien Lacombe (Pierre Blaise). France is clearly a symbolic name, and the story about the young collaborator is a problematic attempt to consider a collaborator as a 'human being' as it were. That in his own way this collaborator manages to save a Jewish girl's life reveals the paradoxes and complexities of the Nazi occupation of France during World War II. For our purposes, it is revealing that once again, it is through the Jewish female body that such an investigation into the "soul" of a Nazi collaborator is made possible.

Lucien's initial attraction to France is sexual, though her 'respectable' middle-class status appeals to him as well.[17] The quick succession of shots and counter-shots that frame the couple's first encounter reveal his fascination with her physical appearance. But in addition, France offers Lucien a chance to prove his virility, and superior rank as a representative of the Vichy government. Spotting her in a shopping line for groceries, he pulls her out, and insists, toting his gun and his insignia that she be served first. France's simple skirts and blouses, bright eyes and curly blond hair suggest a virginal innocence that contrasts with the appearance of other available women. She is a challenging conquest, unlike the waitress Marie, who invites him into her bedroom, or the coquettish actress Madame Beaulieu who flirts with him in front of her boyfriend. In contrast to France's modest and virginal appearance, both women are presented as crass and vulgar, more racist and ruthless than their male counterparts in the Vichy headquarters. When Marie spots Lucien and France dancing in the hallway during the party, she attacks France violently, calling her *"sale Juive"* (dirty Jew) and fulminating about her contaminating power. The film seems to imply that in addition to some sort of archetypal jealousy, an intense anti-Semitism is at play, the kind that is never once evinced by Lucien. The women's Nazi sympathies run deeper, it would seem, than Lucien's rather superficial anti-Jewish platitudes he mouths notably in his confrontations with France's father. If, then, for Lucien France is a worthy conquest, for France, Lucien offers a way out of her Jewish ghetto and of social propriety. Her ability to enjoy herself at the party at the Vichy headquarters dramatizes her complete oblivion to historical context and political reality. It is during that party that France crosses the sexual boundary that previously separated her from Lucien. As she kisses him passionately, she declares *"J'ais mar d'etre Juive"* (I am sick of being a Jew). Here again, the young Jewess is imagined as a sexual object and subject, devoid of any and all moral or political consciousness, as she enjoys complete sensual abandon in the arms of her persecutors.[18]

To her scandalized father, Albert Horn, a high-fashion tailor, France is a whore. Despite his efforts to hide his pretty daughter from the world, much as he tries to enclose her within the piano room in their small apartment, he is unable to put an end to her affair with Lucien. Much of the love story is structured around the conflict between the Jewish father, Albert Horn, and the gentile collaborator, as the former tries to assert his parental authority and the latter stakes out his territory in the small apartment by laying sexual claim to France's body. To appease the father, Lucien goes through the motions of courting France, offering gifts he has looted from French Resistance members and by inviting France to a party in the

Gestapo headquarters. France's conduct leads to her father's death. Determined to find out if Lucien intends to marry his daughter, Albert Horn heads toward the Vichy headquarters in Toulouse, where he is summarily rounded up for deportation and sent off to a concentration camp.

Though she mourns her father's death, France is content to be rescued along with her grandmother, and shows a stunning ability to put the recent past behind her. The scenes that shows France and Lucien cavorting freely in an abandoned hut in the forest, within earshot of her grandmother, shortly after the deportation of her father draw unmistakable analogies between the Jewess's body and the magnificent natural setting.

If as a city girl France continues to resist Lucien to a certain extent, she begins to defer to his authority in the country, where she and her grandmother become completely dependent on his hunting skills. Thus the sequence that shows the couple's postcoital fondling in the city offers a shot of France's back, thighs and buttocks, revealing only part of her face. Lucien's posture and face by contrast reveal his profound fascination with France's body, as he caresses her thigh in quiet contemplation. In the country, however, France is shown to look for Lucien, to call out his name, to follow him, in short, to need him as she becomes gradually and completely dependent on him. Aptly, then, the nude scene that completes this sequence reveals Lucien nonchalantly lying on his back in the meadow, fully clothed, while France emerges naked from a lake near by, her body directed toward him, and her breasts and belly fully exposed to the camera. The sexualization of Lucien's power over France carries unmistakable pornographic connotations.[19] The exoneration of the mysteriously violent man as a lover with a heart of gold and the eventual yielding acceptance of his power by a sexually aroused woman are staples of popular romance, notably of the Harlequin genre.[20] On the visual level what remains problematic is the gradual undressing of the Jewish protagonist, the symbolic peeling off as it were of her outer layers of cultural identity, revealing her at the end as a nude body, a sexual object, an erotic spectacle that is supposed to offer the ultimate clue to her being. The naturalness of this scene is beguiling. There is nothing natural about the cinematic creation of woman as spectacle. As Mary Ann Doane has suggested, the production of visual desire requires much technical effort and sophistication: "Spectatorial desire, in contemporary film theory, is generally delineated as either voyeurism or fetishism, as precisely a pleasure in seeing what is prohibited in relation to the female body. The image orchestrates a gaze, a limit, and its pleasurable transgression. The woman's beauty, her very desirability, becomes a function of certain practices of imaging – framing, lighting, camera movement, angle".[21]

At the end, the postscript to the film reveals that Lucien was captured and executed. His kindness to France was neither acknowledged nor recognized. The postscript does not reveal anything at all about France. She does not seem to require any narrative completion or epilogue. In and of herself, she does not seem to have justified any reference beyond the visual transition she mediates between innocent virginity to sexual experience. The film celebrates this transition, as sexual activity enables France's rescue and survival. It does not show any interest in the story of the Jewess beyond the confines of this imagined sexuality.[22]

Angry Harvest[23]

This film is ostensibly devoted to a moral and psychological inquiry into the rarely represented scenario of a single gentile male rescuer hiding a Jewess. That rescuers have taken in Jews for financial reasons is a proposition that is dramatized in the film itself. That some rescuers may have done so for sexual reasons, availing themselves of the complete isolation and vulnerability of Jewish women is a proposition that is raised in the film, but eventually denied in favor of a more favorable romantic explanation that normalizes and even idealizes the sexual relationship that is at the very heart of the film. The male rescuer in our film is a middle-aged Polish farmer, Leon (Armin Mueller-Stahl), who falls in love with the Jewess Rosa (Elisabeth Trissenaar), whom he takes into his house, feeds, cares for and protects until the end of the war. The disturbing and likely scenario of a rescuer who kills the Jewess in his custody for fear of being accused of exploitative sex even rape after the war is dismissed in favor of more convenient resolution: Rosa slashes her own wrists in Leon's cellar days before liberation. The film proposes that Rosa has taken her own life not because she is tired of serving Leon's sexual needs, but because she has fallen in love with him. The film thus exonerates Rosa of the charge of prostitution, for she does not merely exchange sexual favors for food and shelter, she in effect wants to have sex with Leon because she has fallen in love with him.

On a deeper level, Rosa is an adulterous wife, for she carries on a sexual affair with Leon, while her husband—of whose survival she is unaware—is desperately looking for her. The virgin in the film, ironically, is not the Jewess but the gentile farmer. Catholic to a fault, the repressed farmer has avoided women though somehow they seem to be attracted to him. The pretty and flirtatious servant girl, who will eventually become his wife, the priest's sister and a wealthy widow are all interested in marrying him. But it is only when he meets the attractive, dark-eyed Jewess that the farmer's tormenting inhibitions give way, and he discovers his dormant sexual potential in multiple scenes of orgasmic delight as he unleashes his stormy, long-suppressed sexual energy on her yielding, passive body, whose femininity is only made more appealing by her emotional fragility and physical vulnerability.

But if the farmer's attraction and sexual need for the Jewess emerge as clear motivations in the film by his agonizing nights of masturbatory loneliness and excessive drinking, it is not entirely clear why the Jewess eventually yields to his sexual passion. This puzzling response is made all the more problematic given her ostensible commitment to the memory of her parents, her child and her husband, Dan. On the first night she is permitted to enter the upstairs living room, wearing the dress Leon buys her in the market, she seems shaken by the false possibility that her husband is no longer alive. Leon hides from her the fact that the shawl he hung up in the woods was indeed braided, that her husband did respond by leaving her a signal. Leon hides this crucial piece of information from her only after she has failed to interpret her husband's signal. Even if Dan has indeed disappeared, or just because he may have been killed, should she not have waited for the end of the war to find out what has indeed happened to her husband and child? This moral consideration is erased or overridden by a 'deeper' or rather more conventional one.

Like all romance heroines, Rosa does not seem to be able to resist Leon's declarations and promises of love. What seems to induce Rosa's sexual receptivity is Leon's promise to marry her. As Ann Snitow puts it in her analysis of romance as pornographic imagination: "The hero wants sex; the heroine wants it, too, but can only enjoy it after the love promise has finally been made…"[24] After she appropriately resists his first sexual overture, as he washes her feet in the cellar, her resistance begins to crack after he reveals his love for her. Though she protests vehemently that she will not be bought like a calf in the market, she does yield after Leon shares with her his intention to buy his Jewish neighbor's Rubin's orchard. Rosa demands that Leon help the Jew escape and survive.[25] She sleeps with Leon for the first time after he assures her that he intends to share his wealth with her, and marry her, showing her the money he has stashed away in a crack under the living room floor.

If the first part of the film "explains" the heroine's response by encoding the conventional norms of romance as a story of courtship, the second half of the film explains her increasingly intense emotional involvement with him by encoding the norms of romantic melodrama as a story of domestic strife. Each scene of ever-escalating arguments and violent fights including rape, leads to passionate abandonment, idyllic reconciliation and a renewed commitment to marital love. Presented as the classic heroine of romance living in an eternal present of emotional intensity, Rosa is utterly disinterested in news from the outside. When the two listen to the radio, she requests that Leon tune in to music rather than to news, and she blithely dances, forcing him to dance with her in utter oblivion to the danger that lurks outside. Rosa seems able to find time for passionate romance, partly because she is so well protected, virtually insulated from the dangers of the outside world. Several scenes show her enjoying the sunshine in his yard and on his porch during an idyllic moment showing Leon embracing and kissing her. Rosa is so deeply lulled into the security of romance that she remains rather indifferent to the shots she hears in the background, shots that kill both Rubin and his rescuer. Fully protected and largely indulged, she carries out her housewifely duties, preparing dinners and sewing unperturbed by the political storm and daily tragedies that afflict the Polish citizens in the village. If Rosa indulges in occasional moodiness, singing a lullaby or holding an imaginary conversation with her dead child by candlelight in the cellar, she is clearly haunted by her memories. If she mourns her husband's death, she is clearly tormented by speculation, because as the film later shows, her husband is alive and well (and will eventually marry Rubin's daughter after the war).

It is Leon, rather than Rosa, who is haunted by nightmares of Nazi inspections of his home, and it is Leon who is subject to real and present danger whenever he ventures into the village or the town. Pressured to demonstrate anti-Nazi patriotism by the Underground, he sends off the priest's sister, who is secretly in love with him, on a dangerous mission from which she does not return. Pressured by Fascist speculators to acquire and lay claim to Jewish property, he is terrorized when he finds on this new property the body of an alleged collaborator. Pressured to acquire a wife and settle down, he is forced to ask Eugenia, a wealthy widow, to share his house shortly after her mother dies. Rosa, who is unaware of the contradictory pressures, life-threatening circumstances and tormenting fears to which Leon is subjected on a daily basis, interprets Leon's request that she move to a new hiding place in romantic terms. Suspecting that for Leon she is nothing but a whore he keeps locked up for his occasional pleasure, she is now determined that Leon is trying to get rid of her and to marry Eugenia. Leon's drinking bouts, his sexual passion, his disappearance for days at a time, his keeping her ignorant of the world outside, are erroneously interpreted by the heroine as lack of love. But Rosa, as other Harlequin heroines is wrong. [26]

At the end of the film Rosa emerges as the tragic heroine who chooses death for no reason.The penultimate scene focuses on Leon's genuine grief as he becomes physically ill and refuses to part with his lover's corpse, explicitly evoking Rosa as a deity if not a Madonna (rather than courtesan) as he utters the question *"Mein Gott, warum hastu mich verlassen?"* (My God, why have you forsaken me). Leon, rather than the Jewess, is Christ nailed to a cross, for it is his anguish at having lost the love of his life that we are made to witness. The film thus uses a romantic code to clear the anti-Semitic rescuer of any wrongdoing. The anti-Semitic remarks he makes regarding Jews as Christ-killers, his insistence that Rosa abandon her religion prior to becoming his wife, his accusation of persecuted Jews as rabble, are dissolved and naturalized into a retrospective reconstruction of the narrative as an expression of tormented though genuine love. How can the viewers not condone Leon for his behavior, given the impossible external and domestic and emotional pressures he had to withstand? At the end it is not the anti-Semite who inflicts death on the Jew, but the Jew who imagines danger and risk where they do not exist, thus turning upon himself as his own worst enemy. This problematic implication is naturalized and normalized by feminizing the Jewish victim, a process that draws on the myth of masochistic subjectivity mental fragility as the idealized properties of the romantic (tragic) heroine.

November Moon[27]

A similar presentation of the rescuer as true victim of Nazi persecution appears in *November Moon*, a lesbian romance about Jewish-gentile love during the Nazi occupation of France. Though it does not deny the physical torture and persecution inflicted on the young and attractive November (Gabriele Osburg), it highlights the even greater sacrifice and humiliation exacted from her gentile lover, Ferial (Christiane Millet). Indeed there is something more heroic about Ferial's voluntary choice to help her lover survive, than in November's decision to run barefoot all the way from the South of France to Paris in search for Ferial and a safe haven. Intercutting scenes from the lovers' separate lives, it compares November's relative safety in the country, hidden at a farmer's barn, with Ferial's horror at the Nazification of Paris and her anxiety over her brother, Laurent, who has been deported to Germany. While November is subjected to rape by Nazi officers and turned into a madame after the Nazi invasion of the South, she eventually escapes to safety in Ferial's apartment in Paris. After nursing November back to health, it is Ferial who must suffer the humiliation of becoming the paramour and secretary of the Nazi sympathizer, Marcel, in order to fend off suspicion and to secure the income necessary for November's safe upkeep. Shortly after the end of the war, it is Ferial who is dragged out of her apartment by enraged neighbors, who cut off her hair and threaten to kill her for being a Nazi whore. It is Ferial who in her shorn hair and striped gown resembles a concentration camp inmate, while November, apparently out of danger, comforts and shields her. The scenes showing the two dancing, sleeping, or cavorting together in the meadow earlier in the film present them as mirror images of each other, as both are equally attractive, thin, tall and feminine, though November's features are slightly darker. The symmetrical parallelism between the lovers is sustained both visually and thematically throughout the film that insists on exonerating all the French characters of any and all involvement with anti-Jewish terror, and on establishing an unequivocal moral equality between the lovers.

When November is raped at the Nazi headquarters, the camera focuses on the face of the German officer Hoffman who squirms with disgust and horror at November's shrieks. It is Hoffman who will later be shot for helping November escape from the whorehouse. The scenes showing November spending her days in relative safety in the country are intercut as well with scenes showing her friend, Chantal, terrorized and intimidated by Nazi officers who frequent her bistro. It is Chantal who, early in the film, offers November a job shortly after the death of her father. No French character is shown to harbor any anti-Semitic sentiment. Even Marcel, the Nazi sympathizer and Vichy propagandist, admits to Ferial at the end of the film that he has never harbored any anti-Jewish feelings, and that he has acted because he simply wished to survive the war. Indeed Marcel saves the women's lives, by tipping Ferial off about an imminent search of her house by the authorities.

To be sure, November does not forget her family as easily as do other Jewish heroines in most Holocaust romances. She is shown to hold on to a small book her father made for her as a child, and recalls his memory with fondness. She is shown to spit at the Nazi who raped her and to resist her fate as a prostitute by attacking the German who paid for her services. She is the first in a series of heroines who tries to secure her own livelihood, follows the news avidly, shown to have a political awareness, to be able to reject romantic propositions by dashing young men. The breakdown of the heterosexual politics of romance seems to generate an ability to imagine a more independent Jewess, unconstrained by conventional bias. But at the end, November's identity is constructed as French and lesbian. Her Jewishness is incidental to her suffering, and her suffering is presented as temporary, as something that can be assuaged and redeemed through romantic and sexual love.

Aimée and Jaguar[28]

The representation of the gentile lover as the ultimate and enduring victim of Nazism, on a par with the Jewish victim, is further reinforced in *Aimée and Jaguar,* a biopic based on the lesbian affair between Felice Schragenheim (Maria Schrader), a lesbian Jewish member of the underground in Berlin, and Lilly Wust (Juliane Kohler), a Nazi wife and mother of four during the last two years of the war.[29] To a large extent, the film represents Lilly's romantic interpretation of the affair, as it focuses on her subjectivity and point of view.[30] The frame story introduces us at the beginning and the end of the film to Lilly as an old woman, contrasting her view that love endures forever and conquers all, with the narrator Ilse's more skeptical view of love in general and the affair in particular. The camera vindicates Lilly's privatization of the story throughout the internal story as it focuses on personal and inter-subjective space while lingering only briefly on public scenes of mayhem and destruction.[31] When Felice disappears for periods of time, called by her work in a Nazi editorial office, or her work as a member of the Berlin underground, the film shows us a distraught and lonely Lilly, waiting desperately for the return of her beloved Jaguar. It is her facial expressions and bodily gestures that we identify with as we mourn the unseemly intrusion of public time into the private love story. It is Lilly's family, her parents, her children and her husband, that we alternatively applaud or condemn for supporting (parents, children) or endangering (Lilly's husband, Gunther) the love between her and Felice. The film offers nothing about Felice's sister, her father, Dr. Schragenheim, and too little about her grandmother. The scene presenting the old woman's close relationship with her granddaughter early in the film is just as brief as the one showing her expulsion from her Berlin apartment. When Felice is intercepted in Lilly's apartment, and dragged down the stairs, screaming and kicking, the camera focuses on Lilly's face as she sinks to the floor, shrieking hysterically *"Nein, nein, nein!"* It is Lilly's refusal to give up on Felice, her fateful attempt to visit her in Theresienstadt, and her apparently lifelong mourning for her lost love that the film is interested in, not Felice's fate in Theresienstadt and later in Bergen-Belsen, nor the death march that probably took her life.

The film draws an analogy between Lilly's tragedy as a housewife who is deceived by the false promise of heterosexual marriage (as well as by the false lure of extramarital romance) and the tragedy of Felice who is sexually suppressed as a lesbian and politically oppressed as a Jew.[32] At one point Lilly tells Felice she envies her freedom. *"Du bist frei"* (you are free) she tells her friend admiringly.

Though obviously ironic, the statement is visually vindicated to some extent. The film's beginning sequences dramatize Felice's 'freedom' and Lilly's social and emotional imprisonment as a wife abandoned and neglected by her husband, a soldier on the Eastern Front. While Felice is shown to frequent cafes, enjoy the lesbian high life of Berlin, flirt with her boss in the editorial offices of a Nazi newspaper, Lilly is shown to be the victim of sexist oppression, abused by her philandering husband, Gunther, and sexually exploited by her so-called lover, Ernst. Eventually, Ernst threatens to report her father to the authorities, while later on, Gunther will physically attack her upon discovering her lesbian involvement and in response to her request for a divorce. While it is worthwhile to remember that Nazism was fueled by misogyny and anchored in a deeply entrenched patriarchal bias, it is important to not succumb to a fascistic vision of sameness that reproduces difference in terms of hegemonic norms.

Paradoxically, the representation of Felice as Jaguar, the calm and confident 'butch' who clearly dominates Lilly, the naive heterosexual housewife reproduces the image of the Jewess as femme fatale, as a dangerously seductive siren. Much as it breaks down the old dichotomy of virgin and whore, it constructs Lilly as the "virgin" in this relationship. It is Felice who initiates their early encounters and who manipulates Lilly into inviting her and her lesbian circle into her house. Early in the film, Felice offers Lilly an apple, which Lilly shyly accepts. Felice writes Lilly love letters, parodying and reproducing the conventions of epistolary courtship; she organizes a Christmas party at Lilly's house during which she kisses her for the first time, while Gunther, Lilly's husband, is conveniently whisked away by Ilse (Felice's previous lover) and Felice's other lesbian friends. The camera focuses intently on the initiation scenes in which Felice arouses Lilly to the point of trembling frenzy, using conventional clichés of erotic discourse ("you are so beautiful"; "my sweet girl, sweet girl"). When Lilly finally gives in to Felice's seductive ploys, as she becomes desperately dependent on her, Felice seems to toy with her, suggesting that their relationship is about fun and joy, not about everlasting commitment. The penultimate scene presents Felice coyly suggesting to her circle of trusted friends that she wants all of them, that she does not want 'forever,' that she only wants to remain at the present moment, *"jetzt und jetzt und jetzt"* (now and now and now). Even as an old woman Lilly seems to be tormented by the possibility that Felice may not have been faithful to her, or had she survived may not have stayed with her.

Despite her cautious distance from Lilly she decides at the end to reveal her true identity to the erstwhile winner of a Nazi medal for valiant motherhood. The Jewess is both calculating and reckless, plotting and yet capable of throwing all caution to the wind, thus risking both her own life and the life of her lover. Toward the end of the film, Felice rejects the chance to escape from Berlin, a chance held out by her loving lesbian friends and underground colleagues. Her decision to remain in Berlin is as fatal as her decision to seduce Lilly to begin with. Both decisions eventually sealed her fate. The Jewish lover then is the agent of her own demise. At the end, she and not her German lover is responsible for her own death. That Lilly may have expedited her demise by visiting her in Theresienstadt is a possibility raised by Ilse, whose point of view is suspect because of her obvious jealousy of the woman who had stolen her lover. Within the economy of the lesbian romance, the virgin/whore dichotomy is replaced by the true/ false love dichotomy. That Felice may have used Lilly as a convenient façade is certainly a possibility that enters the film's frame, but it is dismissed in favor of a more romantic interpretation. Though under the historical circumstances of the Third Reich using a Nazi as shield and refuge is an understandable survival strategy, the privatized, normalized code of the romantic narrative excludes this possibility as immoral and offensive to Felice's memory.[33]

The privatization of the tragedy of Felice Schragenheim is facilitated by a structural separation of private and public space in the film, a separation that privileges the former by presenting the latter as mere backdrop. Through a succession of shot/reverse-shot sequences focusing on the lovers' faces; the use of a musical score that enhances the emotional intensity of these shots, and the bracketing of the historical events and the relation of the state and its citizens—the film implies that the personal is apolitical, and more serious and important.[34] While it parodies some of the conventions of heterosexist romance, it re-inscribes the romantic idealization of emotional intensity as the measure of true humanity and morality. Though it parodies on some level conventions of pornographic representations, it enables nevertheless the visual consumption of female (lesbian) sexuality representations as it celebrates the romance of the couple.[35] Though it subverts the image of the Jewess as passive victim of Nazi aggression, and the virgin/whore dichotomy, it nevertheless reproduces the definition of the Jewess as first and foremost a sexual subject, the locus of production and consumption of sexual longing.

Conclusion

Virgin or courtesan, heterosexual or lesbian, the Jewish protagonist of Holocaust romances is constructed in sexual terms. If the narrative ends in death, the Jewess is blamed as the agent of her own demise. The Jewess is both redeemed and doomed by her romantic attachment to gentile men and women, who are portrayed as valiant resisters of the Nazi regime (*Kapo, The Garden of the Finzi-Continis, November Moon*), or naive collaborators (*Lacombe, Lucien, Bitter Harvest, Aimée and Jaguar*). To be sure, Nazi racism is decried and condemned in the cinematic representations that glamorize the Jewess as a celluloid heartthrob. But glamorized as she may be, the Jewess embodies danger and fatal risk for those who are attracted to her. They either pay with their lives or happiness for having succumbed to her irresistible sexuality (*Angry Harvest*) or seductive ploys (*Aimée and Jaguar*). In some way, the elimination of the Jewess is a narrative relief, because Jewish norms of exogamy may interfere—in case of survival—with the romantic desideratum of marriage as resolution. Indeed all films that involve survival erase Jewish identity markers as much as possible.

By privatizing the tragedy of the Jewess, the Holocaust romances we have discussed here universalize and homogenize the historical specificity of the Holocaust. After all, what is the difference between the beloved woman who is lost to illness, to an accident, to pregnancy, and the Jewess who perishes in a concentration camp? By returning the Jewess to the virgin/whore dichotomy the Holocaust romance succeeds in normalizing the Holocaust as a story about sexual innocence and experience, and shifts the subject to a more familiar representational history.[36] More importantly, by presenting the Jewess as a reckless lover, the Holocaust romance shifts the blame from the (male) perpetrator to the (female) victim. To the extent that conventional cinema punishes most romantic heroines for their sexual experience, the Jewess's death is perversely condoned as somehow inevitable, at least in narrative terms. By subtly shifting the blame for her death to the "reckless" victim herself, the Holocaust romance reconstructs and validates the myth of the tragic heroine as the victim of her own actions as it offers up the Jewish victim of the Holocaust as its most generic and profound incarnation.

Notes

1   Livia Bitton Jackson, *Madonna or Courtesan? The Jewish Woman in Christian Literature* (New York: Seabury Press, 1982).

2   Feminist scholarship emphasizes by contrast the frequent reference to family life in Jewish women's memoirs. See for example, Myrna Goldenberg, "Testimony, Narrative, and Nightmare: The Experiences of Jewish Women in the Holocaust," in *Active Voices: Women in Jewish Culture* edited by Maurie Sacks (Urbana and Chicago: University of Illinois Press, 1995), 94-108 ; Joan Ringelheim, "Women and the Holocaust: A Reconsideration of Research" in *Different Voices: Women and the Holocaust* ed. Carol Rittner and John K. Roth Paragon House, 1993), pp. 363- 372. Marion Kaplan, "Jewish Women's Responses to Daily Life in Nazi Germany 1933-1939," in *Women in the Holocaust* edited by Dalia Ofer and Lenore J. Weitzman (New Haven and London: Yale University Press, 1998), 39-54.

3   See my article, "Gender and Representation: Love Stories in Holocaust Films" in Marc Rapahel Lee and Stephen J. Whitfield eds. *The Representation of the Holocaust in Literature and Film* (Williamsburg, Virginia: College of William and Mary, 2003), pp. 29-46. On the Holocaust metanarrative of heroic or atrocity, see Sara R. Horowitz "Women in Holocaust Literature: Engendering Trauma Memory," in *Women in the Holocaust* ed. Dalia Ofer and Lenore J. Weitzman (New Haven and London, 1998), pp. 364-378.

4   Gregory William Mank, *Women in Horror Films, 1940s* (Jefferson, North Carolina and London: McFarland, 1999).

5   See Elisabeth Bronfen, *Over Her Dead Body—Death, Femininity and the Aesthetic* (Manchester, England: Manchester University Press, 1992).

6   On disaster as spectacle see Wheeler Winston Dixon, *Disaster and Memory: Celebrity Culture and the Crisis of Hollywood Cinema* (New York: Columbia University Press, 1999).

7   On the manipulative strategies and gender implications of this genre, see Tania Modleski, *Loving with a Vengeance: Mass-produced fantasies for women* (New York: Methuen, 1982), pp. 35-58.

8   *Kapo*, directed by Gillo Pontecorvo, Italy/France, 1960.

9   See Annette Insdorf, *Indelible Shadows: Film and the Holocaust* (Cambridge: Cambridge University Press, 2003), pp. 148-149.

10 *The Garden of the Finzi-Continis*, directed by Vittorio de Sica (Italy, 1970).

11 On the erasure of Jewish characteristics in the film, see Annette Insdorf, *Indelible Shadows: Film and the Holocaust* (Cambridge U.K.: Cambridge University Press, 2003), pp. 111-115.

12 On the ideal Western feminine body, see Sandra Lee Bartky, "Foucault, Femininity, and the Modernization of Patriarchal Power" in *Writing on the Body: Female Embodiment and Feminist Theory*, pp. 129-154.

13 See Millicent Marcus, "De Sica's *Garden of the Finzi-Continis:* An Escapist Paradise Lost," *Filmmaking by the Book: Italian Cinema and Film Adaptation* (Baltimore and London: 1993), pp. 91-110.

14 De Sica's biopic is based on Giorgio Bassani's autobiographical novel, *The Garden of the Finzi-Continis* trans. William Weaver (New York: Harcourt, Brace, Jovanovich, 1977). While De Sica presents this scene as 'reality,' Bassani presents it as a fantasy, an epiphany of sorts. Bassani eventually distanced himself from the film, objecting to its interpretations. See Millicent Marcus, *Filmmaking by the Book,* above.

15 Ilan Avisar, *Screening the Holocaust: Cinema's Images of the Unimaginable* (Bloomington and Indianapolis, 1988), pp. 173-182.

16 *Lacombe, Lucien,* directed by Louis Malle (France: 1974).

17 Andre Pierre Colombat rejects, rightly, the suggestion that Lucien joins the Fascist collaborators because he wishes to somehow challenge the superiority of the bourgeoisie. See *The Holocaust in French Film, (*Metuchen, New Jersey, 1993), pp. 261-287.

18 See Annette Insdorf on the film's erasure of identifiable Jewish markers, *Indelible Shadows: Film and the Holocaust* , pp. 117-121.

19 Andrea Dworkin, *Pornography: Men Possessing Women.* S. Kappeler, *The Pornography of Representation* (Cambridge: Polity Press, 1986).

20 Tania Modleski, *Loving with a Vengeance: Mass-Produced Fantasies for Women,* pp. 35-58; Ann Snitow, "Mass Market Romance: Pornography for Women is Different," *Women and Romance: A Reader* (New York and London: New York University Press, 2001), pp. 307-322.

21 Mary Ann Doane, "Film and Masquerade: Theorizing the Female Spectator," *Writing on the Body: Female Embodiment and Feminist Theory,* eds. Katie Conboy, Nadia Medina, and Sarah Stanbury (New York: Columbia University Press, 1997), pp. 176-207.

22 In *Summer of My German Soldier*, directed by Michael Tuchner (United States, 1977) a young Jewish girl remains a virgin at the end of a romantic affair with a German POW whom she hides from the American authorities. In *Heavens Tears*, directed by Lloyd A. Simandl (United States, 1997), a pretty Jewish girl who has lost her parents falls

in love with a dashing Nazi officer, who tries in vain to provide her with shelter. The Jewish virgin beseeches the officer to make love to her and the video play exploits every opportunity to offer explicit and often gratuitous shots of her nude body.

23 *Angry Harvest*, directed by Agnieszka Holland (West Germany, 1985).

24 Ann Snitow, "Mass Market Romance," p. 314.

25 In a later idyllic scene showing the couple embracing and kissing in the sunlight, Rosa remains strangely calm after she learns that the shots the two heard have killed both Rubin and his rescuer.

26 The Harlequin romance condones male violence, even sadism, by presenting them as typical male love. As Tania Modleski put it: "The basic premise of these 'mystery' stories is that a good man is hard to detect; the solution usually involves the discovery that the man who had seemed most suspicious and unreliable is the real hero who has been in love with the heroine all along…" See *Loving With a Vengeance*, p. 39.

27 *November Moon*, directed by Alexandra von Grote (Germany: 1984).

28 *Aimée and Jaguar*, directed by Max Farberbock (Germany: 1998).

29 The film does not mention her having won a national medal for her reproductive contribution to the Fatherland. Lilly's past does not enter the film's frame, nor does her marriage after Felice's death enter the frame. See Erica Fischer, *Aimée and Jaguar*: *A Love Story*, (Berlin 1943); trans. Edna McCown (New York: Harper Collins, 1995).

30 Erica Fischer's book offers a much more complex view of Lilly. Fischer refuses to endorse Lilly's self-presentation as the victim of Nazism, always by Felice's side. While the film excludes references to Lilly's Nazi past before her affair with Felice, and while it also excludes reference to her marriage subsequent to Felice's death, the book does provide information that problematizes the romantic premise of the film. See Muriel Cormican, "Aimée and Jaguar and the Banality of Evil," *German Studies Review* volume XXVI no.1 (2003), pp. 105-120.

31 John E. Davidson, "A Story of Faces and Intimate Spaces: Form and History in Max Farberbock's Aimée and Jaguar," *Quarterly Review of Film and Video* volume 19 (2002), pp. 323-341.

32 On the suppression and persecution of lesbians in the Third Reich, see Amy Elman, "Lesbians and the Holocaust" in *Women in the Holocaust: Narrative and Representation* ed. Esther Fuchs (Lanham, Maryland: University Press of America, 1999), pp. 9-18.

33 That Felice may have started her affair with Lilly precisely in order to find herself a safer haven is confirmed by Elenai, a surviving member of the Berlin underground. Her letters to her sister also imply a certain uncertainty about Lilly. *Love Story,* directed by Catrine Clay (New York, 1997), also based on Fischer's book.

34 See John E. Davidson, "A Story of Faces and Intimate Spaces," p.325.

35 The sequence showing the lesbian circle posing for pictures that will eventually be sold to German soldiers as postcards parodies male-centered pornography both by presenting lesbians as alleged prostitutes and by emphasizing the economic benefit and anti-Nazi subversion entailed in the transaction. Nevertheless the male photographer and the nude girls recuperate the ideology of the conventional pornographic economy. On

the convention of the couple (heterosexual or homosexual) as the fundamental trope of cinematic sexual politics, see Robin Wood, *Sexual Politics and Narrative Film: Hollywood and Beyond* (Columbia UP, 1998).

36 To be sure, the erotic representation of female victims of Nazi brutality is not limited to European films. On the erotic representation of the Jewish female victim of Nazi brutality in *Schindler's List*, see Sara R. Horowitz, "But is it Good for the Jews? Spielberg's *Schindler's List* and the Aesthetics of Atrocity" *Spielberg's Holocaust: Critical Perspectives on Schindler's List*. Ed. Yosefa Loshitzky (Indiana UP 1997), pp. 119-139.

Notes on Contributors

Dr. Helga Amesberger and Dr. Brigitte Halbmayr are sociologists and political scientists employed at the IKF – Institut für Konfliktforschung since 1992, lecturing at the University of Vienna. Their main research topics: racism, right-wing extremism, National Socialism and the Holocaust, oral history, integration, and gender studies. Among their mutual publications: *Sexualisierte Gewalt. Weibliche Erfahrungen in NS- Konzentrationslagern*, together with Katrin Auer (Mandelbaum Verlag, 2004); *Rechtsextreme Parteien – eine mögliche Heimat für Frauen?* (Leske & Budrich, 2002); *Vom Leben und Überleben – Wege nach Ravensbrück. Das Frau enkonzentrationslager in der Erinnerung*. Vol. 1: Dokumentation und Analyse, Vol. 2: Lebensgeschichten. (Promedia Verlag 2001); *Rassismen. Ausgewählte Analysen afrikanisch-amerikanischer Wissenschafterinnen, Reihe Konfliktforschung.* (Wilhelm Braumüller Verlag, 1998); *Schindlers Liste" macht Schule. Spielfilme als Instrument politischer Bildung an österreichischen Schulen"*. (Studienreihe Konfliktforschung, Braumüller-Verlag, 1995).

Prof. Judith Tydor Baumel is Chair of the Interdisciplinary Graduate Program in Contemporary Jewry at Bar Ilan University and Professor of Modern Jewish History in its Department of Jewish History. She has written several books and numerous articles about the Holocaust, gender, memory, and the State of Israel. Her current research projects deals with identity and gender among women of the *She'erit Hapleta* (DP Holocaust survivors) and with the commemoration of women soldiers in the State of Israel who died while on active duty. Among her publications: *Double Jeopardy: Gender and the Holocaust* (Vallentine Mitchell, 1999); *A Voice of Lament: The Holocaust and Prayer* (Bar Ilan University Press, 1992.) (Hebrew); *Unfulfilled Promise: The Rescue and Resettlement of Jewish Refugee Children from Germany in the United States 1934-1945* (Denali, 1990).

Prof. Judith Buber Agassi is a sociologist and political scientist. She has held several academic positions around the world, including: Lecturer, Department of Extramural Studies, Hong Kong University; Sponsored Research Staff, Center for International Studies, M.I.T; Fellow of the Radcliffe Institute, Harvard University and Research Project on Jewish Women Victims and Survivors of the Women's Concentration Camp Ravensbrück: a historical and sociological study. Among her books: *A Comparative Study of Women's Pension Rights and Practices: Legal, Social and Economic Aspects*. (Israel Institute of Technology, 1977). (Hebrew); *Comparing the Work Attitudes of Women and Men*. (Lexington Books. 1982); *Mass Media in Indonesia,* (Center for International Studies, MIT, Cambridge, 1969).

Kirsty Chatwood is a Ph.D. student and tutor of European History at the University of Edinburgh. She was a teaching and research assistant at the University of Alberta, Canada. Her dissertation is entitled (Re)constructing Rape Stories: Writing Rape into the Holocaust Metanarrative". She has an M.A. in history with her thesis entitled "Gendered Holocaust Witness Narratives."

Dr. Barbara Distel is Director of the *Dachau Memorial Museum* since 1975 and widely acclaimed as the pre-eminent authority on the history of Dachau. Barbara Distel oversees archival materials dealing with the lives and deaths of more than 200,000 persons interned in this first of the German concentration camps (1933-1945). Barbara Distel has published a variety of papers during her career and currently works with Professor Wolfgang Benz in editing and publishing the annual Dachauer Hefte (Dachau Review) which won the prestigious Geschwister-Scholl-Preis literary award in 1992 for its volume on "Solidarity and Resistance."

Dr. Irith Dublon-Knebel is a historian at Tel Aviv University and a Research Fellow at the Minerva Institute for German History. For seven years she was a researcher on the two joint German-Israeli research projects about the Jewish women of Ravensbrück and its environs. Editor of *A Holocaust Crossroads: Jewish Women in Ravensbrück,* about to be published in the U.S. Her book *German Foreign Office Documents on the History of the Holocaust in Greece* is forthcoming (by Goldstein-Goren Diaspora Research Center at the Tel Aviv University; Hebrew).

Annette Dumbach is an author, journalist and university lecturer who has lived throughout the world. She has received degrees from the City College of New York, the University of Missouri, and the Sorbonne, and currently resides in Munich. She is the co-author (with *Jud Newborn*) of *Sophie Scholl and the White Rose.* (Oneworld Publications, 2006).

Dr. Eva Fogelman is a social psychologist and psychotherapist in private practice, and a Senior Research Fellow at the Center for Social Research at CUNY. She is a co-director of Psychotherapy with Generations of the Holocaust and Related Traumas, Training Institute for Mental Health, and a co-director of the International Study of Organized Persecution of Children in New York City. Dr. Fogelman is an advisor to the United States Holocaust Memorial Council. Among her books: *Conscience and Courage: Rescuers of Jews During the Holocaust* (Anchor Books, 1994); *Children during the Nazi Reign* (co-editor) (Praeger, 1994). She co-produced the film *Breaking the Silence: The Generation After the Holocaust* (1984).

Prof. Esther Fuchs is Professor of Judaic Studies at the Department of Near East Studies, the University of Arizona in Tucson. Among her books are: *Israeli Mythogynies: Women in Contemporary Hebrew Fiction* (State University of New York Press, 1987); *Women and the Holocaust: Narrative and Representation*, (ed.) (Lanham and Oxford: University Press of America, Spring 1999). *Sexual Politics in the Biblical Narrative: Reading the Bible as a Woman* (Sheffield Academic Press, 2000). *Israeli Women's Studies: A Reader* (ed.) (Rutgers University Press, 2005).

Dr. Esther Hertzog: is a social anthropologist at Beit Berl College. She is senior lecturer and head of the Anthropology Program at Beit-Berl Academic college. Her main fields of research are: gender, bureaucracy, immigration, and the welfare state. Among her publicaions: *Immigrants and Bureaucrats, Ethiopians in an Israeli Absorption Center.* (Berghahn, 1999); *Israel: A Local Anthropology* (co-editor, Hebrew, Cherikover, 1998; an English edition, Wayne State University Press, forthcoming). She writes an opinion column in the Israeli daily Ma'ariv. A collection of the articles was published as *Op-Ed, Feminist Social Justice in Israel* (in Hebrew, Cherikover, 2004).

Dr. Vandana Joshi is a feminist historian. She has conducted extensive research in the Gestapo Archives as a Fellow of the German Academic Exchange Service, DAAD – Deutscher Akademischer Austausch Dienst, and the IFU – Internationale Frauen Universität. She is affiliated with the Technical University, Berlin, from which she received her doctorate. She lives in New Delhi, India, with her family. Her book, *Gender and Power in the Third Reich Female Denouncers and the Gestapo (1933-45)* (Palgrave-Macmillan, 2003), is based on her Ph.D. research.

Herta Nöbauer is a Lecturer at the Department of Social and Cultural Anthropology at the University of Vienna. Her research and teaching areas are feminist anthropology, anthropology of the body, cultures of academia, and the anthropology of organisation. She serves as coordinator of the Mentoring Program for Women Academics at the University of Vienna and of the transnational E.U.mentoring project EUMENT-NET. In addition, she teaches gender and culture issues in NGOs. Co-author of *Differenzen. Einschlüsse und Ausschlüsse – Innen und Außen – Universität und freie Wissenschaft*. Materialien zur Förderung von Frauen in der Wissenschaft. Vol. 12. (Wissenschaft und Kultur, 2002).

Prof. Dalia Ofer is a Max and Rita Haber Professor of Holocaust and East European Studies and until October 2002 the academic head of the Vidal Sassoon International Center for the Study of Antisemitism at the Hebrew University of Jerusalem. She is the representative of the Hebrew University on the Yad Vashem Academic Committee and a member of the directorate of the Research Center of Yad Vashem. She is the author and editor of six books and has published numerous articles on the history of the Holocaust, immigration to Palestine and Israel, gender, and the memory of the Holocaust in Israel. Her book *Escaping the Holocaust: Illegal Immigration to the Land of Israel*, (Oxford University Press, 1990) received the Jewish Book Award. She co-edited *Women in the Holocaust* (Yale University Press, 1998).

Dr. Rochelle G. Saidel is founder and director of Remember the Women Institute, New York, and Senior Researcher at the Center for the Study of Women and Gender, University of São Paulo. She is curator of the exhibit "Women of Ravensbrück: Portraits of Courage" for the Florida Holocaust Museum in St. Petersburg. The author of *The Jewish Women of Ravensbrück Concentration Camp* (University of Wisconsin Press, 2004); *Never Too Late to Remember: The politics behind New York City's Holocaust Museum* (Holmes and Meier, 1996); *The Outraged Conscience: Seekers of justice for Nazi war criminals in America*. (*State University of New York Press*, 1985).

Dr. Lidia D. Sciama is a former director of the Centre for Cross-Cultural Research on Women (now International Gender Studies). Her main interests are relations between anthropology and literature, narrative, memory, urban anthropology, gender and crafts. Her publications include articles on "academic wives" and ethnicity and identity with a particular focus on nineteenth-century Italy. With Professor Joanne Eicher, she edited a book on *Beads and Beadmakers*: *Gender, Material Culture and Meaning* (Berg, 1998). Her monograph, *A Venetian Island: Environment, History and Change in Burano* (Berghahn 2003), is based on long-term fieldwork.